PLAY YOUR BEST
STRAIGHT
POOL

PHILIP B. CAPELLE

First Edition
Billiard Press, Huntington Beach

Play Your Best Straight Pool

By Philip B. Capelle

Copyright © 2001

Publication Date: January, 2001

Published by: Billiards Press
P.O. Box 400
Midway City, CA 92655

First Printing

Printed in the United Stated of America

10 9 8 7 6 5 4 3 2 1

Library of Congress Catalog Card Number 00-093073

ISBN 0-9649204-2-5

Acknowledgements

One day I started working on this book with no idea of exactly how it would all come together, but only that I was committed to seeing it through to publication. Then people started to appear who were more than happy to lend their assistance to the project. They once again were a reminder of my favorite wall hanging of an inspirational message by W.H. Murray, which includes the following passage:

"A whole stream of events issues from the decision, raising in one's favor all manner of unforeseen incidents and meetings and material assistance, which no man could have dreamt would have come his way."

Paul Harris worked relentlessly and with great enthusiasm in producing the diagrams and in laying out the book. He also designed the book's cover. I applaud him for a Herculean effort in the face of an onrushing deadline. Thanks also to the rest of the staff at *Pool and Billiard Magazine* for their continuing support for my work.

I spent many afternoons and evenings conducting research sessions with Roy Yamane, Master BCA instructor. And when I had a new idea, he always added valuable insight that would improve upon it. Thanks Roy for many pleasurable hours at the pool table. Thanks also to Regina Giordot, who was a gracious hostess for many of our sessions.

Wayne Norcross, a world class Straight Pool player, kindly shared his knowledge and insights into the game. He was particularly helpful with break shots and the thinking that goes on at the highest levels of play. We spent many hours at the table at Danny K's where he instructs and serves as tournament director. Thanks also to Danny Kuykendall for his support.

Pat Fleming of Accu-Stats was most gracious in his support for the book. I gained many valuable pieces of knowledge from watching the greatest players in the world on tape.I would like to thank him and the staff at Accu-Stats for their work in providing quality tapes of tops pros in action.

Stacy Hurst, a long time friend and a member of the WPBA, graciously volunteered to edit the text. She worked diligently against a tight deadline and was instrumental in improving the quality of the book.

I enjoyed talking Straight Pool with several friends and players who excel at Straight Pool, among them Richard Lingley, Elliott Eisenberg, Leil Gay, Joe Baggio and Todd Fleitman. Thanks also to support from friends such as Emil Egeling, Chris Donnelly, Mike Murad, and Paul Gray.

Dedication

I dedicate this book to all I have met on my journey in pool who have, in one way or another, contributed to my education as a pool player.

Introduction

Straight Pool was adopted as the championship game of pool in 1912. Large crowds used to attend matches and the sport was covered extensively by the press for many years. In fact, in the 1920's and 1930's champions like Ralph Greenleaf were heroes of their day. Willie Mosconi succeeded Greenleaf in the early 1940's as the games top player until he retired in 1956. By that time, pool had lost much of it's popularity. There was a big revival in pool following the release of the film classic *The Hustler* in 1961, and a modest upswing in the game of Straight Pool. In the 1960's and early 1970's the top players included Luther Lassiter, Joe Balsis and Irving Crane. During the 1970's and 1980's the two biggest names in Straight Pool were Mike Sigel and Steve Mizerak. Around 1987 Straight Pool once again lost steam.

Since about 1980, Nine-Ball has taken over as the game of choice in professional play. It is ideally suited to TV and today's faster pace. Still, there are a substantial number of professionals and amateur players who profess an undying love for the game. Major events are still held intermittently in the U.S. and on a more regular basis abroad where the game is growing in popularity.

The Game

Straight Pool has been called the foundation for all other pool games and the most demanding of all pool games. In fact, the game requires precise position play, well thought out patterns, airtight defense, and the ability to stay cool under intense pressure. Interestingly enough, however, new players at the game often feel the game is not hard because you can shoot any ball in any pocket.

When playing other pool games, your turns are of relatively short duration. In Eight-Ball and Nine-Ball, for example, it is difficult to string many racks because of the element of luck involved with the break shot. In Straight Pool, your ability to continue from rack to rack is based almost entirely on skill, not luck. The balls are just sitting on the table daring you to make as many as you can before you must turn the table over to your opponent.

One of the greatest thing about Straight Pool, especially when compared to other pool games and to other sports, is it gives you the opportunity to enter the zone of peak performance for longer periods of time. When you on a run in Straight Pool, there's nothing like it. It is truly just you, the table, and the balls. You are transported into another world where you are completely lost in a place called pool. I'll never forget Paul Newman in *The Hustler* sitting in the park describing to his girlfriend what it is like to be on top of your game when, in his words, "You're right, and you know you're right".

Another attractive feature of Straight Pool is that it allows you to easily quantify your results far easier than other pool games. Every player knows their high run, which is a fairly accurate indicator of a player's level of skill. And most player's long for the day when they exceed their personal best.

Learning the Game

Thinking Like a Straight Pool Player
A great many, but not all, of your skills and strategies from other pool games can be used when playing Straight Pool. Nevertheless, you must adopt a way of thinking pool when playing Straight Pool that often differs greatly from other pool games. You must learn to play defense, pattern the balls, and select your shots like a Straight Pool player.

Comparisons to Other Pool Games
I make reference to other pool games throughout the book because I'm sure that nearly all of you play other games. There are many similarities between Straight Pool and other pool games. If you had to pick the one game that is closest to Straight Pool, it would be Eight-Ball. In both games, you have the freedom to play any of several balls into any pocket. In addition, you must break clusters and play a pattern that ends with a shot on a specific ball. You must also be skilled at short-range position play. Straight Pool is a world apart from Nine-Ball, which is America's second most popular pool game. Since so many readers may have their roots in Nine-Ball, you will find many contrasts between the two games mentioned in the book.

The Correct Way to Play
Perhaps Frank Sinatra said it best with his song "I Did it My Way". Certainly that describes the very best Straight Pool players as none of them plays the game exactly alike. Some like to power the break shots and play a little looser style. Machine Gun Lou Butera and the late Joe Balsis are prime examples. Others, such as the late Willie Mosconi, Mike Sigel, and Ray Martin, are real technicians. All of these players, however, have one thing in common: they became World Champions at Straight Pool doing it their way.

I suggest that you combine the lessons in the book with your particular strengths and preferences and your style of playing pool to create your unique brand of Straight Pool. This should enable you to bring out the best in your game, and to make the game even more enjoyable.

Hotbeds of Straight Pool

In certain areas of the United States there are cities like New York and regions, such as the upper East Coast, where Straight Pool is the game of choice among a fairly high percentage of serious pool players. The game is also becoming quite popular in countries such as Germany, Japan and Chinese Taipei, all of which have produced world-class players.

It certainly can help your game if you are raised on Straight Pool in a hotbed where top players willingly share their secrets, and where you have the opportunity to watch and compete against the best players. But even if you do not live in a hotbed of Straight Pool, you can still learn the techniques and secrets of the masters as revealed in this book. Never forget, there is a great joy in knowing what you're doing.

How to Use This Book

When writing this book, my goal was to provide you, the reader, with the most useful and comprehensive book ever written on Straight Pool. It is designed for players of all levels of skill who have a sincere desire to play their best Straight Pool. The book is also designed to complement my previous books, *Play Your Best Pool* and *A Mind For Pool*, which together give you a well-rounded course in pool an extensive guide to the mental game.

Since each one of you is at your own unique place in your development as a pool player, I suggest you develop your own specific course of study based on the needs of your game. For example, if you are losing control of the cue ball on break shots, you will want to study Chapter 5. If your end of rack pattern play needs work, you'll find help in Chapter 5.

You can design your current course of study by making extensive use of the detailed table of contents. Read through it and make a list of the things that you want to work on right now. Once you have mastered the subject matter, pick out your next course of study. I recommend you eventually read the entire book, but only over an extended period of time. You need to take your time, just as any student would when studying a topic in great depth. I also suggest that you view the book as a reference source and as a refresher course.

You can certainly play a respectable game without knowing much of the material in the book, but if you wish to play your very best Straight Pool, you eventually have to know it all, and then some, for no book can cover everything. Although there is much to learn, you have a lifetime to enjoy the fruits of your labor. As an example, a week ago as this is being written, a good friend of mine who is 63 ran 162 balls!

Understanding the Game

The book explains the principles behind concepts like position play, pattern play, breaking balls and so forth. Once you understand a principle of play, you can apply it to a wide variety of situations. For example, one theme that runs throughout the book that applies to countless situations is the need for precise execution. Another is the need for intelligently planning your work.

• Newcomers Guide to the Book

Those of you who are new to Straight Pool have a long and rewarding journey ahead of you. To help you get started, I have identified those sections of the book I feel you should learn first. There is an • next to them in the expanded table of contents and in the matching sections throughout the book that. All told, these lessons represent about 25% of the book. Once you have the basics of play mastered, then it is time to move on to the additional principles and finepoints that are also scattered throughout the book.

The Illustrations

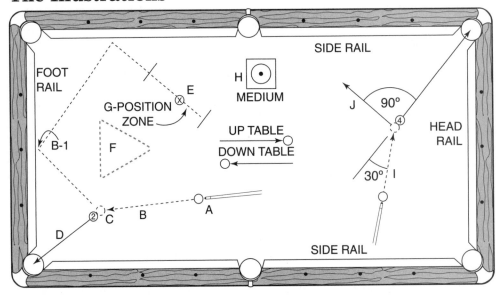

The illustrations have been drawn perfectly to scale so that you can see exactly how the shots and strategies really work at the table. There are no balls that won't fit into the pockets or other techniques that detract from the realism of the shots. Let's take a few moments to go over how the diagrams work.

A   The cue shows which direction the cue ball is being shot. When english is being applied, the cue will be positioned to either the left or right of center. You can gain the shooter's perspective by turning the book so you are looking straight down the cue stick, just as if you were playing the shot.

B   The dashed line shows the path of the cue ball to the object ball, as well as its path after contact.

B-1 The cue balls path is shown by where the center of the cue ball is traveling. As a result, the line will never touch the rail.

C   The dashed circle shows the cue balls position at contact with the object ball.

D   The solid line shows the path of the object ball. In most, but not all cases, it will be to the called pocket. On certain shots, the line into the pocket will be purposefully drawn to one side of the pocket or the other.

E   The cue ball with an X inside shows where the cue ball has come to rest. When you see a series of cue balls with an X on one shot, they are illustrating several possible stopping points for the cue ball. On straight in shots when the cue ball stops dead at the point of contact, this cue ball is used to show both contact and the cue balls ending location.

F   The outline of the triangle is present on all diagrams (except those showing the initial break shot of a new rack). The triangle is an important point of reference for a very high percentage of the shots you play in Straight Pool. (Note: In professional tournament, an outline of the triangle is always drawn on the table.)

G   You will find descriptive text on the diagrams where appropriate throughout the book.

H   Whenever the speed of stroke and cueing are particularly important to your understanding of a shot, you will find a box with a cue ball inside.

I   It is important for you to understand the ideal cut angle for a wide variety of shot in Straight Pool. You will therefore find cut angles labeled throughout the book.

J   You will find numerous references to the tangent line. It is simply a line that shows the cue balls path after contact at a 90-degree angle from the object ball's line to the pocket.

Glossary

There are many terms that are used for pool in general, and many more that are specifically used in Straight Pool. In the process of writing this book, I coined additional phrases that I believe can help you to easily grasp and retain the meaning of a particular lesson. If you have any question on the terminology used in the book, I suggest you look for the definition in the appendix.

Tips

There are a series of tips in the book. Each is designed to be a concise lesson related to the topic discussed just above it. Nevertheless, they can be read independently of the text. They provide you with a valuable piece of information to add to your game.

Using the Donuts

BCA Master Instructor Roy Yamane first gave me the idea for using the same hole reinforcements that you use for three ring binder paper as an inexpensive, but powerful training tool for pool. You can quickly and accurately mark the position of the balls when practicing so you can play the same shots over and over until they are mastered. Throughout the book hole reinforcements are referred to simply as donuts.

Use of the Masculine Pronoun

I would like to make it perfectly clear that I am 100% in favor of women playing pool. For style purposes only, however, I chose to use the masculine pronoun throughout the book as I find it awkward to be constantly alternating between he and she. To women readers I ask that you understand that he really means he/she in the book.

Author's Note: How This Book Came into Being

Straight Pool has been my favorite pool game since I started playing pool over 30 years ago. Even so, I had no plans to write this book anytime soon. But four days after the conclusion of the 2000 U.S. Open 14.1 Championships, something compelled me to start writing about Straight Pool. After a couple of weeks of furiously writing notes on every thing that came to mind about the game, my momentum had built to a feverish pitch. I knew I couldn't stop now until this book was complete.

The highest runs in Straight Pool happen when a player is in the zone and are playing on automatic pilot. Writers experience the same thing, which can turn what could be a tedious grind into a joyous experience. I similarly took off on a writer's high run for the next 5 months as I worked on the book 7 days a week. I wrote, drew diagrams, watched tapes, conducted research sessions, asked questions and basically thought about little else but Straight Pool. The end result is the book you are now reading. I hope it helps you to enjoy the great game of Straight Pool more than ever before, and that you run more balls than you ever imagined possible.

Reader Comments

I would like to hear your comments and suggestions for improving future editions. You can write to me at:

Billiards Press
P.O. Box 400
Midway City, CA 92655

ABRIDGED CONTENTS

Contents - New Players Guide (•)

CHAPTER 2   Pattern Play

XVI

CHAPTER 8 Strategy

CHAPTER 11   All About High Runs

Appendices

CHAPTER 1

POSITION PLAY

How to Master the Cue Ball for Playing Straight Pool

Excellent position makes the game of Straight Pool look so easy when a master is at the table. There is no big mystery to how the experts control the cue ball as well as they do. The concepts they use to run rack upon rack are presented to you in this chapter. It all boils down to knowledge and execution. On any given shot, you need to decide where you want the cue ball to end up, and how you are going to get it there. Then you've got to have the skill to implement your plan. It is as simple as that. In this chapter you learn the 21 principles of position play and then be shown the position plays required to play shape like a master. There is much to learn, so take your time and enjoy the journey as you witness your skills climb on an almost daily basis.

The 21 Principles of Position Play

• #1   Fine Tune Your Speed Control

The heart and soul of Straight Pool is speed control. If you can consistently apply the proper force to the cue ball, then you will have taken a huge step towards mastering the game. If you fail to develop this skill to at least a reasonably high degree of proficiency, you will forever be struggling to play position in Straight Pool, or any other pool game for that matter.

Speed control is crucial to playing pool well, and yet I have witnessed so many experienced players who continue to have trouble with this part of their game. Perhaps they are unaware of their deficiency, or feel they lack the skill to improve in this vital area. In any case, don't you become one of them. Understand the importance of controlling the speed of your stroke and continue to refine this crucial component of your game. In doing so, you'll improve faster, play better, and gain a substantial edge on your competitors. My sales pitch for developing your speed control to the "n"th degree has now mercifully come to an end as I trust that you've got my point. Agreed?

I introduced a spectrum of force in *Play Your Best Pool*, but I'm going to present it again with a few refinements that are geared towards Straight Pool. The spectrum uses the familiar 1-10 scale to illustrate the various possible speeds of stroke.

1	Extremely Soft	7	Hard
2	Very Soft	8	Very Hard
3	Soft	9	Extremely Hard
4	Medium Soft	10	The Break Shot (for Nine-
5	Medium		Ball and Eight-Ball,
6	Medium hard		not Straight Pool)

The scale is geometric, which means that the speed of stroke increases in higher increments as you move up the scale. For example, a medium hard stroke (#6) is approximately four times as fast as a soft stroke (#3), not twice as fast as the number on the spectrum suggests. In essence, stroke speed on the scale rises in the same manner as the magnitude on a Richter Scale used for measuring earthquakes.

The spectrum is designed to help you understand the variety of speeds needed if you happen to play all pool games.   Stroke force #10 is never used in Straight Pool, but is reserved for blasting open the rack in Eight-Ball and Nine-Ball. The vast majority of shots in Straight Pool will be played with speeds in the #2-#6 range, but you must still be able to make use of higher speeds such as #7 & #8 and, on rare occasions, #9 when it's called for.

Since Straight Pool is such a precise game, you must also master a variety of speeds of stroke in the lowest ranges of the scale. To help you visualize the possibilities, I'll break the scale in the lowest range (#1) into fractional increments. Let's start with the lowest speed possible, which is a mere nudge of the cue ball. This "speed" is used when your goal is to play an intentional foul by moving the cue ball perhaps an inch or two. We'll call that stroke speed .1, or 1/10 of extremely soft. Now let's say you need to tap in a pocket hanger from 6" and send the cue ball a scant 2" off the rail. That would probably rate .2, or less than 1/5 of extremely soft. The variations of speed are truly endless. The more you can refine your touch and fill in the gaps between the grades of the spectrum, the more control you will exert over the cue ball.

The example in the diagram demonstrates the concept of filling in the gaps with a very challenging position play. The only way to obtain excellent shape on this break ball is to have near perfect speed control. Using a medium soft stroke (#4) would cause the cue ball to come up short, while a medium stroke (#5) would send the cue ball way past the position zone. Notice how even small gaps between speeds #4 and #5 (4.2 to 4.5) create radically different cut angles on the 10-ball. Now I'm not suggesting you think about speeds 5.4 vs. 5.5, for example, when preparing to shoot unless, of course, that can actually help

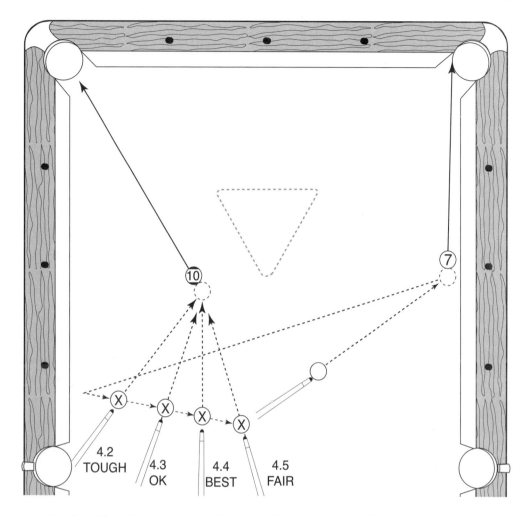

4.2
TOUGH

4.3
OK

4.4
BEST

4.5
FAIR

you to play the shot correctly. Rather, the purpose of the scale is to increase your awareness of the wide variety of speeds that need to be employed to perfect your position play.

For most players there is a range on the scale where they feel most comfortable. A soft stoker's favorite range may be #3-#4 while a player who favors a firm stoke may prefer the #5-#6 range on the scale. You should become aware of your favorite zone so you can play to your strengths. Knowing your preferred speed of stroke can also lead to improvement in areas outside your comfort zone as you strive to create a more well rounded approach to playing position. You should also understand that fine-tuning your shape in the #1-#2 range and the #7-#9 range is especially challenging for all players. It is much easier to come within a certain percentage distance of your target when you are not hitting the cue ball at either high speeds or with extreme delicacy.

4   PLAY YOUR BEST STRAIGHT POOL

Our discussion of speed control is supposed to alert you to the challenge of using correct speed control. You simply must gain a feel for distance and speed on a wide variety of shots. Those of you who play games such as golf or basketball, where you need just the right touch, may be able to transfer some of your skills to pool.

Tips for Improving Your Speed Control
1. Use a light grip and a smooth stroke.
2. Make sure to feel the speed of the shot during warm-up strokes.
3. Observe the results of your shots. Do you typically end up long or short on certain shots? If so, make the necessary adjustments.
4. Remember your successes. Your memory is key, since there are a variety of shots that will continue to show up over and over again.
5. You must learn to raise your level of execution on difficult position plays. Record these shots and work on them during practice sessions.
6. Use progressive drills during practice. Start with the shorter versions of a shot and gradually increase the distance.

• #2   Right Side/Wrong Side

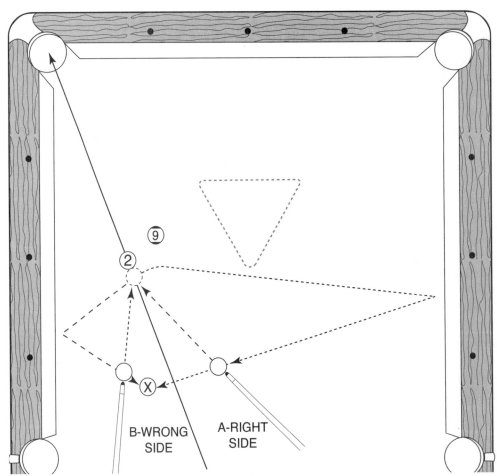

There are two sides to nearly every shot on balls that are off the rail. At times you can play shape from either side, but usually there is a big advantage to having the cue ball on a particular side of the object ball. There are also times when being on the wrong side can eliminate any chance at all of playing position on the ball you had chosen next in your pattern.

In Diagram A, your objective is to pocket the 2-ball and arrive at Position X for excellent shape on the 9-ball break shot. From the right (correct) side of the 2-ball (Cue Ball A), the position play off the rail to Position X is a routine shot. On the wrong side, with the cue ball at Position B, you are faced with a position play that's easily ten times harder since you must now draw across the table, and back, to land at Position X.

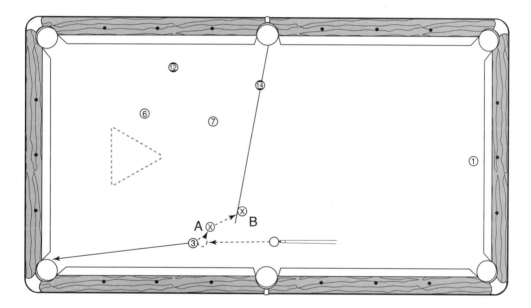

The position in Diagram B shows how a little mistake can destroy a pattern. The ideal pattern goes like this: 3, 14, 1, 12, and the 7-ball in the side for a perfect break shot on the 6-ball. This can easily be accomplished as long as you get on the right side of the 14-ball, shown at Position A. If, however, you happen to mistakenly draw the cue ball back a few inches to the wrong side of the 14-ball at Position B, then you can no longer get from the 1-ball to the 14-ball.

As part of your planning process, you must be careful to arrive on the correct side of the object ball. This is not always as easy as it seems when playing Straight Pool. Quite often you will be playing for a shallow cut angle where a few inches could easily put you on the wrong side of the object ball.

• 3 Plan for Three Balls at a Time

Most Nine-Ball players are familiar with the need for planning for three balls at a time. Even though you can theoretically play any ball at any time in Straight Pool, the principle still applies just as much, if not more so in this game. With Straight Pool, you will get far better results by following a well chosen pattern rather than just shooting the easiest shot available. That means when you are playing the first ball you should nearly always be playing position for a second ball so you can easily get shape on a third ball.

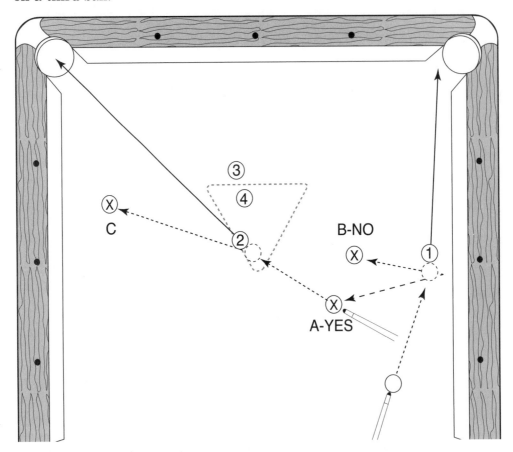

Position angles in Straight Pool are often much narrower than in Nine-Ball. In the example, you need to be on the correct side of the 2-ball after playing the 1-ball. As part of the planning process for three balls at a time, you also need a shallow cut angle on the 2-ball which will enable you to roll forward to Position C for ideal shape on the 3-ball. If you make the mistake of only playing position for the next ball by sending the cue ball to Position B, you could no longer get the shot you wanted on the 3-ball.

You seldom have to perform heroic deeds playing Straight Pool. Instead you must exercise pinpoint control over short distances. That means playing precise shape that enables you to maintain your plan for three balls at a time through those parts of the rack where it is feasible. Some of the obvious exceptions to this principle include break shots, secondary break shots, and Plan B position that changes your pattern.

#4 Play to the Long Side Whenever Possible

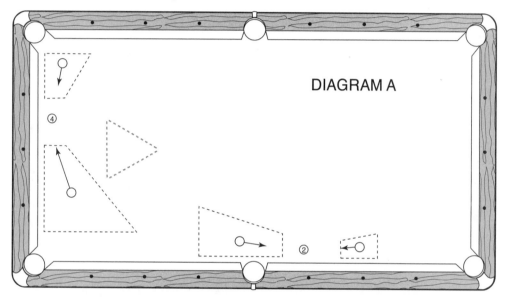

DIAGRAM A

Playing position on the long side of the object ball whenever possible definitely increases your chances of getting good position. Diagram A illustrates this principle. The position zones illustrate the areas in which various shots on the object ball are routine for a Straight Pool player from either side of the object ball. The zones are smaller than those for similar positions in Nine-Ball because of the need for accuracy in Straight Pool where misses are not treated lightly. Smaller position zones are also favored in Straight Pool because you want cut angles that are typically less steep.

When playing Nine-Ball, there are not many exceptions to the long side principle because you are typically moving the cue ball longer distances and therefore need larger target zones for position. In Straight Pool, however, you will encounter many more exceptions to this rule.

Exceptions to Principle #4
- Position on the short side is more easily accessible.
- The short side is integral to playing the pattern correctly.
- The congestion of a typical Straight Pool rack may result in the long side pocket being blocked.
- You need to be on the short side for a better break shot.

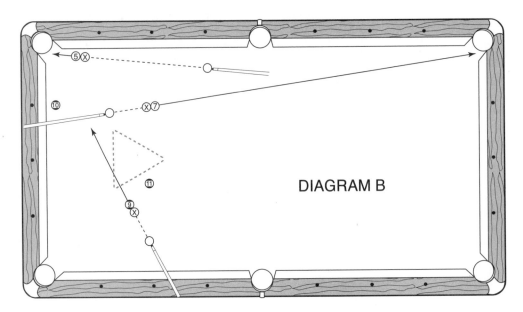

DIAGRAM B

Diagram B illustrates a few exceptions to the rule. Position on the 10-ball is a cinch by playing a stop shot on the 5-ball. Playing the 7-ball in the far corner is a tactic used to simplify or preserve a pattern. The shot on the 9-ball is also a typical short side shot that comes up repeatedly in Straight Pool. The shot on the 9-ball is especially useful in making room for a break ball, such as the 11-ball.

• #5 The Correct Angle and Distance Equals Position

There are two major components to position: the cut angle, and the distance of the cue ball from the object ball. When the cut angle is just right, it is much easier to send the cue ball where needed. When the cue ball is the right distance from the object ball, your accuracy is increased. The correct distance also eliminates stretch shots, which can appear with great regularity in Straight Pool if you're not careful.

I'm are going to refer to various cut angles throughout the book, so let's take a moment to go over how to measure them correctly. A line that extends from the effective center of the pocket through the middle of the object ball as shown in Diagram A is the straight-in line. Cue Ball A in Part A shows a straight-in shot on the 4-ball with a 0-degree cut angle. Cue Ball B depicts a 30-degree cut shot. This is calculated by measuring the angle of the line the cue ball travels to the straight-in line. Notice that the cue ball's line of travel is the center of the cue ball prior to being shot to it's center point at contact with the object ball. Some players mistakenly measure cut angle to the center of the object ball, which in this example would incorrectly reduce the cut angle to 27 degrees.

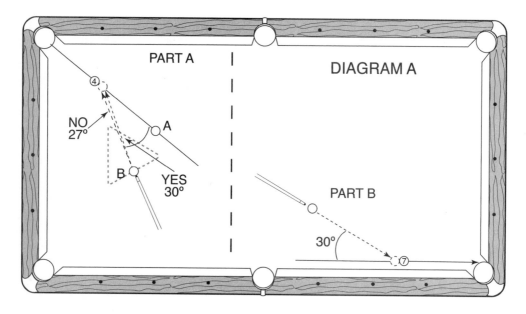

Part B of Diagram A shows another 30-degree cut shot, only this time the object ball is close to the rail. Notice how the effective center of the pocket has shifted to the left side of the pocket. The effective center of the pocket must be considered when calculating cut shots that are not close to being on a diagonal line from the pocket. Note that the shot in Part A of Diagram A was on the diagonal line from the pocket.

I mentioned previously that Straight Pool is a game of fairly shallow cut angles. Shallow angles help contain and control the cue ball and raise your pocketing percentage as well. At times, however, you'll need a sharper cut angle to move the cue ball across and around the table and, of course, to play break shots. Diagram B illustrates a typical shot from a variety of cut angles. On one side of the 11-ball the cue ball will go towards the rail, while it will be traveling away from the cushion on the opposite side.

I would suggest that you take a few moments to look at the shot on the 11-ball from the shooters position behind all eleven cue balls. What does each position suggest to you regarding the difficulty of pocketing the ball? Also consider where you could send the cue ball at various speeds using centerball, draw and follow. If you just considered soft, medium and hard strokes, that alone would result in 99 possible shots (11 x 3 x 3 = 99). Now imagine if you added other speeds (remember our scale), used english, and also shot from additional increments such as 15 degrees, 25 degrees, etc. The possibilities are endless. The point of this exercise is to alert you to reinforce the importance of understanding how various cut angles affect your position play.

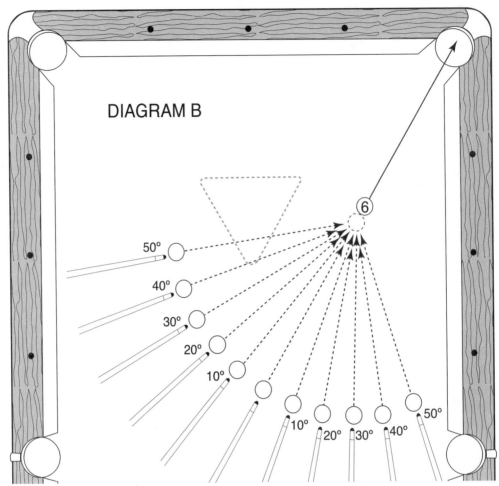

DIAGRAM B

Ideal Cut Angles for Achieving Different Objectives

- Stop shots, 0-3 degrees.
- Stun shots, 3-15 degrees.
- Follow shots, 0-30 degrees.
- Draw shots, 0-30 degrees.
- Floating the cue ball, 5-20 degrees.
- Holding the cue ball on the rail, 0-15 degrees.
- Traveling across and around the table, 20-50 degrees.
- Secondary break shots, 15- 40 degrees.
- Break shots, 30-50 degrees.

You can determine the optimal cut angles for your game by using the general guidelines above, and by fine-tuning them to your style of play, as well as to the conditions. Those who favor a firm stroke will play position for shallower angles. Those who prefer a soft touch will play for slightly steeper angles. A fast table will require that you reduce your cut angles. On a slow table, you will need to play for larger cut angles.

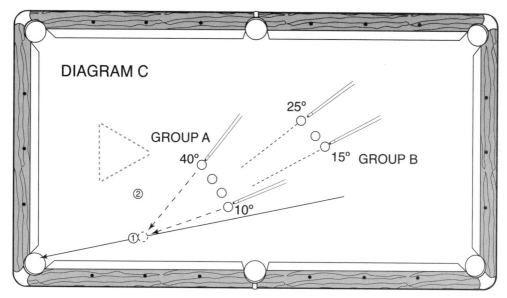

DIAGRAM C

GROUP A

25°

40°

15° GROUP B

10°

②

①

Distance is a critical component in playing position. In Diagram C, your goal is to play the 1-ball and come back off the rail to Position X for the 2-ball break shot. When the cue ball is close to the object ball, you have much more flexibility in playing position (assuming you're not stretching excessively). The four cue balls in Group A are each within 20" of the 1-ball. At this distance, you could reasonably expect to arrive at Position X by pounding the cue ball when the cut angle is only 10 degrees, or by using a soft draw stoke with the cue ball at 40 degrees.

Now let's consider playing position from Group B, which is 3fi' from the 1-ball. Notice how distance has compressed the acceptable cut angle. Now you wouldn't want to pound the cue ball with anything less than a 15-degree cut angle because that would require excessive force. On our 1-10 scale, you'd need to use an extremely hard stroke (a #9), which dramatically raises your chances of missing the 1-ball. You would also not want a cut angle of greater than 25 degrees on this shot because it's very difficult to hold the cue ball with a big cut angle at long range.

#6   Know the Boundaries of a Position Zone

It is best to shoot for an area that guarantees you'll be able to play the next shot as planned. Position zones come in all sizes and a variety of shapes. The position zones in Straight Pool tend to be rather exacting. The good news, however, is that you will normally be traveling short distances from zone to zone.

It is important to know the boundaries of the shape zone on every shot. If you land within the position zone, the cue ball will not be too close or too far from the object ball, and you will not be faced with a cut angle that's too steep or too shallow. On many occasions, you can still play the next shot successfully even if you miss the zone. The diagram shows a typ-

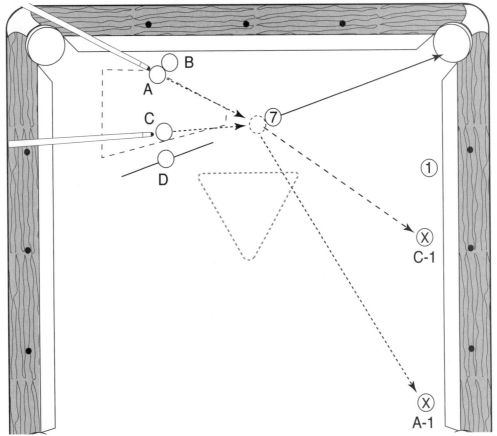

ical Straight Pool position play. The plan is to shoot the 7-ball and follow to the top rail for shape on the 1-ball. As long as the cue ball is within the zone, you shouldn't have too much trouble getting on the 1-ball. With the cue ball at Position A it should strike the rail just below the side pocket at A-1. If the cue ball was over a couple of more inches at Position B, a scratch would have been likely.

Position C is a much shallower angle, but you can still reach the 1-ball with a stun/follow shot. Over a couple of inches at Position D, however, and you are now out of the position zone. Now you would be forced to draw the cue ball off the rail and across the table for shape on the 1-ball. This position zone is large, but you would pay a high price for missing it. Sometimes when you miss a zone it just means that you will have to play a recovery shot to get back in line with your pattern.

#7   Enter the Wide Part of a Position Zone

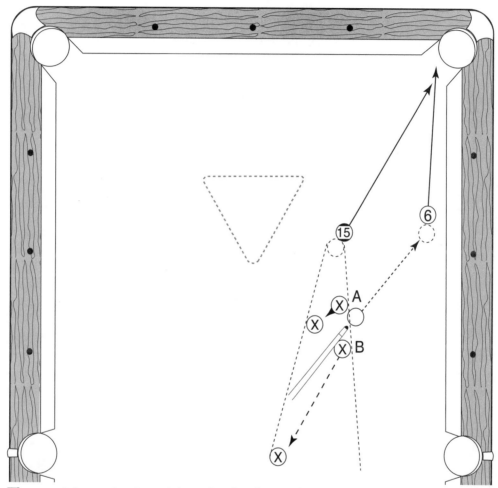

The most important position play by far in Straight Pool is for the side of the rack break shot, so I have chosen it to demonstrate the importance of crossing into the wide area of a position zone. The objective is to cut the 6-ball and float gently off the rail for an ideal shot on the 15-ball break shot. The secret is to get the correct angle so you can effectively open the rack. If you tried to get too close to the 15-ball, you could easily lose your angle as the distance across the position zone is very narrow at Point A.

By drawing back a little farther, you can enter the position zone at Point B, which is a much wider spot. Crossing into the zone at Point B greatly increases your odds of obtaining a cut angle that's in the acceptable range. Notice that the path along the wider part of the zone (B) is, in this example, three times as long as the narrow part (A)!

#8 Playing Down the Line of a Position Zone when Possible

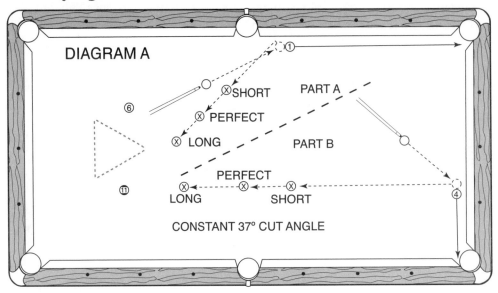

When the cue ball is traveling towards the ideal position line at an angle, as in Part A of Diagram A, then your speed has to be nearly perfect to give you the ideal angle for the next shot, or at least something close to it. The steeper the angle of approach, the better your speed needs to be. Notice how difficult the break shot becomes in this example if the cue ball stops a few inches short, or long, of the ideal position angle.

Part B illustrates the principle of playing down the position angle whenever possible. The plan is to cut the 4-ball and roll down for the 11-ball break shot. The cue ball is traveling directly towards the exact location where it will contact the 11-ball on the next shot. As it rolls down the table, the cue ball maintains the same 37-degree cut angle. You will have that same cut angle whether or not you hit the position bulls-eye.

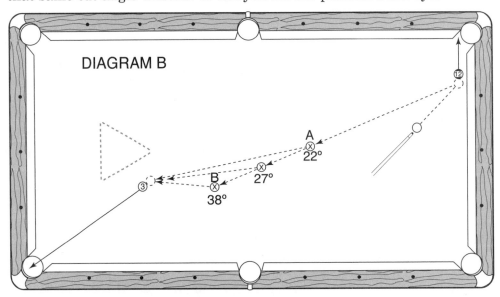

Diagram B shows a variation of the principle. Top right english will send the cue ball down a position line in which the angle for the next shot is constantly increasing. On many occasions such as this, you may want the angle to change slightly. In this example, you may prefer a shallower angle on break shots from long range at Position A and a much sharper angle for the break ball with the cue ball up close at Position B.

• #9 Survey the Table Before Shooting

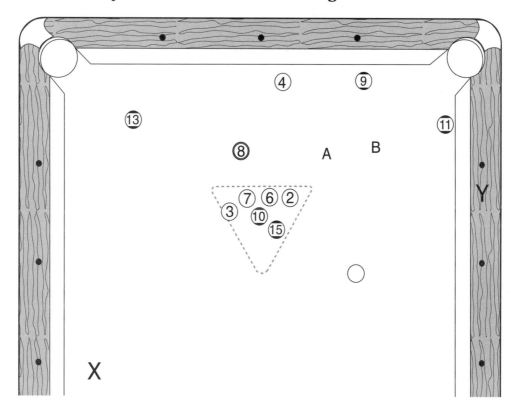

The great Willie Mosconi was always circling the table checking out the layout from any and all appropriate vantage points. I advise that you do the same. In our example, while standing at point X you've decided to spin the cue ball softly off the rail when playing the 11-ball to Position A for a secondary break shot on the 8-ball. The 9 and 13-balls are your insurance balls. This may, in fact, be a great plan. But before proceeding further, it would be wise to double-check the shot on the 8-ball from another perspective. From Position Y you can see that there is only half a pocket for the 8-ball, thanks to the 13-ball. This bit of intelligence should convince you to play the 11 more softly to Position B for a very acceptable break shot on the 4-ball.

The following list gives you just a few of the many possible objectives that you will want to accomplish at various times when surveying the table.

Possible Objectives when Surveying the Table

- Choose the best shot.
- Discover if there is a better shot or pattern than the one you're now considering.
- Find dead balls in the rack.
- Discover if a particular ball will go or not.
- Plot your position zone.
- Set your rail target.
- Check the entry point into the rack, or into a secondary cluster.

#10 Ball in Hand Shape

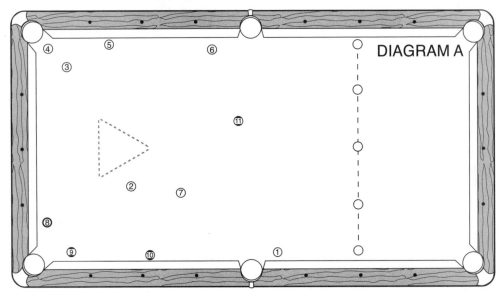

When your opponent scratches in Straight Pool, you can place the cue ball anywhere behind the head string. While this limits your choices compared to Eight-Ball or Nine-Ball (where you can place the cue ball anywhere on the table), it nevertheless gives you ample opportunity to play a successful shot most of the time. You should therefore consider your choices wisely.

On many occasions, your first priority will be to pocket a long shot and get in sync with the remainder of the balls. Since all object balls stationed past the side pockets are long shots, you should, in most cases play the easiest shot that will still get you back into play with the rest of the balls. Diagram A presents several typical shots to the far corner pockets that appear regularly in Straight Pool.

Take a moment to rank them in order of their difficulty. Assume that the pocket is not blocked on any shot. If you are ranking the 6-ball, for example, assume that the 4 and 5-balls aren't there. Let's also figure that you can get good position on the next ball on any shot you choose. Your selection should then be based on which ball gives you the best pocketing percentage. The cue balls along the head string give you just a few of the many positions where you could place the cue ball with ball in hand.

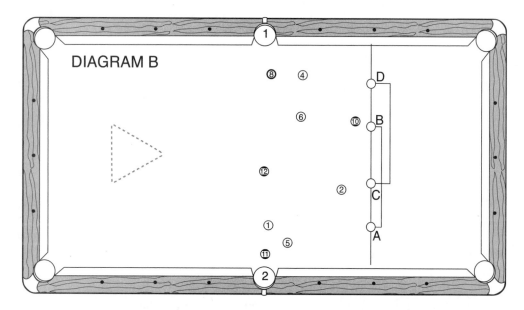

DIAGRAM B

Diagram B shows some of the typical shots that you'll play into the side pockets with cue ball in hand. The side pockets are excellent stepping-stones to the rest of the balls down the table. Cue ball positions A-B show the range of locations where you should place the cue ball for a shot at side pocket #1. C-D shows where it should go for shots into side pocket #2. Some side pocket shots with ball in hand also make excellent secondary break shots because you can precisely control your route down into the stack. You could, for example, play a secondary break shot by placing the cue ball at Position D for a cut shot on the 12-ball into pocket #2 (again assume the other balls are not there).

#11   Play Natural Shape as Often as Possible

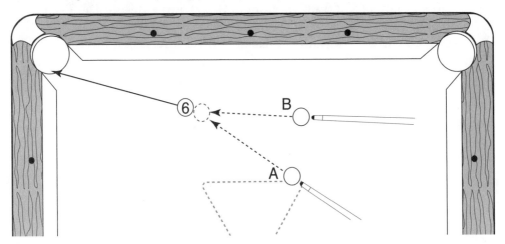

Your efforts to achieve the highest pocketing percentage possible will be much higher if you play natural shape whenever possible. You can discover 100% pure natural shape on any shot by playing it with centerball using a speed of stroke with which you are very comfortable. The route the cue ball travels after contact with the object ball when you do nothing special to alter its course is called natural shape. As a practical matter, you are also playing natural shape when you apply draw or follow to the cue ball along its center axis.

Natural shape can also be augmented with english providing it enhances the natural roll of the cue ball. In the diagram the 6-ball is cut into the corner from both sides of the ball. With the cue ball at Position A, right english and draw is natural shape. If the cue ball were at Position B, follow with left english would also be considered natural shape. In Position B, using right english would go against the grain of the cue ball's natural tendencies. There will be many occasions, however, when you will have to make an exception to this principle.

#12   Use Rail Targets

The diamonds adjacent to the rails of the table can be used for establishing intermediate targets for the cue ball as it travels across and around the table. The position in Diagram A on the following page illustrates a fairly common route to a key ball on the side rail next to the break ball. The goal is to arrive near or at Position X for the 2-ball. You certainly do not want to scratch in the side. You would also want to avoid sending the cue ball too far down the table. The correct route will take you towards the first diamond past the side pocket. The first diamond can be used as your rail target.

In Diagram B, your objective is to play a tricky draw shot on the 11-ball to the side rail and out for a down-the-rail break shot on the 2-ball.

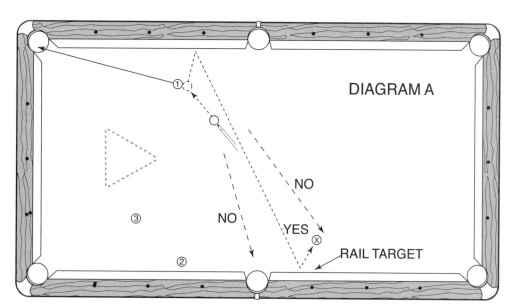

DIAGRAM A

NO

NO

YES

RAIL TARGET

You could aim somewhere on the side rail, but it helps to have a point of reference. By telling yourself that you need to hit the cushion 1/ diamonds above the corner pocket, you give yourself positive reinforcement that should help in executing the shot correctly.

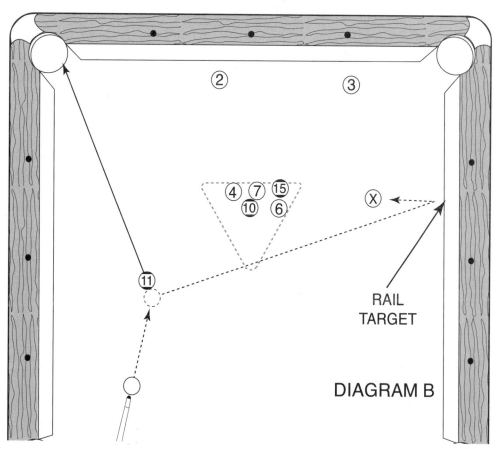

RAIL TARGET

DIAGRAM B

13 Plan Your Route and Avoid Obstructions

In Straight Pool, the cue ball will be traveling short distances for position most of the time, but your routes must nevertheless be very precise. One little unwanted kiss in route to your position zone could easily lead to disaster. Furthermore, the often congested quarters of a Straight Pool layout can make precision routing a must as well as an exacting challenge. So be sure to plan your position route very carefully, especially when there is heavy traffic along the way.

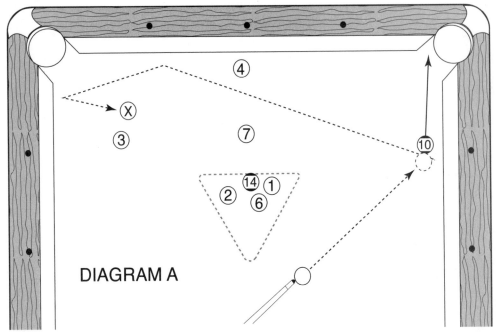

DIAGRAM A

Diagram A illustrates a route fraught with danger, but must be played since it is the best way to get through the rack. The plan is to send the cue ball three rails to Position X for a secondary break shot on the 7-ball. When playing the 10-ball, the cue ball must be struck with just the right amount of top left english as well as the correct speed to land at X. If you use too much left english, you could run into the 4-ball, and if you use too little, you could scratch. The only way to succeed at shots like this is to carefully plan your route and cueing, and then execute the shot to the best of your ability.

Diagram B on the next page shows an around-the-table position route that appears quite frequently when you have a severe cut angle on a ball near the end rail. There are several variations of this around-the-table shot, including the route to the secondary buster in the illustration. The key on this shot is to hit the far end rail before the lower side rail. And, of course, excellent speed control is a must in this situation.

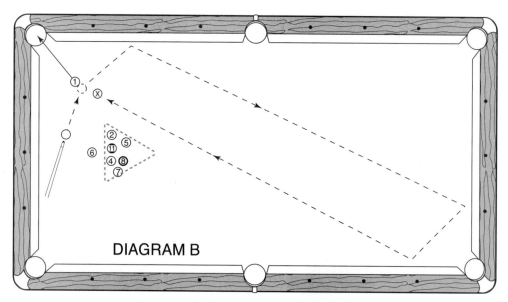

DIAGRAM B

#14 **When to Play Area Shape**

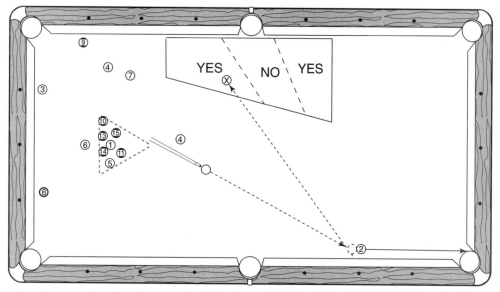

On the vast majority of your position plays in Straight Pool, you will be aiming for a relatively high degree of precision. Occasionally, however, your best strategy is to focus on pocketing the ball while sending the cue ball to a large position zone. You have a long shot on the 2-ball, which requires that you really focus on pocketing the ball. You are fortunate to have a substantial position zone for the 9-ball, which is the next logical shot. This is no time to get too cute by trying to play precise shape to Position Y when it's not needed. Just concentrate on making the ball and getting the cue ball anywhere within the position zone, and be sure not to scratch in the side pocket.

When to Play Area Shape
- When you have a long or difficult shot.
- Your next shot is close to a pocket.
- You're playing for the game ball.
- There will a choice of shots after pocketing a tough shot.
- Break shots.

#15   Margin for Error

Perfect shape is always a worthwhile goal. Because you are a person playing a difficult game, it is only prudent to make some allowances for human error. In Straight Pool, your tolerance on any given position play may range from as little as an inch (yes, that small) to perhaps a foot or even more. It all depends on the shot you are playing, and your unique capabilities for controlling both the speed and direction of the cue ball.

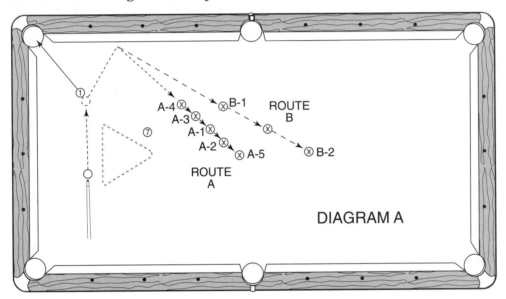

Diagram A shows a key ball position play where speed is the most critical component of the shot. If you possess a superior touch, you may choose Route A, which will leave you with a relatively short and easy shot on the 7-ball break shot. (Note that the break ball is sitting high up on the rack.) Cue ball A-1 is in prefect position for the break shot. If you came up a little long to A-2, you would still have a very workable shot. The same is true if you came up short at A-3 as long as you don't mind a semi-tough backcut. The five inches short and beyond A-1 give you a margin for error on this shot of plus or minus five inches.

Now let's carry this a step further. On this position play, if you stopped short of A-3, at A-4, you would have no reasonable shot at the break ball. In contrast, if you went a little past the ideal position zone to A-5, you could still play the break shot even though the cut angle is relatively shallow. To be on the safe side, you should play for a spot between A-1 and A-2. By aiming for the long side of the position zone, you will give yourself an extra margin for error. This will help you guard against committing the worst mistake, which is to come up short at A-4.

In this example, you could also increase your margin for error by sending the cue ball down Route B. By playing for a longer shot, your position zone is 2 1/2 times larger than with Route A. This route should be favored by shotmakers and those who don't have a well refined feel for distance. Note that this approach is the same as entering the wide area of a position zone (Principle #7). If you are just learning the game, you should consider playing position along Routes like Route B. As your game progresses and your feel for distance improves, you can tighten your position routes.

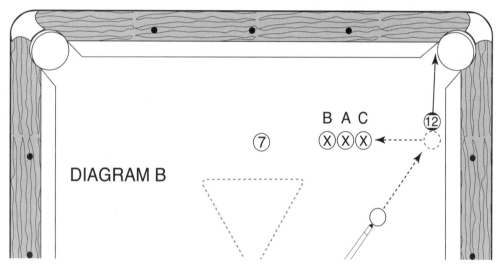

DIAGRAM B

Diagram B shows a delicate position play for a behind-the-rack break shot. Your margin for error is only plus or minus 2 1/4". This cut shot requires an extremely soft stroke and an acute sense of where your allowable margin for error lies. Position A is perfect. Position B is 2 1/4" long, while Position C is 2 1/4" short.

#16 Play the High Percentage Sequence

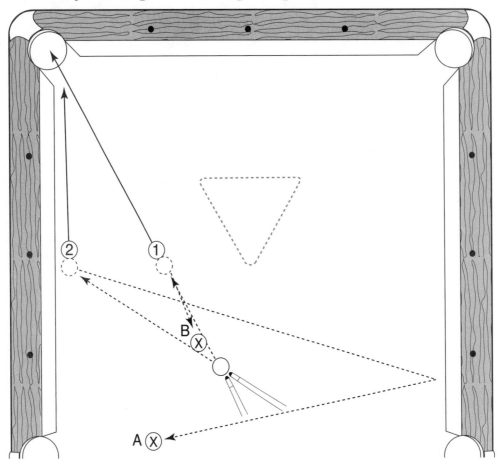

Playing great pool is largely about choosing the best percentage sequence of shots in any given situation. Let's assume you have left yourself with too much of a cut angle on the key ball shot on the 2-ball. To arrive a Position A for the break ball, you must now send the cue ball across the table and back with near perfect speed. A far better percentage play would be to draw straight back a foot or so on the 1-ball to Position B for a down-the-rail break shot on the 2-ball.

At times like this, your best percentage play is to accept your mistake and shift to Plan B. The odds of opening the next rack by playing the 1-ball, then the 2-ball break shot are probably about 95% for an "A" player. I would guess the odds for the same player opening the next rack successfully by playing the 2-ball first is about 40-50%.

#17 Avoid Scratching

Straight Pool presents many challenging situations where the risk of scratching must be successfully managed. There are three broad categories of scratches:

- The cue ball goes directly into the pocket after contacting the object ball.
- The cue ball strikes one or more rails before scratching.
- The cue ball bounces off another ball and continues into a pocket

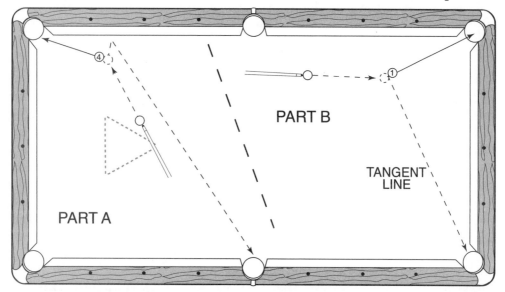

Part A demonstrates a type of scratch in which the cue ball first contacts a rail. These kinds of scratches result from improperly routing the cue ball, which usually results from insufficient knowledge about the cue ball's path as it travels across and/or around the table. The solution lies largely in evaluating shots like this on which you have scratched, and then practicing them to learn the correct route.

Part B of the diagram shows a direct-into-the-pocket scratch in which the cue ball closely followed the tangent line as it traveled across the table and into the corner pocket. Now don't feel too bad if you've scratched in a similar fashion since this foul was committed by one of the best players in the world in a major tournament. The point I'm trying to make is that no one is immune from scratching.

You can severely limit your direct-into-the-pocket scratches by understanding how the cue ball reacts after contacting the object ball. If you think a scratch is likely, first check out the cue ball's path after contact. Is the tangent line pointing at or near a pocket, as it is in our example? Then figure how you can adjust your cueing to avoid a scratch. In the example, a softer follow shot or a draw shot would have averted a scratch.

The third category of scratches occurs when the cue ball strikes another ball after contact with the object ball before heading into a pocket. These include:

- Scratching off the rack on break shots.
- Kissing off a ball when you miss your position route.
- Scratches off of secondary break shots.

Most scratches are a result of poor play, not bad luck. If you continue to look at scratches as a form of torture handed out by the pool gods, then you will fail to learn the valuable lesson that each one of them can teach you. Yes, some scratches are bad rolls, but in Straight Pool probably 80-90% are from caused by an error in judgment or execution.

#18 Pay Attention to Details

If you relish details, then Straight Pool is the game for you. The more detail oriented you become, the more position plays you will discover, any one of which can help you to meet an important positional objective at any moment during your run. When writing this book, I was tempted to gloss over a number of topics to simplify matters. I then convinced myself that you, the reader, are not going to read the book in one sitting, but will be using it as a reference for all matters about the game for years to come. Furthermore, if I left out an important detail, perhaps it might take you years to discover it through trial and error, if at all. I certainly know that it took me a long enough time to learn what's in this book, and I'm still learning new things daily.

There are numerous examples of the detail of the game throughout the book, but we'll go over one more here to further illustrate the extreme to which the very best players go in their attention to detail. The rack is nearly over and you have a perfect pattern to the 3-ball break shot. A detail-oriented player would first survey the table (see Principle #9) from Position A just to make sure that stop shot on the dead straight in 1-ball is what's best. The cue ball at Position B (which is where it will rest after a stop shot) is now lined up at a slight angle to the cue ball at Position C and the side pocket. This isn't bad, but its not quite good enough for a detail-oriented position play master.

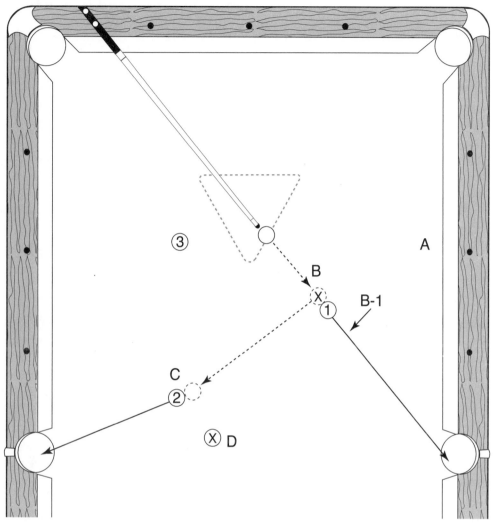

The slight cut angle on the 2-ball will cause the cue ball to end up in Position D. At Position D, you will have lengthened shot on the break shot and reduced the cut angle on the 3-ball. After playing the 1-ball, the cue ball should be in a direct line with the cue ball at Position C and the side pocket. This can be accomplished by drifting the cue ball 4" forward to B-1 after it contacts the 1-ball. Now when you play the 2-ball, the cue ball will stop at Position C for a much better break shot.

#19   Keep the Cue Ball Away from the Rails and Other Balls

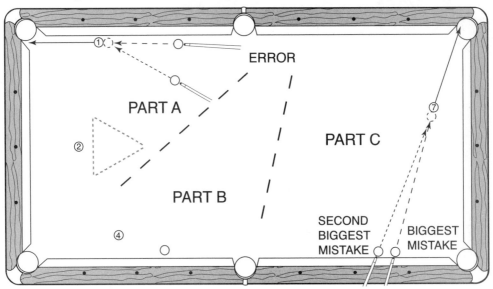

You will find the cue ball stops a little closer to the rail more often in Straight Pool than in Nine-Ball or other pool games. The cue ball tends to hug the rail because of the congestion factor, and because you are playing shorter shots that don't require as long of a bridge or as much clearance from the cushion. Nevertheless, as a general rule, you should still attempt to keep the cue ball at least 2" from the rail, if not more.

In Part A, the goal was to get a slight angle on the 1-ball so you could follow down and off the rail for a good shot at the 2-ball. You still retain your cueing options (draw or follow), with the cue ball adjacent to the rail, but you will be forced into playing the next shot from the cushion.

Part B shows a break shot, which provides an exception to the rule about keeping the cue ball away from the rails. In this position, having the cue ball near the rail gives you an excellent cut angle for a powerful break shot.

Part C Shows one of the biggest mistakes in pool, the dead straight in shot with the cue ball frozen to the rail. The second biggest mistake is to have a small angle with the cue ball frozen to the rail. This error is often compounded by the tendency to over-stroke the next shot in an failed attempt to recover position. This can easily lead to a missed shot.

The congestion factor in Straight Pool causes a higher percentage of shots in which you must bridge over intervening balls. Although you should avoid getting jacked up whenever possible, you will nevertheless end up shooting over balls quite often. Plan on mastering the skill of shooting over balls rather than fearing these shots whenever they appear.

#20 Play Your Game

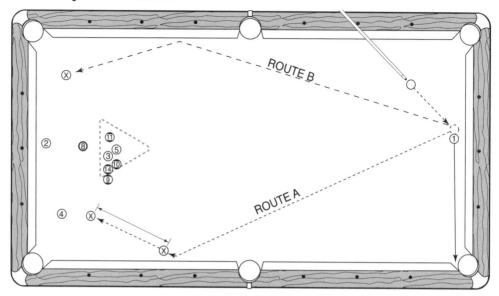

There are many styles of good Straight Pool position. Some players would rather play up close to the balls, while others may feel more comfortable maximizing the size of their position zones by setting up for longer shots. When it comes to shot selection, what is a hanger for some players may look like a high-risk venture to others. These preferences, and several others, will help determine your style of shot selection and the way you play your patterns. The idea is to maximize your game by tailoring your style to take full advantage of your talents and to minimize the impact of your weaknesses. As a further refinement of this principle, you may even alter your shot selection to better fit the way you are playing at a particular moment, or to mesh better with the conditions.

The position play is to shoot the 1-ball and travel down the table for a secondary break shot on one of the balls behind the rack. A shotmaker might choose Route A for shape on the 2-ball. Notice the ample size of the position zone. The shotmaker just wants a shot on the 2-ball and is not too particularly concerned with the difficulty of the shot. A position player with a refined sense of speed and above average directional control, on the other hand, might choose Route B. Their goal is to play the 2-ball first, then break the cluster with the 8-ball.

21   Use Your Imagination

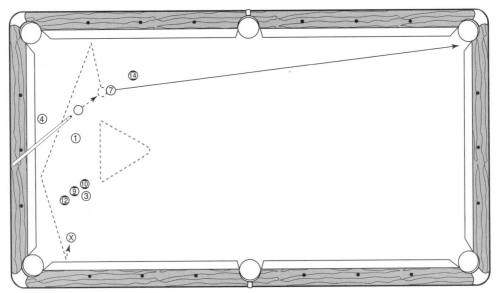

After you've played enough Straight Pool, the vast majority of position plays will become somewhat routine. Still, you will occasionally run up against a position that challenges you to get your creative juices flowing. When faced with an unusual position play, you can begin to discover a workable solution by quickly eliminating what is not feasible. The next step is to sift through some potential solutions. Let's follow the process with the help of our example.

A look at the table reveals that the only remotely reasonable shot is the 7-ball into the far corner pocket. That quickly eliminates the other balls from consideration. Since you've got to shoot the 7-ball firmly, position on the 4-ball is out. How about a two-rail route into the cluster? That's not an option because the 4-ball is in the way. And, of course, the 1-ball blocks the one rail route to the cluster. You could cross the table and out for shape on the 3-ball next, but the 3-ball won't go because the 10-ball is partially obstructing it. You could conceivably cross the table twice for shape on the 14-ball, but that would require a hard stroke with inside english, which greatly raises your chances of missing.

Wait a second! What if you concentrated on pocketing the ball and playing natural shape? What would that give you? Bingo, the three rail position route to Position X shown in the diagram. The lesson: sometimes you've got to take a little extra time to sift through a few possibilities before the winning position play pops out at you as a result of you putting your imagination to work.

22 Know the Exceptions to the First 21 Principles

Now that your on your way to mastering the 21 Principles of Position Play, I'm going to risk alienating you by suggesting that there will be times when you will have to fly in the face of each and every one of them. The exceptions would probably take another book, so instead I'm going to leave you with this thought: it takes years of work and experience to master the principles we've just discussed, and several more to learn the exceptions to the rule. In this instance, experience is the best teacher.

There will be times (but not many) where your best play is your only play, and that may be to turn the cue ball completely loose. So be it. At other times you will have a position play that requires such precision that you have no margin for error. It's even possible that you may have to play a shot off the rail that looks like a dead scratch in the hopes that you have miscalculated the scratch angle. Many of these lessons and more can only be learned through exercising your best judgment on each and every shot. Accept the results, learn from them, and move forward with your game.

Position Play, Straight Pool Style

Playing good position is a necessary ingredient for excelling at any pool game, and the basics of fine position play are the same for all. But each game has it's own particular requirements. In Nine-Ball, for example, you must master moving the cue ball long distances across and around the table. When playing Straight Pool, you must move the cue ball short distances with a high degree of precision. You must also fine-tune your cut angles. It is not sufficient to merely get on the correct side of a ball. And you must be able to consistently send the cue ball into other balls and come away with good position after contact. This section covers the most commonly recurring position plays in Straight Pool. If you master the shots and concepts in this section, you will be able to handle 99% of the position plays that you encounter when playing Straight Pool.

Cueing

You can significantly alter the path of the cue ball on any given shot by changing the position of your cue at address and by using different speeds of stroke. The most basic position plays are on the center axis. The illustration shows a stop shot, a follow shot hit one tip above center, and a draw shot hit a tip below center. You run the risk of miscueing when you go much at all beyond a tip off of center. When playing Straight Pool, you almost never have to exceed the limits of draw and follow shown in the illustration. As a matter of fact, on the vast majority of shots, you will use less than what is shown.

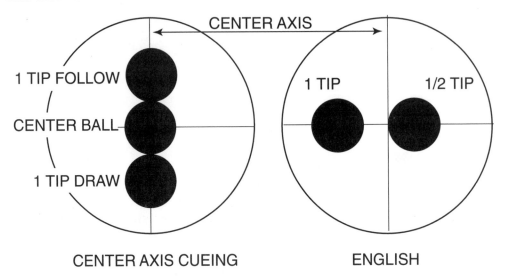

CENTER AXIS CUEING   ENGLISH

Many of the greatest Straight Pool players in history advocate that you play upwards of 80-90% of your shots on the center axis. There are, however, many fine players who feel they do best by spinning a majority of their shots, but this technique takes years and years of practice.

You will need to learn to use english effectively when playing Straight Pool so you can fine tune the movements of the cue ball. I recommend, however, that you limit how far you cue off the center axis. There is no point in using any more english than is absolutely necessary. Besides, the effects of english on aiming become exaggerated the farther you cue away from the center axis. The illustration shows you what both a fi tip and 1 tip of english looks like. In the diagrams that follow you will learn how to adjust your cueing to achieve a wide variety of positional objectives. Although there is a separate chapter on practicing, most of the shots in this section should also be practiced until mastered.

• Stop Shots, and Adjusting Stop Shots

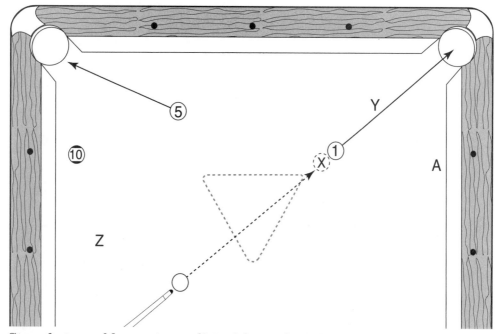

Stop shots enable you to predict with nearly 100% accuracy where the cue ball will rest for your next shot, which makes it one of the most useful positional tools for a Straight Pool player. The stop shot is traditionally thought of as a straight in shot. The objective is to have the cue ball stop dead in its tracks upon contact with the object ball. However, perfectly straight-in shots are somewhat of a rarity even in Straight Pool. For practical purposes, we're going to define a stop shot as a short range shot with a cut angle of about 3 degrees or less. On a stop shot, there is little or no sideways movement after contact.

Stop shots are hit with centerball, a medium firm stroke, and a level cue. The cue ball will slide across the cloth and stop dead upon contact as long as it is within 2fi' – 3' of the object ball. When the cue ball is over this distance from the object ball, you will need to apply draw to the cue ball for it to stop dead.

A stop shot on the 1-ball will leave you with a straight-in shot on the 5-ball. When planning a stop shot, be sure to calculate the cue ball's new position from the spot adjacent to the object ball. This is shown with the cue ball marked X. Is a stop shot precisely what you need? Or should you adjust your cueing slightly? You may wish to hit the cue ball slightly above center to arrive at Y so you'll have an angle on the 5-ball. You could then follow to Z for position on the 10-ball.

Tip: Before shooting a stop shot, it would be wise to walk over to where you'll be playing your next shot to determine if a stop shot is exactly what is required (Position A in our example).

• **Soft Outside Draw**

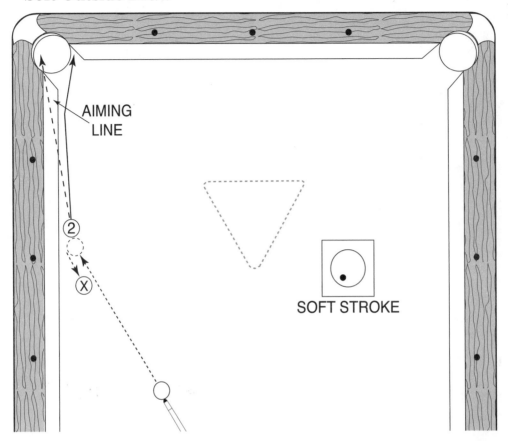

On this down-the-rail cut shot of 30-degrees, your objective is to have the cue ball bounce off the cushion as little as possible. This shot comes up quite often when you are shooting two or more balls in close proximity or when playing shape on a break shot. Play the shot with low outside english. Use the softest stroke that will allow you to get the object ball to the pocket with a few inches to spare, avoid a roll off (if the table is not level), and enable you to maintain your accuracy. Since you are shooting softly, you can also cheat the pocket. The english will also help pull the cue ball backwards after it strikes the rail instead of straight out.

In this example, the combination of cheating the pocket and spinning in the object ball turns a 30-degree cut shot into approximately a 23-degree cut shot, which helps keep the cue ball much closer to the rail.

Inside English

When playing Straight Pool, inside english is a required tool for routing the cue ball through traffic and for playing position. Using inside english may initially challenge those of you who are used to playing other pool games where outside english is the mainstay of position play on off center axis position plays.

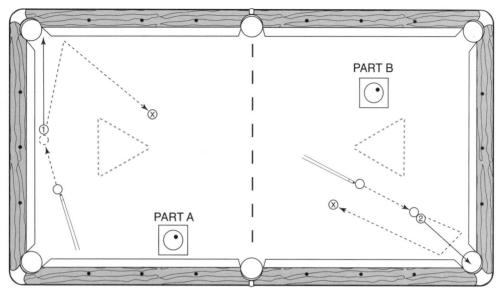

While inside english is universally blamed by pool players for missed shots, in Straight Pool it is not nearly as difficult to use as in other games. With Straight Pool, virtually all inside english shots are played from close range, which minimizes the need to allow for deflection. They are also played with a softer stroke than in other games such as 9-ball, which also minimizes deflection. Using inside english on short shots with a soft to medium speed of stroke takes little away from your accuracy once you get used to using it in this manner.

Part A shows a two-rail follow shot, which is one of the most commonly occurring uses of inside english in Straight Pool. Your goal is to escape the end rail and return to the middle portion of the table.

Part B shows what can sometimes be a troublesome two-rail position play using inside english. The 2-ball is nearly straight in. When using inside english on shots like this, you must guard against having the cue ball's path diverted slightly in the direction of the inside english. In the example, the cue ball would turn to the right and follow the object ball into the pocket. To avoid this disaster, you should aim to cheat the pocket slightly to the outside.

You'll also need to use inside english on a variety of break shots when the object ball is near the rail (see Chapter 4). These shots require that you shoot from a shorter range at higher speeds of stroke.

Tip: If you have difficulty using inside english, try practicing it with a series of progressive drills. Try shooting short-range two-rail follow shots with the object ball near the pocket and the cue ball within a foot of the object ball. Concentrate on using a smooth stroke. Note your misses and adjust your aim accordingly. Gradually increase the distance of the shots and your speed of stoke as your progress allows.

• Draw Speed Control

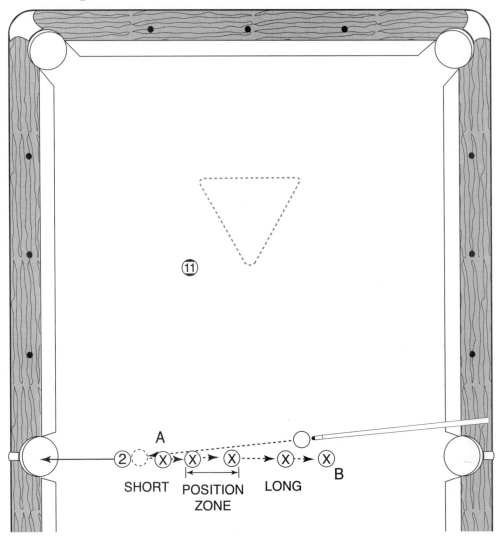

Excellent speed control on draw shots is one of the biggest dividing lines between an average player and one who excels at Straight Pool. I believe that most players can master the art of draw speed control at shorter ranges by taking the time to work on this vital positional skill with a series of progressive drills.

The example shows some of the potential pitfalls to playing draw shots when precise shape is required. The goal is to shoot the 2-ball and draw back within the position zone for excellent shape on the break shot (the 11-ball). There are two errors that commonly occur in this situation. While playing the shot you may, in mid stroke, become fearful of drawing back too far. This erroneous thought can cause your arm to tighten up, which reduces draw and leaves you with a tough backcut at Position A. The other mistake occurs when you tell yourself that you're not going to come up short. Now the cue ball will go long to Position B.

In this example, the worst of the two errors is coming up short at A, because you failed to stroke the shot. Error B arises mostly because you do not quite know yet how to regulate the amount of draw your stroke produces at short range, not because you didn't stroke the shot. Draw speed control comes from developing the skill in practice and then having the confidence and decisiveness to play the shot as planned. Once you are down over a short-range draw shot where precision is a must, make a commitment to the speed required. You've got to feel the speed before the final stroke and then just let the shot go. You're best chance for success lies in executing the shot as positively as possible.

There are a variety of techniques for achieving short-range draw control. You can always cue in one position, such as fi or 1 tip below center. When using this approach, you are relying only on speed of stroke for achieving the proper draw distance. Another approach is to change your tip position while at the same time regulating your speed control. For example, you may wish to use fi tip below center with the cue ball a foot from the object ball when your goal is to draw the cue ball back only 6-8". When the cue ball is, let's say, two feet' from the object ball and you need a foot of draw, you might then use 1 full tip of draw.

Tip: If you favor a soft stroke, you may wish to cue lower than those who favor a firm stroke on draw shots for precise shape in Straight Pool. Those who like to use a firmer stoke may wish to cue a little closer to center.

• Stun Shots

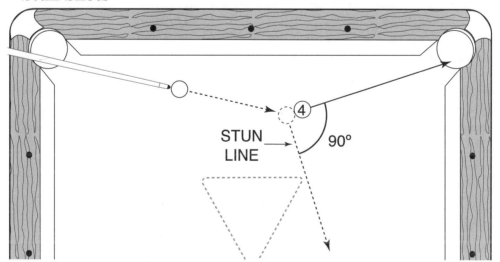

On cut shots stroked with a centerball hit and medium firm stroke, the cue ball will travel down a path that's at a 90-degree angle to that of the object ball as shown. This bit of knowledge is extremely useful since it allows you to predict the cue ball's direction with great accuracy. Viewing the cue ball's path from Position A can be useful in planning your position route, breaking clusters and shooting break shots. You may need to slightly adjust the path forward with follow or backwards with draw to achieve your objectives for the shot.

Tip: When playing stun shots with a cut angle under 15 degrees, you must be very precise in your cueing. Proper cueing is needed to achieve the desired path because of the force required to move the cue ball more than just a few inches with accuracy on small cut angle stun shots.

Draw/Stun Shot

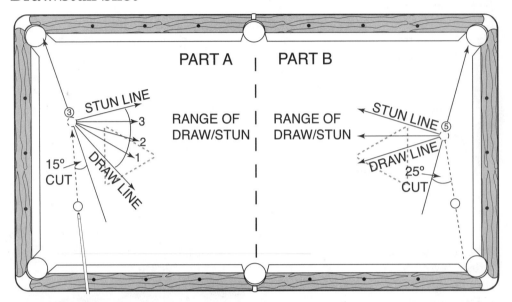

Straight Pool position is largely played without going to a rail. This is particularly true when balls are located in the area of the triangle. You must become adept at guiding the cue ball from place to place using the proper cueing and speed of stroke. Part A shows a 15-degree cut shot. Notice the path of the cue ball if you use either stun or draw. Also observe the gap between the two lines. How do you send the cue ball to the various locations within this zone? The answer is what I call the draw/stun shot, which is a hybrid of both the draw and stun shots.

There are a number of combinations of draw and stun that will enable you to send the cue ball anywhere within the zone. These involve using various amounts of draw and a variety of speeds of stroke. To simplify the shot, just keep in mind the following three combinations of draw and stun. These should enable you to achieve nearly all of your positional objectives within the zone. Because of the cut angle, note that the zones start some distance from the point of contact.

In Part A, the cue ball will travel down Line 1 using fl draw and/ stun. The cue ball will follow Line 2 by using fi draw and fi stun. The cue ball will travel down Line 3 using/ draw and fl stun.

Part B shows a range of possible draw/stun shots on a 25-degree cut shot. Note that the gap is much narrower than on the 15-degree cut shot in Part A. At this angle you can simplify matters by using fi draw and fi stun to access the middle of the gap. On cuts shots over approximately 35 degrees the gap narrows to the point where it's not worth attempting to split it with a draw/stun shot.

Follow/Stun Shot

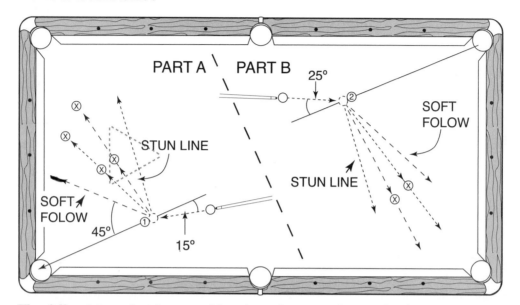

The follow/stun shot is a combination of a stun shot and a "typical" follow shot played with a medium soft stroke. When your cut angle is relatively shallow (under 10 degrees) you can play the follow/stun shot by using a medium firm stroke (the same as a stun shot). Strike the cue ball slightly above center, and it will drift forward. Another technique is to let up slightly on the speed (versus the stun shot) so that the cue ball rolls forward of the stun line. The follow/stun shot is easiest to gauge on cut angles under about 15 degrees. It is also easiest to control when the cue ball is within three feet of the object ball.

   The objective of the follow/stun shot is to access the zones shown in both parts of the illustration that could not be reached with either a pure stun shot or a soft follow shot. Part A of the illustration shows a 15 degree cut shot. When played with a soft follow stroke, the cue ball will roll forward at a 45-degree angle to the line of the shot. The cue ball will roll quite some distance when using a stun follow shot at over 15 degrees. You can expect the cue ball to roll at least as far as those in Positions C and D. If you need to access a part of the zone closer to the object ball, such as at cue balls E and D, then you need to play a soft draw shot. Gauging the speed on this shot is definitely a challenging proposition.

   Part B shows a Follow/Stun shot on a 25 degree cut shot. The cue ball will roll several feet when using a stun stroke with follow to at least Position A or B. You can cut down on the cue balls rolling distance, as in part A, by playing a soft draw shot. The cue ball would then stop at either C or D.

Pounding Balls with Speed and Accuracy

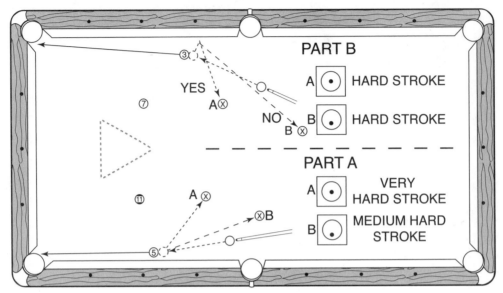

At times you will find yourself with a smaller cut angle than is required to comfortably play position for your next shot. Part A shows a situation that comes up repeatedly: you're too straight on the 5-ball and you need to get the cue ball away from the rail and out for position on the break ball (the 11-ball). You could pound the cue ball off the rail (Path A) using a hard stroke with about a/ of draw. You have to really let your stroke out and shoot with confidence when playing this shot. Use a few extra warm-up strokes to really get comfortable over the shot and develop a feeling for the smooth, powerful acceleration you're going to use on the shot. From the original position, another option is to draw back to Position B. This gives you a longer break shot, but it straightens out the cut angle without having to use a hard stroke.

Part B is a similar situation that calls for you to pound the shot. This time the cue ball is further from the rail. Since the rail slows down the cue ball, you've got to really stroke this shot to send the cue ball very far off the cushion. When the object ball is off the rail the cue ball will naturally come backwards with centerball and a hard stroke to Position A. A common mistake is to apply too much draw, which would send the cue ball further back down the table to Position B.

Holding Up the Cue Ball

On small angle cut shots of about 7-10 degrees or less, you can reduce the sideways drift that would normally accompany a stop shot by what's called holding up the cue ball. The shot is played with low draw (1 to 1fi tips) and a soft stroke. To reduce the amount of sideways drift, the object ball should enter the pocket at the slowest possible speed you feel comfortable without having the object ball roll off. On shorter shots, you may also consider cheating the pocket.

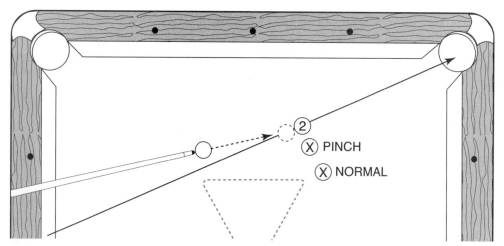

The objective is to have the cue ball rolling forward at the slowest speed possible with a lot of backspin. The backspin will transfer into follow on the object ball, helping to propel it to the pocket. Many players also like to aim for a fuller hit on the object ball while using outside english. In our example, that would be right english.

Drawing Across the Table and Out

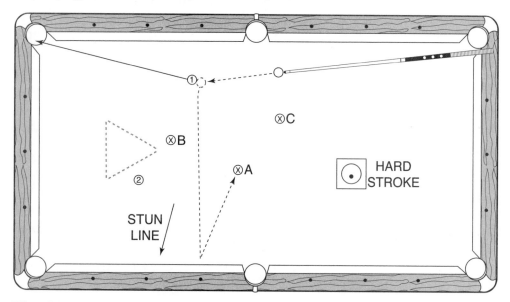

The objective on this shot is to send the cue ball across the table and back out for shape on the 2-ball break shot to Position A. While this shot may appear routine, it is not nearly as easy it looks. You need to regulate both your speed and cueing, which is difficult because the shot must be played with a hard stroke. If you fail to apply enough draw, you'll wind up at Position B, and if you use too much speed and/or draw, you'll end up at Position C. A hard stroke with a fi tip of draw should work. This very useful position play demonstrates the challenge of using a hard stroke when going for precise shape.

Floating Follow at Higher Speeds of Stroke

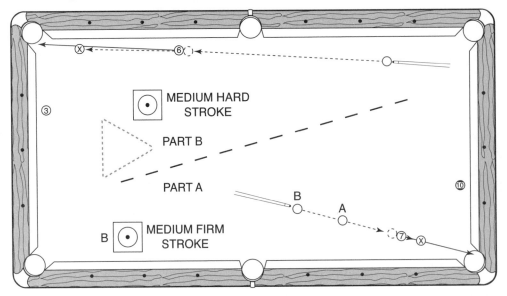

When playing Straight Pool, you'll be faced with numerous straight in or small angle follow shots of about 5 degrees that are not virtual pocket hangers. Often, your objective on these shots will be to send the cue ball a short distance past the object ball. In Part A, your goal is to pocket the 7-ball and follow a short distance for position on the 10-ball. You could slow roll the cue ball, which is no problem when the cue ball is at Position A. If the cue ball is further from the 7-ball, such as at Position B, then slow rolling the cue ball takes away from the accuracy of the shot. The answer is to float the cue ball forward. Use a stun stroke (medium firm) and/tip of follow.

At longer distances such as the shot in Part B, the cue ball will roll forward with a stun stroke and a centerball hit. Naturally the secret to this extremely valuable positional tool lies in practicing it over and over again at various distances using a variety of speeds (medium firm on up). Also experiment with adjusting the position of your tip. The shot takes some getting used to, but once you've got it down, you'll eliminate those misses that come from weakly slow rolling shots that are really out of the slow roll range.

Bending the Cue Ball with Follow for Position

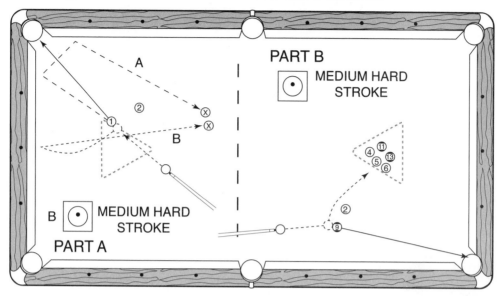

Line A in Part A shows the conventional route from the 1-ball to break shot shape on the 2-ball. This shot is played with follow and right english. This path, however, requires that you cross the position zone. A better approach would be to play the shot with a medium hard follow stroke. The cue ball will at first travel down the tangent line, before bending forward. By the time it strikes the rail, the cue ball will be headed in a new direction. Now it will travel down Line B for perfect shape on the 2-ball.

In Part B, your objective is to break open the cluster. It appears as if the 2-ball is blocking the cue ball's path to the rack, which prevents you from breaking the balls with the 9-ball. The 9-ball is not, however, in the way as the cue ball will travel down the tangent line before bending into its new route, which will take it directly into the cluster.

Tip: The mysteries of the cue ball are often hidden by the naked eye. As a matter of fact, I picked up the shot in Part A after playing a video over and over again in slow motion. I suggest you do the same. Once you gain an increased awareness of how the cue ball really behaves in actual flight, you'll open up to a whole new world of position play possibilities.

Pounding with Follow

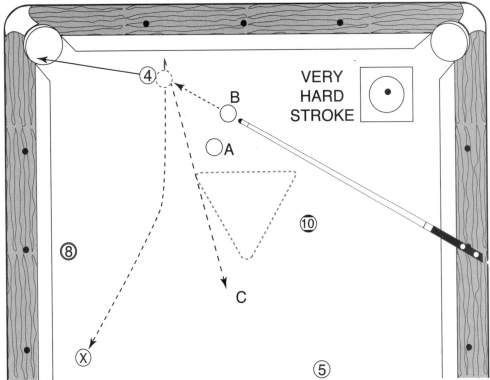

Pounding a shot with follow will help get you out of many a jam when you've failed to position the cue ball at a sufficient cut angle. It would be easy to send the cue ball from Position A to Position X. With the cue ball at Position B, however, you have very little angle to work with. By pounding the shot with centerball, you would send the cue ball down Line C. By applying a half tip of follow with a very hard stroke, the cue ball will bend forward and arrive at Position X for ideal shape on the 8-ball.

Bending with Draw

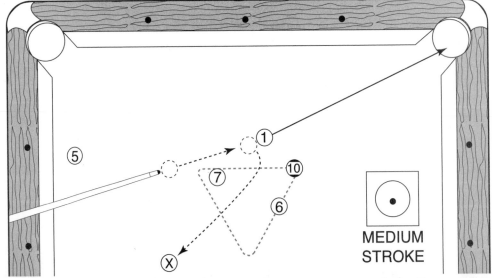

Your goal on this shot is to play the 5-ball next. It looks, however, as if the 10, 6, and 7-balls are in the way. But we learned from a previous section that looks can be deceiving. In this case, the cue ball will travel a short distance down the tangent line before bending into its eventual path towards Position X for the 5-ball. Notice how the 7-ball is on a straight line from the cue ball's point of contact and its eventual resting point. Like magic, the cue ball went right past the 7-ball for position.

Tip: The cut angle and the speed at which you stroke draw shots will affect where the cue ball starts to bend. When using a hard stroke on cut angles of around 20 degrees the cue balls bend will more closely resemble a big loop.

Floating the Cue Ball for Precise Shape

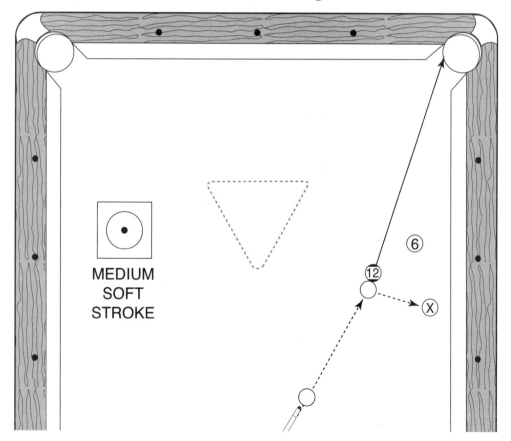

On shots with a cut angle of about 10-20 degrees, you can float the cue ball relatively short distances sideways with great precision. The shot is played with a soft draw stroke. You want just enough backspin so that the cue ball does not roll either forward or backward. The illustration shows a precise position play where you need to have the cue ball float a short distance up close to the rail for a good cut angle on the break ball.

Concepts and Fine Points of Position Play

It is possible to work you way through a rack with a seemingly endless series of recovery shots, or shots where your position is not quite right. On a vast majority of your position plays, however, you will make running out so much easier by adding a degree or two of precision to your game. Perhaps, for example, a 15-degree angle could be greatly superior to a 20-degree angle on a particular shot. And an inch or two here or there could make all the difference in getting good shape on a break ball. In this section, you will learn many of the concepts and fine points of position play that should keep you out of trouble and that should add crispness to your position play.

Complementary Angles

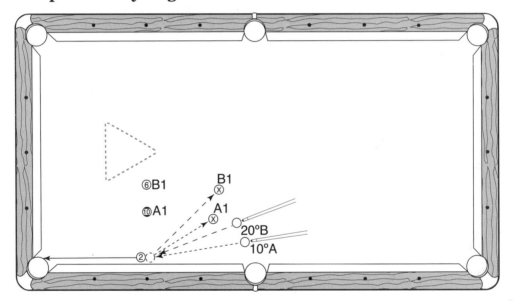

When playing position on down the rail cut shots your goal is to wind up with a cut angle that maximizes your chances of both making the ball and getting excellent shape on the next ball. The ideal angle would enable you to avoid having to pound the cue ball, or to shoot so softly that you lose accuracy.

There are certain cut angles on down the rail shots that are match up perfectly with specific position plays. In our illustration, a 10 degree cut shot enables you to easily get position on the 10-ball (A to A1). A 20-degree cut makes it easy to come further out for position on the 6-ball (B to B1). Going from A to B1 requires a pound shot. Playing from B to A1 requires a very soft touch.

Whenever you play position for a cut shot, there is always an ideal angle that enables you to most easily get position on the next ball. Your awareness of that ideal angle on critical position plays, and ability to achieve it, will help add a great deal of precision to your game.

Tip: Your ideal angle depends on both the speed of the table and your preference for using a soft, medium, or firm stroke on most shots.

• Using the Rail Increases Your Options

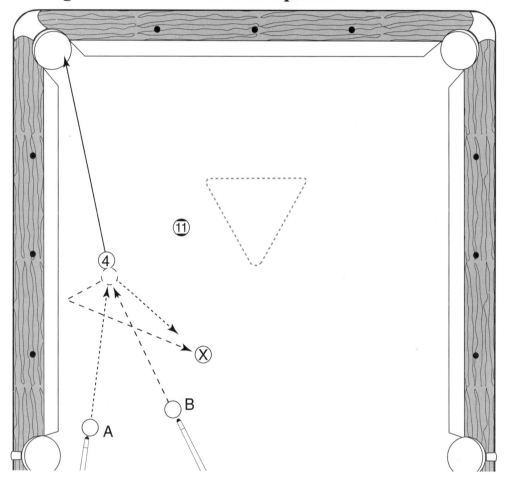

When the object ball is within about 6" of the rail, it is much easier to go to the rail and back out for position rather than floating the cue ball across the table from the opposite side of the object ball. In the example, the goal is to get shape on the 11-ball, which is the break ball. From Position A, you would have to play a very delicate draw shot to arrive at Position X. With the cue ball at the same 15 degree cut angle, but on the opposite side of the 4-ball at Position B, you can use the rail to help exert maximum control over the shot. The rail reduces cue ball speed, which enables you to play the shot with authority. In addition, you can freely use english to alter the cue ball's path if necessary.

Balls Near the Rail – Ideal Angles

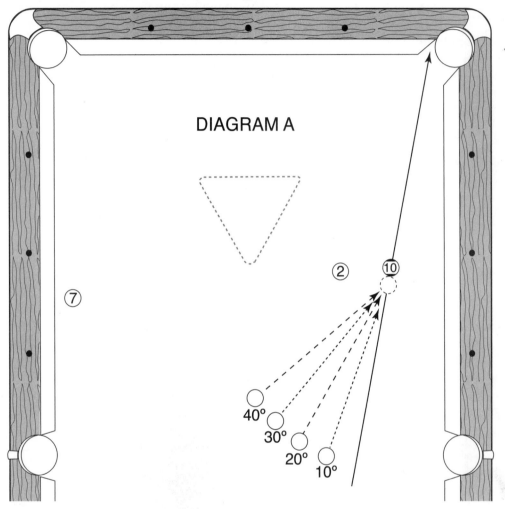

DIAGRAM A

The ideal cut angle for shots near the rail depends on several factors. These include:

- Where you need to send the cue ball.
- How close the object ball is to the rail.
- The speed of the table.
- Which stroke speed you feel most comfortable using.

In Diagram A, the object ball is 6" off the rail. A cut angle of 30-40 degrees is ideal for sending the cue ball to the other side of the table for the 7-ball. An angle of less than 30 degrees is best for playing shape for a ball on the same side of the table, such as the 2-ball.

When the object ball is very close to the rail, as in Diagram B, the ideal cut angles are significantly less compared to Diagram A. To cross the table for position on the 15-ball, a cut angle of about 25-30 degrees is ideal. Position on the 9-ball is most easily reached with a cut angle of about 15-20 degrees.

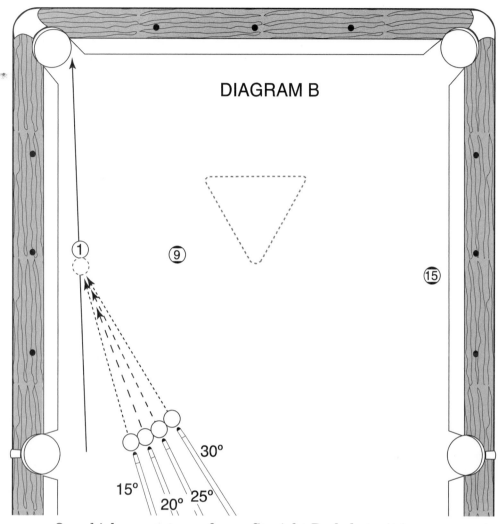

DIAGRAM B

On a high percentage of your Straight Pool shots, it is necessary to have the ideal cut angle, or something very close to it. Getting the perfect angle is as difficult as trying to get straight-in shape. When playing position, you will no doubt miss landing perfectly on the ideal angle more often than not. But if you know, prior to playing a shot, where position on the ideal cut angle is located, then you have a target to shoot for. In most cases, if you end up close to the target angle, you will be able to easily play position on the next ball.

Tip: If your only goal when playing position in Straight Pool is to stay on the correct side of the object ball and you pay little attention to fine tuning your cut angles, then you will forever find yourself pounding and killing shots to make up for deficiencies in the cut angles that you've left for yourself.

• Balls in the Open – Ideal Angles

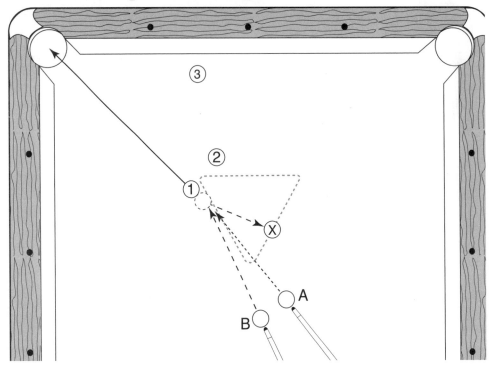

When playing position from ball to ball in the middle of the table without the use of the rails, which are where a number of shots in the area of the triangle are located, then you must really limit your cut angles. As a general rule, you'll want cut angles of no more than about 10-degrees. With cut angles of over 10-degrees, the cue ball travels some distance sideways after contact. The diagram shows a 7-degree cut on the 1-ball at Position A. The objective is to slide over just far enough for the 2-ball so that you stay on the correct side of the 2-ball. If the cue ball stops on the correct side of the 2-ball you can easily drift over for the 3-ball.

If the cue ball were at Position B with a cut angle of 20-degrees, then it would not be possible to play this three ball sequence in the same manner. Notice that Position B is only 3" from Position A. When playing shape from ball to ball in the open, you must be very aware of the ideal angles since a slight positional error, as our example shows, can change your sequence of shots dramatically.

Tip: When working in the open, you can recover shape easier with a soft stroke and a small cut angle. When your cut angle is too great (see our example), then you will most likely need to play a recovery shot to keep your original pattern intact.

• How Pocketing Affects Position

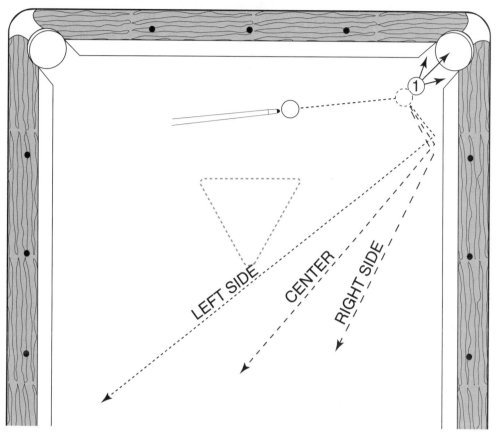

I went over earlier how you can enhance your efforts when playing position by cheating the pocket. Along the same lines, you can also miss position by failing to shoot the ball into the right portion of the pocket. The distance you miss position is related to the distance the object ball was from the pocket and how far off-line the object ball is to your target (which is usually the center) when it enters the pocket.

When the center of the object ball is on a diagonal line 6" from the pocket, you can "miss" by 10 degrees to either side of the center of the pocket and still make the shot with room to spare. But "missing" into the pocket is no guarantee of shape. The diagram shows the position that results from playing a stun shot into each side of the pocket at the same speed. Notice the difference in both direction and distance that pocketing makes in this somewhat extreme example.

Tip: The cue ball travels further when the shot is overcut (Line A) and a shorter distance when it is undercut (Line B) than when the object ball enters the center of the pocket (Line C). Remember also that the closer the object ball is to the pocket, the more wildly the cue ball can be thrown off course when not shot into the correct portion of the pocket.

Nine-Ball Shape to a Straight Pool Position Zone

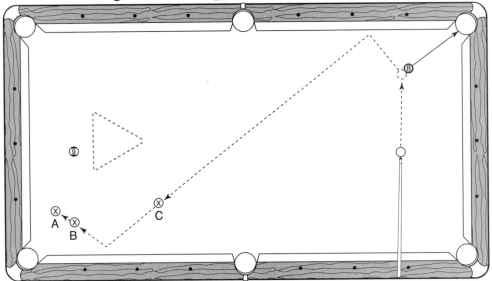

One of the more challenging aspects of Straight Pool is the need to occasionally play Nine-Ball type of position to a Straight Pool sized position zone. The objective is to play the 8-ball and travel across the length of the table for position on a behind the rack break shot on the 9-ball. Now imagine for a moment that this was a game of Nine-Ball. You would have a reasonably simple shot on the 9-ball if the cue ball landed anywhere between Positions A and C. In Straight Pool, your zone of acceptable shape shrinks to between A and B.

To execute Nine-Ball type position plays with Straight Pool precision, you must first recognize the challenge and then plan your route very carefully. Once you've got your route mapped out, it all comes down to executing the shot with perfect speed. You've simply got to rise to the occasion and give the shot your very best. Feel the speed during your warm-up strokes and let the shot go with your very best effort.

Tip: Because of the degree of difficulty factor, you should not expect perfection on long distance position plays to small shape zones. Adopting the attitude that you can only give it your best will free you up to play the shot as well as you can at that moment in time.

Short Range Position – the Essence of 14.1

The series of diagrams that follow are some the most important in this book because they demonstrate the precision required to play Straight Pool at a very high level. The illustrations show the benefit of obtaining the correct position in tight quarters. They also show how missing position by a couple of inches can, in certain situations, entirely change the complexion of a runout. The type of position shown in this series is the kind masters like Mosconi played that made running out look so easy when it's really not.

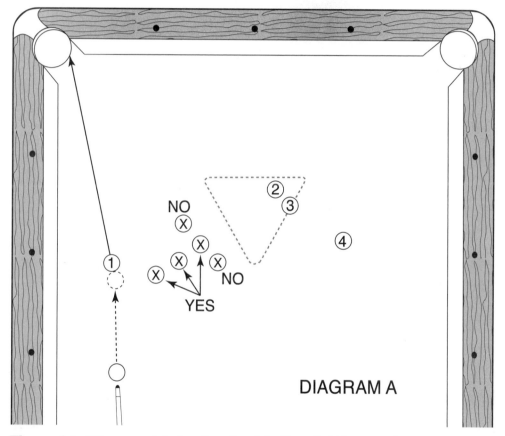

DIAGRAM A

The goal in Diagram A is to play the 1-ball and slide over for a straight-in shot on the 2-ball. The 3-ball comes next. The series of cue balls along the straight-in line are in perfect position for the 2-ball. When you have two balls that are close together at the end of the rack, position play can be substantially more difficult than it appears. If you miss your angle by even as little as an inch or so, your pattern can be radically altered.

Tip: When you are playing for straight-in shape, it is wise to have a recovery plan in place in case you miss position.

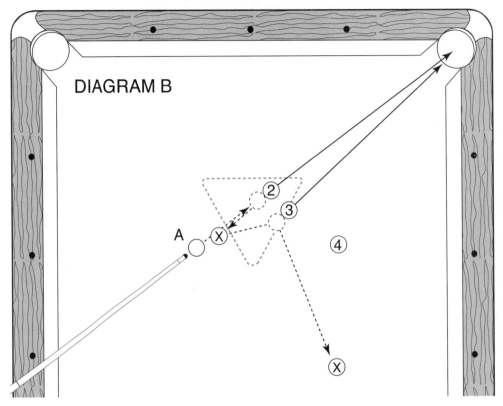

DIAGRAM B

Diagram B shows the happy result of getting perfect position on the 2-ball at Position A. Now all that's needed to get excellent position on the break ball (the 4-ball) are short-range draw shots on the 2-ball, and then the 3-ball.

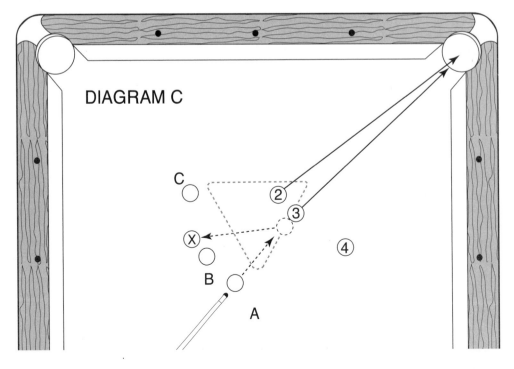

DIAGRAM C

Diagram C shows the problem that arises from missing shape slightly above the target at Position A. Now you've got to stun/draw the cue ball over for the correct angle on the 2-ball. If you are successful and the cue ball stops at Position X, then you will have recovered position. You can now easily slide over for shape on the break ball. Note what happens if your recovery attempt comes up short at Position B or long at Position C. In these positions you will be hard pressed to get anywhere near the same quality of shape on the break ball as you can when playing from Position X.

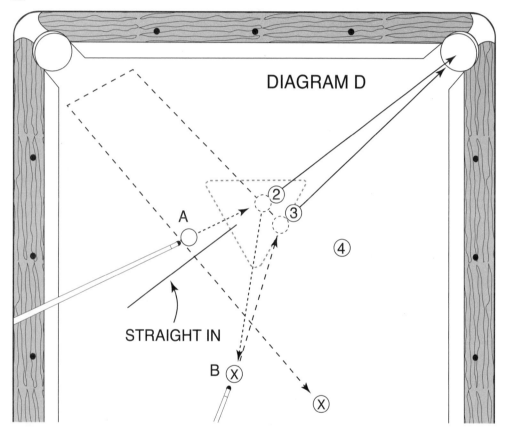

DIAGRAM D

A

STRAIGHT IN

B

Diagram D illustrates one of several challenging solutions to recovering position when the cue ball ends up at Position A, which is below the straight-in line on the 2-ball. The play now is to shoot the 2-ball and draw back to Position B. Then go two rails on the 3-ball for position on the break ball at X.

Tip: We started this series with an innocent looking short distance position play. You learned that all hell could break loose if you are off by even an inch or two in certain situations. Straight Pool does not always call for the type of precision needed in our example, but when it does, you must learn to recognize the need for precise play, and then plan and execute with the exactness of a surgeon.

Using Your Knowledge of the Balls to Play Position

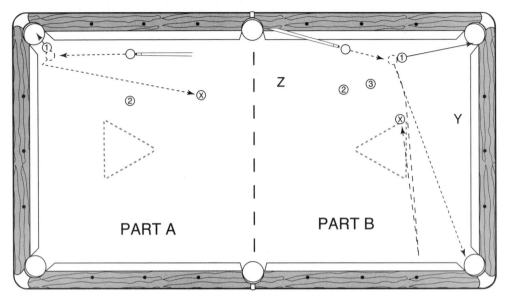

On position plays that you encounter sporadically, and especially for those that you may have never experienced before, you must use your knowledge of the balls to create and execute an effective shot. Some of the choice bits of information that may go into your calculations include:

- The cut angle.
- The location of both the cue ball and object ball.
- Where you need to send the cue ball.
- Obstructing balls, if any.
- Which rail(s) can be accessed.
- Use of english, cueing.
- The tangent line off contact.

Position A shows position on the break ball from the 1-ball, which is not exactly your typical key ball. As you know, the cue ball can easily spiral out of control on pocket hangers. This bit of knowledge immediately tells you that the shot must be aimed with great care. You also know that if you hit the shot a fraction full, it will kill the cue balls speed coming off the rail. If the shot is hit too full, the cue ball could run into the 2-ball. That is a far worse mistake than hitting the shot too thin, which is very difficult to do from the position shown. Your best play is to hit the 1-ball almost as thin as possible (but not as thin as you can) and reverse its return angle with a / tip of right english. Now that you know the cuing, direction, and aim, you must calculate the correct speed, which is in the range of very soft. Wow!

In Position B, you need to play shape on the 2-ball. You immediately know that you can't hold the cue ball with soft follow (at Position Y) because the angle is too great. You also know that position anywhere near Position Z is out. Your only choice is too somehow get position for the side pocket or the far corner pocket. This can't be done by hitting the end rail first. The tangent line is pointing towards the pocket. At this cut angle, it's possible to draw to the side rail and back across the table. The right english that's picked up at contact, and the cue ball's angle of approach to the rail, need to cancel each other out so the cue ball can return across the table on about the same line as it took when approaching the rail. A full tip of draw and a medium hard stoke should work to complete the picture on this rather demanding and unusual position play. **Tip**: On shots you're not familiar with, but are nevertheless very playable, you should take a few extra moments to weigh the appropriate variables so you can arrive at the best possible position play.

Elevating Your Position Play when Necessary

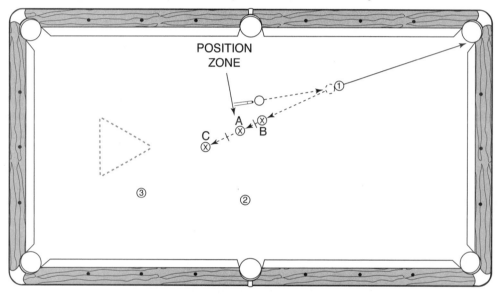

There are a number of Straight Pool type position plays that will definitely challenge your skills, just as the Nine-Ball shot did in the section above. In this example, you need to draw back into Zone A for shape on the 2-ball in the side pocket. Again, you must carefully plan your route and feel the speed of the shot to the best of your ability. Top players like to say that you must be able to "come with a shot" when faced with a difficult shot. Well, in Straight Pool, you must also be able to "come with a tough position play" when it's called for.

On troublesome shots like this, there is often a particular side of the position zone where it is best to land in case you miss the ideal position zone. The big mistake on this shot is to come up short at Position B. From there it would now take an exceptional shot on the 2-ball to arrive back near where the 2-ball is presently located for break shot shape on the 3-ball. In sharp contrast, it would be not be very difficult from Position C to get workable, if not ideal shape, on the 3-ball.

Playing Position off a Combo

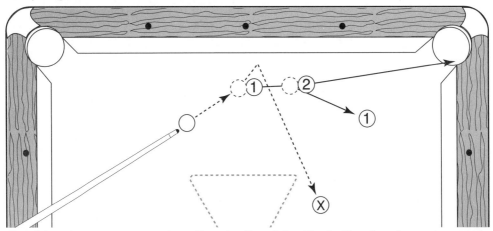

Combinations appear quire often in Straight Pool. Combo shape is another of those all important little things that many players overlook that could eventually loom large some day when you're in the middle of your record run. Most combos in Straight Pool are reasonably straight in, so determining the future location of the first ball should not be much of a problem. On many combos you'll need to play shape on the first ball of the combo on your very next shot. At other times you'll need to control the first ball so it doesn't create an unwelcome obstruction. In our example, the 1-ball will cut the 2-ball slightly to the left, sending the 1-ball forward and to the right. Knowing this, you would want to use follow to send the cue ball to X for position on the 1-ball.

Tip: I suggest that you pay special attention to both your combos as well as those of your opponents so you can gain an even greater understanding of how the first ball reacts in a variety of situations. You should also consider practicing combos and closely observe where the first ball goes as well as how to play shape on it from a number of positions.

Side By Side Position

Quite often balls will be positioned side by side, especially around the area of the rack where the balls tend to break off from the stack in rows. Because of this, mastering position with the balls side by side, will greatly simplify your patterns. You want to maintain a fairly shallow cut angle on the first ball so you can play a short-range draw shot with maximum control. With the balls in Part A of the diagram, a 10-degree cut angle on the 1-ball is just about perfect for drawing back for position on the 2-ball.

In Part B, the 1 and 2-balls are in a similar position, but now you have a 20-degree cut on the first ball, which will cause the cue ball to end up at Position X. There is nothing wrong with arriving at X if your goal is to have an angle on the 2-ball. If you have more than two balls in a row, you'll definitely want a small cut angle on the first ball that will send the cue ball towards the second ball.

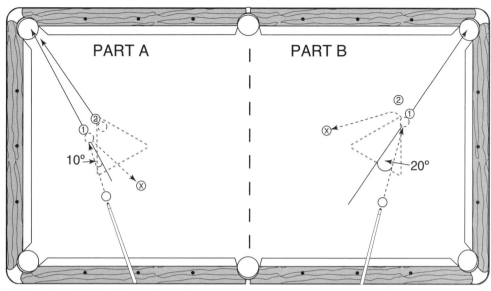

Side By Side Position Zones

Part A shows the size of the position zone if your objective is to play either ball first followed by the other. A shot on the 1-ball from Cue Ball A will leave you with a shot on the 2-ball at Cue Ball A-1. And a shot on the 2-ball from Cue Ball B will give you a shot on the 1-ball at B-1.

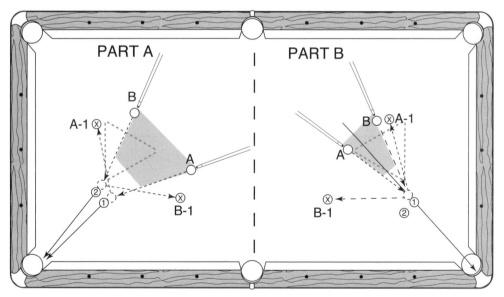

In Part B, notice how the zone shrinks significantly when your objective is to sink a specific ball first, then the other. In this example, a shot on the 1-ball from Cue Ball A will give you position on the 2-ball at A-1. And a shot on the 1-ball from Cue Ball B will send the cue ball to B-1 for the 2-ball. Note the range of possible positions for the 2-ball, which range from A-1 to B-1. Your position on the 2-ball depends on your shape on the 1-ball.

Using the Cue Ball as a Target

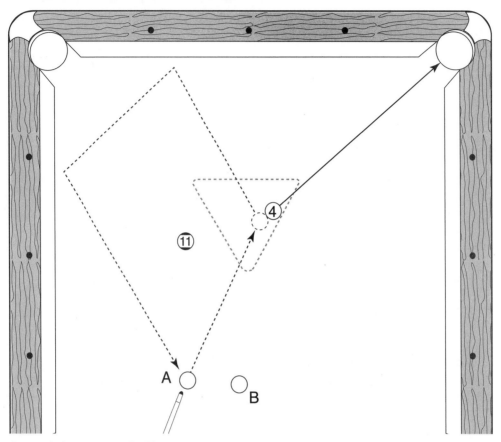

One of the many challenging aspects of playing position is that your target for the cue ball is an undistinguished spot on the green cloth. When you get ready to shoot, you have no real point of reference for where you want the cue ball to wind up.

In the diagram your goal is to play the 4-ball and go two rails and out to the exact spot where the cue ball is now stationed for position on the 11-ball. Your efforts to achieve the desired position can be enhanced by using the cue ball as a target. Now lets assume that the cue ball was originally located at Position B for the shot on the 4-ball. Instead of using the 4-ball as a target, you can use it as a point of reference. Now your objective is to send the cue ball to a position about 7" closer to the rail at Position A. In both examples, the cue ball's position helped give you something positive on which to place your attention, helping to ensure a successful shot.

Tip: You can choose any spot on the table as a target. You could aim to send the cue ball to a spot near or at the ball you are now playing. Or you could pick out a ball and set a target some specific distance from the ball. If there are no landmarks near where you want to send the cue ball, you can point to a spot on the table and fix that in your mind as your target.

The 2 1/4 Inch Rule

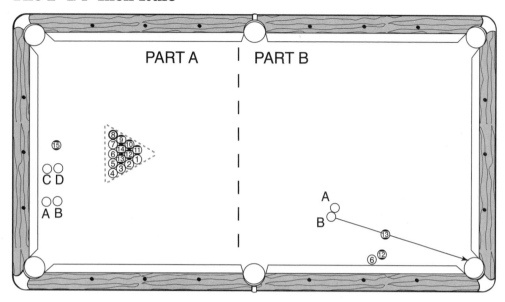

To achieve the precision necessary to play top-flight Straight Pool, consider the 2 1/4" rule, which happens to be the width (diameter for purists) of the cue ball. The rule states that **everything about a shot can and very often does change within the space of 2 1/4".** As a corollary to this rule, the closer the cue ball is to the object ball, the more pronounced are the effects of the 2 1/4" rule.

Consider Part A of the diagram, which illustrates a behind the rack break shot on the 15-ball. At Position A, you have a good chance of peeling off a few balls from the corner of the rack. With the cue ball 2 1/4" over at Position B, however, the shallower cut angle suggests that your run is likely over. With the cue ball at Position C, you have an excellent break shot. Move the cue ball a scant 2 1/4" over to the right to Position D and you have much less of a chance of continuing your turn at the table.

In Part B, your objective is to break the 6-12 cluster off the 10-ball, which is easy enough with the cue ball at Position A. Move it over 2 1/4" to Position B and you have now lost your opportunity to take care of a potentially run ending problem.

Tip: The purpose of the 2 1/4" rule is help you gain a necessary appreciation for the exactness that the game often calls for, as well as to assist you in planning position for the cue ball. This rule will also help you reduce your tolerances when playing shape. It is not, however, intended to make you tighten up or frustrate you while seeking a level of perfection that's beyond your unique capabilities

• Minimize Cue Ball Movement

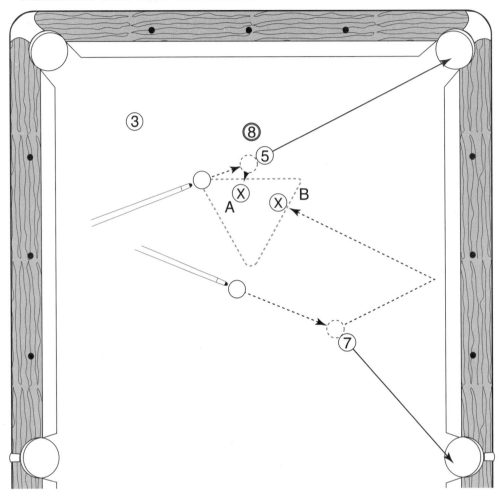

As a general rule, the shorter the distance the cue ball must travel, the more precise your position play will be. Your goal is to arrive at Position A for a stop shot on the 3-ball. Good shape on the 3-ball will enable you to open a new rack using a behind the rack break shot on the 8-ball. The short-range draw shot on the 5-ball is a cinch to give you excellent position on the 3-ball.

Now let's assume your shot before the 3-ball was the 7-ball into the side pocket. The cue ball has to now travel nearly 3" (as opposed to 4") to arrive at Position B. Obviously there is much more that can go wrong when the cue ball must travel several feet off the rail. These examples show the importance of minimizing the cue ball's traveling distance as much as possible, especially towards the end of a rack.

• Bumping Balls – The Basic

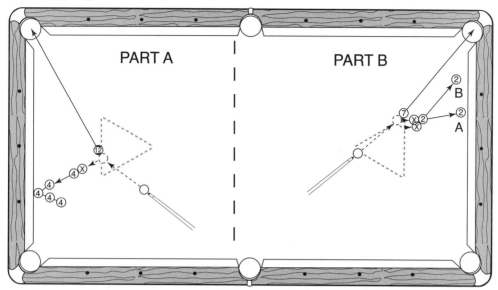

Bumping balls skillfully is one of the subtle nuances of Straight Pool that can go a long way towards extending your runs. Specifically, bumping balls is a short-range maneuver in which the cue ball, after contact, repositions a nearby object ball to a more advantageous location. Bumping balls can help you play shape, manufacture a break shot, clear a pocket, and accomplish a host of other worthwhile objectives.

The secrets to bumping ball are:
• Determining where you want the bumped ball to go.
• Controlling the cue ball's initial direction after contact with great precision.
• Using the speed of stroke necessary to send the bumped ball where you want it. The speed is determined largely by the cut angle and the fullness of the hit on the ball to be bumped.

Most bump shots are played from close range and at fairly shallow cut angles, which can makes these shot quite easy. Part A shows the basic bump shot. Controlling the hit on the ball to be bumped is simple because the cue ball is nearby. In this position, you can hit the 4-ball on target by sending the cue ball down the tangent line. The main variable on this shot is choosing where you want to send the 4-ball. This means that stroke speed is the key component for achieving the desired results on this shot. Notice just a few of the possible locations for the 4-ball.

Part B illustrates a bump shot in which the direction of the ball being bumped can be altered significantly by your choice of cueing. A soft follow stroke would send the 2-ball to Position A. The degree of difficulty rises dramatically when you use a stun/follow stroke to propel the 2-ball to Position B. The key to success on this shot is to use stun and follow in the correct proportions. If you use too much stun you'll miss the 2-ball altogether. Employ excessive follow and you'll cut the 2-ball too thinly.

Playing Position on the Bumped Ball

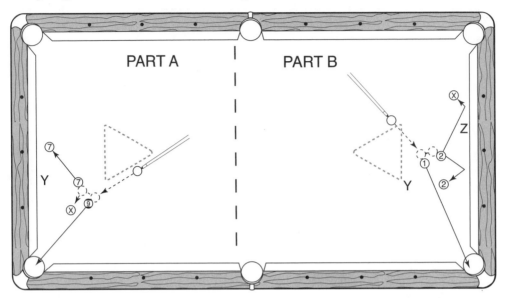

This position play is a classic example of the intricacies of Straight Pool. To play the 9 and 7-balls in order you must, when playing the 9-ball, control both the cue ball and the 7-ball.

Sending the cue ball and 7-ball to the positions shown is not hard if you know what you're doing. A delicate touch and proper cueing are the keys to this shot. Most players, especially those who have mostly played Nine-Ball, have a tendency to shoot too firmly in situations like this. If you use excessive speed, you could scratch. Another mistake is to use soft draw. The 7-ball would then relocate at Y, and the cue ball would end up about where the 7-ball is now, leaving you with no shot on the 7-ball.

A big mistake that happens quite often when playing position for the 2-ball in Part B is to hit the 2-ball too fully. The 2-ball goes to position Y while the cue ball ends up at Z, leaving you without a shot. The secret to this shot lies in the planning stage. You need to examine the cue ball's path down the tangent line and make any necessary adjustments if needed. Then you must decide on the proper cueing and speed of stroke. In this example, if the cue ball travels down the tangent line it will send the cue ball and the 2-ball to the positions shown. The shot is played with a soft draw stroke, not a much firmer stun stroke.

Tip: Many easy shots, like the ones in the examples, have been missed because the shooter took their eyes off the shot to watch the second ball. So be sure your eyes on the ball you are shooting when bumping balls.

Bumping Balls with Spin

You can subtlety, but yet significantly, alter the way the balls react on bump shots by using english. It would be easy to commit the error of hitting the 2-ball too fully, which would send it to Position Y. To avoid

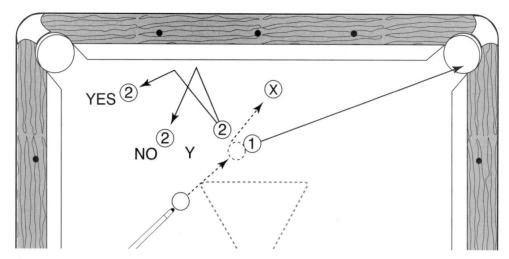

this potential problem, play the 1-ball with a soft stroke and right english. The right english enables you to hit both the 1 and 2-balls a little thinner. The right english also throws the 2-ball to the left, causing it to rebound more softly off the cushion from a shallower angle of approach.

Precision Ball Bumping

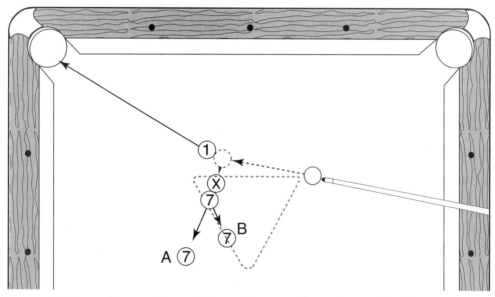

On a slight angle cut shot, it is easier to adjust the path of the cue ball than on a thinner cut angle where the cue ball will initially travel for a longer distance down the tangent line. The idea is to bump the 7-ball a few inches to Position A to create an ideal break shot. If you merely played a stun shot, the 7-ball would remain in the triangle at Position B. By adjusting the contact point on the 7-ball with draw, you will cut the 7-ball into ideal break shot position. The key is to determine the cue ball's path down the tangent line as well as to adjust your cuing to create the desired point of contact with the ball you're going to be bumping.

Avoiding a Double Kiss

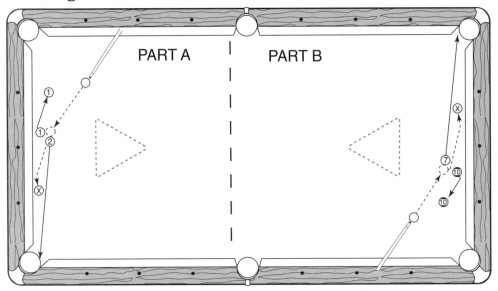

When the ball your going to bump and the object ball are close together and they are near the rail, you've got to be very careful to avoid a double kiss. In Part A, a double kiss is definitely "on" because the cue ball's position at contact with the 1-ball is on a line that extends directly through the 2-ball into the rail. Recognizing this, you can avoid getting stuck by using follow and /or a fi tip of left english. The cue ball and 2-ball will double kiss, but on the second kiss, the cue ball will be slightly forward and the 2-ball will be a hair closer to the near corner pocket. These minute changes in position for the second half of the double kiss will help squeeze the balls apart to the positions shown.

Part B shows the same shot, only this time the 1-ball is a⁄" past the 2-ball. This tiny change in position allows you to avoid a double kiss entirely. The secret is to use a soft stroke with left(inside) english. You could also separate the two balls by using draw with right (outside) english. The balls will separate on the second kiss similar to the way they did in Position A..

• Using Balls to Stop the Cue Ball

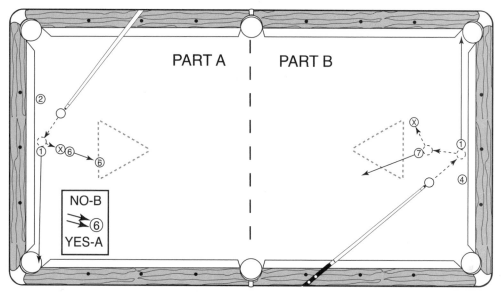

With the cut angle illustrated in Part A, it would be difficult to hold the cue ball near the rail for shape on the 2-ball. In this case, however, the 6-ball can act as a backstop for the cue ball. The key is to fine-tune the cue ball's route off the rail so that it contacts the right portion of the 6-ball, which acts a backstop. In this case, a fi tip of left engligh gets the job done. Make sure to slightly favor hitting Side A of the 6-ball. If you strike it too thinly on Side B, you will lose position on the 2-ball.

The position in Part B looks very similar to Part A but there is one big difference: the two balls on the rail are 6" closer together. To avoid an overly steep cut angle on the 4-ball, you've now got to hit the right half of the 7-ball. This will divert the cue ball over to Position X for excellent shape on the 4-ball.

Tip: There are a zillion opportunities to use balls as backstops. These backstop balls can enable you to play position on shots that would be difficult if not impossible to do were it not for the braking action of these most helpful balls. So be on the lookout for backstops, and learn to hit them precisely where you want to.

Glancing off Balls for Shape

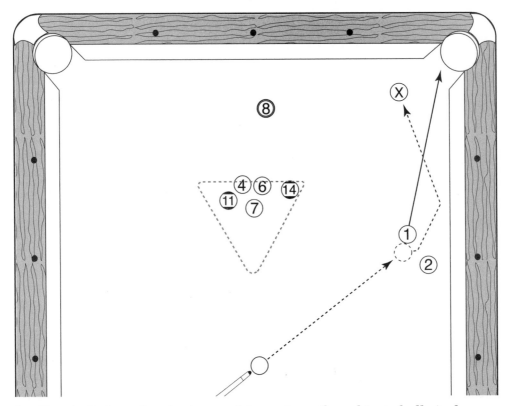

Another technique for playing position using other objects balls is demonstrated in the diagram. In this position, the objective is to play shape on the 8-ball so you can break the cluster on your next shot. Now imagine for a moment how you would get to the 8-ball from the 1-ball if the 2-ball was not there. You probably couldn't. The dashed line shows the cue ball's path to Position X. It first hits the 1-ball, then 1/3 of the 2-ball, and off the side rail and down for perfect shape on the 8-ball.

Tip: You would be wise to experiment with variations of this shot so you can accurately predict the cue ball's path after hitting the glancing ball in a number of degrees of thickness.

CHAPTER 2

PATTERN PLAY

How to Read the Table
and Plan Your Runs

Straight Pool can be deceivingly easy because you have the choice of shooting any ball in any pocket. But that doesn't mean you should just fire away at the defenseless array of available shots. Instead, you should develop patterns that should be followed as closely as possible. Pattern play can be defined as the order in which you play the balls. The correct pattern will enable you to meet any of several objectives such as separating a cluster, clearing an area, or getting on the break ball.

The top 20 players in the world would play a Nine-Ball pattern almost identically. If you put the best 20 Straight Pool players to work on a rack of Straight Pool, you could easily see 20 different patterns for running the same rack, any and all of which could be correct.

Although the balls never break the same way twice, there are nevertheless commonly recurring patterns that are easily recognizable. With a trained eye, you can learn to quickly spot them and plot the appropriate course of action. In this chapter you'll learn the many principles, concepts and components of pattern play. Later in Chapter 6, you will be shown how the lessons in this chapter are applied to running racks from start to finish.

Principles of Pattern Play

The list below summarizes the most important principles of pattern play, which are presented throughout this chapter. The principles, and other concepts in the chapter, are designed to help you read the table so you can make the best possible decisions on how you are going to attack it. I advise that you be patient as you learn to incorporate this information into your game. If you keep at it long enough, you will discover that reading the table and planning the optimal patterns will become more and more automatic. You may wish to copy this list and keep it with you refer to it when you go to the pool room to practice. You could then pick out one of the topics to emphasize during your practice session.

- Use process of elimination planning.
- Play the table, don't force the issue.
- First things first – learn to prioritize.
- Let the shot help determine the pattern.
- Simplify the table.

- Save balls for a specific purpose.
- Label each ball correctly.
- Work the table (areas).
- Use all six pockets.
- Play shots with multiple possibilities.

- Look to accomplish multiple objectives when possible.
- Move balls to advantageous locations (break ball, key ball).
- Know when to play for luck.
- Execute with precision and care.
- Managing risk.

- Keep an open mind.
- Be prepared to improvise at any moment (plan B).
- Have a Plan B ready.
- Timing – develop a sense of (cluster breaking, etc.).
- Eliminate problem balls – clusters, on the rail, etc.

- Avoid trouble whenever possible.
- Clear obstructions.
- Don't play position when you've already got position.
- Don't overplay a shot.
- Conflicting agendas – judgment calls.

Planning

Process of Elimination Planning

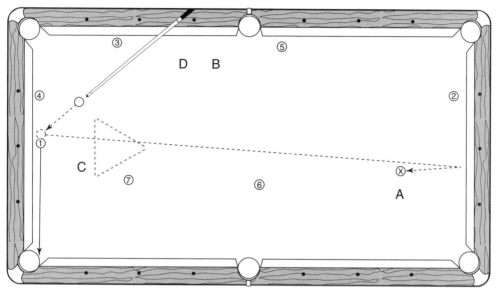

When you reach the later stages of a rack and the balls are spread nicely, it's time to plan the sequence of shots for the remainder of the rack. You can use what I call the process of elimination method to plot your course. The steps to the method are:

1. Identify what ball(s) you can possibly play first.
2. Select your break ball, key ball and the ball before the key ball.
3. Select which ball(s) tie parts one and two together.

The 1-ball is your only reasonable shot, and it is perfectly positioned to send the cue ball up table for the troublesome 2-ball next. Part One is now complete. The 7-ball is the obvious choice for the break ball, and the 6-ball is in perfect position for the key ball. Floating a short distance off the rail after playing the 5-ball will give you the shape you need on the key ball. That takes care of step two. Now all that's left is to tie the two parts together.

Since the decision has been made to play the 1-ball to get on the 2-ball, we'll pick up the planning process with the cue ball at Position A. One possible sequence is to go from the 2-ball to Position B for the 3-ball. Next, play a follow shot on the 3-ball to Position C for the 4-ball. Finally, a follow shot on the 4-ball will produce shape on the 5-ball at Position D. Let's do a quick recap of the process:

- The 1-ball is your only likely first shot, and it leads to the 2-ball.
- The 5, 6 and 7-balls are saved for last.
- The 3 and 4-balls connect the first and last parts of the sequence.

By applying this type of logical, common sense to planning your patterns, you will take a lot of the mystery and confusion out of the later stages of a rack of Straight Pool.

Play the Table – Don't Force the Issue

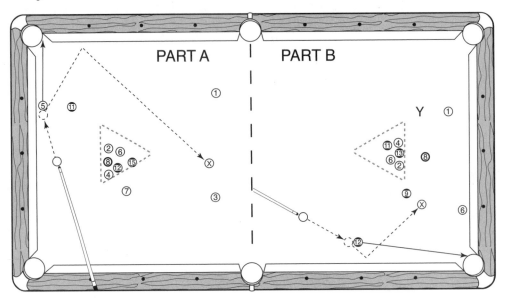

When you fight the table and the physics of pool, it is usually a losing battle. Take the layout in Part A of the diagram. You have a 15-degree cut on the 5-ball. It might be tempting to use that as a secondary break shot, especially since you have the 11-ball as an insurance ball. At this angle, however, the cue ball would be approaching the cluster with very little speed. The better play is to follow two rails for the 7-ball, which is an excellent secondary break shot.

In Part B at Position X you would have a secondary break shot on the 8-ball. The drawback to this choice is that you only have a little over half the pocket for the 8-ball. A better approach is to play position from the 12-ball to the 1-ball, and use the 1-ball to get on the 8-ball on the other side of the table at Position Y.

There are several instances where fighting the table is a losing proposition. And, sadly enough, most of the time when a player forces the issue they have other shots available that have a much higher chance of success.

Common Instances of Fighting the Table
- Playing a very tough shot, especially when a safety is available.
- Shooting to half a pocket.
- Playing balls that are almost dead.
- Breaking with too shallow of an angle.
- Trying for position to a tiny shape zone.
- Playing position routes that are totally unrealistic.

Forcing the issue can be caused by impatience and the feeling that you just want to get on with your turn. Over aggressiveness can lead to forcing the issue, as can the desire to make up for a mistake right away by inadvertently committing another one.

Tip: Develop a little warning bell in your mind that tells you to stop and reconsider the situation when you are about to play a shot that you know is fighting the odds.

- ## Labeling the Balls Correctly

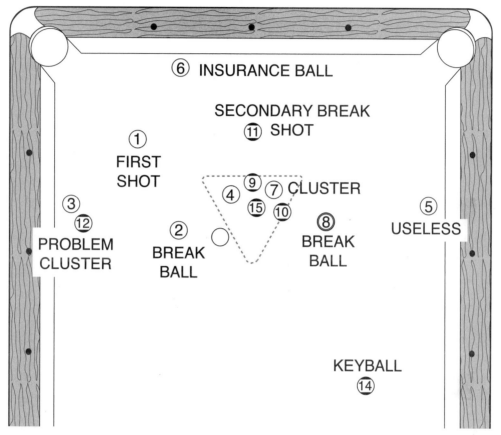

At any stage of the rack, every ball or group of balls carries with it a label that defines its current position on the table. Learning to label the balls correctly can help in reading the table and establishing your plan of attack. The illustration gives you an example of how the balls are labeled in this post break-shot layout. Labeling can help you establish order out of chaos. You've got:

- Balls to be saved: break balls (2-ball and 8-ball) and a key ball (14-ball).
- Shots to be played very soon: the first ball (1-ball) and the secondary break shot on the 11-ball.
- A problem to be solved when the time is right: the 3-12 cluster.

Don't Play Position When You Already Have Position

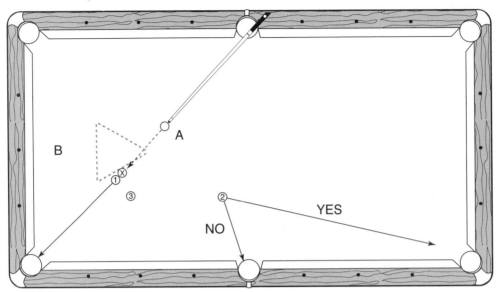

What could be easier than this end of rack position? Just pocket the 1-ball and draw back to Position A for a stop shot on the key ball, which is the 2-ball. Right? Wrong. A lot can go wrong when playing a draw shot for position, even at close range. There is a much better choice that virtually guarantees you'll have the shot you need (straight in) on the key ball. If you take a quick walk over to Position B, you will discover that a stop shot on the 1-ball will put you in perfect position for a straight in shot on the 2-ball (the key ball) into the far corner.

By choosing this sequence, you don't have to play position on the 2-ball because you will already have it just by playing a stop shot on the 1-ball. While the shot on the 2-ball is admittedly a long shot, it is the kind that you should be able to pocket with regularity when playing Straight Pool.

Let the Shot Determine the Pattern

The 2-ball is definitely the correct shot. It will be difficult to control the rolling distance of the cue ball as it must travel to the other end of the table. Because of this, you should let the shot determine the pattern. If the cue ball stops at Position A, then a break shot on the 5-ball is the best bet. With the cue ball at Position B, you might want to play the 7-ball into the side pocket and send the cue ball to Position D for a break shot on the 1-ball. Should the cue ball stop at Position C, the right pattern is a soft follow shot on the 3-ball for shape on the 4-ball..

It is nice to know you have several choices available, especially on long distance position plays where the outcome of the shot is uncertain. When these positions exist, let the shot determine the pattern.

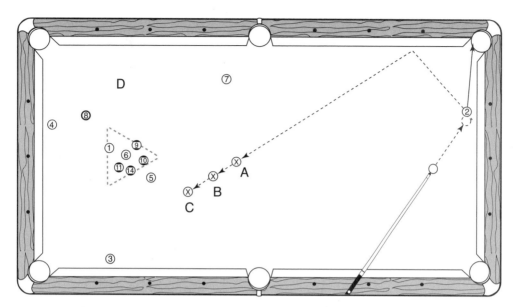

First Things First

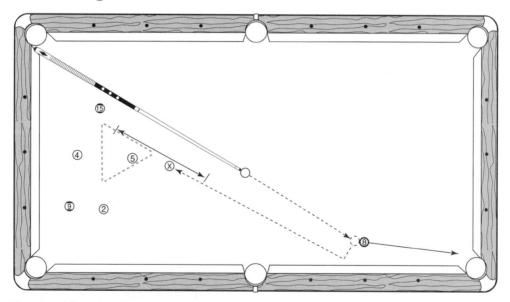

You could pick off some of the balls around the 4-ball, which is going to be the break shot. This could, however, you limit your options for playing this pattern, especially later on when you have to go up table for the pesky 8-ball. Simplifying the pattern is a worthy objective, but it must wait until you take care of business on the other end of the table. Play the 8-ball right now while you have a sufficiently long position zone to get back in play with the rest of the balls. Remember, Straight Pool is largely about prioritizing your objectives, just like they suggest you do in books on time management. Take care of the A's first and so on.

Simplify the Table

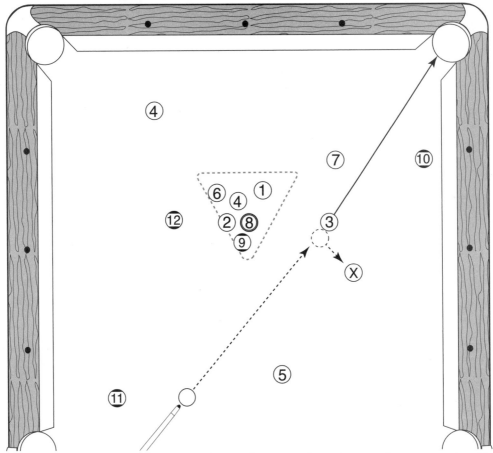

I remember my chess playing days when my favorite tactic was to simplify the board by trading pieces. My plan was to try to win in the end game. This tactic is certainly analogous to Straight Pool where you want to eliminate balls and solve problems so you can win in the end game, which is to have good position on a break ball.

You could play the 12-ball secondary break shot right now while you have shape on it. This would follow the rule of not playing for position when you already have it. In this case, however, your first concern should be to simplify the layout. This would reduce the chances of a ball in the cluster getting tied up with the 3,7, or 10-balls. One possible pattern that can simplify the table is the 3, 10, and 7-balls in that order. You could then use the 4-ball to get back to the 12-ball.

Managing Risk

Straight Pool is a game that is fraught with risk. Scratching, missing balls, missing position and freezing up against a ball are just a few of the most common risks. A million things can go wrong, and yet skillful players are able to somehow manage these risks and go on to run 50, 100,

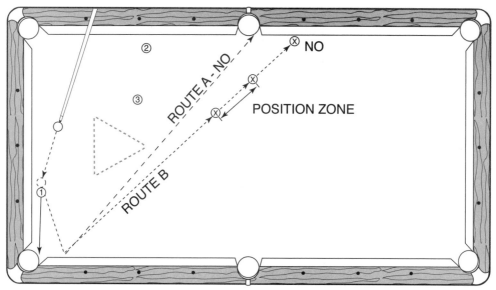

200 balls and more. How do they do it? By understanding the risk factors that are inherent in any shot and then dealing with them successfully.

When the risk of a scratch is high, for example, top players don't just go ahead and shoot and tempt fate. Instead, they will choose another shot, or change their cueing to reduce or eliminate any possibility of scratching. There is a chance of scratching in the side pocket when playing shape on the 2-ball on Route A. A player who manages risk well will use a little more left english when playing the 1-ball and send the cue ball down Route B. Incidentally, the player managed risk on this shot by using the principles of allowing for a margin for error, and entering the wide side of a position zone.

To manage risk successfully, you must learn to plan not only for what you want to have happen, but also for what you want to avoid. Before playing a risky shot, stop for a moment and ask yourself what could go wrong, and what you can do to prevent it from happening. This isn't being negative, just practical. The list below will alert you to some of the most common situations where risks are particularly high.

When Risks Are Particularly High
- The break shot.
- Break shots at shallow cut angles.
- Secondary break shots behind the rack.
- Secondary break shots without an insurance ball.
- Long range position plays.
- End of the rack pattern play.
- Breaking clusters on the rail.

There are strategies for minimizing risk in each of these situations and even more that are discussed in the appropriate sections of the book.

Pocket Choice

Testing Top Professionals

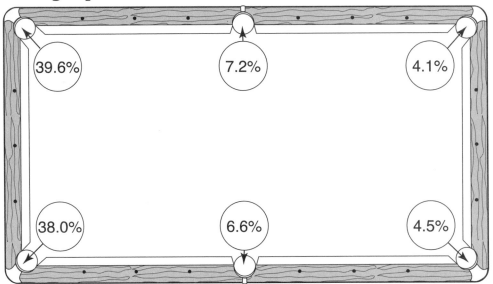

Perhaps you've been told that Straight Pool is a four-pocket game, that you should avoid the far corner pockets. Or perhaps you have been led to believe that you should avoid the side pockets and play most of your shots into the two corner pockets nearest the rack. I wondered about these pearls of wisdom, so I decided to gather some empirical data on the pocket choices of the worlds leading players. I tabulated the results of over 2,000 shots by leading professionals, at which point I decided that was good enough to be pretty close to 100% accurate. The results are shown on the diagram. The difference from one side of the table to the other may be attributable to the fact that more players are right-handed, and therefore send more balls to the opposite side of the table when playing right-handed break shots.

  The table below shows the average number of balls in a typical 14 ball rack that are played into the two corner pockets at the break end of the table, the two side pockets, and the two far corner pockets.

- 10.864 - corner pockets at the break end
-   1.934 – two side pockets
-   1.203 – two far corner pockets

  We can conclude that the two nearest corner pockets are where the vast majority of shots are played, a whopping 77.6% in fact. The main reason is that the rack is located closest to these pockets, and that most break shots are played off the side of the rack, which tends to drive balls towards those pockets. The reason shots are played primarily into these pockets is not because it is the right thing to do, but because that's where most of the balls are located.

The other 22.4% of the balls are played into the side pockets and into the far corner pockets. That computes to 3.14 balls out of every 14 ball rack. That's a very significant number when you consider the troublesome balls at the far end of the table and the critical role that the side pockets often play in getting on the break ball. So while the four "other pockets" are only the target on a little less than 25% of the shots in a typical rack, those are a mighty important 3+ balls per frame. The primary uses of the three groups of pockets are:

Near corner pockets - routine shots, break shots, secondary break shots, insurance balls.

Side pockets - key balls, diagonal patterns, shape for balls on the rail, insurance balls, first shot after the break shot.

Far corner pockets - strays from break shots, preserve pattern from rack end of the table.

• Side Pocket Shotmaking

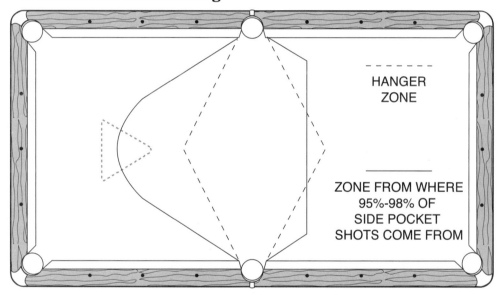

HANGER ZONE

ZONE FROM WHERE
95%-98% OF
SIDE POCKET
SHOTS COME FROM

This solid line in the diagram shows the zone from which probably 95%+ of all shots into the side pockets are played. The dashed line illustrates the boundaries of the "hanger zone". Any ball within the zone has an effective pocket opening of about 5" or more. This illustration should be useful in alerting you to the opportunities for shots into the side pockets.

I urge you to become very comfortable shooting into the side pockets because of their importance in patterning the balls correctly. Don't be like the Tennis player who avoid their backhand at all costs. Replace "I hate the side pockets" with "they are my friends because they give me so much more flexibility in playing the rack".

• Using the Side Pockets to Their Full Advantage

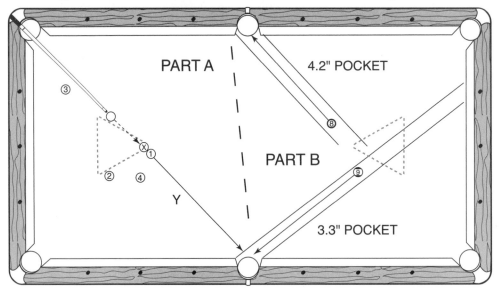

The pros play an average of nearly two shots per rack into the side pockets. We also discovered those are two mighty important shots. For example, side pockets are often the source of the first shot after a break shot. They can also be useful in getting position on the break ball.

If you avoid the side pockets, you will often have to play awkward patterns, especially at the end of the rack. Take Part A in our example. The 1-ball is an easy shot to the side pocket even though it will be approaching the pocket from an angle. The pattern is a cinch (1, 2, 3, 4-ball break shot) if you play the 1-ball into the side. Now imagine how much trouble you would have getting to Position Y for shape on the 1-ball into the corner pocket if you chose to play it later in the pattern.

Most shots into the side pockets from the area of the triangle usually have little or no cut angle, which greatly reduces their degree of difficulty. It may also comfort you to know the effective size of the pocket from this area of the table. In Part B of the diagram, the 8-ball has an opening 4.2" wide, or nearly twice as wide as the 8-ball (which measures 2.25"). The 9-ball has an opening of 3.3", which gives you a margin for error of a little more than .5" on either side of center pocket. Both of these examples assume a regulation table with 5.25" side pockets.

Shooting to the Far Corner Pockets At the Break End
The end of rack position in Diagram A on the next page shows how valuable the far corner pockets can be in playing patterns correctly. Neither the 11-ball nor 4-ball will go into the upper left corner pocket. Because of this, many players would make the mistake of trying to separate them when playing the 9-ball so as to have a shot at a nearby pocket.

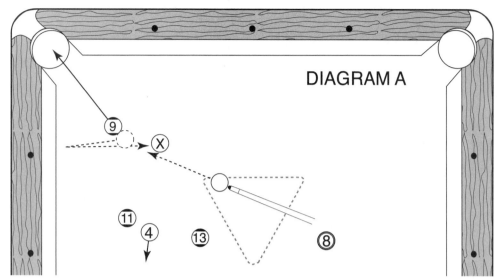

A better choice is to accept the position of the balls as they lie. You will eliminate the luck factor that comes with breaking a so called cluster. A soft follow shot on the 9-ball will send the cue ball to Position X for a relatively easy shot into the far corner pocket on the 4-ball. Variations of this position play come up over and over again so you should always be looking to play simple long straight in shots to the far corner pockets.

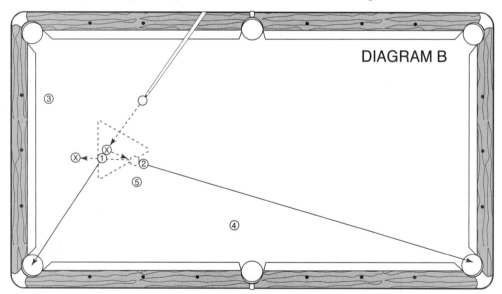

Diagram B illustrates the same concept, but from another position. In this example, the 2-ball will go into the upper left corner pocket. Getting good position on the 2-ball for that pocket won't be easy. A far superior choice is to play a stop shot on the 1-ball. This will give you a straight in shot into the lower right-hand corner pocket. This pattern also removes the risk (remember our discussion on risk?) of knocking the 5-ball break shot out of position.

Learn to Think Diagonally

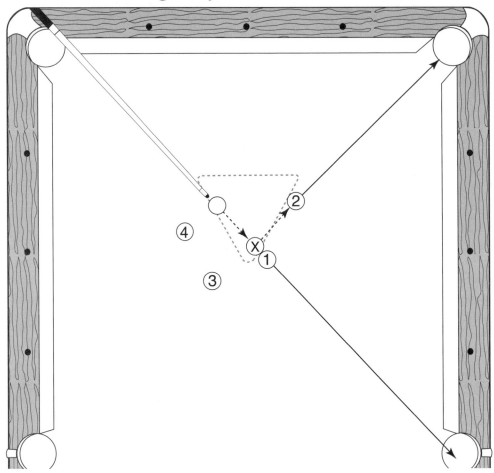

Many shots in the later stages of a rack come from balls scattered within the area of the triangle. This can lead to a series of position plays away from the rail where you must be able to control the cue ball in the open without the benefit of "working it" off the cushion. When playing a pattern within the area of the triangle, your four primary targets are the near corner pockets and the side pockets.

The diagram shows you the benefit of thinking diagonally when playing end-of-the-rack patterns. The best way to complete this rack is to play the 1-ball diagonally into the side pocket. Then play the 2-ball diagonally across the table into the corner pocket, followed by another diagonal shot into the other side pocket on the 3-ball. You will minimize the cue ball's traveling distance greatly by using the closest pockets in this manner.

Connecting Balls

Diagram A on the next page shows a series of shots on the 1-ball. On each one, a stop shot will position the cue ball for a straight-in shot on the 2-ball. The 1-ball is in essence, connected to the 2-ball because playing the 1-ball with a stop shot will automatically give you position on the 2-ball.

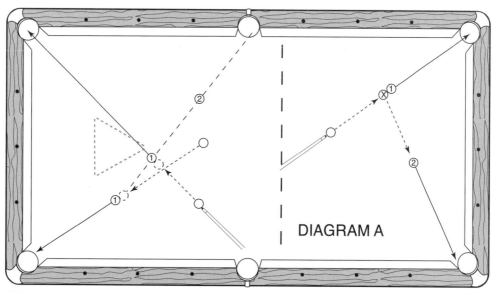

DIAGRAM A

Whenever you have a straight in shot, check to see which ball it connects with. This can be an especially valuable planning tool if you are playing in congestion where shape is uncertain, or on long shots where you want to maximize your chances of making the shot by stopping it dead.

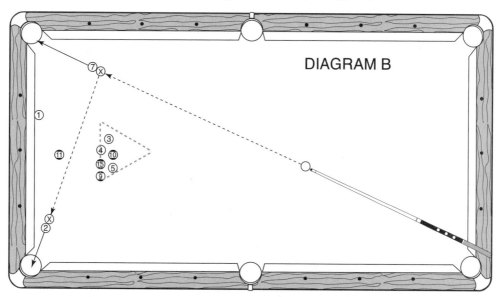

DIAGRAM B

In Diagram B, your immediate goal is to pocket the 7-ball and get down to the end rail from where you will be playing the next couple of shots. The congestion at that end of the table could make position a tricky proposition. In the diagrammed position, however, you have a stop shot on the 7-ball that connects with the 2-ball. You really don't have to play shape in situations like this, you just have to let the position of the balls work to your advantage.

Multiple Possibilities

• **Resorting to a Plan B**

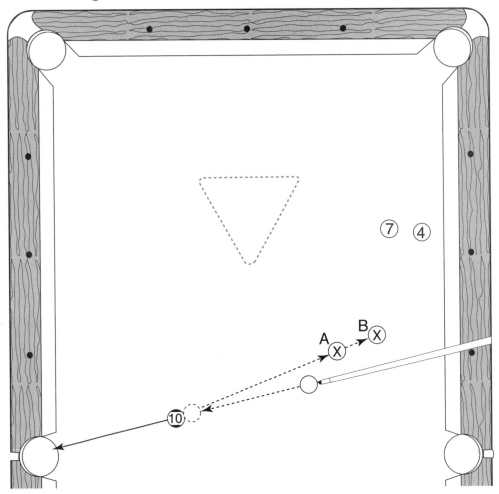

Most of the time you will be playing an ongoing series of mini-recovery shots. Your recovery efforts could involve playing the ball you had originally intended, but in a slightly different way. Your Plan B could also cause you to shoot another ball. It is to important for you to always keep an open mind as you proceed through a rack, especially when you make a positional error. The original plan was to shoot the 10-ball into the side pocket and draw back to A for the 7-ball, then the 4-ball. Unfortunately you've landed at B. Since your goal was also to clear both of these balls while in this location, to accomplish this you should now play the 4-ball first, then the 7-ball.

Tip: When your goal is to clear two balls on the same rail, it is usually easier to play the outside ball first.

Have a Plan B Ready

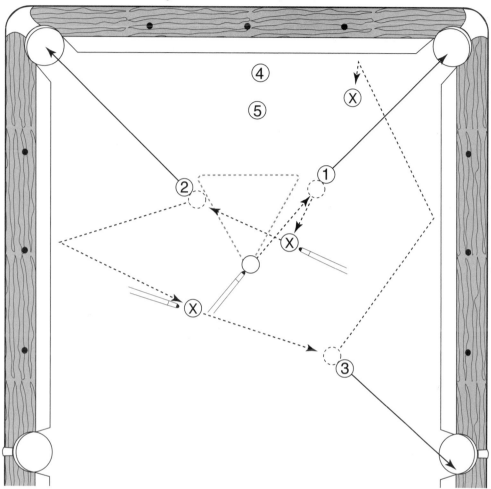

In this example, the pattern was to play the 1, 3, 2, and then 4-balls in that order. The 4-ball would be used to get position on the 5-ball for a behind-the-rack break shot. The draw shot on the 1-ball was targeted for Position A, but was under-hit, causing the cue ball to stop short at Position B. Because of the cut angle on the 3-ball, it's no longer the best choice. Plan B calls for changing the order to the 2-ball next, followed by the 3-ball into the side pocket, and down for the 4-ball.

Small errors at the end of a rack can lead to a big change in the way you play the rest of the balls. It is therefore wise to have a very workable Plan B waiting in the wings. Now if you already have a Plan B waiting, you would know, even before shooting the 1-ball in the example, that you could easily finish the rack if you came up short at Position B.

Two-Way Shots

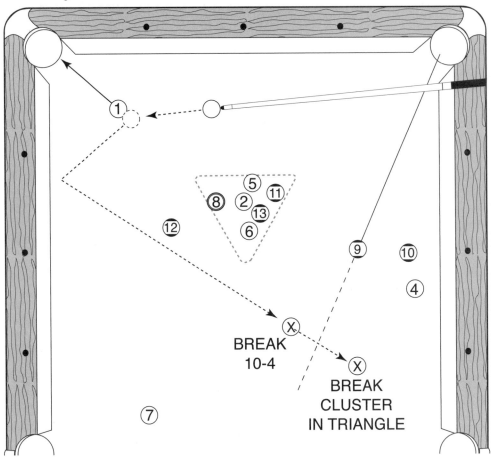

BREAK
10-4

BREAK
CLUSTER
IN TRIANGLE

When you are faced with a reasonably challenging position play, you are often given the luxury of playing position on either of two possible targets. Let's assume for a moment, that the 10-ball and 4-ball weren't there. To arrive at Position A for a break shot on the cluster in the triangle would require near perfect speed when playing the 1-ball With the 10-ball and 4-ball in their present location, you could separate the two balls when playing the 9-ball. Note that you still have the 12-ball available for a break shot.

Tip: The beauty of a two-way shot is that you are not covering a mistake with a less favorable choice, as is so often the case when resorting to Plan B. Instead, you are going to be, in effect, playing for either Plan A-1 or Plan A-2.

Accidental Two-Way Shape

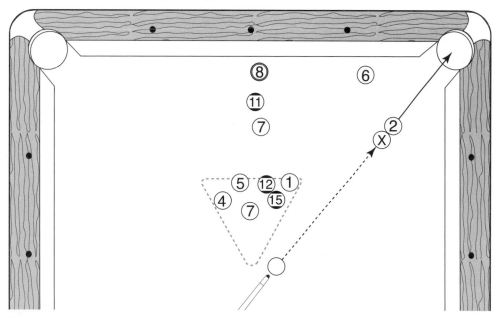

You have achieved your original goal, which was to play a stop shot on the 2-ball to get position to break the cluster with the 7-ball. Upon arriving at Point A, however, it dawns on you that you could also play the 11-ball first and draw back for the 8-ball. Then you would have a relatively easy route to break shot shape on the 7-ball. The 6-ball is left alone for now as it guarantees that you'll have a shot after the break shot. The change in plans allows you to clear the end rail of a couple of potentially troublesome balls while you have the chance.

Tip: Even though you may realize a positional goal to perfection, you should still remain open to the possibility that a better choice may present itself that you may have overlooked while planning your first shot.

Clearing Obstructions

• Clearing a Pocket and then Some

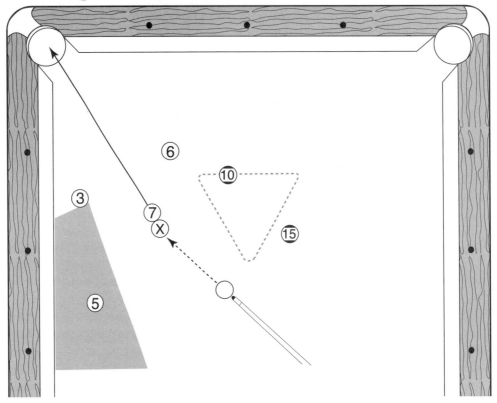

The illustration shows that the 3-ball is blocking a sizeable area from access to the near corner pocket. In this position you could:

- Play the 7-ball to get on the 3-ball, next followed by the 5-ball into the far corner pocket.
- Shoot the 5-ball after the 7-ball, and then the 3-ball.
- Play the 7-ball, come off the rail and bump out the 5-ball, then shoot either the 3-ball or 5-ball or perhaps something else.
- Play the 7-ball, then the 3-ball and draw off the rail and out for shape on the 5 into the same pocket.

Clearing pockets is always a worthwhile goal. This exercise shows that even in a simple position such as this you may have several options for unblocking the pocket. Any one of the four options shown could easily be the best selection. It all depends on the layout of the rest of the balls.

Opening Up Room for the Cue Ball

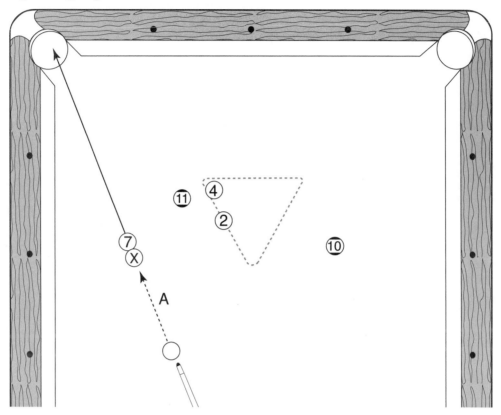

There are many players who make the big mistake of viewing all groups of balls as clusters that need to be broken. In the example, they might shoot the 7-ball with draw to Position A so they would have an angle on the 2-ball to break the balls apart. In this position the 4-ball and 11-ball each will have a clear path to the same pocket once the 2-ball is removed. You don't need to clear an obstructing ball from in front of the 4 and 11-balls. Instead, you must remove the 2-ball, which blocks the cue ball's position.

Tip: You should always be on the lookout for groups of balls that can be cleared off without being broken.

Clearing the Way for a Secondary Break Shot

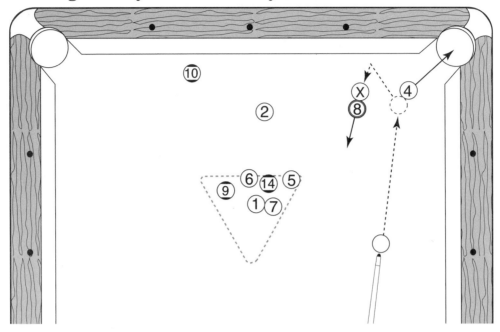

Getting the stack open is one of your most important goals as you proceed through a frame of balls. The 8–ball is in a position where you must have the cue ball to break the rack. On numerous occasions, an excellent potential secondary break shot, such as the 8-ball, needs to be liberated from an obstructer so you can use it to its full advantage.

Clearing a Pocket of a Row Blocker

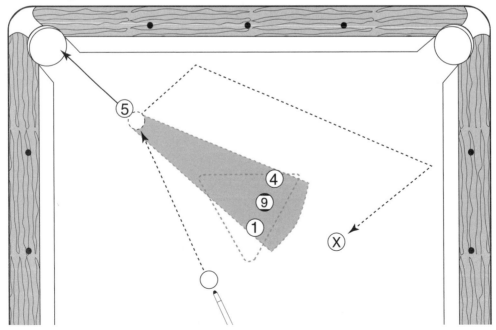

The balls tend to form certain patterns that appear over and over again following breaks shots. One of the most common is a row of balls in the area of the triangle, such as the 1,4, and 9-balls in the diagram on the previous page. Quite often there is also an obstruction like the 5-ball that blocks an entire row of balls from access to a corner pocket. A ball like the 5-ball that's out in the open gives the appearance of being a useful ball until you realize that any ball that's touching the boundary lines of the zone is blocked by the 5-ball from the upper left corner pocket.

By playing the 5-ball as shown, you will give three balls access to the same pocket. All three can now be played into the same corner pocket with the cue ball on the correct side of the row at Position X.

Common Patterns

Circling the Table Picking off Balls

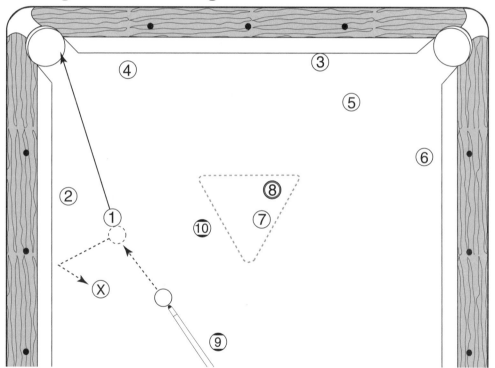

This pattern is extremely effective as it minimizes the amount of distance that the cue ball must travel between shots. The idea is to pocket balls on one side rail, then move to the end rail for more easy shots followed by a shot(s) on the opposite side rail. You simply go with the flow. In the example, the order in which the balls should be played is the number on the balls (this was done for simplicity, and should not to be confused with Nine-Ball).

Circling Behind the Rack and Back Out

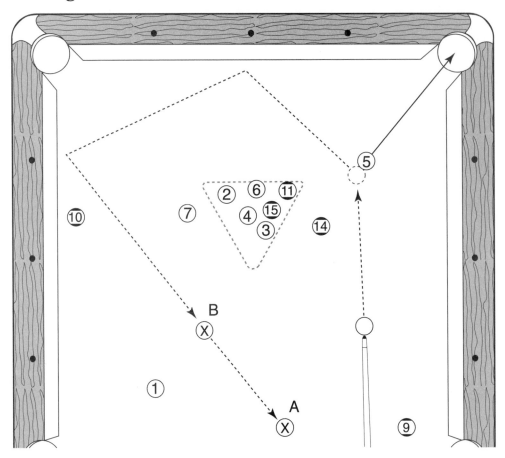

Two-rail position is the bread and butter shot of all Nine-Ball players. Two-rail shape is also a very useful position route in Straight Pool. When playing two-rail position you must be alert to certain balls, such as the 10-ball, which could through the cue ball off course. And naturally, because this is Straight Pool, you may need to play the shot with perfect speed or have multiple shots waiting when the cue ball returns to the center of the table.

In the example, shooting the 5-ball clears the pocket for the 14-ball. If the cue ball stops at Position A, you could open the rack with the 14-ball. If it came to rest at Position B, you could break the cluster with the 7-ball. Note that each break shot has a safety valve. You could play the 9-ball after the 14-ball, or the 1-ball after the 7-ball.

Useless Balls

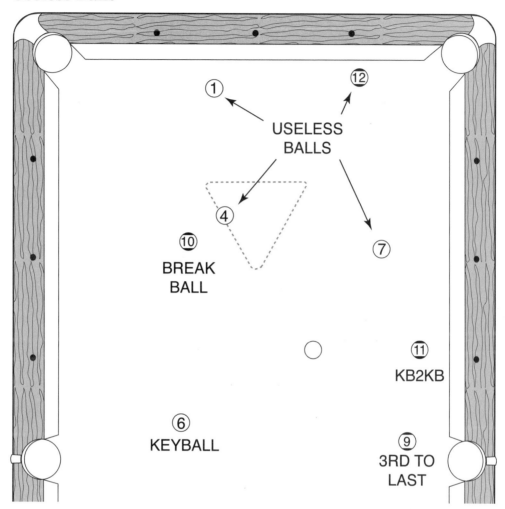

It looks as if you have a zillion ways to play this end of rack pattern. But upon sifting through the clutter, you can quickly spot a can't miss, four ball, end-of-the-rack pattern. The 10-ball is the break shot. The 6-ball is an ideal key ball. The 9-ball followed by the 11-ball will get you set up for a stop shot on the 6-ball. There are any number of ways of playing the remainder of the rack. Two possible patterns are the 4, 1, 12, and 7-ball, or the 7, 4, 1, and 12-ball. Both patterns lead up to the 9-ball.

When the balls are laid out this easy and serve no real purpose, such as breaking a cluster or setting up the break shot, then they are really useless balls. They are no more than target practice. But you must not slack off on these gimmes as they can bite you if you're not careful. If you were wondering if there was ever such a thing as a "breather" in Straight Pool, the first four balls of this pattern are it.

Balls High Up in the Triangle

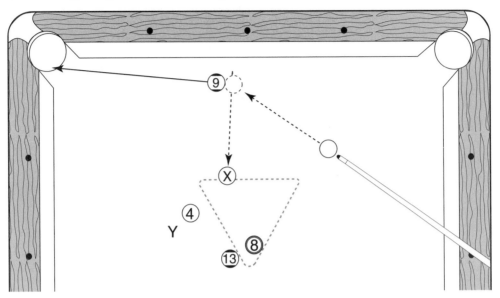

A ball or two stationed high up in the triangle can provide you with a deceptively tricky situation. Balls in this position often block the break ball. At times they are a real pain to get good shape on. This is especially true late in the rack when you want to preserve your break ball, and your choices for maneuvering around the problem are nil.

The example shows a touchy situation. You've got to play the 6-ball and get on either the 8-ball or 13-ball. Position for a shot into the far corner pocket is the high percentage play. If you have super directional control and a fine touch, you could chose to bump the 4-ball to Position Y and play the 13-ball in the side pocket.

Linking Balls

It's a good idea to clear the balls at the far end of the table as long as you are in the vicinity. In the diagram on the next page, the next logical destination after shooting the 4, 7 and 2-ball is the foot rail. Once there, you can play the 11-ball, followed by the 1-ball to break the cluster. The key to completing this plan successfully is the 2-ball. The 2-ball links one part of the pattern (4, 7, 2) with the next. A linking ball makes it much easier to move from an area where your work is complete to another, such as the foot rail in our example.

The ideal linking ball is one close enough to a pocket where you can focus on controlling the cue ball with maximum precision. To more fully appreciate the value of linking balls, notice how difficult it would be to play the 7-ball to get to Position A. Although this shot is routine in Nine-Ball, it is the kind best avoided in Straight Pool. Look for linking balls and use them whenever possible.

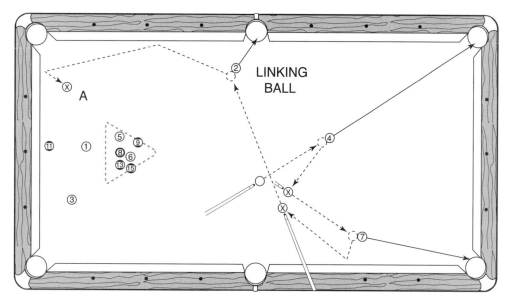

One Shot– Two Big Results

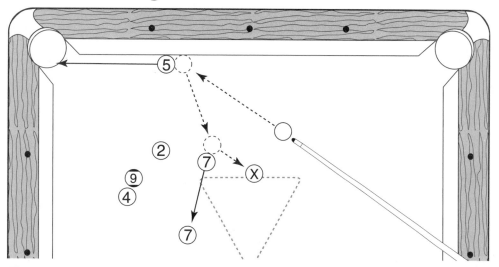

This end-of-the-rack position is fraught with danger, and yet loaded with opportunity for brilliance. A precise hit on the cue ball will, after pocketing the 5-ball, send the cue ball off the rail and into the left side of the 7-ball. This will reposition the 7-ball for a break shot. In addition, you can easily break the cluster when playing the 2-ball. The keys to this shot were recognizing it in the first place, and then executing with a high degree of precision. Notice that the cue ball traveled slightly backwards off the cushion to contact the 7-ball right on target.

Controlling the direction of the cue ball off the rail when the object ball is this far from the cushion is one of the most useful and challenging position plays in Straight Pool. If you can consistently execute shots like the one in the diagram, then you're in an elite class of Straight Pool players. Practice, practice, practice.

• Working on an Area

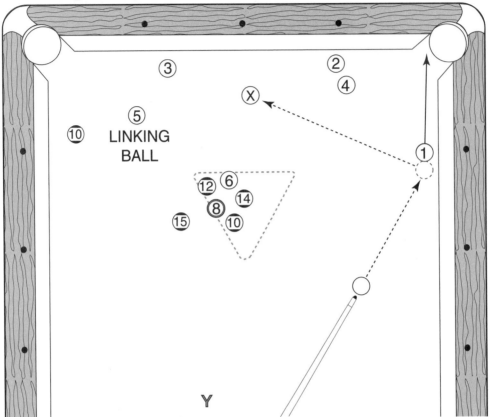

While you're in a specific area of the table, you should consider clearing all of the balls in that section before moving elsewhere. In the diagram, the correct sequence is the 1-ball first, followed by the 2, 3, 4 and 5-balls. Note that the 5-ball is a linking ball to Position Y for the 15-ball. The 10-ball should be saved as an insurance ball for the break shot. Clearing the balls off the rail in this example also makes room for the balls that are now in a cluster in the triangle.

A Game Plan for Preparing to Clear an Area
- Identify the area to be cleared.
- Plan the most logical sequence.
- Decide if any balls should be left behind for future purposes.
- Decide where you want the cue ball after clearing the area.
- Identify your linking ball to the next sequence or shot.

When a Cluster is Not Really a Cluster

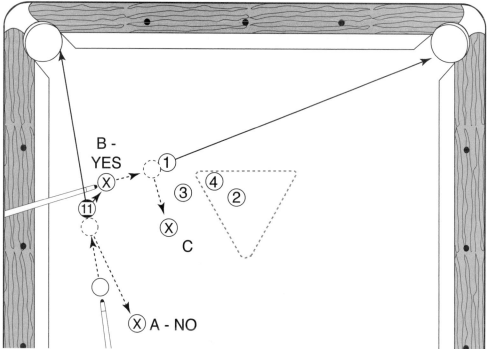

A cluster is normally thought of as several balls that are so close to one another that they need to be broken apart for you to have a shot on any one of the members of the group. At first glance, the 1, 2, 3 and 4-balls seem to fit the definition. But wait a second. Perhaps it possible to play the balls without facing the uncertainty that comes with breaking a cluster. Here are the steps in the planning process:

- What ball(s) in the group could be shot first?
- What side of the first ball must the cue ball end up on?
- What ball(s) does shooting the first ball open up?
- What ball comes next?

You could draw back off the 11-ball to Position A for the 2-ball, but then you would have to break the "cluster" to have another shot. A soft follow shot on the 11-ball puts the cue ball at Position B. This gives you an angle to stun the cue ball to Position C for the 2-ball. After the 2-ball, you have shots on either the 3-ball or 4-ball. The end result is four super easy shots in which you didn't have to touch another ball.

Working the End Rail With Inside English

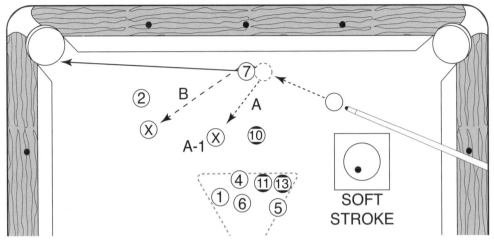

Using inside english is one of the big secrets to playing position on the end rail because you are constantly rolling past the next ball for shape on it, and inside english is instrumental in getting a proper cut angle. On most position plays behind the rack, you will be using a stroke in the soft to very soft range

In the example, you are preparing to shoot a secondary break shot that comes up repeatedly. You have to travel to the other side of the 10-ball because the 2-ball blocks the 10-ball for the upper left corner pocket. The play is to shoot the 7-ball and follow past the 10-ball and off the rail for a secondary break shot. If you use straight follow, the cue ball will bounce too abruptly off the rail and follow Route A. You would then have to have incredible speed control to land at Position A-1. But if you play the shot with a little softer stroke and a tip of left (inside) English, the inside english creates a flatter path off the rail which gives you a much greater margin for error in getting to Position B for the 10-ball.

Multiple Objectives in Congestion

When you are working in close quarters where you can exert maximum control over the cue ball, it is sometimes possible to accomplish several worthy objectives on a single shot. This is especially true once you train yourself to look for these opportunities. In the position in the diagram on the following page, you can do five things in one shot:
- Pocket the 1-ball.
- Bump the 12-ball into ideal position for a break shot.
- Clear the pocket for the 8-ball.
- Get position on the 6-ball.
- Get an angle on the 6-ball that enables you to easily play position either the 8-ball or 9-ball next.

Wow! You accomplished five things on one innocent looking shot. Remember, when you are working in congestion, keep a sharp eye out for the number of things you can accomplish on one shot.

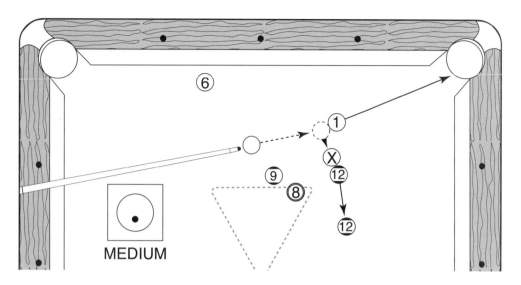

Back and Forth Across the Table

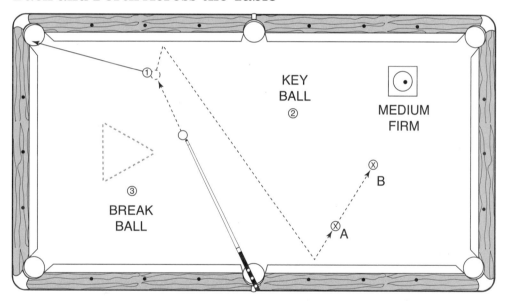

This position play gives Nine-Ball players a chance to let their stroke out. It also shows that Nine-Ball type position routes can, at times, play a vital role in extending your run. The angle on the 1-ball is too steep to hold the cue ball for a shot on the 2-ball into the upper right hand corner pocket. Even if you could hold the cue ball, it is extremely difficult to get the correct angle on the 2-ball for the corner. Your best bet is to cross the table and out for shape on the 2-ball in the side pocket. Use right english. On this route, it is tough to come up short of Position A. You also don't need to worry about rolling past Position B because the rail and a bit of reverse english (off the second rail) will help slow the cue ball down.

Shooting Easy Combos Can Preserve Your Pattern

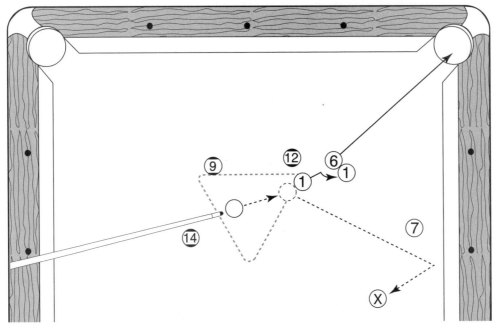

Many players learn to avoid any and all combos that are not lined up dead in the pocket. This aversion to combos, however, can play havoc with your patterns in Straight Pool. Passing on simple, high-percentage combos can, at times, totally disrupt your pattern.

When to Play a Relatively Easy Combo
- It is a high percentage shot, even for the combo averse player.
- Taking a small risk seems well worth it for the gain in position.
- The alternative plan for working around the combo is cumbersome.

In the diagrammed position, you have several choices:
- You could cut in the 9-ball and come off the rail into the 1,6,12 "cluster".
- You could stun/follow the 12-ball slightly forward and play the 1-ball in the far corner pocket.
- You could play the easy combo.

The combo seems well worth the "risk", especially when considering the alternatives. By playing the combo, you'll be able to remove the troublesome 7-ball on the next shot. The 1-ball should drift slightly to the right after contact with the 6-ball. Once the combo is down, the remainder of this rack should be a breeze.

Tip: When playing combos in traffic, always figure the new location of the first ball. Make sure it won't be relocating to a disadvantageous position.

Picking off a Ball on the Far End of the Table

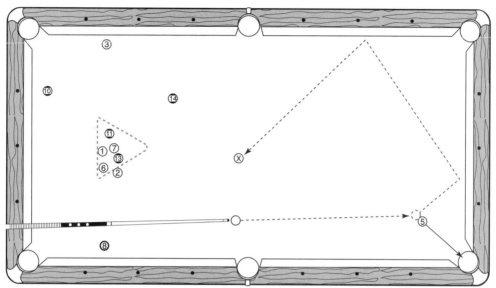

Stray balls located at the far end of the table can be troublesome, especially in the later stages of a rack. This rule of thumb, however, is loaded with exceptions. The big key to removing balls at the far end is timing. You've got to pick what you feel, and what the pattern suggests is the right time to play a shot such as the 5-ball. Some of the key considerations in shooting balls at the far end include:

- You have a very makeable shot at it right now.
- The route back has no scratch risk.
- The ball will not likely be of any value later in the rack.
- You are not sacrificing good shape on another ball.
- You can play the stray and easily get back in line with the rest of the rack.
- You might even be able to get good position for meeting a valuable objective on the next shot, such as a secondary break shot.

After examining the shot on the 5-ball, you can see that it meets nearly every one of these objectives. If the cue ball were at Position X prior to playing the 5-ball, then the secondary break shot on the 2-ball would be a far superior choice. Remember, it's all about timing.

One-Rail Twice or Two-Rails Twice

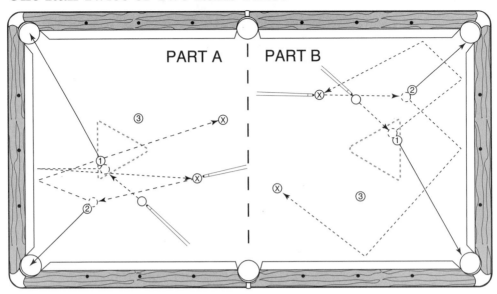

The diagram shows two patterns for playing the exact same layout. In Part A, the 1-ball is shot using follow for one-rail position on the 2-ball. Then it is one-rail and out on the 2-ball using top left english for position on the 3-ball break shot.

In Part B, the 1-ball is played first again, only this time the cue ball is going two-rails for shape on the 2-ball. Next it's two-rails and out for the break ball.

In both cases, the pattern was played to perfection. So which sequence is better? In this case, it is really a matter of personal preference. The big key is the first shot. Some players prefer going one-rail, and don't mind using inside english. Other players, when given a choice, would just as soon play the natural two-rail route.

Keep an Open Mind

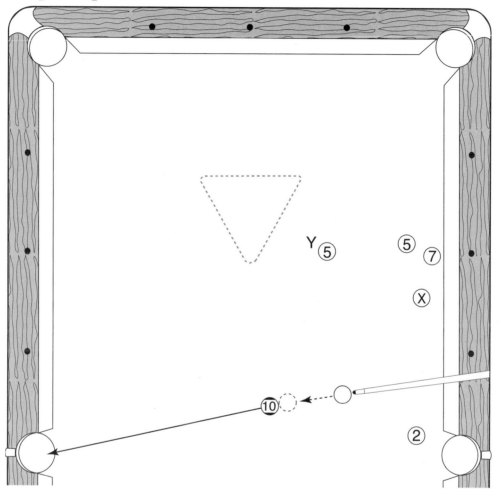

There are many rules in Straight Pool that, if followed regularly, will enhance your game tremendously. However, there are also as many exceptions to the rules, as I've stressed throughout this book. You must learn keep an open mind for exceptions to the rules in a high percentage of the positions you will encounter.

As a rule of thumb, when you are setting up a side-of-the-rack break shot, you want your last shot before the break shot to be an easy one into the side pocket. This will enable you to exert maximum control over the cue ball. This rule implies that you should play the 10-ball into the side pocket and draw back for the 7-ball. Next shoot the 2-ball into the side pocket for shape on the 5-ball break shot. This would be the better sequence if the 5-ball were at Position Y. In this case, however, you can raise your chances of getting excellent position by defying conventional wisdom. Play the 2-ball after the 10-ball. Then use the 7-ball to place the cue ball at X for the 5-ball break shot.

Grinding it Out

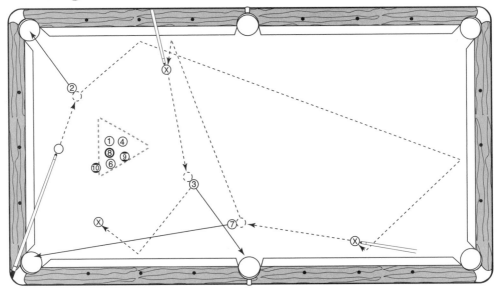

You've got to learn to grind it out if you want to finish off racks that are not roadmaps to the break ball, then. This means exercising your gray matter to come up with a creative solution to a layout that is anything but routine. Some elements of a "grind it out" run include:

- A tough and /or unusual position play.
- A creative sequence of shots.
- Working your way to a secondary break shot.
- Moving balls at the end of the rack to better positions.

In the example, the cluster in the triangle must be broken, but how? It would be tough to get the proper angle on the 3-ball for a secondary break shot. It would also be difficult to get on the 2-ball for a side pocket break shot. The 10-ball is a very workable secondary break ball providing you can get to it. The solution is shown in the diagram. Notice that it includes around the table shape for the 7-ball followed by a precise cross table route to the 3-ball. Finally, a soft touch follow shot will send the cue ball to Position X for the 10-ball break shot.

While you may never encounter this exact pattern (I only have once and it turned out as shown), you will be constantly challenged to find creative solutions to puzzles just as difficult if not more so, to keep your inning alive.

Tip: Perhaps the biggest secret to grinding it out is to have the discipline to stop and think, really think, about the layout. An approach that is guaranteed not to work is firing away, hoping a miracle will be bestowed upon you.

Playing for Luck

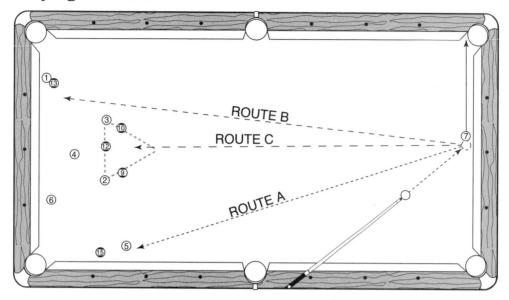

In the early stages of a freshly broken rack you may, to your surprise, discover a shortage of open shots. When the balls separate widely from the triangle, they sometimes have a tendency of getting in each other's way. In this position, your only shot is on the 7-ball. You must then travel down table for a shot on the ? –ball. You read correctly. Your next shot is a big question mark.

There are three routes to a possible shot, each of which is going to require a dose of luck. If you follow Route A and hit the 5-ball on the wrong spot, you could end up without a shot. You could also miss the 5-ball and scratch in the lower left-hand pocket. Route B requires that you travel the length of the table to a very small position zone for shape on the 6-ball. If you come up short or long, you'll be faced with the 4-6 combo.

Route C is the best choice as it is the easiest to control (you are coming straight off the rail) and it greatly reduces the chance of scratching. With Route C you will need some luck, but the odds are definitely in your favor of coming away with a shot. It all depends on which ball you contact where, and at what speed. Playing for luck definitely goes against the grain, but it can be your best shot, especially if the alternatives call for extremely demanding position plays that are, in essence, lucky shots since no one can pull them off with any consistency. **Tip**: When playing for luck, it's better to play for what you could call controlled luck. Design the shot so that even though you need some good fortune, you would be really unlucky not to get another reasonably makeable shot.

Conflicting Agendas

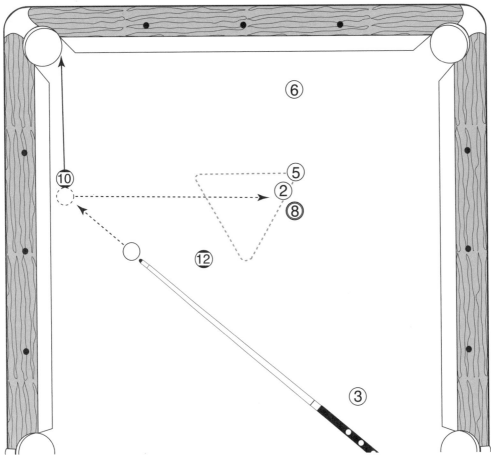

It is getting late in the rack and you're going to need to get rid of the mildly troublesome 10-ball very soon. In fact, you could play it right now. The cue ball would then roll into the 2-ball, separating a cluster that doesn't need to be broken. The 3-ball is an insurance ball that guarantees a shot after the 10-ball. Playing the 10-ball now solves a problem, but it could also create another one. It all depends on the roll of the 2, 5 and 8-balls.

Although you've got to take care of the 10-ball, should you at the risk of running into balls that don't need to be moved? You could play the 6-ball first for position on the 5-ball next, but you might have trouble getting back over for the 10-ball later in the rack. In positions like this, there may not be a clear-cut best answer. When you could just as well play one shot or the other, you've got conflicting agendas. The best solution lies in exercising your best judgment, all things considered, then commit to executing your chosen shot as well as possible.

Saving Two Break Shots on the Same Side

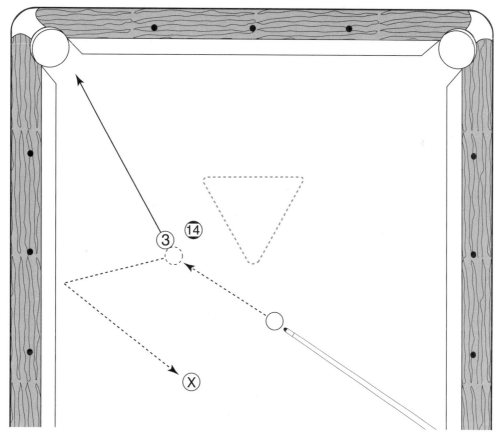

It is a good idea to save two break balls for as long as possible providing it doesn't upset your pattern. If both balls are the last two balls and are on the same side of the table, one of them can serve as a very effective key ball for the other. In most cases, such as the one in the illustration, you will want to shoot the ball closest to the rail first and come back out for break shot shape on the other ball.

Saving Two Break Shots on Opposite Sides

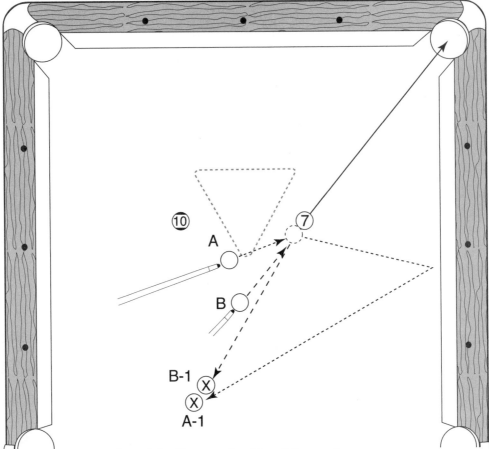

When you save a break ball on each side of the rack, you can open up your options for patterning the other balls. It's comforting to know that another break shot is still available. If you run into a jam, you can shoot one of the break balls sooner than you'd originally planned and still have one available. If both break balls survive until the end of the rack, then either ball can serve as a key ball for the other. When this happens, your selection for the break ball and key ball depends on:

- Whether you are right or left handed.
- Which ball is in the better break ball position.
- Which ball is easiest to get good shape on.

You have a choice between the 7-ball and the 10-ball for your break shot. We'll assume you are a righthanded player. With the cue ball at Position A, you can come off the rail to A-1 for the break shot. From Position B, a draw shot will send the cue ball to B-1.

Using Balls on the Side Rail

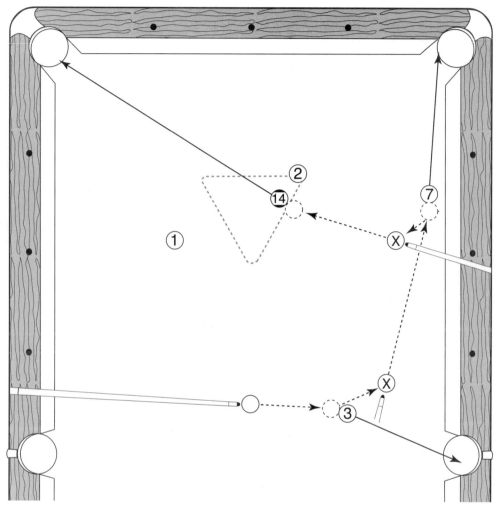

Many players believe you should remove balls from the rail as soon as possible. This is another generalization that has many exceptions. You will regularly encounter instances where a ball in a location such as the 7-ball can be useful for getting shape on balls in the area of the triangle. This pattern could arise at any stage of the rack. The 7-ball in the diagram is ideally stationed for playing position on the 2-ball and 14-ball. The ball on the rail is especially useful as a stepping stone when you need is to obtain a precise angle on a ball such as the cut shot on the 14-ball.

• Taking Balls off the Rail

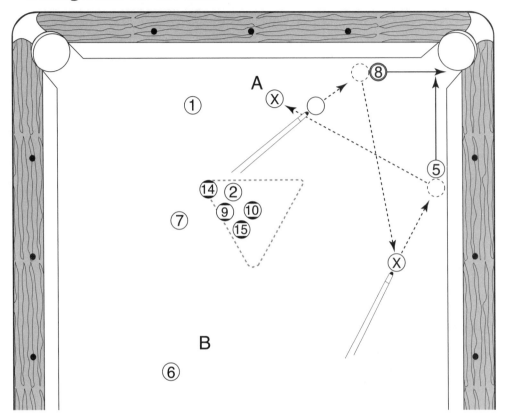

Your goal in the near future is to break the cluster with the 7-ball. There is some work to be done, however, before playing the 1-ball to get on the 7-ball. Now is a good time to clear the 8 and 5-balls from the rails. These balls serve no useful purpose, and they could get clustered up with one of the balls that are now in the triangle when they are broken apart.

     The decision of whether or not to first remove the 8 and 5-balls in this position also depends upon your ability to re-establish position on the 1-ball at cue ball Position A so you can use it to move to Position B for the secondary break shot. If your short-range position play is a little suspect, you may chose to follow out for the 7-ball right away.

Short Side for Balls Along the Side Rail

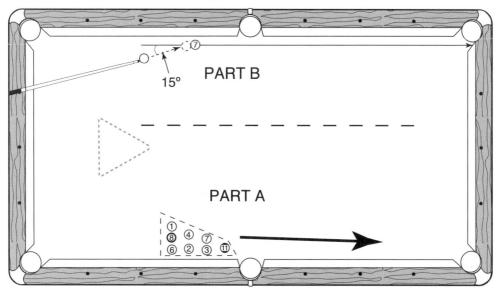

It is often easier to play shape for the far corner pockets for balls along the side rail on the foot end of the table that are at least /″ off the rail. The zone in Part A shows a number of typical ball locations for shots that are often played into the far corner. The reason to play balls from the short side is that the majority of balls you can use to get on the balls in the zone are located at the break end of the table. The key is to leave a shallow cut angle of no more than about 15 degrees, as shown in Part B. **Tip:** It is better to cut towards the rail, as this puts a touch of spin on the object ball that can help it into the pocket (left in Part B of this example).

Neutral Balls

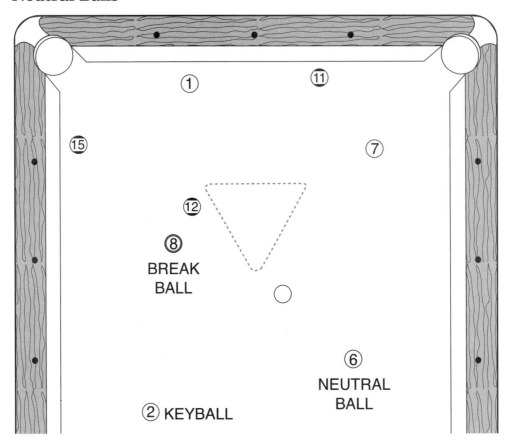

A neutral ball is easy to get shape on from a variety of positions and it is doing no harm in its present location. The 8-ball is the break ball and the 2-ball is the key ball. The most immediate concern are the 12 and 15-balls. Either the 7-ball or the 1-ball could be used to get on the key ball.

What about the 6-ball? It could also be used to get on the key ball, but we decided that the 7 or 1-balls will be used for that purpose. The 6-ball is really excesses baggage. It serves no real purpose, but also presents no particular problem. So should you play it now and get it out of the way, or save it for later? It's really a judgment call. With neutral balls like the 6-ball, you can shoot it now, or shoot it later.

Dealing with Trouble and Avoiding Problems

Clearing the End Rail of Trouble

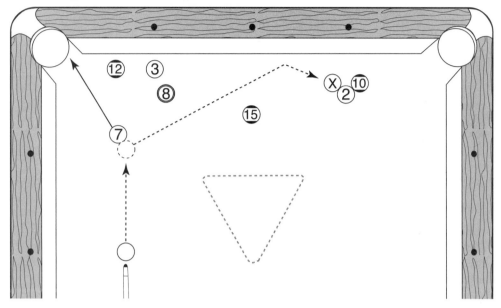

At times half the rack will relocate around the end rail after a break shot. The balls could present you with a series of ducks that will quickly add 4-5 or even more points to your score. Balls on the end rail could also, however, present you with a serious challenge to your run. Due to the congestion factor, you should be prepared to:

- Play exquisite short-range position.
- Pattern the balls perfectly.
- Shoot a combo.
- Play a carom or billiard.
- Go rail first.
- Squeeze in a ball between the rail and another ball.

All of the above become viable options when maneuvering on the end rail because the balls are so close together. When working the end rail, you will often find yourself playing many shots you may never consider in the open spaces on the rest of the table.

The diagram shows a mess along the end rail. You've got to deal with a combination, a cluster, a blocker (the 8-ball) and the 15-ball, which could block a shot on either pocket. Take a few moments to develop a plan for dealing with this basket of problems. Here's a possible the plan: Cheat the pocket to the right side when playing the 7-ball to avoid running into the 8-ball, and send the cue ball into the 2-10 cluster. Use a soft draw stroke. This shot requires precision, not power. The idea is to hit the 2-ball left of center at a slow speed. The shot on the 7-ball will also set you up for the easy 3-12 combo. Your next shot could be the 10, 12 or 8-ball. At this point the hard work should be over.

- **Access Balls to a Danger Zone**

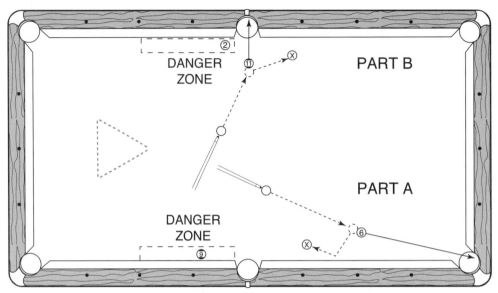

The two side rails from the second diamond to the side pocket are poten-tially troublesome areas of the table because you often have to go out of your way to play position on balls in these zones. Balls left too long in these zones can be especially annoying at the end of the rack. The dia-gram shows how access balls can help you get to balls in these zones. In Part A, a ball along the same side rail can give you easy access to the both-ersome 9-ball. The 11-ball can be played into the side pocket in Part B to give you position for removing the 2-ball, which is a real run wrecker.

Tip: The further a ball lies up the rail, the more troublesome it becomes.

Access Balls to Trouble Balls

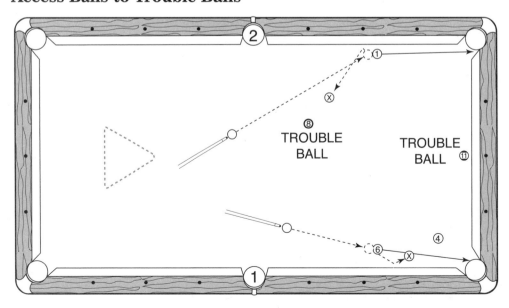

Balls at the far end of the table can be troublesome, especially if the are by themselves. The 8-ball and 11-ball in the diagram on the previous page are both examples of balls that can easily derail your run if not handled properly. Quite often, however, there will be other balls at the same end of the table that can provide easy access to the trouble balls.

The 1, 4 and 6-balls all provide a means of getting on the 11-ball. They also keep you from having to play difficult position from the opposite end of the table. The 1, 4 and 6-balls also give you easy access to the 8-ball. The 8-ball can be played into side pocket #1 or #2 after the 1-ball, or into side pocket #2 after the 4 or 6-balls. The diagram shows just two of the many possibilities for using access balls to take care of trouble balls.

Avoid Tying Up Balls That Are Already Broken

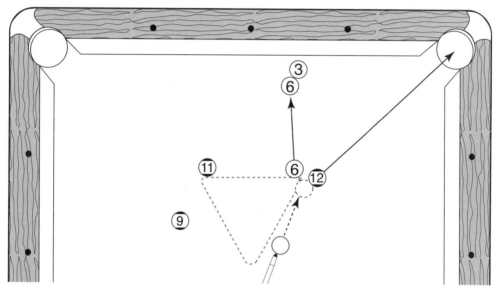

When you've worked hard to separate the balls, there's noting more aggravating than tying them up again. This outright blunder is one of the biggest run killers among average players and experienced professionals alike. Tying up balls out in the open is usually a result of firing away without taking notice of where you will be bumping a ball that is close to the object ball.

The 12 and 6-balls look like a cluster that needs to be broken, but it's not since both balls go into the upper right hand corner pocket. After the cue ball contacts the 12-ball it will drift to the left at just the right direction to send the 6-ball directly towards the 3-ball. One way to avoid a disaster like this is to take notice of what ball the cue ball could hit after contact and what direction the ball will be going.

Another way to avoid tying up balls is to recognize the possibility it could happen, and to play a pattern that eliminates any contact with a second ball. The 11-ball could be shot first, followed by the 3-ball, and then either the 6 or 12-balls next. Problem solved

Don't Overplay a Shot

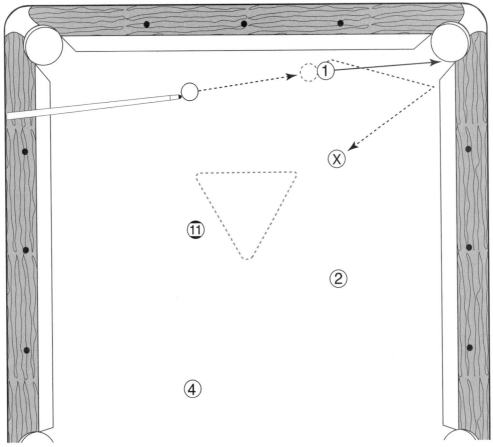

When you miss position, sometimes there is a tendency to try to make up for the mistake on the next shot. Don't let ego, anger or poor judgment cause you to make this mistake. Instead, accept your error and go about playing the next shot in the most favorable manner possible.

In the illustration, you're too straight on the 1-ball. You can still run out providing you accept your medicine and don't do something foolish like trying to pound the cue ball off the rail at such a shallow angle. A soft follow stroke with right english will send the cue ball to Position X for a perfectly acceptable shot on the 2-ball.

Tip: You don't want to cover a mistake by overplaying the next shot. Sometimes two not so difficult shots in succession can do the work of one overly difficult shot. Besides, two wrongs don't make a right.

Avoiding the Domino Effect

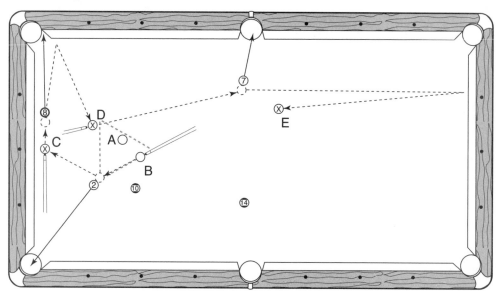

There was a rock song by The Fixx called "One Thing Leads To Another". The title of that song is the definition of the dreaded domino effect. One little mistake at the wrong time can cause your whole pattern to unravel. At worst, you're run out will disintegrate entirely. What's so insidious about the domino effect is that your mistake may not become visible until several shots later when it's too late to do anything about it.

The plan was to draw back on the first ball (not shown) to Position A for a stop shot on the 2-ball. With the ideal angle on the 8-ball, it would be easy to float up for the 7-ball in the side. A stop shot on the 14-ball would then have you in great position for the break shot on the 10-ball.

Now let's see how quickly a pattern can unravel when the dominos start to fall. The first shot was drawn back a few inches too far to Position B. Now a soft follow shot was played for position on the 8-ball. The risk of getting the incorrect angle was realized as the cue ball stopped at Position C. With almost no angle to work with, the best play was to Position D for a cut shot into the side pocket on the 7-ball. The shot on the 7-ball left the cue ball at Position E, a maddening 5" short of position for the key ball. From Position E, it will take a super shot to get on the break ball in the vicinity of where the 14-ball now rests.

The big mistake in this pattern occurred on the first ball, but its total effect was not felt until four shots later. The best way to avoid the domino effect is to plan and execute with great care. I know, you've heard that before. Another safeguard is to recognize the first little mistake when it happens and to make every effort to play an effective recovery shot. In our example, you could have played the 2-ball very softly with inside (left) english for an angle on the 8-ball. You could have also drawn into the left side of the 8-ball to try to manufacture a shot on it, knowing that you've got the 7-ball as a safety valve.

A Hall of Fame Member's Mistake

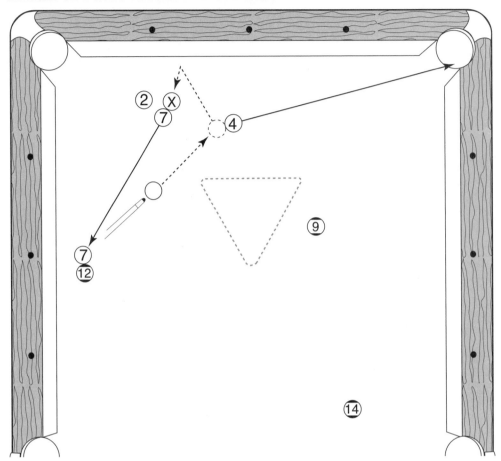

Did I mention earlier that anyone can commit the blunder of tying up balls? In the second diagram, a member of the Hall of Fame broke the 7-2-ball cluster and created another with the 7 and 12-balls. His mistake may have come from executing the shot poorly (perhaps he meant to hit the 7-ball with less speed or on the left side). The error could also have occurred because he failed, under the pressure of tournament play, to take notice of the danger. Luckily enough for him, the 7-12 lined up dead and he was able to continue his run well past 100 balls.

Tip: Maybe it's true that the better you play, the more the pool gods smile upon you.

When the Obvious is Not So Obviously Wrong

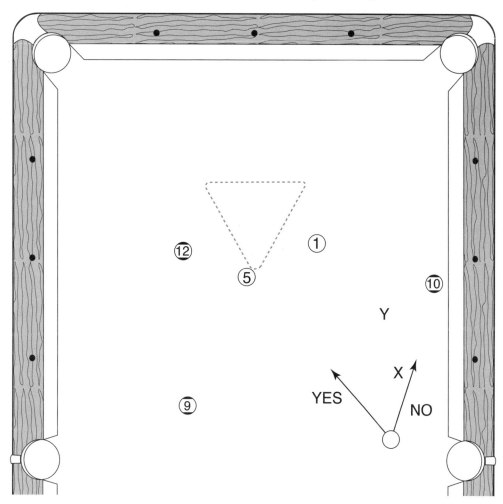

Even though you are only four easy shots away from the break ball and the balls are spread nicely, a lot can still go wrong. In this position, the natural inclination is to remove the 10-ball from the rail while you've got the chance. After all, it does give the appearance of being your last trouble ball. Here are two possible patterns: 10, 1, 5, 9 or 10, 5, 1, 9.

While either of these obviously "correct" patterns could work, there is a better plan that gives you a 99% chance of success. Play a stop shot on the 5-ball. Then cut the 1-ball into the corner and slide over to Position X for the 10-ball. After the 10-ball you should be at Position Y for a stop shot on the key ball.

Tip: The best shot prior to a key ball is the one that can help you get on it with virtually no risk of failure.

Two-Rails to Avoid Trouble

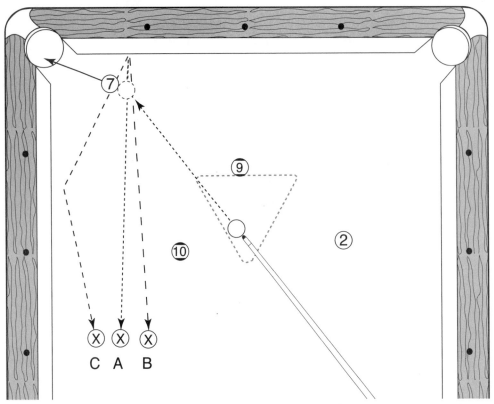

This shot illustrates one of the finer points of position play that separates truly great players from those a notch or two below. The goal is to get from the 7-ball to the 10-ball. That seems easy enough. You could go straight up the table along Route A. This would put you in good shape for the 10-ball and then the 9-ball. The problem with Route A is that if you make a slight error in execution, you could travel down Route B. This would make it triple tough to get from the 10-ball to the 9-ball.

You can remove the risk from this position play by using inside (left) english to go two-rails along Route C. This route ensures that you'll not land too close to the 10-ball with the wrong angle, as is the case if the one-rail route goes astray. This into-the-rail-and-out position play using inside english is a valuable tool that has a thousand and one uses for keeping you out of trouble.

Beware of the Middle

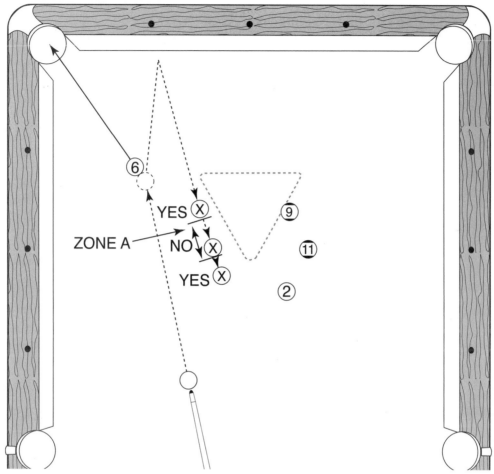

You're nearing the end of your pattern where precision is a must, but there should be no problem as you are playing shape on either of two balls. If you land short, you can play the 2-ball in the side pocket, and if you come up long, you can play the 9-ball first. That's all well and good, but what if you stop in Zone A? Now you're in the dangerous middle. This is pool's equivalent of the Twilight Zone. When you shoot either ball, you're going to destroy your break shot. This mistake is easy to make when you are playing tight shape on either of two balls.

In this example, the solution was to recognize that playing shape for either of two balls is no guarantee of success, especially in tight quarters. The better pattern was to play the 9-ball first, then either the 2-ball or 6-ball next. There is a middle zone (see if you can find it) between the 2-ball and the 6-ball. But even if you were to land in it, you could still run out without wrecking the break ball.

Stuck in the Middle

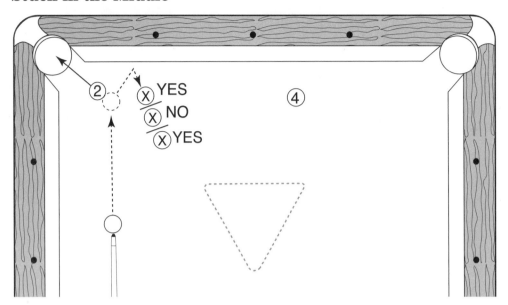

This innocent looking position play has sunk many a fine player. Just roll in the 2-ball and drift off the rail for the 4-ball. All you want is a workable angle on the 4-ball so you can escape the end rail and head out to the middle of the table. If you play either short or long of the middle, then you'll have position to exit the end rail. The danger lies in getting stuck in the middle with not enough angle to work with. Don't just casually approach this position play with the idea that it's such an easy shot that's is bound to give you something playable. The key to avoiding this mistake is to commit to playing for one side or the other of the middle zone.

Long Shots In the Middle of the Table

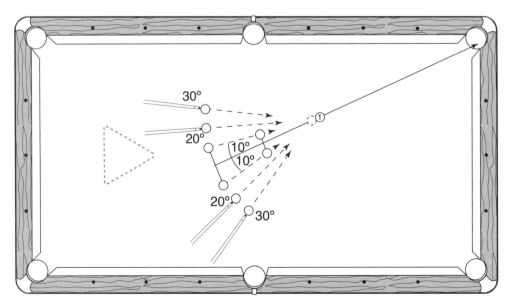

When playing shape on a solitary ball in the middle of the table past the side pockets, your ideal positional zone is very small. The diagram on the previous page shows a typical shot to a far corner pocket. Notice the size of the position zone, which is bordered on either side by the 10-degree cut angle. With a 10-degree cut, you can easily control the cue ball without going to a rail. I suggest that you now turn the book so you can look down the line of the shot to gain the players perspective. Ask yourself what the shot looks like to you when the cue ball is both in the zone and out. At the higher cut angles of 20 and 30 degrees, you now most certainly must send the cue ball to the rail.

Tip: Going to a rail is usually preferable when a ball in close to the rail. It is generally better to avoid going to a rail when a ball is near the middle of the table.

Balls Frozen To the Rail Next To the Side Pocket

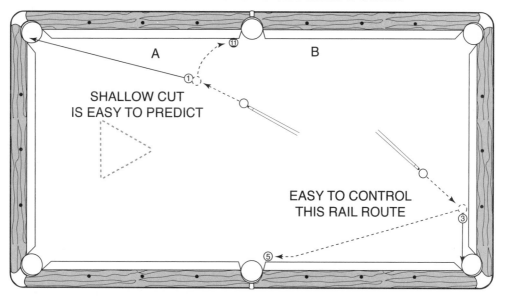

When a ball is frozen to the rail next to the side pocket, it can end your run about as surely as anything. The reason the 11-ball is such trouble is that it is so easy to miss when shooting it from Position A. The point of the side pocket seems to have a way of jumping out at the ball. It's equally as tough to get a fraction of an inch off the rail to shoot the 11-ball into the opposite corner from Position B.

When a ball is frozen next to the side pocket, it should be considered unplayable. You should make every effort to remove the ball from the cushion. Two of the best strategies for ridding yourself of these pests are shown in the diagram. It is easy to control the cue ball's path into the frozen ball in both positions, and they each carry no risk of scratching.

When to Shoot a Break Shot Away

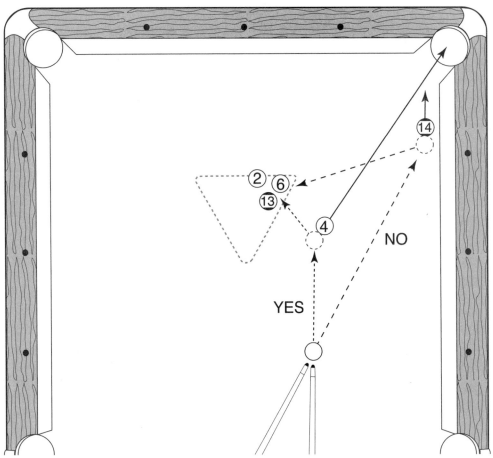

It really hurts when you have to shoot a classic break ball, such as the 4-ball, in the later half of the rack when their value rises greatly. Straight Pool, however, is largely about establishing your priorities. Survival often takes precedence over maintaining your break ball.

Your choice of shots is between the 4-ball and the 14-ball. Playing the 14-ball will preserve your break shot for now, providing you don't hit the 4-ball instead of the cluster, which is far from guaranteed. If you do contact the cluster, you may not come away with a good shot. A soft draw shot on the 4-ball will separate the cluster nicely and you will almost assuredly have a very easy shot on one or more of the three balls. One of the balls might even stop in good position for a break ball. Even in the worst case scenario, you have the 14-ball as a side rail break shot.

Tip: It is ok to shoot a break shot if you absolutely must, but don't make the mistake of running into break balls and destroying them in your normal course of business.

Balls At the Far End of the Table

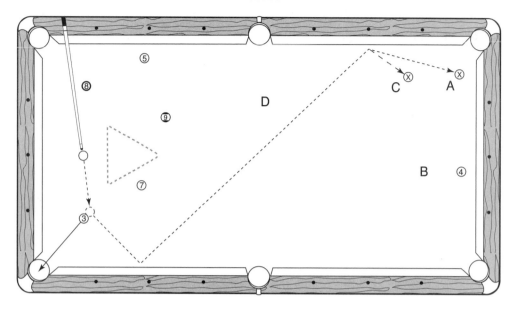

The shotmaking demands of Nine-Ball dictate that you play tougher shots on a regular basis that have a higher probability of being missed than those you'll mostly be playing in Straight Pool. When you're playing Nine-Ball and you miss position, you may still fire away at a harder shot because the penalty for missing is usually not nearly as great. Interestingly enough, in Nine-Ball you also have more opportunities to play safe when you miss position because you only have to prevent your opponent from making one ball, not any ball as in Straight Pool.

When you are playing a Nine-Ball type of position play in Straight Pool, you must execute the shot with great precision. This is especially true when you don't have another shot you can easily switch too if you make a positional error. In the example, your goal is to get from the 3-ball to the 4-ball at the far end of the table. Now if the game was Nine-Ball and the cue ball stopped at Position A, you could play a modest recovery shot to Position B for the 5-ball. When playing Straight Pool, you really need to avoid the kind of error that leaves the cue ball at Position A, because you don't want to be shooting a shot that can be easily missed like the 5-ball. You need the cue ball at Position C so you can send the cue ball back down table to Position D for an easy shot on the 5-ball.

Manufacturing Break Shots

After playing the initial break shot of a new rack or any subsequent break shots, one or more balls may be positioned as break shots for the next rack. In the course of running out, you may have to play a ball that could have served as a break ball, or you may accidentally knock a break ball out of position. In any case, you will often have to create a break ball for the next rack by skillfully bumping a ball into position. Manufacturing a break ball takes:

- The right opportunity. The balls have to be in the right places.
- A soft touch.
- Excellent directional control of both the cue ball and object ball.
- The right timing.

You'll quite naturally want to manufacture the classic side of the rack break balls. But that doesn't mean you should overlook the opportunity to create a wide variety of other break balls that can enable you to proceed into the next rack. And when you have a break ball that's in a fairly decent location, that doesn't mean you shouldn't look for an opportunity to nudge an inch or two to an even better position.

• Manufacturing a Break Shot

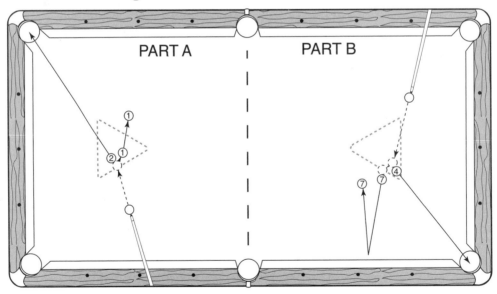

You can extend your runs by manufacturing break shots. Most of the time manufactured break balls will come from the vicinity of the triangle. Part A shows the classic example. Play the 2-ball with enough speed to get it just past the entrance to the pocket. You want the cue ball to bump the 1-ball so softly that it only rolls about a foot, or a little past the triangle. The key to this shot is a shallow cut angle on the first ball and a soft stroke so that the new break ball can be struck with little force.

Occasionally you may find that the last two balls on the table are in the position shown in Part A. When this happens, the play is to leave the cue ball in the triangle. You can then shoot the break shot with ball-in-hand from the head string.

The cut angle is much more severe in Part B, which means that you will have to shoot harder. Now your best play is to send the break ball you're manufacturing to the rail and out as shown.

Make a Break Shot and Play Shape on It At the Same Time

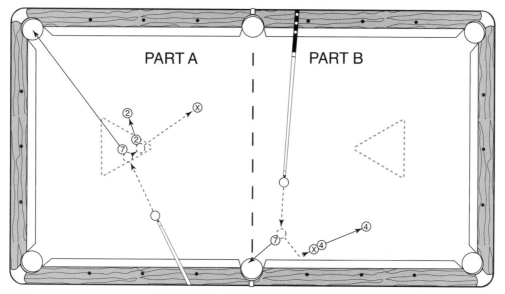

When running a particularly challenging rack, sometimes you are fortunate to get to the point where you have two balls remaining on the table, even if neither is a break ball. When there are only two balls left and you don't have a break ball, it's time to make one, if at all possible. Unless you can leave the cue ball in the triangle (for ball-in-hand), then you must simultaneously play shape on the break ball.

In Part A, the shot is to use a soft draw stroke on the 7-ball. This will create a thin hit on the 2-ball, sending it about 6" to position for a break shot. At the same time, the cue ball will continue to Position X for ideal shape on the 2-ball.

In Part B, the key is to contact the 4-ball with a full hit so that it relocates in the position shown. The cue ball will pretty much stop dead at the point of contact. This shot also requires a soft stroke. The keys to this shot are determining how much of the 4-ball to hit, as well as visualizing what the resulting break shot would look like. Both of these simple looking shots are really more examples of the finer points of Straight Pool at the very highest levels of play.

Two Rails to Create a Break Shot

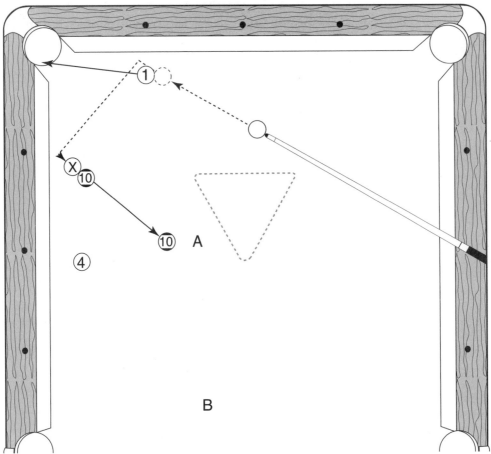

Time is growing short for creating a break shot. The solution is to go two-rails into the 10-ball with good speed to knock it out to Position A. Now you can play a follow shot on the 4-ball to Position B for the break shot. This shot is another example of high level Straight Pool. A whole new world of possibilities will open up to you when you can control the balls with the precision shown in this, and the previous, illustrations.

Skillful Ball Bumping to Create a Break Shot

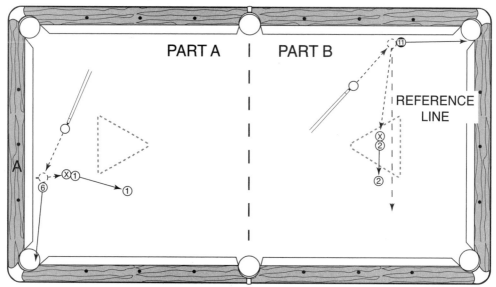

In Part A, you have a cut shot down-the-rail with the object ball very close to the rail, as well as the potential break ball in good position to be bumped up next to the rack. The key is to walk over to Position A and check out the direction the cue ball will be taking off the rail. Is it going to cut the 1-ball as shown with centerball, for example? Or do you need to make some adjustments in cueing to strike the 1-ball where required?

Part B shows another high precision shot. The 11-ball is very close to the rail, and you have enough cut angle on the 1-ball that the cue ball will travel straight off the rail. Under these conditions, you can predict the cue ball's path across the table with a high degree of accuracy. It should follow a line at about a 90-degree angle to the rail. The line can then serve as a point of reference. In the example, about a/tip of left english will help send the cue ball slightly above the reference line into the 2-ball, which should then relocate as shown.

Manufacturing a Break Ball Using English

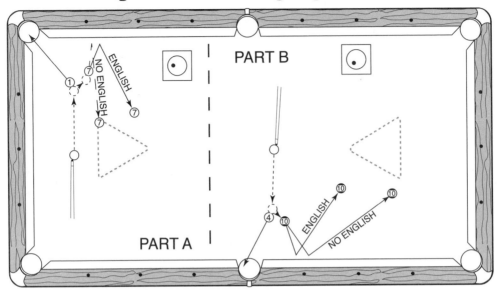

Sometimes the ball you'd like to turn into a break ball is slightly out of position. We covered one instance of how to deal with this challenge a moment ago when the balls were near the rail. In these examples, the future break balls can be thrown onto the proper path by using english. In Part A, the 7-ball would follow Path A, which certainly isn't going to get the job done. But add some inside (left) english and now the 7-ball will head to Position B. Two forces helped create the new path, thanks to the inside english: 1) the thinner hit on the 1-ball led to a thinner hit on the 7-ball; and 2) the 7-ball was thrown to the right causing it to hit a little further up on the cushion.

Part B demonstrates a similar shot, only this time you can use outside english to create a sharper rebound angle off of the cushion. Notice the different paths of the 10-ball with and without english.

Tip: The technique using english in these illustrations to create a break shot can also be used throughout the rack to send non-break shots to more advantageous locations.

Advanced Break Ball Manufacturing

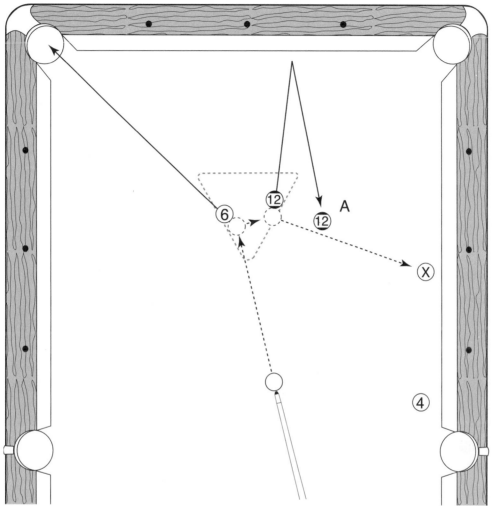

Remember that in difficult situations one of our Principles of Position Play is to use your imagination. Here's an example. The shot is to control the speed and apply just the right amount of draw so that you can cut the 12-ball in the right place with the correct speed to send it to Position A. The 4-ball is conveniently stationed for use as a key ball. The keys to this shot were seeing it in the first place, and then executing it to perfection.

Manufacturing an Insurance Break Ball

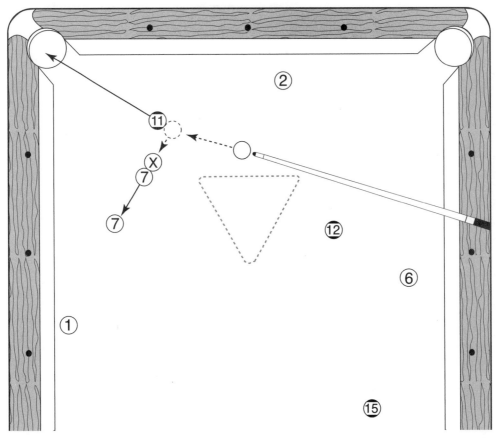

You may wish to create an additional break shot or two even if you already have a good one. Extra break shots can serve as insurance in case you have to shoot the ball you'd originally selected for a break shot. The 12-ball is in good position for a break shot. Furthermore, the 15-ball makes an excellent key ball. The 6-ball on the upper side rail could pose a problem later in the rack. In fact, you may need to use the 15-ball to get to it.

Your most immediate shot is on the 11-ball. If you play it just right, you could bump the 7-ball into position for a back-up break shot. The 13-ball can get you to the 1-ball at the end of the rack. The 1-ball is an excellent key ball for your newly manufactured break ball. With just a little foresight you can adjust the layout so that you have a great chance of getting on a break ball on either side of the table.

• Manufacturing Break Balls From All Angles

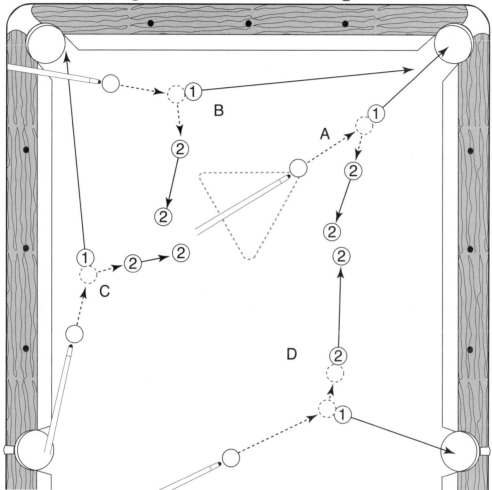

There are a zillion possible positions in which you can manufacture a break shot. You can use draw (A), stun (B and C), and follow (D) as shown in the illustration. You can knock balls off rails, use english, and exercise your creativity in challenging end of rack positions, all of which we've covered in previous sections. In short, there are countless situations for creating break shots.

The break shots you create don't, by any means, have to be classic side-of-the-rack break shots. Just about any break shot that you will learn in the chapter on break shots is a candidate for manufacturing, as long as you can pocket a shot and drive the cue ball into a second ball. So when you are in need of a break shot, keep your mind open to the possibilities.

Getting Position on the Break Ball

Break shot shape is by far the most important in Straight Pool. It can oftentimes be the toughest to get right because of the typically small position zone for the break ball. The difficulty factor is compounded by the fact that you can't cover your mistake by shooting another ball to get back in line. What you play is what you get.

It's been said that Nine-Ball is a game of angles. Well, Straight Pool break shot shape is one of precision angles; it's much more exacting. To get the best shape possible, you've got to make getting on the break shot as easy as possible. This is accomplished by using a key ball, which is the ball before the break ball.

Grading Your Key Ball Position

It may be helpful to visualize several different grades of key balls when you practice running balls. This will alert you as to the quality of your end-of-the-rack patterns. If you have an easy stop shot, or short-range position play for the break ball most of the time, then you know you're playing your patterns well. On the other hand, if you are playing Nine-Ball type of position plays on the key ball, that's an indicator that your end-of-the-rack patterns really need work. The scale below lists 5 grades of key ball positions. I suggest you use it to evaluate the quality of your end-of-the-rack performance. You will go a long ways towards achieving high runs if the vast majority of your position plays from the key ball to the break ball are confined to categories 1 and 2.

1] A stop shot is the best as shape on the break ball is guaranteed.
2] The cue ball must travel a very short distance for shape on the
   break ball. Good shape is almost guaranteed.
3] You must play a typical position route you'd encounter throughout
   the rest of the rack. You will probably have a workable angle to
   break the balls, but it could be less than ideal.
4] It takes extra effort to get good position on the break shot.
5] Heroics are now required. These shots are typically Nine-Ball
   type of position routes to a Straight Pool sized shape zone.

Tips that Can Help Your End-Of-The-Rack Play

- The key ball order of preference is: 1] Position via a stop shot, 2] Down the line position on the break ball, 3] Cross the line position on the break ball.
- Fight to keep your break ball.
- Each type of break shot has an ideal key ball associated with it.
- Even pros rarely get the classic straight in key ball, so expect to have to play position on the break shot.
- When playing for shape on the break ball, it is best to minimize the cue ball's traveling distance.
- Getting in line at the end of a rack greatly raises your chances of extending your run.

Tip: If you are having trouble with your speed control, play back in the position zone for the correct angle on the break ball.

Tip: Straight Pool is a very exacting game. Shape that might be very acceptable in another pool game is not in Straight Pool.

• Characteristics of the Ideal Key Ball

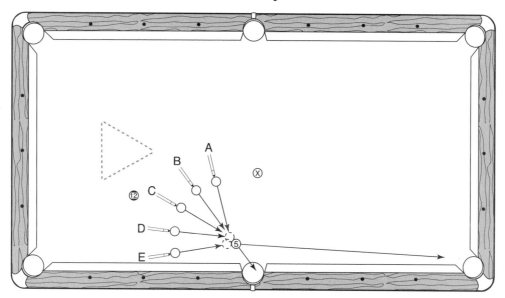

The objective when playing the 5-ball is to arrive at Position X for an excellent side-of-the-rack break shot. Position X can be reached from any of the cue balls labeled A through E. Positions A through D can be played in the side pocket. Position E is the worst-case scenario, as the 5-ball must now be played into the far corner. This kind of key ball gives you a sizeable margin for error. In addition, you need only send the cue ball about 1fi" after contact with the 5-ball to arrive near or at Position X.

The ideal key ball has most, if not all, of the following characteristics:
- The cue ball is close to the key ball.
- The key ball is close to the pocket.
- The key ball is close to the break ball.
- You can recover from an error in position on the key ball.
- You can play the key ball into more than one pocket.

The Can't Go Wrong Key Ball

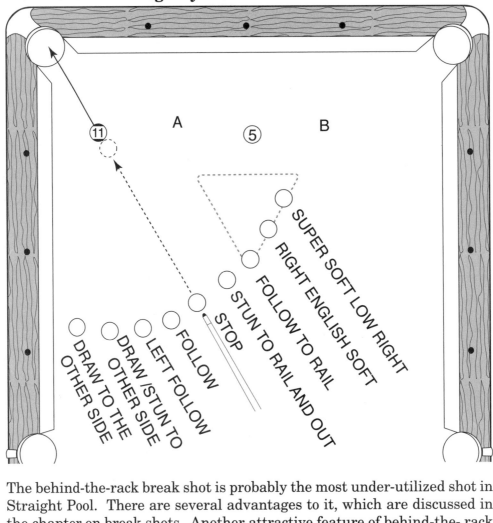

The behind-the-rack break shot is probably the most under-utilized shot in Straight Pool. There are several advantages to it, which are discussed in the chapter on break shots. Another attractive feature of behind-the- rack break shots is that you may have, in many positions, such a wide variety of options for playing the key ball. Just look at the many choices for playing the 11-ball to get on the 6-ball.

One reason why you have so many options is that you can play shape on either side of the 5-ball. Shape on the break ball at Position A, however, is certainly easier than arriving at Position B. You can also go to either the side rail, or the end rail first, before coming back out for shape just in case you fail to have a stop shot. In short, you have many options for getting on the break ball should you fail to leave yourself a straight-in stop shot.

An Excellent Second Choice Key Ball

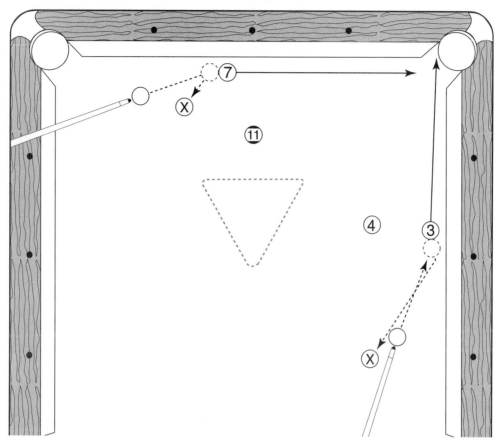

A ball that is located near the rail (but not frozen to it) can make an excellent key ball. The key is to have a relatively shallow cut. This can enable you to play the shot with the speed of stroke you feel most comfortable with. While most players favor side pocket key balls, a down the rail key ball is a close second choice and one that appears repeatedly. The illustration shows a down-the-rail key ball shot for a side-of-the-rack break shot as well as a behind-the-rack break shot.

Tip: Set up a variety of positions and practice coming off the rail until you can consistently get the ideal angle on the break shot.

Stop Shot Key Balls

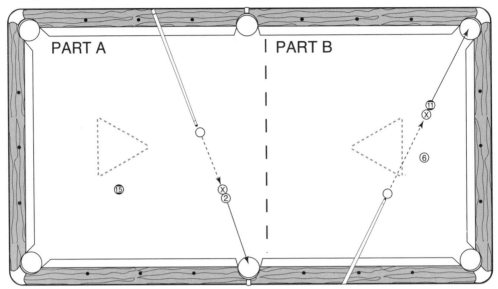

The best shot on the key ball is a stop shot. With a stop shot, you know you're going to have exactly the shot you want on the break ball. The shot on the 2-ball in Part A is a prime example of the perfect stop shot key ball. In Part B, it also looks like a stop shot will leave you with a good break angle on the 6-ball. But don't forget that the cue ball stops 2 ⁄" short of where the object ball lies, it doesn't replace it. So in Position B, you should follow 3" for a sufficiently great cut angle on the 6-ball.

Tip: Stop shot keys balls work great if you get nearly straight-in shape on them. Keep in mind that that is an awfully big if.

When to Shoot a Key Ball Prematurely

It is one the most annoying moments in Straight Pool is when you have to shoot a break ball prior to the end of the rack. It is almost as bothersome as having to shoot a key ball that is perfectly positioned for getting on the break ball. In the illustration on the following page, the 1-ball is your only reasonable shot. A soft follow shot on the 1-ball will allow you to roll over to Position A so you can remove the potentially troublesome 2-ball. Of course the 2-ball then links to the 3-ball, which is the key ball you were saving for the 7-ball break shot.

Even though you've removed the key ball, there is still a very playable route to the break shot. Shoot the 5-ball first, followed by the 4-ball into the lower left corner pocket. When playing the 4-ball, the goal is to slide the cue ball over to Position B for a key ball shot on the 6-ball.

Tip: If shooting a key ball prematurely reduces the risk of runout failure, then you should sacrifice it for the good of the cause.

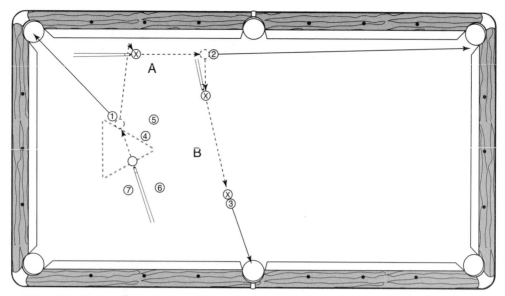

• **Key Ball in the Rack**

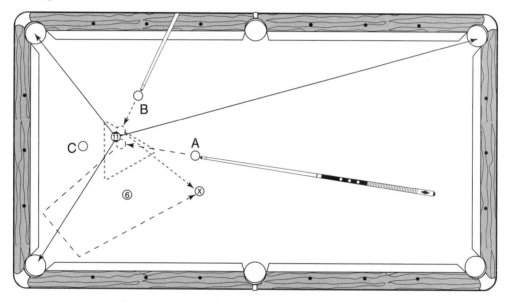

There are several ways to get on a side-of-the-rack break ball when the key ball is in the area of the triangle. One possibility is the natural two-rail route to the break shot as shown with Cue Ball A. In Position B, you can send the cue ball to the identical spot as in Position A by playing a stun shot. When playing a key ball like this, you may have to use a variation of the stun shot, such as stun/draw or stun/follow. It all depends on the position of the balls. With the cue ball in Position C, the only way to get on the break ball is to play a stop shot, then play the 6-ball with ball in hand behind the head string.

Side Pocket Key Balls

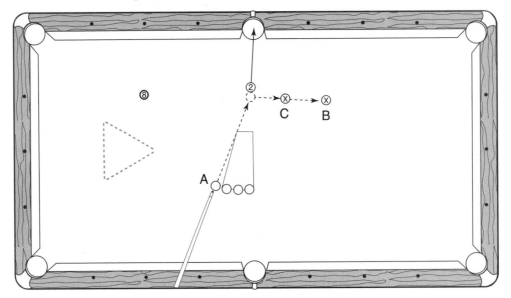

Side pocket key balls that enable you to play a stop shot for position on the break ball are highly valued. The diagram shows the size of a position zone for a typical stop shot key ball. The dimensions of the zone take into consideration the possibility of playing the 2-ball into either side of the pocket (cheating the pocket) should you fail to line up with the dead center of the pocket. As you can tell, there is some margin for error in playing shape on this shot, but not much.

Let's assume you end up a ball's width out of the zone at Cue Ball A. Now you run the risk of traveling much further down the table for the break shot, especially if you want to maintain the same cut angle. From this distance, a stun shot could easily send the cue ball to Position B. A soft draw shot could also help maintain the same cut angle and it would probably leave the cue ball at Position C.

Once again, you can see how little errors loom large in Straight Pool, especially at the end of the rack. As I'm sure you're well aware by now, this is a constant theme that runs throughout the book. Once you are apprised of the dangers that are inherent in position plays like the one in this illustration, you can take the appropriate action to reduce the risk, if not eliminate it all together. More on this later.

Side Pocket Key Balls (2)

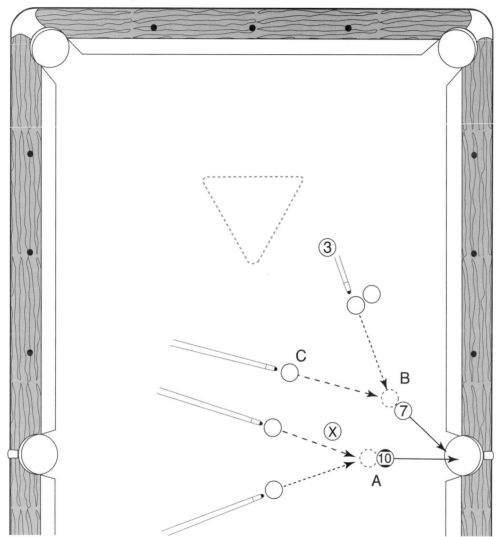

I'm really emphasizing side pocket key balls because playing them successfully can be instrumental in your achieving high runs. The 10-ball key
ball shot in Position A is similar to the one in the last section, only this
time you need to draw the cue ball back about 8" for position on the 3-ball.
Take notice of the size of the position zone. From Position A-1, the cue ball
would end up at Position Z.

The 7-ball at Position B can also serve as a very effective key ball.
It gives you several more options for playing shape on the break ball. From
Position C, you could go to the rail and back out using inside (right) english. And should you miss the zone at Position D, you could always play the
7-ball into the far corner and still arrive at Position X for the break shot.

Another advantage to a key ball located below the side pocket is that
it should be easy to play shape on, because it is likely that the ball before
it will be located further down the table towards the break end of the table.

A Key Ball Shot With Many Possibilities

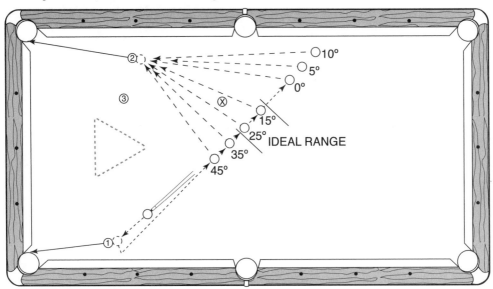

Playing position using a key ball located several inches off the rail, as the 2-ball is in the illustration, is never easy, even if your cut angle falls in the ideal range shown. Should the cue ball come to rest outside the ideal range, getting on the break ball requires that you play an extremely difficult position play.

- 45 degree cut – cross the table and back to X.
- 35 degree cut – draw with outside english spin shot to X.
- 25 degrees – a typical draw shot, no tricks needed to get to X.
- 15 degrees – use a pound/draw shot to arrive at X.
- 0 degrees – draw straight back to Y.
- 5 degrees on side B – draw back to X.
- 10 degrees on side B – use a super smooth draw stroke to hold the cue ball at Position Z if you're lucky.

As we went through a number of possible shots, perhaps you were reminded once again of why you don't want to be playing Nine-Ball position plays in Straight Pool. The example also demonstrates why crossing into the ideal position zone is such a high risk venture.

Position Concepts at the End of the Rack

The concepts in this section will help sharpen your position play and decision making as you navigate your way through the end of a rack.

• Down-the-Line Shape on the Key Ball

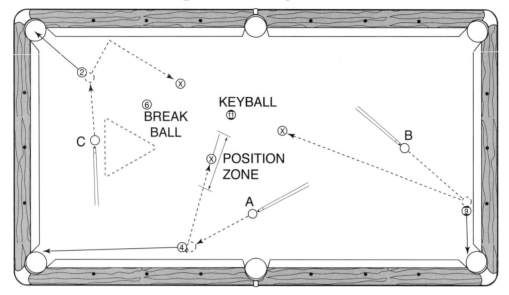

Employing the principle of playing down-the-line position whenever possible can be especially valuable when you're goal is to next play a stop shot key ball. To play perfect, no risk, down-the-line position on the key ball, three things must be in line:

- The pocket the key ball will be played into;
- The key ball; and
- The path of the cue ball as it approaches the key ball.

In Position A, notice that the side pocket, the 11-ball (key ball) and the cue ball's line of travel after pocketing the 4-ball, are all in perfect alignment. In this position, nothing can go wrong as long as your speed control is good enough to send the cue ball to any point in the position zone.

Positions B and C show two other examples of the value of playing down the line shape on the key ball. In each of these positions, applying the principle makes what could be a very difficult position play a relatively simple matter.

A Difficult Across-the-Line Position Play on the Break Ball

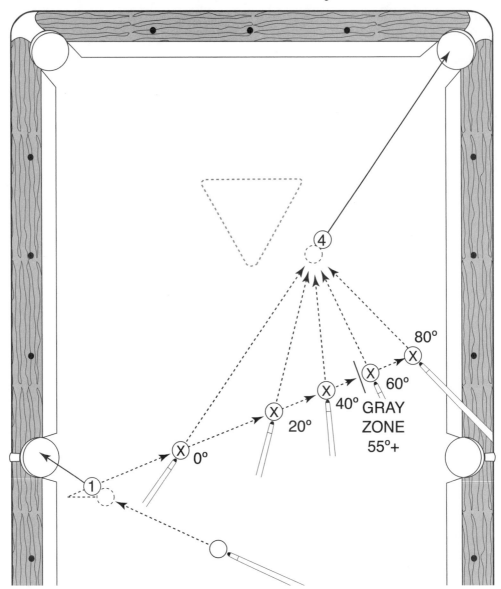

You want to avoid difficult speed control shots on the key ball when you must cross the position zone. In the example, your best break shot position is a 40-degree cut angle. Before playing shape on the break shot, you must take your game into account. You need to decide what would be the bigger mistake, coming up short for a 20-degree break shot, or rolling too far to a 60-degree cut angle. Then give yourself a little margin for error by aiming for a spot a little short, or beyond, the 40-degree position.

　　Should you roll past 60 degrees, you will have entered the gray zone. Now your decision of whether or not to play the 5-ball, or play a safety, depends largely on the game situation and your confidence in making the shot.

Maintaining a Constant and Shallow Cut Angle

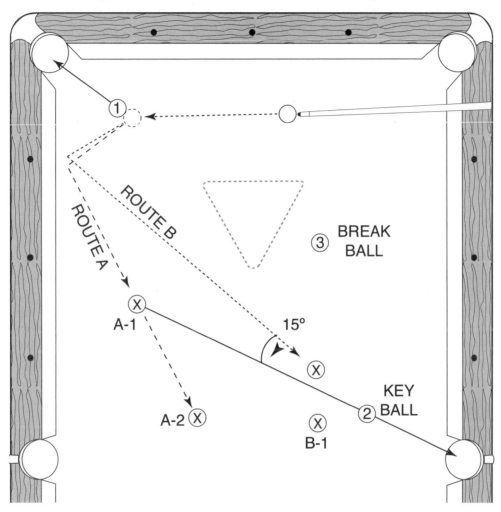

You could gamble that your speed will be near perfect by sending the cue ball down Route A. If you are successful (and very lucky), the cue ball will stop at A-1 and you will have a straight-in shot on the key ball. But look what you'll be stuck with if the cue ball rolls to A-2. Once again you have witnessed the perils of crossing over the position line.

Following Route B after pocketing the 1-ball will send the cue ball directly at its point of contact with the 2-ball. While the cue ball is rolling across the table, it will be maintaining a constant cut angle on the 2-ball. The relatively shallow 15-degree cut angle will enable you to easily control the cue ball when playing the key ball. With the cue ball anywhere along Route B, you'd be able to send the cue ball to Position B-1 for ideal shape on the break shot.

Using a Shallow but Variable Angle to the Key Ball

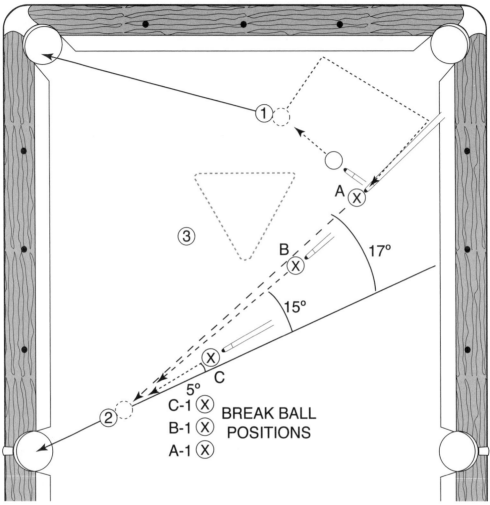

The position of the ball before the key ball will often prevent you from playing perfect down-the-line shape, or for position using a constant shallow angle, as we've discussed in the previous two sections. When neither of these choices is available, you may still have a route to the key ball where the cut angle changes in small increments as the cue ball is rolling across the table.

Notice how the cut angle only changed from 12 degrees to 5 degrees while the cue ball rolled a full 2' from Position A to Position C. Even though the cut angle is constantly changing, it is doing so in small enough increments that it won't change the way you play the next shot much at all.

When to Take the Second Best Break Shot

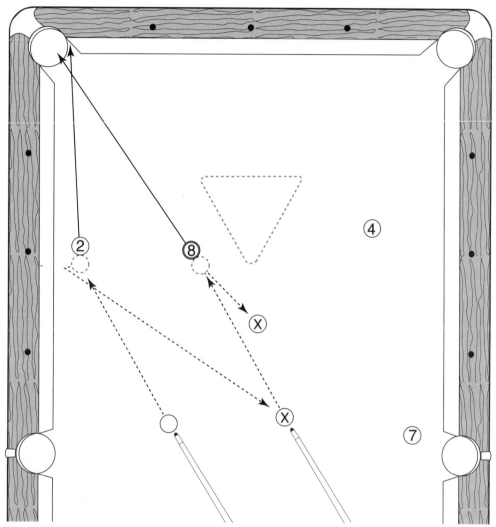

The 8-ball is a better break ball than the 4-ball, all other things being equal. But all things aren't equal. To get on the 8-ball you could play the sequence of the 2, 4 and 7-ball or possibly the 4, 2 and 7-ball. But no matter what pattern you chose to get on the 8-ball, you're going to have to play a skillful shot to arrive at Position A.

On the other hand, you can hardly go wrong getting to the 4-ball break shot. The pattern is to play the 2-ball and then the 8-ball, which should leave you with a stop shot on the 7-ball (key ball) for excellent shape on the 4-ball break shot.

Tip: When you have two perfectly acceptable break shots, take the one that is easiest to get on. As your ability to play a wide variety of break shots increases, you will find this strategy increasingly more valuable.

Risky Versus Conservative

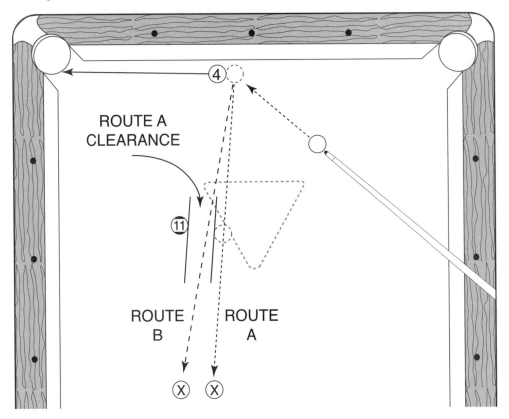

It is a huge blunder to hit the break ball while playing the key ball. In the illustration the cue ball will be passing close by the break ball on the key ball shot. Path A gives you ample clearance. If your directional control is extraordinary, you could gain a better angle on the break shot by passing a little closer by the 11-ball down Path B. Before playing position like this, you should very carefully weigh the risk versus the reward.

Manufacturing a Key Ball

You should be on the lookout to manufacture a key ball since it is the all important ball that enables you to get position on the break shot. Some considerations in manufacturing a key ball include:

- You don't currently have a key ball.
- The balls are in good position to manufacture one.
- You already have a key ball, but you could use a better one or an extra key ball just in case things go wrong.

The diagram shows two of the thousands of possible for manufacturing a key ball. In Part A, a stun/follow shot will drive the 4-ball up close to the side pocket. In Part B, you will have an easy two rail shot on the 2-ball for position on the 3-ball, which is the key ball you've just manufactured. To manufacture a key ball you must recognize the need and the opportunity, and execute the shot with great precision.

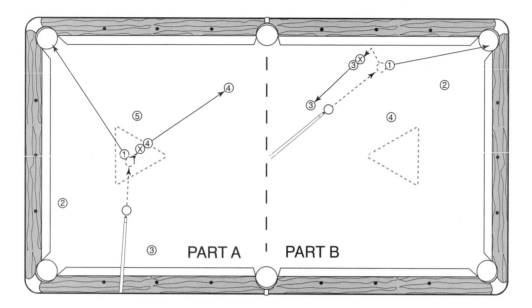

Risk is Well Worth the Reward

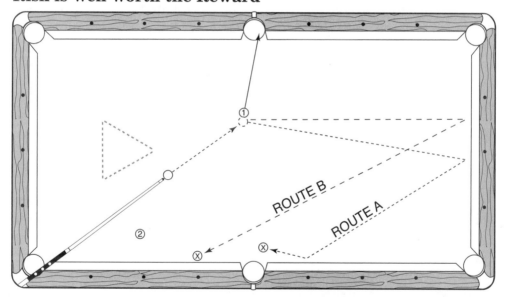

It's not often that you'll want to tempt the scratch demon, but this position is an exception. Route A is a conservative play that will keep you out of the side pocket. But there is not much of a payoff as you'll have to hit the break shot firmly (which increases the chances of a miss) from a cut angle of only about 17 degrees. Playing Route B increases the risk of a side pocket scratch, but you will be rewarded with a 37-degree cut shot from a much closer range. This break shot should really open up the rack. If you happened to scratch, your opponent will have to play a spot shot, which would make getting on the break shot a difficult proposition.

Covering a Mistake With Ball In Hand

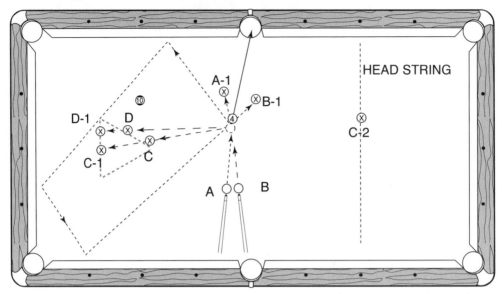

Your goal was to have a straight-in shot on the 4-ball. From Position A you could play a simple follow shot to A-1 for great shape on the break ball. Unfortunately, the cue ball came to rest at Position B. You could try to power the cue ball three rails to B-1, but that would take a Herculean effort.

Whenever you miss position on the key ball, stop for a moment to consider whether you have easy access to the triangle. In our example, you have a short range draw/stun shot to a 14" long target, providing you approach the triangle at the top edge as shown. If the cue ball stops anywhere between Positions C and C-1, you'll have ball-in-hand. Position C-2 is a likely spot to place the cue ball for the break shot.

Since only a small fraction of the cue ball has to be touching the rack, your actual target is much bigger than it appears. Don't forget to have the cue ball approach the widest part of this "position zone" (as it did in the example), especially if there is any question about your being able to stop the ball in the triangle. Notice how much smaller the "position zone" is between Positions D and D-1.

End of Rack Patterns

If you can play your end-of-rack patterns to perfection, you will have taken a major step towards increasing your ability to string racks together. When there are 4-5 balls left on the table, the break ball should have already been chosen most of the time. Under the ideal scenario, there will be a very well defined sequence of three shots that result in great shape on the break ball. They are:

- A third ball prior to the break ball that enables you to get good position on the key ball to the key ball.
- A ball before the key ball that you can use to get excellent shape on the key ball.
- The key ball, which enables you to play perfect shape for the ideal angle on the break shot.

• The Key Ball to the Key Ball (KB2KB)

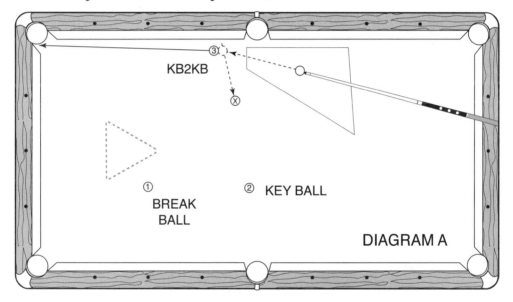

We've discussed the importance of getting good shape on the key ball. To help you accomplish this, you should make use of a key ball to the key ball whenever possible. We're going to use a Y2K-type abbreviation for this of "KB2KB". A well placed KB2KB can virtually guarantee that you'll have a simple position play on the key ball. And in many cases, a KB2KB will lead to the much sought after stop shot on the key ball.

You've possibly been counseled to remove balls near the rails as soon as possible. There is, however, a huge exception to this rule. In the diagram, the 2-ball, is the key ball for the 1-ball break shot. The 3-ball is on the rail directly opposite the 2-ball. Notice the sizeable position zone for the 3-ball. With the cue ball anywhere within the zone, you should have little trouble sending the cue ball to somewhere very close to Position X for an ideal angle on the 2-ball.

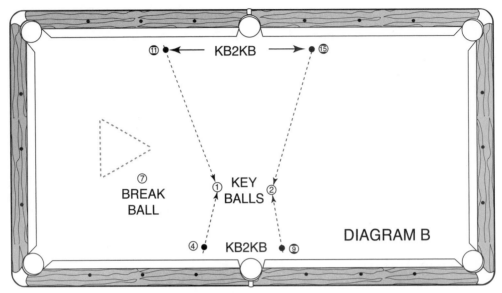

Diagram B shows other examples of KB2KBs that are located near the rail. Notice in every case that the cue ball's position at contact with the KB2KB, the key ball, and the pocket for the key ball all form a straight line. For example, the cue ball's position at contact with the 15-ball, the 2-ball (the key ball) and the opposite side pocket are all in a straight line. A stop shot on the 2-ball will give you perfect shape on the break ball.

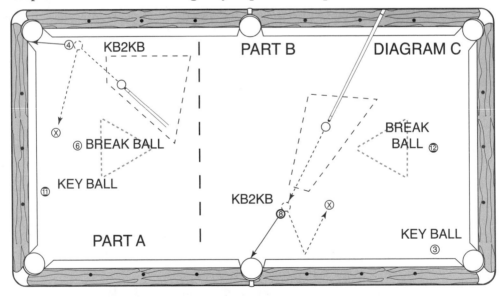

Diagram C shows a couple of KB2KBs for break balls on the end rail. Notice that the position zone for the KB2KB is very large in both positions. This is often the case when playing position for a key ball to a behind the rack break shot. This diagram shows why behind the rack break shots are fairly easy to get shape on.

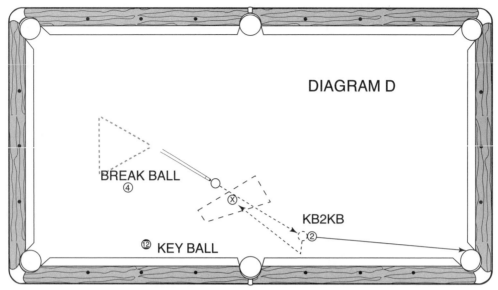

DIAGRAM D

The KB2KB shown in Diagram D appears quite frequently. You have some room for error with your directional control. Your speed control must be very precise, since you will be crossing the position zone no matter where you enter it. Note that you could reverse the order by playing the 12-ball and then the 2-ball as the key ball.

You must be very precise with your position on the key ball for the side pocket break shot in Diagram E. Cue Ball A shows a stop shot on the KB2KB (3-ball). With the cue ball at Position B, you will be able to play down-the-line position to X for shape on the 1-ball.

Tip: As the rack comes to an end, your position should get tighter and tighter until it culminates with a short-range position play on the key ball. A KB2KB helps you to help accomplish this.

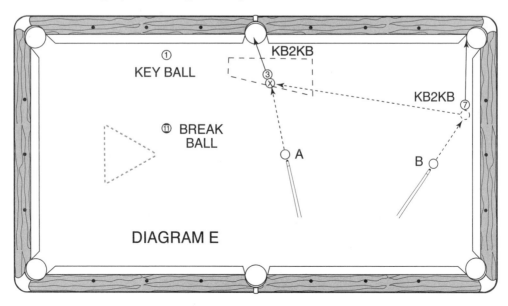

DIAGRAM E

• The Three-Ball End-of-the-Rack Pattern

Another big secret to playing highly effective rack-ending patterns is to really focus on the last three balls prior to the break ball. You know you want an easy shot on the key ball. You also know now that a KB2KB can help you get the key ball shape you're after. Now to complete the picture, you need to have a third ball that can enable you to send the cue ball to the typically generous position zone for the KB2KB.

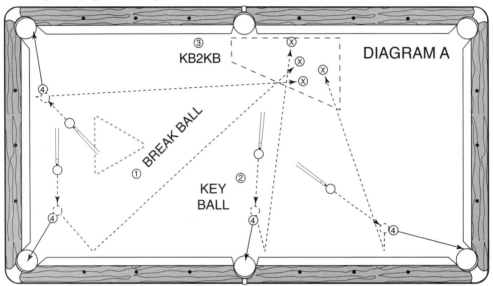

The KB2KB (the 3-ball) in Diagram A is very strategically positioned on the table for easy position on the key ball (the 2-ball). In contrast, there may be a wide variety of positions for the third ball.

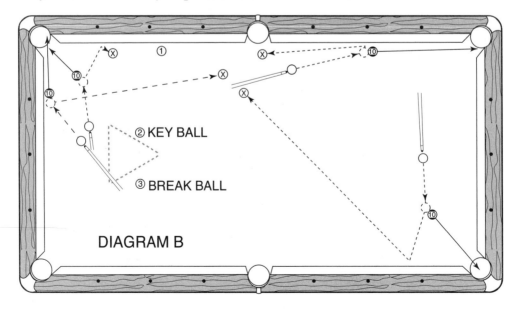

Diagram B show four of the many possible routes that can be used to send the cue ball into the position zone for the KB2KB (1-ball). As you can see, your positional requirements for the KB2KB are not nearly as stringent as they are for the key ball.

To recap, the ideal end-of-the-rack pattern goes like this:

- A shot on the third ball that makes it relatively to send the cue ball into the position zone for the KB2KB.
- An easy shot on the KB2KB that makes getting on the key ball a cinch.
- A simple shot on the key ball that results in great shape on the break ball.

Tip: There are scores of rack ending three ball patterns that show up repeatedly in Straight Pool. It could help your game tremendously if you became familiar with as many of them as possible, much like a Chess master who has memorized the opening moves of a number of sequences.

A Perfect End-of-Rack Pattern

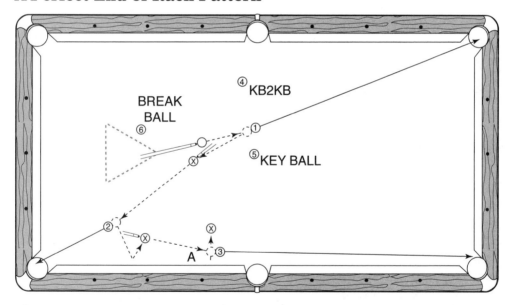

The pattern here shows several key elements to a successful end-of-rack run out. The 1-ball is deceptively troublesome as it is located between two other balls. Now is a good time to play it. The 2-ball is an access ball to the 3-ball, which is problem ball #2. Before playing the 3-ball, it is a good idea to survey the table from Position A to make sure you will get the shot you are after on the 4-ball. Stop shots on the 4-ball (KB2KB) and then the 5-ball (key ball) will complete the run.

The Magic 20-Degree Cut Shot

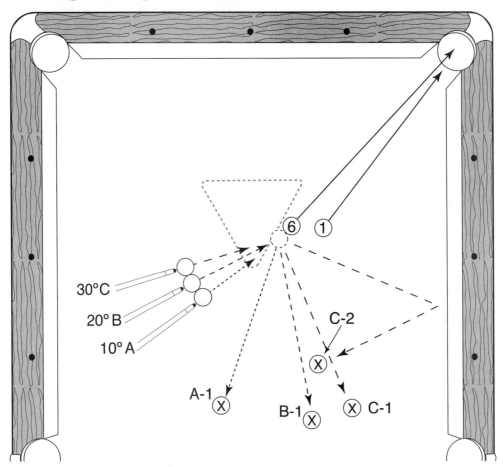

This key ball shot is one of the most important, and yet most often mis-played position plays in Straight Pool. On several occasions I have even seen world class players mishandle this shot. Try it yourself. The big secret is to set up a cut shot that enables you to play a medium soft draw shot. With the correct cut angle, you don't have to do anything tricky that could cause you to lose control of the cue ball. Let's consider the three cue ball positions in the diagram

With the cue ball in Position A, you have a 10-degree cut shot on the 6-ball. If you use draw, the cue ball will end up at A-1. Now you are stuck with a 5-degree cut shot on the break shot. That's certainly not going to work. To arrive at B-1 for an ideal break shot from Position A, you're going to have to play a draw/stun shot (see chapter on Position Play) with a hard stroke.

The cue ball in Position B is perfectly placed to send the cue ball to B-1 for a 32-degree cut shot on the break shot. A medium soft draw shot is all that's needed. Having the correct angle in the first place makes this a simple position play. The 20-degree cut angle is a nearly perfect angle for playing this kind of shot. It is neither too steep nor too shallow.

Now let's move over to the cue ball at Position C, which is a 30-degree cut shot. With this thinner cut angle, the cue ball will end up at C-1 if you play a soft draw shot. This would leave you with a 47-degree cut on the break shot. There is no way to reduce the cut angle unless you sent the cue ball to the rail and back out as shown by Route C-2. In this example, you are fortunate to have this option available. If the break ball were a little higher up, however, you would run into it, as is often the case.

It's So Easy to Go Wrong

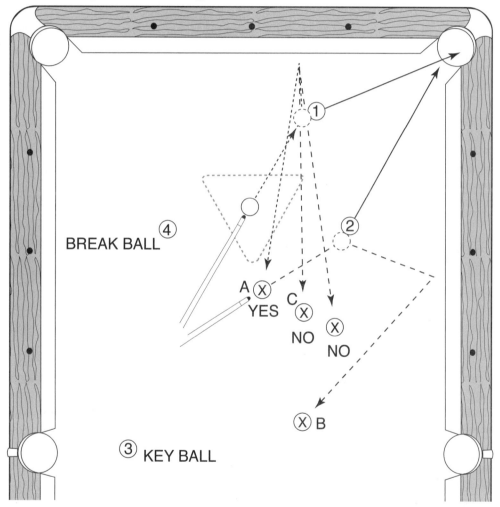

You are only three easy shots from finishing off the rack in style. Play a follow shot to Position A, then draw softly off the side rail for shape on the key ball at Position B. Easy enough, except that this is the kind of layout where it is so easy to go wrong. A top champion in this position sent the cue ball to Position C and then had to use the bridge to continue his run. **Tip**: No one is immune from silly little end-of-the-rack errors, so you must play with precision and care right up to the very end.

A Classic Stop Shot Pattern

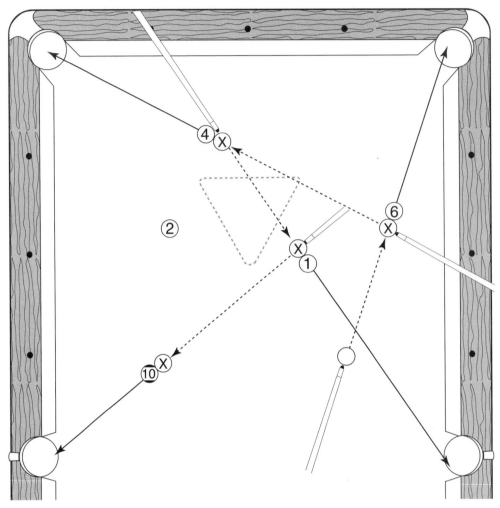

The diagram illustrates a classic pattern that is every true Straight Pool player's favorite way of ending a rack. It is a series of stop shots that end up positioning the cue ball perfectly for the break ball. In real life, you will seldom have a pattern that is as textbook perfect as this, but many will come close. A series of near stop shots where the cue ball has to travel a very small distance on each shot with the stop shot on the 10-ball is a close second. You can help create layouts such as the one in the example by leaving a few neutral balls in the area of the rack. They may then turn into a roadmap run to the break ball once the rest of the balls have been cleared from the table.

A Creative End-of-Rack Pattern

There are four balls remaining and a few things are for certain: the 4-ball is the break ball, the 2-ball is a problem ball, and the 1-ball is your first shot. The 2-ball is a lousy key ball, which suggests that the proper sequence is the 1, 2 and the 3-ball. The 1-ball is a straight-in shot.

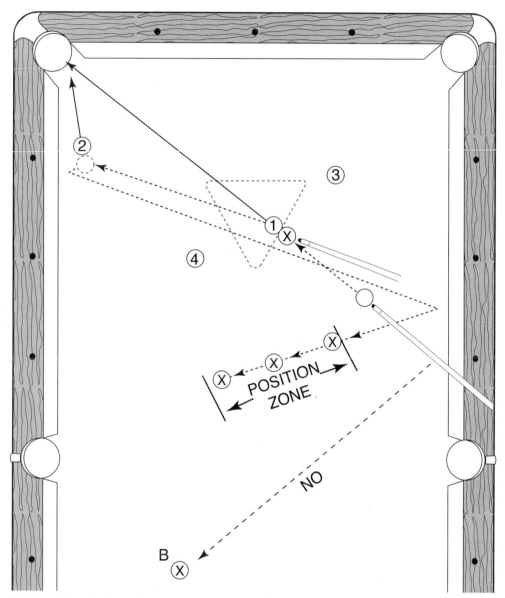

Your only choices for getting on the 2-ball are to play a stop shot at Position A, or a massive off-the-rail draw shot to Position B. The stop shot is clearly the better choice. The question now becomes how to play the thin cut on the 2-ball for shape on the 3-ball, which is going to be your key ball.

The illustration shows a creative solution: use the thin cut to your advantage by playing across the table and back out to the position zone. The 2-ball can be shot confidently with a firm stroke because the second rail will really slow the cue ball down, enabling it to glide to a stop in the zone. The route on the 2-ball is a Nine-Ball type of shot to a rather large shape zone with little risk of anything going wrong.

Work With What You've Got

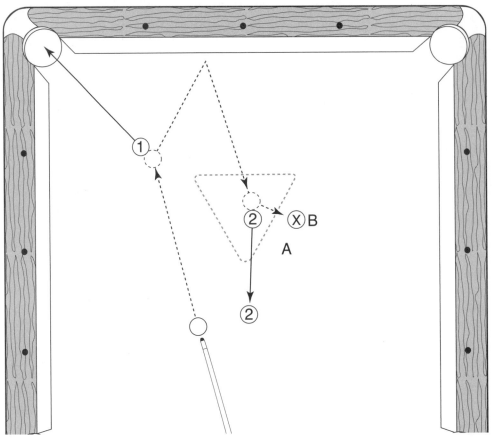

You are no doubt very familiar with the principle that says you've got to play the table. When you start fighting the position of the balls, it's a case of ego or poor judgment overruling plain old common sense. Trying to make something out of nothing can be very damaging when you are nearing the end of the rack and you have no chance to recover from a mistake.

I have mentioned errors by world class players to let you know even best make mistakes. Here's another: the player tried to come off the rail and bump the 2-ball into position as a break ball. While this is a worthy objective, in this position, cutting the 2-ball to Position A is a 10 on the 1-10 scale of difficulty. The player mishit the shot and the cue ball wound up at Position B. His run soon ended. The wiser play would have been to shoot the 1-ball or 2-ball first, and then the other. The objective would be to wind up at either Position Y or Z for a side pocket break shot.

Tip: Accepting what the table gives you is often a much higher percentage play than trying to make something out of essentially nothing.

A Common Rack-Ending Pattern

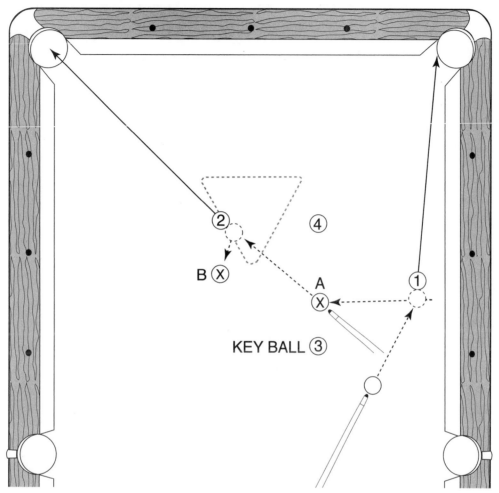

The diagram shows one of the most reliable rack-ending patterns. A soft follow shot with a/tip of right english will send the cue ball to Position A for the 2-ball. The 2-ball is in the area of the triangle, which makes it a good ball for getting on a side pocket key ball. This is especially true if there is a relatively straight-line relationship between the 2-ball, the key ball (3-ball) and the side pocket. A stop shot on the 2-ball will leave it at Position B for perfect shape on the 3-ball.

Leaving Balls in the Area of the Rack

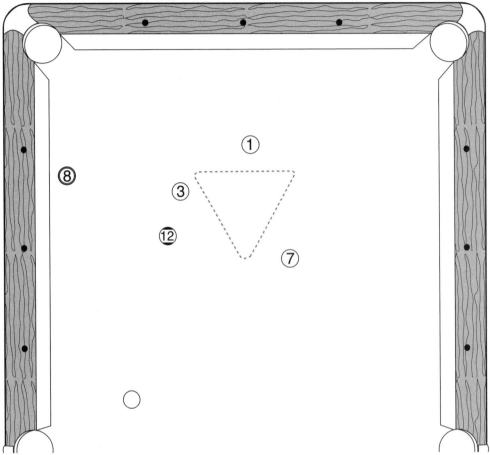

If the layout permits, it is a wise strategy to leave several balls in the area of the rack at the end of the frame. This enables you to play a series of short distance position plays that can help you hone in on the key ball and break ball. Leaving balls in the area of the triangle may also provide you with an abundance of potential break balls should you miss position on a ball or two. The layout in the diagram appeared in the 2000 BCA U.S. Open. The player had five balls remaining, any of which could have been used as a break shot!

Which Way Is Better?

In this end-of-rack position, it would be very tempting to play the 4-ball first and save the 1-ball for the key ball. Unless the cue ball stops within the position zone, you're going to have trouble getting on the break ball. A better choice is to play a stop shot on the 1-ball first, then draw back off the rail for shape on the 5-ball break shot. This sequence guarantees that you'll come away with a decent shot on the break ball, which is certainly not the case if you attempt to get on the 1-ball for your key ball and fail. The thinking that produced this sequence is the kind that is needed to avoid playing what would seem like the right shot when it's not really the best percentage play.

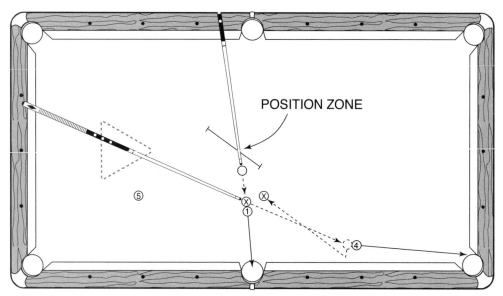

POSITION ZONE

A Very Typical End-of-Rack Pattern

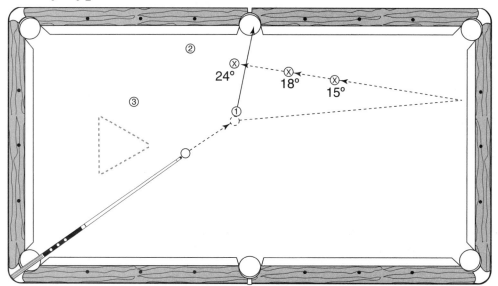

While it would be nice to have a series of two or three stop shots to complete every frame, reality says that you will quite off be cleaning up the table right until the very end. Hopefully this can be done in a manner that poses little risk to your run.

The diagram shows a typical end-of-rack scenario: play the 1-ball in the side and go to the end rail and back for a down-the-rail key ball shot on the 2-ball. Notice that the cut angle on the 2-ball increases slightly as the cue ball travels down the table. This kind of end-of-the-rack layout is half cleaning up of a problem and half position on the key ball.

CHAPTER 3

SECONDARY BREAKSHOTS

How to Break Clusters
in the Area of the Triangle

A secondary break shots is used to separate balls that remain clustered around the area of the triangle after the opening break shot of each rack. At times you may play two or more secondary break shots if the rack remains stuck together. Secondary break shots are used to break large cluster of more 5 or more balls. There are different techniques for breaking smaller clusters of 4 balls or less which are discussed in the following chapter. Smaller clusters usually are located away from the triangle.

The best secondary break shots are versions of the classic side-of-the-rack break shots, and behind-the-rack break shots. Off-the-rail secondary break shots also can be used very effectively. You should be very aware of your positional objectives when playing secondary break shots. Ideally there will be a ball or two that you know you can get shape on. Shots usually come from an insurance ball (more on these in a moment), or from a ball that was in the cluster.

Generally speaking, the more you know, the more you will be able to predict the results of your secondary break shots. This enables you to have a clear shot after a break shot and to stay out of trouble. Nevertheless, there will be times when you have to shoot and hope for the best as certain positions are inherently very unpredictable.

• Key Concepts for Playing Secondary Break Shots
- Proper cueing allows you to hit the stack in the right place.
- Generally speaking, the smaller the cluster, the less speed is required.
- Most secondary break shots are played with a medium soft to medium speed of stroke.
- Avoid trouble, such as scratching.
- Do whatever you can to maximize your chances of having a shot.
- Try to avoid playing secondary break shots when you can't generate much speed into a large cluster.
- Avoid having a fast moving ball collide with your break ball before it gets to the pocket.
- Your goal on some secondary break shots is to loosen up the balls for a second secondary break shot. You may also wish to pick some balls off the edges of the remaining cluster.
- Sometimes you just have to play for a roll on a secondary break shot.

• Your Next Shot After a Secondary Break Shot
- An insurance ball virtually guarantees you'll have a shot after the secondary break shot.
- Have an insurance ball on the same side on which you broke the balls if possible.
- Have a cluster that should separate widely or predictably.
- Have a ball in the cluster that you can get shape on.
- Take your chances. Now is the time to break the balls and none of the other options are available.
- Sometimes your next shot will come from the cluster.

• Know When to Stop Breaking the Balls
Many players make the mistake of plowing into balls in the area of the triangle after they have been sufficiently spread apart. Once the balls are reasonably well spread, they should be left alone. Going into the rack unnecessarily can create problems where none currently exist. You should stop breaking the balls when:
- When none are touching or blocking a pocket;
- There are clear paths to all pockets; and
- You have an acceptable break shot.

Three Ball Patterns to Secondary Break Shots

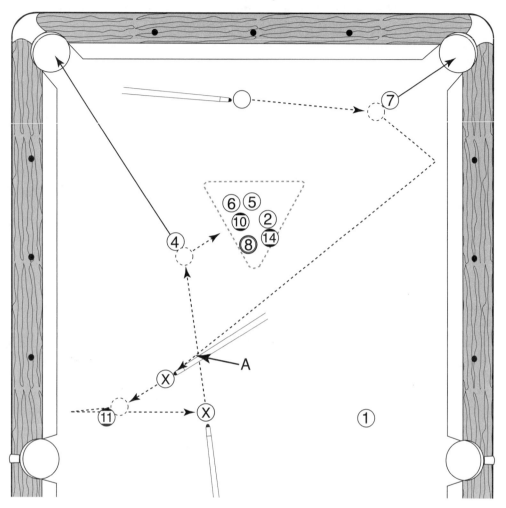

Getting position on a secondary break shot can be just as critical to maintaining your run as getting on the break shot for a new rack. You can use three ball patterns to meet your positional objective. The 7-ball could lead to shape on the secondary break shot at Position A. More than likely, however, you will need a shorter-range position play on the 11-ball to give you the shape you require on the 4-ball. The 11-ball should really be thought of as a key ball. This is the same concept that you would use to get on the break ball at the end of the rack.

• Precision Secondary Break Shots

When playing the break shot of a new rack, your target ball on the rack should be very well defined. The power you put into an initial break shot is also largely governed by the type of break shot you are about to play. As you gain experience, playing the break shot of a new rack becomes highly systematic. This is not necessarily the case with secondary break shots. You may need to hit a specific side of a ball in the cluster to get the desired results. The very same secondary break shot (the position of the cue ball and break ball) might be played in many different ways, which depends on the position of the balls you are separating.

On most secondary break shots, your goal is to hit a specific ball in the cluster, or even a specific a part of the ball. Hitting the chosen spot on the target ball in the cluster allows you to separate the balls in the best way possible. Precisely targeting you point of entry into a cluster also allows you to maintain as much control of the cue ball as possible, given the oftentimes random nature of secondary break shots.

The position of the cue ball and break ball determine the possible paths that the cue ball can take into the cluster. There are two main variables that can affect the cue balls path into the rack after it contacts the break ball:

- The distance of the break ball from the rack. You have more flexibility in determining the path of the cue ball the break ball is farther from the cluster.
- Shallow cut angles of 15-25 degrees allow more flexibility than steeper angles. When the cut angle is over 40 degrees, you can't do much to change the path of the cue ball over a short distance.

In the example on the next page, you have a secondary break shot on the 1-ball. The break ball is about a foot from the rack, which gives you some flexibility in where you contact the cluster. With the cue ball at Position A, you can contact the cluster in a variety of places because of the relatively shallow cut angle. Routes A-1 and A-2 show how you can alter the cue ball's path with either follow (A-1) or draw (A-2).

The cut angle is significantly sharper with the cue ball at Position B. This limits how much you can alter the cue ball's path from the tangent line. You could now contact the cluster between B-1 (using follow) and B-2 (using draw).

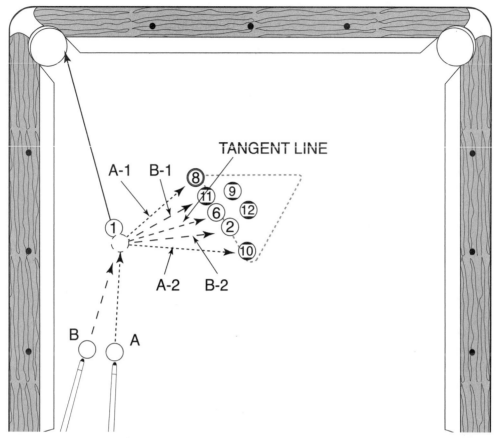

Steps for Playing Precision Secondary Break Shots
- Determine where the cue ball will strike the rack if it follows the tangent line.
- Decide if the path down the tangent line leads to where you want to contact the cluster.
- Choose a new point of contact, if needed. Be sure to consider the distance of the break ball from the cluster and the cut angle.
- Apply the proper cueing and speed of stroke to the shot.

Tip: Use shallower cut angles on secondary break shots because you typically need more control and less power than on the initial break of a new rack.

Tip: Occasionally you will want to use a steeper cut angle on a secondary break shot when the balls aren't breaking very well, or the cluster is very large.

• Insurance Balls

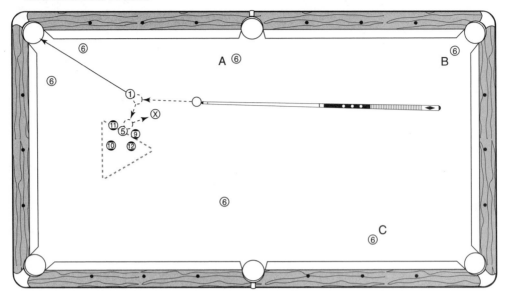

If you time your secondary break shots properly, you'll be rewarded an insurance ball or two. An insurance ball guarantees that you will have a shot when the cluster is broken. It is quite possible you will chose another ball after the secondary break shot, but it's still nice to know you have the insurance ball just in case it's needed. If the 6-ball were in any of the locations shown on the diagram, it would serve as an insurance ball for the secondary break shot on the 2-ball.

There are different ranges of "coverage" with this kind of insurance. A ball that is reasonably close to the pocket and is close to the cluster is probably best. That would be the 6-ball at Position A. A ball in the jaws of a distant pocket such as the 6-ball at Position B can also be very effective. And if nothing else better is available, the insurance ball at Position C can be used to get you out of a jam.

The Pinball Effect

When the cue ball enters a partially scattered rack, it oftentimes acts like a pinball as it bounces off ball after ball while chewing its way through the rack. This action usually occurs when there is a hole in the rack that the cue ball can nestle into, and when the balls have been loosened up a bit. You can also encourage this action by using maximum follow on the break shot.

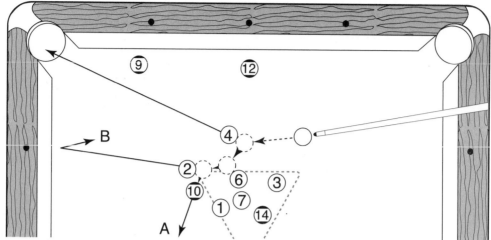

At times you can even predict the outcome of the pinball-like action with a fair degree of accuracy. In our example, the cue ball is going to bounce off the 6-ball and into the 2-ball. It will then proceed into the 10-ball. You may be able to plot where one or more of the balls will stop. The 10-ball, for example, could roll to Position A and become your break shot for the next rack, or the 2-ball might bounce off the rail to Position B and become your next shot.

Secondary Break Shots to an Open Table

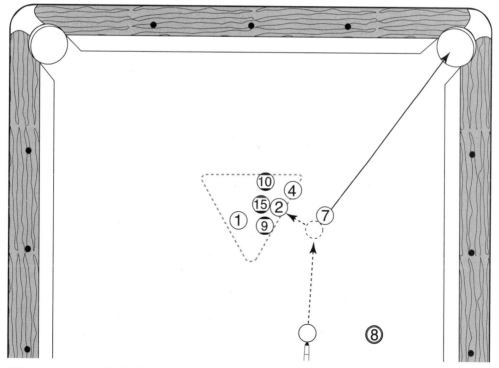

When you are breaking a relatively small group of balls to a wide open table, and you have an insurance ball (the 8-ball), there is little that can go wrong. The position in the illustration resulted from clearing the table first before playing the secondary break shot.

Partially Breaking a Cluster

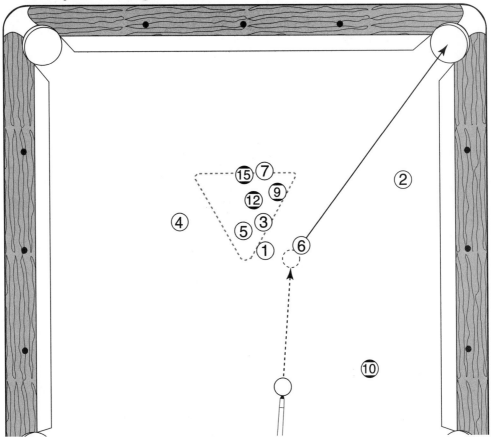

It would be tempting to blast away at the cluster, especially since you have the 10-ball as insurance. Upon closer inspection though, you can see that the cue ball is going to hit the 1-ball if played with follow, and the 1-ball is probably going to miss hitting the 5-ball. The cue ball might then graze off the 3-ball or miss the rest of the cluster entirely. This position is an example of one of the most devious traps you can fall into when playing secondary break shots: blasting away at a super looking break shot that's really not.

To get the most out of this position, shoot the break shot with a soft draw stroke. This will enable you to knock the 1-ball into the 5-ball, freeing two balls from the stack. Within the next shot or two after the break shot, you should be able to break the remainder of the cluster with the 4-ball.

Tip: Sometimes you have to break apart secondary clusters in sections.

Now return to our original position for a moment and imagine that the 7-ball and 9-ball weren't there. After playing the 6-ball as before, the 3,12 and 15-balls will all go into the upper righthand corner pocket.

Off the Rail Secondary Break Shots

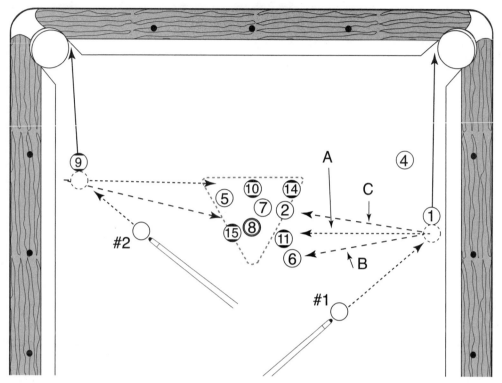

There is much to be said for off-the-rail break shots such as the one at Cue Ball #1. There are three key lines of travel to keep in mind. Line A is at a 90-degree angle to the rail. This line serves as a point of reference. If the break ball is within a fraction of an inch of the rail, the cue ball will travel almost directly down this line.

Most down-the-rail break shots, however, are probably an inch or two off the rail. When the break ball is an inch off the rail, the cue ball will rebound slightly above the reference line along Line B when played with follow and without english. You can, however, easily alter the cue balls path into the cluster on down-the-rail break shots with the use of english. In our example, the ideal target is the upper half of the 2-ball, which can be hit using about a/tip of left English, which will send the cue ball down Line C.

The reference line for Cue Ball #2 on the other side of the rack is pointed just below the 5-ball. The 9-ball is an inch off the rail, so the shot can be played with center ball. It should enter the cluster between the 5-ball and 15-ball as shown.

Breaking Clusters on the Good Side

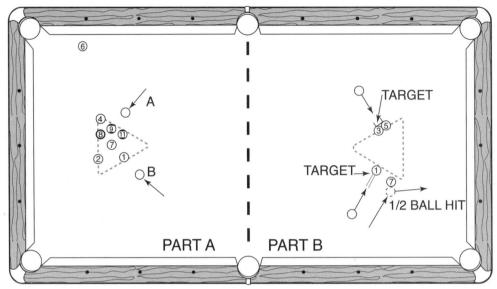

PART A | PART B

It is much easier to go into a cluster when you have a line of two or three balls as your target. In Part A, you would be much better off breaking the stack from the direction of Cue Ball A. Hitting the rack from the direction of Cue Ball B is a much riskier proposition because you'll need to hit the 1-ball dead-on to maintain control of the cue ball.

Part B shows the size of the target zone for hitting two balls side by side versus a solitary ball. Notice the target zone for contacting the 3 and 5-balls. You will lose the cue ball if you hit the 1-ball much to either side of the target. Notice how the cue ball will be thrown far off-line if it contacts half of the 7-ball.

A Kiss to Watch Out For

On thin-cut secondary break shots with the break ball on the near side of the stack, you must guard against a ball shooting out of the cluster and into the path of the object ball. In the example on the next page, the 8-ball will be traveling at a relatively slow speed because of the thinness of the cut. The majority of the cue ball's energy will be applied to the 9-ball. The 9-ball, in turn, is linked to the 11-ball and 2-ball.

The 2-ball is going to definitely cross the path of the 8-ball. The big question in this position is timing. Will the 2-ball and 8-ball collide? It's purely a judgment call. Let's say you are considering playing the shot one of two ways in an effort to avoid the kiss: with a soft stroke and just enough speed to get the 8-ball to the pocket, or a hard stroke. Your choice would be based on the belief that one of the two speeds offers less chance of producing an unwanted collision between the 8-ball and 2-ball.

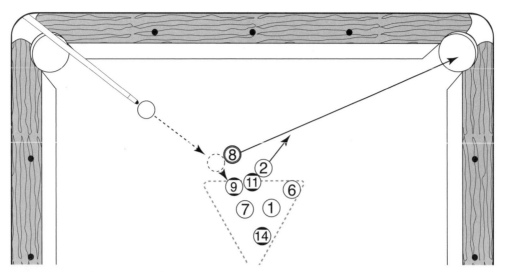

The Overdrive Follow Break Shot

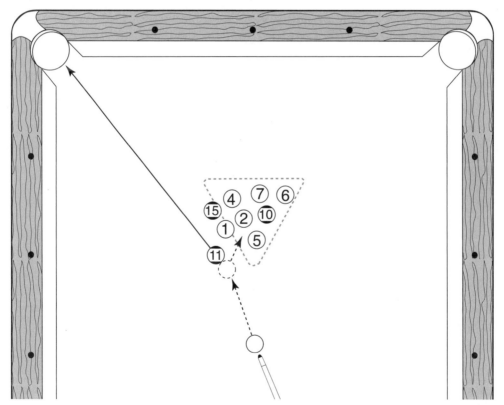

The break shot on the 11-ball probably won't do much damage because of the tight cluster and the shallow cut angle. You've got to get the balls open and there is, thankfully, a solution. Use a follow stroke with a closed bridge. Lift the base of your hand off the table so that you are hitting down slightly on the cue ball. This semi-jump shot will help propel the cue ball up into the balls and the topspin will chew them apart. When executed properly, this is one of the prettiest shots in pool.

Explosion Balls

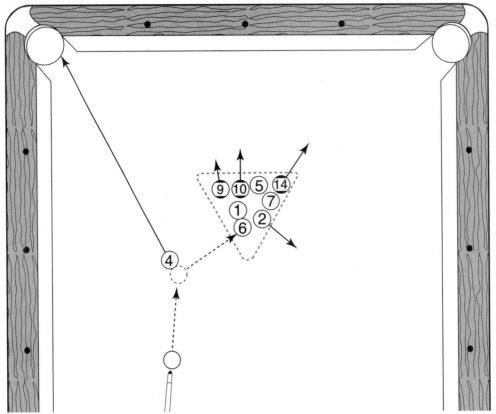

On a good percentage of your secondary break shots, you won't have to power the break ball or chew through the rack with topspin to separate the balls. All that is needed is for the cue ball to hit the right ball at the correct angle with adequate speed to set off a chain reaction.

The 6-ball in the illustration is what you could call an explosion ball. If the cue ball contacts the 6-ball fully as shown, the rack should easily blast apart. The force of the 6-ball will push the 2-ball out. There should be enough force on the 2-ball to drive the 7-ball into the 14-ball, knocking it free. Plenty of energy from the 6-ball should also help break open the 1, 9 and 10-balls.

Tip: When planning your secondary break shots, look for a ball you can hit that can cause an explosion throughout most of the cluster.

Breaking Without Insurance

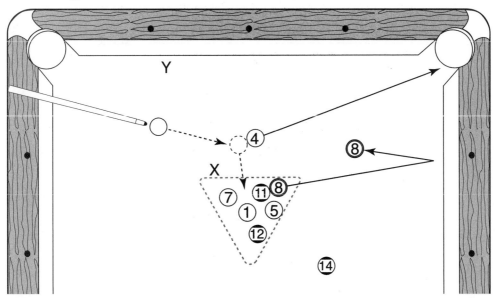

There will be many occasions when you will not have the luxury of an insurance ball. When you are not "covered", you could blast into the balls and hope for a shot. This strategy might work often enough to trick you into thinking that it is the best way to play a secondary break shot without insurance. Often, however, the layout will be very predictable, even without the presence on an insurance ball. Then you can use your knowledge of the balls to play shape on a particular ball in the stack.

The illustration shows a behind-the-rack secondary break shot that appears quite frequently. It would be nice to have an insurance ball for this kind of break shot, but such is not the case in this example. If you blast and hope, you could drive some balls to the opposite end of the table. Furthermore, the cue ball could wind up at Position Y, leaving you with no shot.

A better approach is to study the cluster carefully to determine what the balls might do with a more controlled break shot. A soft draw shot will send the cue ball into the 11-ball on the right side. It will then push the 7-ball out of the triangle and possibly into position for a break shot. A soft and relatively thin hit on the 11-ball should send the 8-ball to the rail and out, while the cue ball should stop at Position X. Your next shot should be on the 8-ball. This approach to playing cluster breaks without insurance will increase your knowledge of the game and improve your chances of having a good shot after the break.

Driving a Second Ball Into the Stack

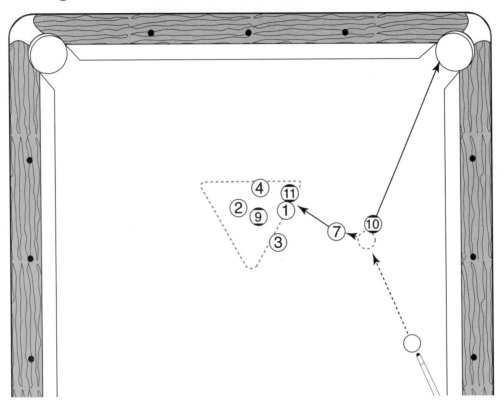

You've missed position on the 7-ball which was supposed to be the secondary break shot. There still is hope for opening the rack. Play a billiard off the 10-ball into the 7-ball, which will continue into the cluster. The 7-ball will receive less of the cue ball's energy since you are hitting about 1/3 of the 10-ball. At this cut angle you will therefore have to shoot a little harder than if you were sending the cue ball straight into the balls without interference from the 7-ball.

Beware of Drawbacks on Break Shots

It appears as though you've got an excellent secondary break shot on the 9-ball in the diagram on the following page. You've also got an insurance ball (6-ball) close by. The shot is going to be played with draw to keep the cue ball from possibly glancing off the 12-ball and rolling into the upper left corner pocket. When playing break shots with draw, you must guard against the cue ball sliding across a ball or two, which could propel the cue ball way back up the table as shown in the diagram.

The best way to avoid trouble starts with recognizing the danger signs before shooting. In this position, you might decide to play a draw/stun shot instead of using straight draw. The cue ball will hit the 12-ball slightly fuller and with far less backspin, which should keep the cue ball from shooting up table to Position X.

A Very Dangerous Break Shot

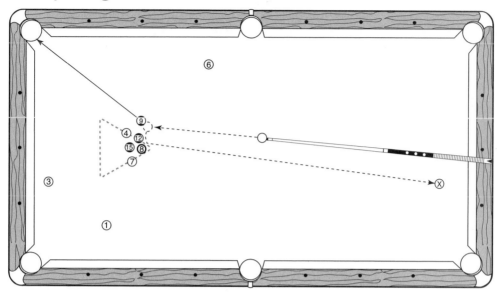

The position in this illustration is somewhat similar to the one in a previous section, only this time your results are far less predictable. You have no insurance ball, you're breaking from behind the rack, it's hard to predict where the next shot will come from, and it will be hard to escape the lower end of the table. Whew! In positions like this, a controlled blast and hope may be your best and only choice. You should, however, try to at least get the cue ball away from the rack and keep it from going to the end rail.

Breaking Into Jagged Edges

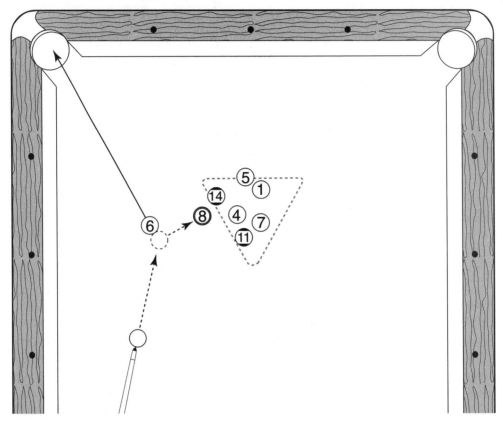

Sometimes you have no choice but to play a secondary break shot into a ball that is slightly outside the cluster. These shots have a way of disappointing players who are expecting great results because of the excellent position of the cue ball and break ball. Unless you hit the 8-ball squarely, you could easily lose control of the cue ball. And if you cut the outside ball too thinly, in some positions you may barely disturb the cluster at all.

The best solution is to avoid these kinds of break shots altogether, if possible. But if you must play a break shot to a cluster with a jagged edge, recognize the difficulty so that you can plot you course into the outside ball. Don't just hit and hope.

CHAPTER 4

CLUSTER MANAGEMENT

How to Separate Small Groups of Balls with Maximum Effectiveness

Clusters are small groups of four or less balls that do not have open pockets available to them. Clusters are different from secondary clusters, which usually contain five or more balls and are always located in the area of the triangle. Clusters usually are formed by balls that have broken free from the triangle, only to come together again on another part of the table. Clusters, however, can also result from a few balls that remain in the area of the triangle that are refugees from a secondary break shot.

Breaking clusters properly is more about finesse than power. It only takes a light hit to separate three or four balls. A two ball cluster can be broken with just a nudge, unless the balls are on or near the rail. When separating clusters, you still retain the objectives that go with a regular shot, such as playing position and managing risk as well as the situation allows. Timing is also crucial to breaking clusters. The rules below should prove useful in helping you to play cluster breaking shots with maximum effectiveness.

- **Rules for Breaking Clusters**
    - Timing is crucial. Generally the sooner the better.
    - Precision is better than power, especially with small clusters.
    - Try to break clusters from short distances.
    - Identify, if possible, exactly where you want to hit a cluster.
    - Estimate where each ball will end up.
    - Plan for position.
    - Avoid long distance, low percentage breakouts, if possible.
    - Beware of hooking yourself.
    - Break clusters away from the break ball for the next rack.
    - Beware of scratching.
    - Avoid breakouts where you might miss the cluster and a disaster could result.
    - Be extra careful when breaking clusters in heavy traffic.

- **Using the Tangent Line**

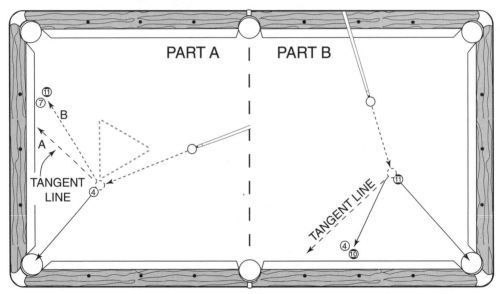

Another use for our old friend, the tangent line, is in predicting the cue ball's path into a cluster. In Part A, a stun shot down the tangent line would send the cue ball along Route A. This would cause the cue ball to miss the cluster. This tells you that you'll need to use some draw to send the cue ball down Route B to breakup the cluster.

In Part B, the tangent line points above the cluster. This indicates that a follow shot is what is needed to break apart the 4-10 cluster.

How the Cut Angle Determines the Path Into a Cluster

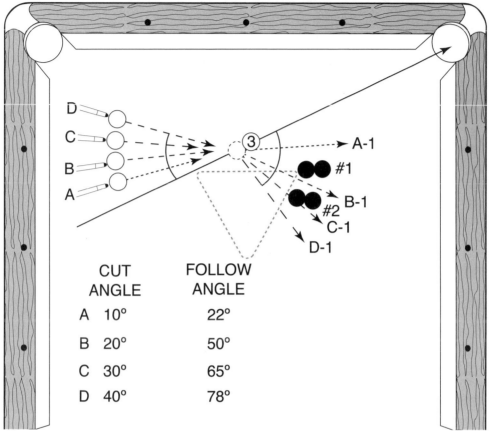

	CUT ANGLE	FOLLOW ANGLE
A	10°	22°
B	20°	50°
C	30°	65°
D	40°	78°

This illustration can help you plot your course when following into a cluster. It can also tell you what cluster breaks are possible and those that are not. The four lines showing the cue ball's path after contact all correspond to the cue balls original position (A to A-1, etc.).

    With the cue ball at Position A, you have a 10-degree cut angle. A soft follow shot will send the cue ball along Line A, missing cluster #1 on the low side. You can, however, still hit the cluster by adding a little speed. >From Positions B, C and D, it is impossible to hit cluster #1, even with a soft follow shot, because the cue ball will be traveling above the cluster after pocketing the 3-ball.

    The cue ball at Position C will strike the right side of cluster #2 when played with a soft follow stroke. Cluster #2 could also be hit from Positions A and B by applying additional speed to the shot. From Position D you will miss either cluster on the high side.

    By knowing the cue ball's follow angle after contact, you can tell which clusters can be broken. You can also determine those which you will miss to either side of the cluster. It is important to remember that you can increase the follow angle to hit a cluster, but you can't reduce the angle below its minimum. That's why the cue ball at Position D will miss any cluster below the line (D-1) that shows it's minimum follow angle.

The Ideal Cluster Busting Scenario

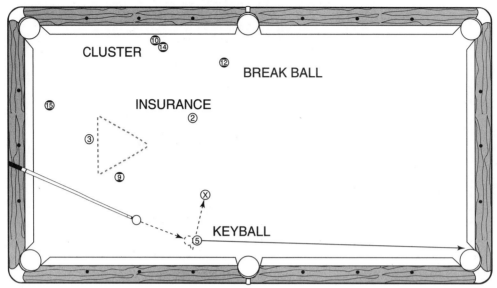

The ideal scenario for breaking a cluster is really no different than that which leads up to a secondary break shot and, in many respects, an initial break shot. In the illustration, the 5-ball is the key ball that puts the cue ball into position for breaking the cluster with the 12-ball. The 2-ball acts as an insurance ball when you go into the 10-14 cluster. In addition, there are open spaces near the cluster so that neither ball will become tangled up with another ball.

Tip When you have a short-range cluster break, you can exercise maximum control over the cue ball. You should take advantage of this by devising and executing a plan to send each ball to a very favorable location.

The Perfect Cluster Break

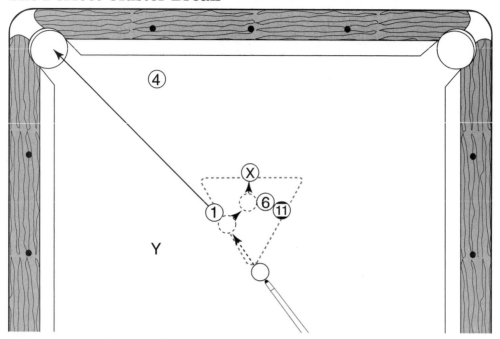

Quite often a cluster will remain in the area of the triangle after you have played one or more secondary break shots. These in-the-rack clusters can be broken with great precision using another ball within the vicinity of the rack. Two-ball clusters in the triangle are also offer the opportunity to manufacture a break ball.

In the illustrated position, there are only 4 balls left and there is no break ball. A stun shot on the 1-ball will open the cluster and, at the same time, drive the 11-ball into position for a break shot. A follow shot with a touch of left english on the 4-ball will send the cue ball to Position Y for shape on the key ball (the 6-ball). Notice how it looked like the run could be over, and how moments later the layout was in great shape, all thanks to a precise cluster break.

Busting a Cluster When the Timing is all Wrong

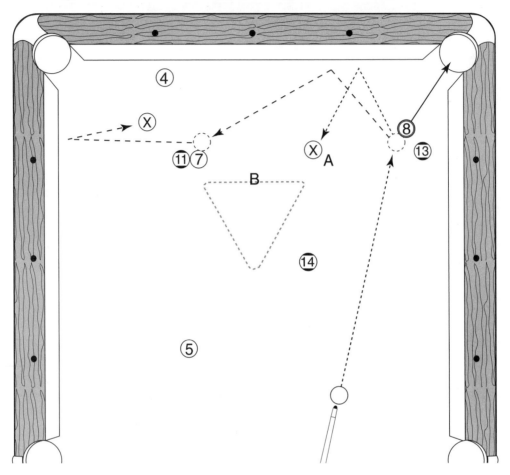

It may appear as though now is the right time to use the 8-ball to break the 7-11 cluster. After all, you should come away with a shot on the 13-ball or perhaps even the 4-ball. You will have to hit the 8-ball rather fully. Keep in mind that you may be taking a risk when you come into the back of a cluster off the bottom rail. The example shows one way that you can lose position when playing an improperly-timed cluster break.

The low risk way to break the 7-11 cluster is to play a soft follow shot on the 8-ball to Position A. Now you have a short-range cluster break that allows you to exert maximum control over the cue ball. If you hit the left side of the 7-ball, you should end up near Position B for the 13-ball or 5-ball.

The Cluster Busting Double-Kiss of Death

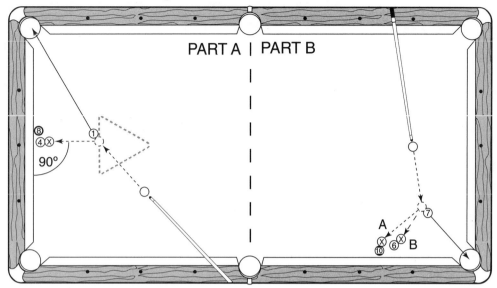

When a cluster is located near or on the rail, you have to be especially careful about where you hit the contact ball. If you hit the first ball squarely, a double-kiss could result. In Part A, the cue ball double kissed the 4-ball, wasting an opportunity to solve a big problem. If the aborted cluster break attempt comes early enough, you may get another chance. It is never, however, a good idea to use two shots to solve one problem. Naturally the solution in the example is to hit far enough to the side of the 4-ball so that the cue ball can get out of the 4-ball's way and exit the rail.

In Part B it looks as if nothing could go wrong as the cue ball will be approaching the cluster at an angle down Line A after pocketing the 7-ball. But that's not the case as the cue ball could still hit the 10-ball twice and pinch it to the rail. In this position, a follow shot along Line B will send the cue ball into left center of the 6-ball, which should separate the cluster with no problem.

Tip: Always remember that accuracy counts more than brute force in breaking small clusters.

Playing a Not So Obvious Cluster Break

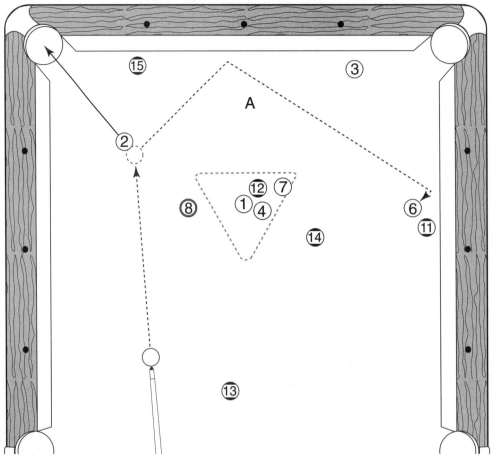

Breaking clusters is one of those problem solving activities where you have to seize the opportunity whenever it is present, as long as it doesn't clash with the rest of your strategy for running the rack. Often these cluster breaking activities are somewhat disguised as you are going about your business as usual.

The diagram shows a position where you might be planning to roll down to Position A for either the 3-ball or 15-ball next. But wait a second! Over on the side-rail is the 6-11 cluster, which needs to be broken sometime, so how about right now? You have a perfectly natural route to the cluster, and you will most assuredly have a shot on either the 15-ball or 13-ball after the shot.

Tip: Quite often clusters are located on the other side of the table (like the one in our example), which may incorrectly eliminate them from your train of thought. So remember to keep conscious of any clusters so you are ready to break them up whenever the opportunity presents itself.

Long Distance Cluster Busting

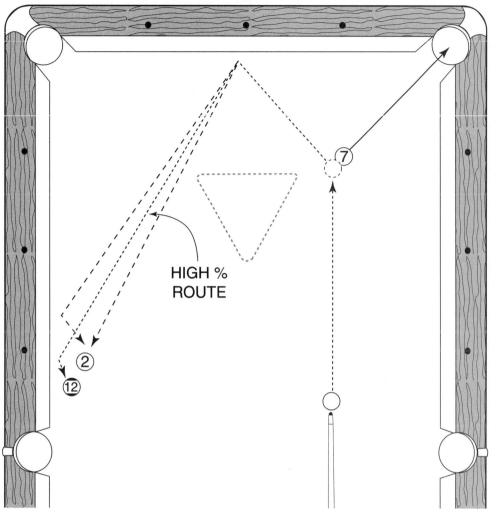

HIGH %
ROUTE

When playing a long distance cluster buster, the first rule of thumb is to hit the cluster somewhere, anywhere. This is especially true late in the rack. You don't want to get too cute trying to clip the edge of one of the balls and run the risk of missing the cluster altogether. Play the shot that gives you the best chance of hitting the cluster and hope for the best.

It is best if there is a natural route to the cluster so you don't have to do any fancy maneuvering that could cause you to miss either the ball or the cluster. The illustration shows a natural path towards the 2-12 cluster after pocketing the 7-ball. You should follow the center of the channel to the cluster. Should you then miss a little to either side, you will still make contact with the cluster.

Precision Routing Can Save a Break Shot

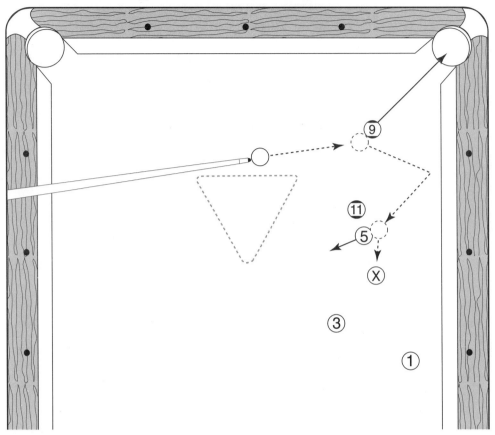

I've mentioned the need to exercise control over force when playing clusters. This is especially true when you need to hit one ball in the cluster while totally avoiding the other to accomplish a valuable objective. The illustration shows a common scenario: you have an opportunity to bounce off the side rail and break a cluster that contains what will hopefully be your break ball. Now is the time for you to exercise your skill at short-range cue ball control. When you really hone in on a smaller target, such as the left center of the 5-ball, you increase your ability to play an exacting shot such as the one shown.

CHAPTER 5

BREAK SHOTS

How to Break a Full Rack With Maximum Control

In nearly every pool game, the objective of the opening break shot is to spread the balls widely across the table. There are, however, two notable exceptions. When playing One-Pocket, the opening break is a defensive measure designed to send several balls toward your pocket while positioning the cue ball on the opposite side of the rack. In Straight Pool, the opening break is also a defensive shot in which your goal is to leave your opponent with a long and difficult shot, or perhaps no shot at all. Once you have finished the first rack, the goal on all subsequent break shots is to pocket a ball and simultaneously open up a fresh new rack.

The break shots I'm going to discuss now are the ones that are played at the beginning of every rack after the initial break shot. At the end of the chapter is a discussion on the opening break.

All About Break Shots

To those who are new to Straight Pool, the last ball (the 15th ball) remains on the table while the other 14 balls are racked after each rack has been played. Your goal is to leave the cue ball and the 15th ball in such places where it will be easy for the cue ball to hit the rack after pocketing the break ball (the 15th ball).

There are multiple objectives when shooting a break shot. You've got to pocket the ball, break the rack, and control the cue ball, all at the same time. Many players make the mistake of thinking about these things while they are playing the shot. While you need to accomplish so much on a break shot, it still comes down to execution as with any other shot.

You should do all your planning before you get down into your stance, then go 100% into execution mode. Make your decisions before you get into your stance so you can focus on playing the shot. Don't let the sight of a full rack adjacent to the break shot intimidate you. And don't worry about where the cue ball is going. Your preshot planning should take into account any requirements for the break shot so you can fire away with complete confidence.

Break shots come in all varieties. You can easily open the rack with some break shots, while on others you are just hoping to knock out a ball or two that can be used to separate the rest of the rack. The difficulty of pocketing the ball also varies greatly.

Characteristics of the Ideal Break Shot:
- You have a relatively easy shot.
- You can easily control the cue ball.
- Several balls will break loose from the rack.
- You are 98% guaranteed to have an easy shot after the break.
- You can work open the rest of the rack without too much trouble.

Tips for Playing Break Shots
- Place a rack on the table to determine if a potential break ball is in the rack or not.
- Avoid destroying the break shot as you play the rack.
- As a rule of thumb, less knowledgeable players should hit break shots a little harder, as they lack the skills to pick a rack apart.
- Avoid playing low percentage break shots, especially from the far end of the table.
- Play for less angle early in a game until you're in stroke.

Pocket Openings On Break Shots
The size of each corner pocket is theoretically the same no matter which angle the ball approaches. While this is true on softly struck shots, such is not the case when you are playing a rather forceful shot, such as the break shot. When the object ball approaches the pocket on a cut shot down the rail, for example, such as the 1-ball in the illustration, the pocket opening is much smaller than normal.

Now contrast the effective pocket size for the 1-ball with the opening for the 2-ball, which is straight out from the corner pocket. The effective opening for the 2-ball is significantly larger. The effective size of the pocket opening can affect your choice of break shots, as well as the speed at which you play them.

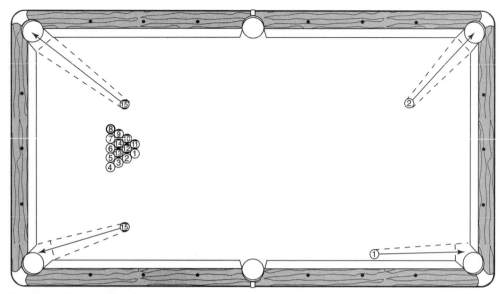

Break Shot Variables

There are several variables that affect the outcome of a break shot. Once you become completely familiar with these variables, you will increase your ability to consistently plan and execute successful break shots. The variables include:

1] Which ball you hit in the rack:
- Determines largely how the rack opens.
- Affects where the cue ball goes.
- Determines whether there is a chance of getting stuck.

2] What part of the ball you hit in the rack:
- Affects the path of the cue ball.

3] The speed you hit the cue ball:
- Affects the spread of the balls.
- Affects cue ball position.
- Determines your chances of scratching.

4] The angle you hit the contact ball in the rack:
- Affects the direction of the cue ball.

5] The action (spin) on the cue ball:
- Affects cue ball position.
- Can be used to avoid trouble.

6] The playing conditions:
- Determine which break shots you select.
- Affects how you play a break shot.
- Affect how the balls spread.

Attacking the Rack

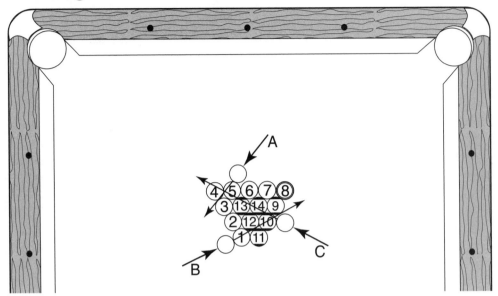

Straight Pool break shots are completely different from those of Eight-Ball and Nine-Ball where you whale away at the head ball in an all-out effort to spread the balls all over the table. In Straight Pool, you must take each and every break shot on a case by case basis. Part of your analysis should include the point on the rack where you expect to make contact. The diagram shows three of many possible angles of attack. They illustrate the necessity of hitting the rack properly.

The cue ball approaching the rack on Line A has a 4fi" long mass it is attacking that is comprised of the 3, 4, and 5-balls. The cue ball certainly won't destroy the rack at this angle, but it will knock out some balls, and there is no risk of sticking to the stack.

The cue ball traveling down Line B has a 6fi" long mass it is attacking that includes the 1, 10, 11, and 12-balls. This break shot should dislodge a good portion of the upper part of the rack.

The cue ball approaching the rack from Line C has it's work cut out for it, as the mass of balls it is attacking is nearly a foot long. In addition, there are balls to either side of the line of attack. It's going to take a precise hit on the 10-ball with a lot of power to bust the rack. There is also the risk of getting stuck on the side of the stack. However, under certain conditions, if the cue ball hits the middle balls just right, it should create a table full of open shots.

The Contact Point on a Ball

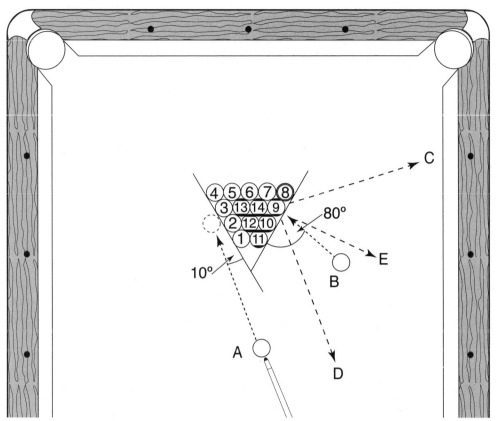

When the cue ball approaches the side of the rack at a fairly shallow angle, it is very likely to follow a predictable path after skimming off the stack. In the diagram, for example, the cue ball in Position A has been shot directly at the rack at a 10-degree angle. It will rebound off the side of the rack at the same angle, or within a few degrees one way or the other.

In sharp contrast, when the cue ball in Position B enters at an angle of about 80-degrees, it could rebound straight back out, up the table, or down towards the corner pocket. It largely depends on which part of the ball in the rack the cue ball contacts. That's why you can shoot what appears to be the same type of break shot as before and have the cue ball go off in a radically different direction.

When the cue ball hits the lower part of a ball it will go forward along Line C. When it hits the top part of the ball, it will rebound up the table on Line D. If you hit the outer edge of the ball just right, it will rebound directly away from the stack along Line E. When you consider the many points of contact on the ball in the rack, you can see the many directions the cue ball can take on certain types of break shots.

Speed of Stroke

Many newcomers to the game may be surprised to learn the range of speeds of stroke employed in a variety of Straight Pool break shots. The spectrum of speed, which appeared in the chapter on position play, is also presented below. I've included my guesstimates of how often each speed is used to play a break shot. This is not a scientific study, but it should give you a working model you can incorporate into your game.

Speeds of Stroke on Break Shots

1 Extremely soft – 0%   6 Medium hard – 40%
2 Very soft – 0%   7 Hard – 20%
3 Soft – 0%   8 Very hard – 10%
4 Medium soft – 5%   9 Extremely hard – 5%
5 Medium – 20%   10 The Break Shot – 0%

You will notice that you never use the same force you would on an opening break shot in Eight-Ball or Nine-Ball. The upper ranges (#8-#9) are only used when you have a nearly straight in shot and you need to generate sufficient power with very little cut angle. The lower ranges (#1-#3) are never used, because you do have to apply some power to the rack, even if you are breaking it at a weak point in the corners. Ranges #4-#5 will open up the rack reasonably well when you are attacking the end balls at the proper angle. The majority of break shots (80% by my estimate) are shot in the #5 to #7 range.

Six Factors that Determine the Speed of Stroke on Break Shots

- The cut angle.
- Which part of the rack the cue ball will be contacting.
- The cue ball's angle of attack.
- The degree of difficulty of the shot.
- The need to control the cue ball.
- The playing conditions, or how the balls are breaking.

Let's evaluate three break shots using the criteria above. Let's assume the balls are not flying apart, nor are they stuck together (criteria #6, the conditions). On break shot A, the cut angle of only 15-degrees is not at all difficult. This shallow cut angle does mean you will need to supply the power with a very forceful stroke. You will, however, be contacting the lower part of the top ball, which means that you are hitting the rack at a weak spot. You shouldn't have too much trouble controlling the cue ball, as it should drift back above the rack. After considering the relevant variables, this break shot should be played with a very hard stroke (#8 on the 1-10 scale).

Break shot B is a thin cut of 50 degrees, so the cue ball will retain much of it's energy for breaking open the rack after contacting the 15-ball.

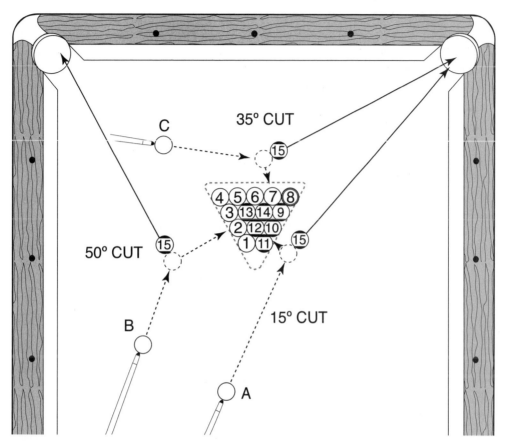

The shot is of moderate difficulty, which says it should be shot at a speed with which you feel confident. The cue ball is taking on the rack at about its strongest place, so this indicates the need for power. Cue ball control is not an issue on this type of shot. You can let the cue ball go with the understanding that you should come away with a shot. Play it with a medium hard stroke (#6) to hard stroke (#7).

Break shot C is a relatively short and easy cut shot of 35 degrees, so pocketing the ball is a minor concern. The cue ball will be hitting the end balls at an angle, which indicates that it won't take much power to get the cue ball away from the rack. You will be attacking the rack at a weak spot, so you should be able to knock out several balls. Cue ball control is the main issue on this shot. You need to use a speed that will send the cue ball to the rail and out to the middle of the table. All relevant factors considered, this break shot should be played with a medium stroke (#5) to medium hard stroke (#6).

The three examples we've just covered should alert you to the need for learning the optimal speed for playing each kind of break shot. You will give yourself the best chance of learning how to play the wide variety of break shots by applying the criteria mentioned above and carefully evaluating the results. The evaluation process will become automatic once you gain enough experience.

How Cueing Affects the Cue Balls Path

The cue balls path after contacting the rack on most break shots is far from a random happening. As a matter of fact, experienced players play shape on break shots. This is done by using proper cueing and speed of stroke that will put the cue ball in position for one of several balls which typically land in certain areas of the table. Draw, follow and stun can all be used to get the cue ball away from the rack and to help send it where needed. English is also employed on some break shots to maneuver the cue ball off the rails and around the table for shape. The diagrams on specific break shots will indicate the correct cueing for each shot.

Why the Cue Ball Sticks to the Rack

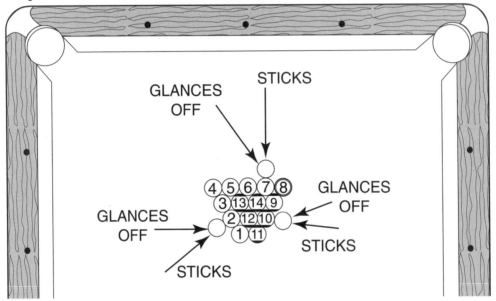

Having the cue ball stick to the rack with several balls in the clear on other sides of the rack ranks right up there with scratching as a major source of dismay for Straight Pool players. The primary reasons why the cue ball sticks include:

- The cue ball hits the side of the rack at a slow speed
- The cue ball makes full contact with a ball.
- The balls are not breaking very well (humidity, unclean balls).
- The cue ball is taking on the interior balls at the rack's strongest point.

The diagram shows a couple of angles of approach where the cue ball is in danger of sticking to the rack. It also shows how the cue ball will glance off the rack if it hits the same point on the object ball but at a different angle. Now that you know why getting stuck happens, you will be able to recognize high risk situations and be able to take protective measures against getting stuck.

Scratching off the Side of the Rack

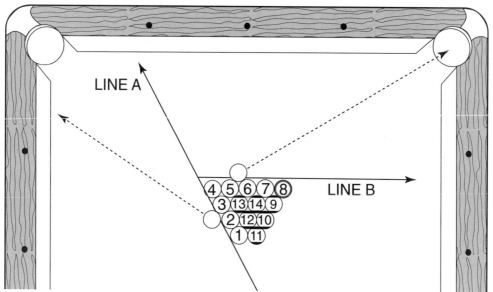

Scratching can be a real problem for many players on side-of-the-rack break shots. Notice in the diagram that the side of the rack is pointed towards a position on the rail (Line A) less than a diamond inside the corner pocket. The uneven "surface" of the side of the rack also contributes to scratching. If you hit a certain part of a ball just right with a certain spin, it will shoot straight towards the pocket. For example, if the cue ball hits the 3-ball at the wrong angle with follow, it will curve into the corner pocket. Now add incorrect cueing to these physical characteristics of a pool table and balls and you have the recipe for a scratch. In other words, the game has been designed so that scratching is a highly probable event unless you take protective measures.

The good news is that scratching directly into the corner pocket is a rare occurrence on behind the rack break shots. Line B shows you why. Observe that the edge of the rack is pointing over a diamond above the pocket. The cue ball that's contacting the 6-ball is headed straight for the corner pocket, but if enough follow has been applied, it should bend forward and strike the side rail. On any point of contact other than the gap, the cue ball should have no trouble hitting the side rail. Scratching on behind-the-rack break shots usually occurs in the opposite corner pocket because the player failed to use english properly (more on this later).

Dangers on the Break Shot

Missing the Break Shot

The main thing that can go wrong is missing the break ball and leaving your opponent a wide-open table. The primary causes and cures for missing are presented below:

Cause #1: Shooting too hard

Cure: There are only a select group of break shots that should be played with a hard stroke. Most break shots are played with a medium hard stroke for control and accuracy. Hitting the right part of the rack is usually more important than hitting it with full force.

Cause #2: Shooting hard break shots

Cure: If you typically are faced with long break shots or steep cut angled shots, it is an indication that your end-of-rack patterns need work.

Cause #3: You're sharked by the rest of the rack

Cure: You must totally focus on how you are going to play the shot. Give it your best aim and stroke.

Cause #4 You're worried about the cue ball

Cure: Your preshot planning is designed, in part, to eliminate the possibility of a scratch. Your decisions on where you are going to hit the rack, your cueing, and your speed of stroke should all account for the possibility of scratching. Once you are over the ball, you should only be thinking about making the shot.

Scratching on the Break Shot

How it happens:
- Off the side of the rack into the corner pocket or side pocket.
- Double kiss scratch.
- Hit too hard, turn the cue ball loose, and kissed into a pocket or travel into a distant pocket.

Cure: Learn to apply the proper cueing and speed to each kind of break shot. Also learn how the cue ball reacts off different contact points on the rack. You also must stroke break shots so that the cue ball will react properly.

Sticking to the Rack

How it happens:
- On low angle break shots.
- When the cue ball hits an interior ball squarely at a slow speed.

Cure: Learn the break shots that lead to the cue ball getting stuck, and either avoid them or learn to get the cue ball away from the rack. Don't get greedy on break shots where the cue ball might get stuck.

No Shot or No Easy Shot [didn't play shape off the break shot]
- Certain break shots are inherently difficult to control.
- You were just unlucky. Bad rolls do happen on well played shots.

Cure: Learn how to play shape on all the various break shots.

Blasting Balls Everywhere, Creating Problems All Over the Table
- You may get lots of easy shots.
- You could also wind up with some big problems, including clusters on the rail.

Cure: Don't hit break shots too hard, even when they are the kind you can blast the rack on. Learn to pick apart a rack in sections.

The Cue Ball is on the Far End Rail After Contact
The cue ball may head towards the far end rail for any of the following reasons:
- Too much draw on a side-of-the-rack break shot.
- Too much english and speed on a behind-the-rack break shot.
- Glanced off the side of the rack, such as often happens on a down-the-rail break shot.

Cure: Solve this problem by checking out contact better, cueing properly, and by learning the most probable route for the cue ball on each kind of break shot.

Missing the Rack Entirely
This error can result in the cue ball coming to rest at the opposite end of the table. In this position, you will probably have to play an intentional foul. The missing-the-rack error occurs when you:
- Play long distance break shots.
- Misplay a break shot.
- Miss shape on a break shot and play the shot anyway, even though you'll almost certainly miss the rack.

Cure: Become very familiar with the path of the cue ball on all of the various break shots, especially those where the cue ball has to travel some distance to hit the rack.

Side of the Rack Break Shots

• The Classic Break Shot

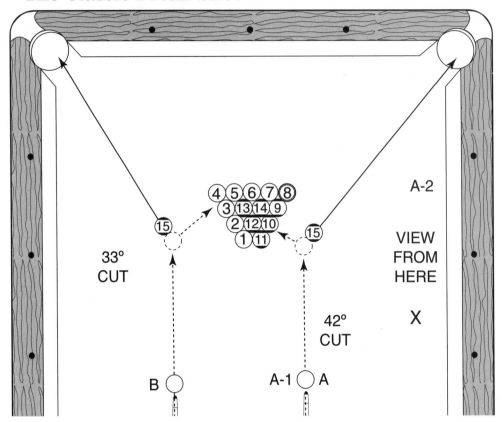

Break Shot A is a classic break shot. The cue ball is lined up parallel with it's point of contact with the break ball and the side rail. The 42-degree cut angle ensures that the cue ball will retain a good deal of it's speed going into the rack. The contact point with the rack can make a big difference in how the cue ball reacts off this break shot. I suggest getting in the habit of viewing break shots from a 90-degree angle from the break ball's path to the pocket. This will enable you to pinpoint exactly where the cue ball will be hitting the rack. You need to draw a line from the middle of the cue ball's position at contact to the rack as shown. The cue ball will hit just slightly above the middle of the 10-ball. You can't change the contact point on this break shot because you will be using a firm stroke and the break ball is so close to the rack. This break shot should be hit with a half tip of draw and a medium hard stroke. The cue ball should come back to A-1. If the cue ball was going to contact the lower half of the 10-ball, it would end up at A-2.

Break Shot B looks similar to A since the cue ball is once again parallel with it's point of contact and the rail. There are, however several important differences, which illustrates how seemingly small changes in the position of the break ball and cue ball can impact a shot.

The break ball is farther from the rack, which reduces the cut angle to 33-degrees. This means less of the cue ball's energy will be retained for opening the rack than with Break Shot A. The cue ball is lined up to hit slightly below the center of the 3-ball, which is a much lower contact point in the rack than with A. You can alter the point of contact on this break shot because of the distance of the break ball from the rack. For example, by using draw you could hit higher up on the 3-ball. Some players in this situation might prefer to use follow instead of draw since the cue ball would be attacking the lower portion of the rack, and would guarantee that they would come away with several open shots.

• A Control Break Shot

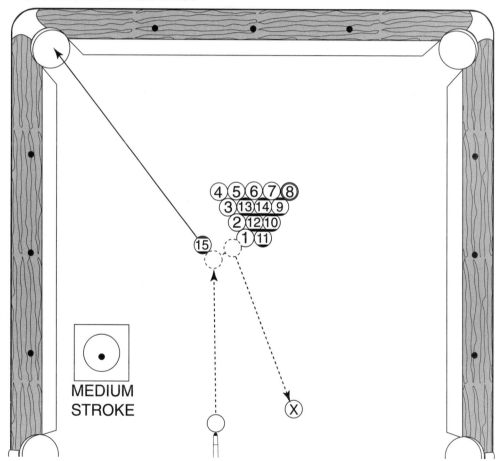

The break shot in this diagram is a favorite of many top players because it allows you to attack the rack at a weak spot, which enables you to knock out 5 and 6-balls without much effort. You can control the cue ball by using a medium-speed stroke and a half tip of draw. The shot is really a stun/draw shot. There is no chance of getting stuck to the rack since the ball you are contacting on the rack is going to be dislodged from the stack. The cue ball should ease its way back to the center portion of the table, from which you should have a choice of at least two or more shots.

Back-Cut Rack Blaster

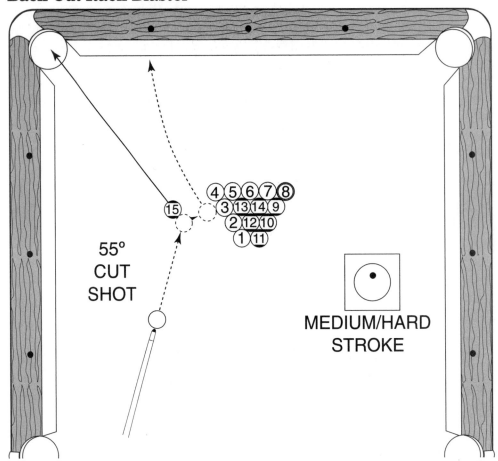

This break shot was the great Willie Mosconi's favorite. Even though the cut angle is 55 degrees, it's not that tough of a shot since the cue ball is relatively close to the break ball. In addition, you don't need to worry about the cue ball since it usually emerges from the mayhem in good shape even though you can't control it as precisely as you can in other break shots. The shot is played with a medium-hard to hard follow stroke.

Close-To-the-Rail Break Shots

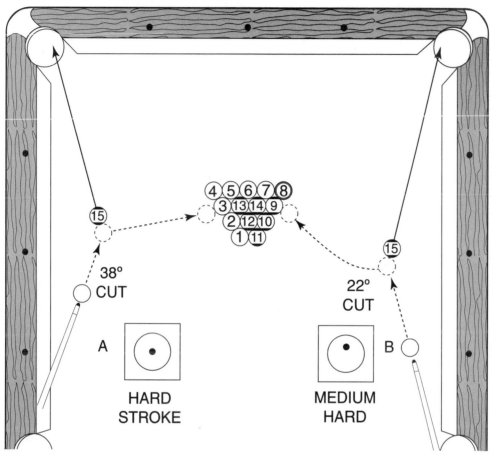

When the break ball is within 6-8" of the rail, you still have the opportunity for a very successful break shot. The secret is to play shape close to the break ball so you can create a sufficiently sharp cut angle. In Part A, you have a 38-degree back-cut. From this close you can use a hard stroke while maintaining accuracy. It is tough to precisely control the contact point from this distance, so you will need just a little luck. The cue ball will, however, be striking the rack at a slight angle, which should lessen the chances of it sticking to the pack

The cut angle is only 22 degrees in Part B, and the break ball is a little further up the table. In this case, you need precision over power. The idea is to attack the lower corner of the rack, which you can access by using a medium-hard stroke with a full tip of follow. You should emerge with a shot on the foot-end of the table.

Shallow Cut Angles (P)

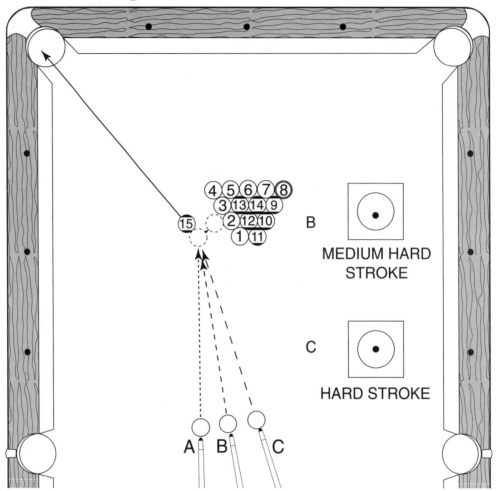

Break Ball A and it's point of contact with the break ball are parallel with the rail. The cue ball is slightly right of parallel on Break Shot B. This 27-degree cut shot gives you adequate power to knock out several balls with a medium-hard draw stroke and a half tip of draw. The key to this shot is to give a decent blow to the side of the rack, and then escape to the middle of the table. Regulating the speed and cueing of this shot is crucial.

Break Ball C is quite a bit over from parallel and has a cut angle of only 20 degrees. When the cut angle is this shallow, the cue ball will lose much of it's power after contacting the break ball. You must provide the power by using a very smooth and powerful pound stroke. It is best if you can hit directly on a ball, such as the 2-ball, and then escape by bouncing off the side of the rack. This will open the balls better, but at a higher risk. If you try to draw back up-table with a less forceful stroke, you run the risks of not separating the balls very well, and ending up near or on the opposite end rail. If the break ball was a little higher up you could contact the 1-ball. The shot would then be to draw off the 1-ball and break out a few balls from the top of the rack.

• The Distance Principle On Break Shots

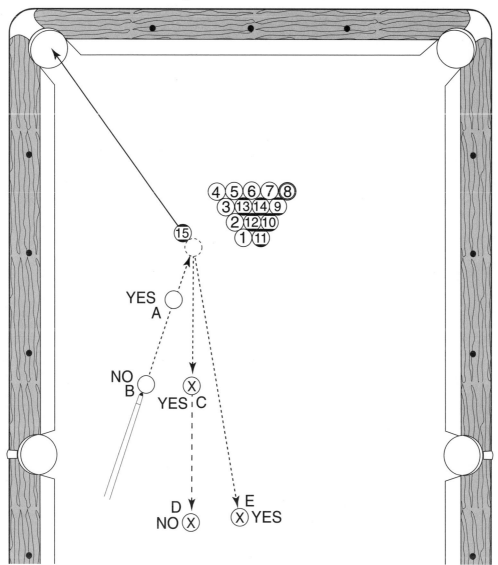

There is a high cost to missing break shots, so you must always balance accuracy with your desire to blast open the rack. In the example, Cue Ball A is within 8" of the break ball, so a cut angle of 50 degrees does not make this a very difficult shot. Lengthen the shot to Cue Ball B though, and the risk factor rises greatly. The break shot at Cue Ball C is not too tough, but if you move it back along the same cut line to Cue Ball D, then the shot becomes somewhat more challenging. From this distance you might prefer to have the smaller cut angle at Cue Ball E to insure the accuracy of the shot.

The Ideal Draw-Back Distance

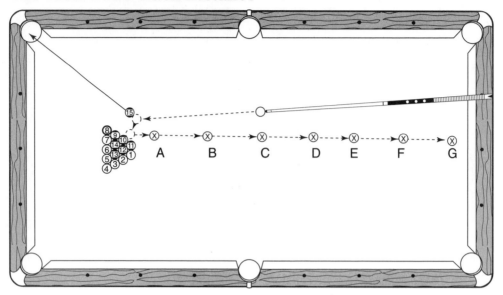

One of the biggest challenges on a great many side-of-the-rack break shots is in controlling the distance the cue ball draws back off the rack. With the cue ball at Position A, you may limit your shot selection. If you try to land here, you are running the risk of sticking to the rack. Cue Balls B-D show the ideal draw back zone. At these distances you have a good view of both sides of the table, and a relatively short shot. You have also regulated the cue ball's return to avoid sticking to the rack, or traveling too far up table. Shots with the cue ball in zone E-F increase the chance of a miss greatly. With the cue ball at G or beyond, you are hoping to have a pocket hanger at the other end of the table to bail you out of trouble.

- **Break Shot Stretch Distances**

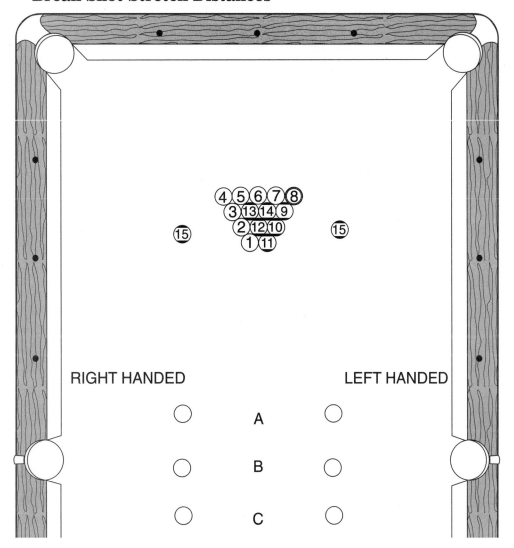

For most side-of-the-rack break shots, you'll want the cue ball within an easy reaching distance. Most players find they can set up comfortably for the shot with the cue ball somewhere between cue balls A-C. It all really depends on your physical characteristics (such as your height and length of your arms) and your shooting style. For example, a player who likes to shoot low to the table may prefer to have the cue ball further down the table than a player who stands higher over the ball.

I advise you to set up break shots, like the ones in the illustration and establish your personal comfort zone. The goal is to balance power with accuracy. If you do this, when you are in a game, you will know exactly where to position the cue ball for side-of-the-rack break shots.

Tip: When the cue ball could end up much past the side pockets (towards the direction of the rack), set up for the imaginary break shot before you play shape on the break shot This will enable you to tell whether or not you are playing shape for a stretch shot on the break ball.

Above the Rack

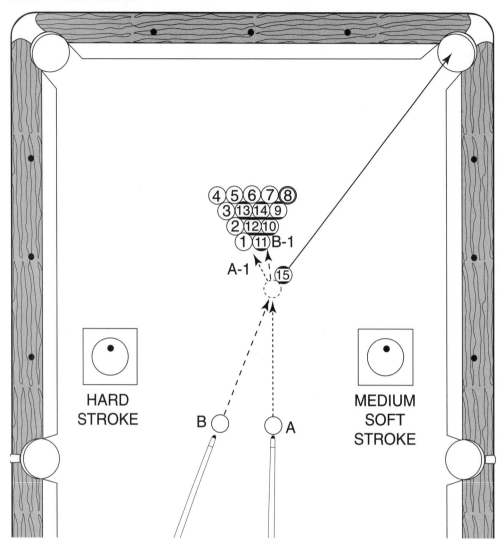

When the break ball is above the rack, as in the illustration, you still have a very playable break shot. With the cue ball at Position A, you must resist the urge to get too much out of the shot. If you use excessive force, the cue ball could miss the rack entirely. The secret in Position A is to back off on the power and go for a precise hit on the 1-ball. Use a medium- soft stoke so the cue ball will travel down Line A-1. This will do sufficient damage to the rack and give you an excellent chance of extending your run. In addition, you should be able to maintain control of the cue ball.

With the cue ball at Position B, the objective is to send the cue ball down Line B-1 to strike the upper right-half of the 11-ball. This shot requires a powerful follow stroke as you have such little angle to work with.

Follow Back Out off the Low Balls

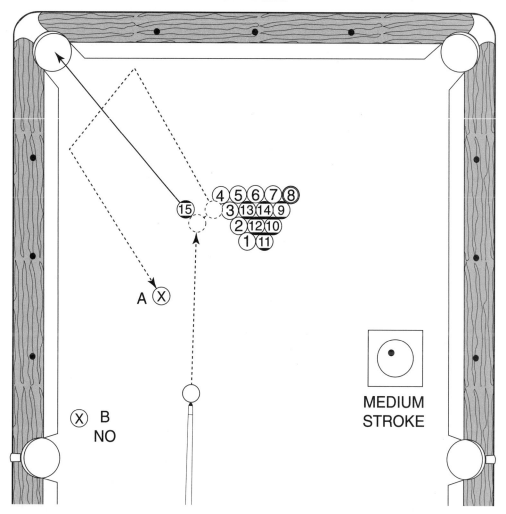

You can attack the rack more forcefully by using follow when the break ball is down low, as is the case in the illustration. Use a medium hard stroke with top-left (inside) english. The cue ball will go two rails to Position A. Be sure to allow for deflection by aiming for a fuller hit on the 15-ball. If you are not comfortable shooting at higher speeds with inside english, you could play the shot with straight follow. You run the risk, however, of the cue ball stopping along the side rail at Position B.

Shallow-Angle Follow Shot

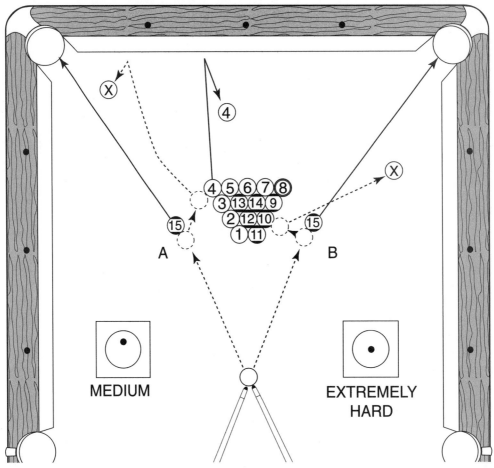

You may occasionally get too straight-in on a break shot at the side of the rack, but you can still continue your run. In Position A, you could try to pound off the side of the rack, but with only a 10-degree cut angle chances are you'll stick to the stack. A better bet is to back off the speed and go for the corner ball. If all works out as planned you could end up with a secondary break shot, such as the one on the 4-ball.

In Position B, you can't hit the corner ball. Now your shot is to play a power stun shot off the side of the rack. Use center ball and an extremely hard stoke (probably the most forceful stroke you will ever use on any shot in Straight Pool). If you strike the side of a ball, you can reduce or eliminate your chances of sticking to the side of the rack. You want the cue ball to bounce one way or the other away from the rack.

Ball-in-Hand Break Shots (P)

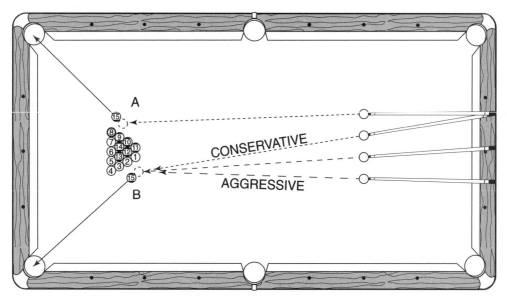

When playing break shots with ball-in-hand, you know you have a long shot, which makes pocketing the ball the first priority. With this thought in mind, you will want to place the cue ball in a position that minimizes the difficulty of the shot, while still providing you with enough cut angle to do some damage to the rack. When the break ball is low to the rack as in Position A, a follow shot works best. When the break ball is higher up, as in Position B, use a draw stroke. You should practice with the break ball and cue ball in various positions to determine your comfort zone, and to discover which approach works best for you with each shot (draw, follow, etc.). Be sure to keep in mind the distance principle mentioned in a previous section.

Low Break Shots

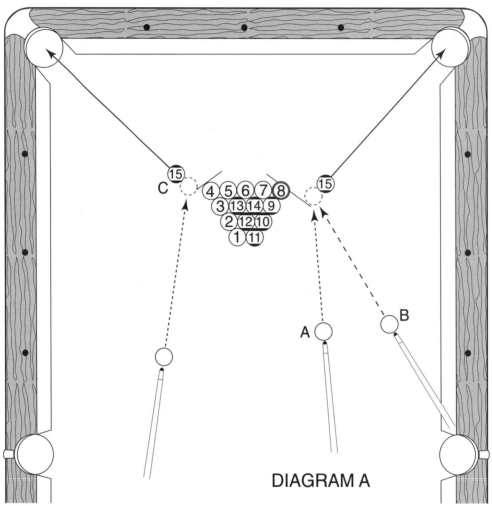

DIAGRAM A

When the break ball is very low to the rack, you must guard against missing the rack entirely. You don't want is to inadvertently play a "safety" on yourself by scoring a point, missing the rack, and sending the cue ball to the far end of the table. When the best you can probably expect is to contact the corner ball, your primary goal is to get a shot or two that you can use to open up the rest of the balls.

You can determine if the cue ball has a chance of hitting the rack by lining up the top edge of the position the cue ball will be in at contact with the corner ball of the rack. The cue ball in Position A, in Diagram A, is lined up to hit the edge of the 8-ball, assuming you hit the cue ball firmly in the center. By applying draw you can, at this moderate cut angle, contact just a fraction more of the 8-ball. If you use follow on this shot, you might miss the 8-ball, thus committing the error we mentioned a moment ago. With the cue ball in Position B, you should use draw with outside (left) english to ensure that you will hit the rack.

The 15-ball in Position C is a half-ball lower, and the cut angle is greater than the break shot in Position A. Notice how the edge of the cue ball at contact lines up with the edge of the 4-ball. Since you're not going to hit much of the rack, you must guard against missing it entirely. You must also take extra steps to control the cue ball, as it will only be skimming off the 4-ball.

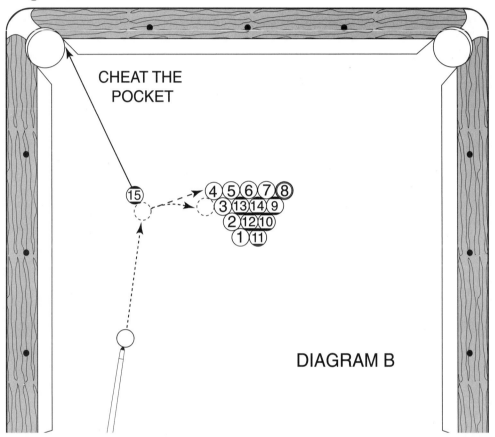

CHEAT THE POCKET

DIAGRAM B

The further the break ball is from the rack, the more you can alter its path to the rack by using draw and a softer stroke, providing the cut angle is not too severe. You can also create a higher hit on the rack by using outside english and cheating it towards the outside part of the pocket. This is shown in Diagram B. The 15-ball is to be played into the right side of the pocket with right english. This will enable the cue ball to strike the upper side of the 4-ball rather than the lower side, which will do more damage to the rack.

Side-Rail Break Shots

• A Basic Side-Rail Break Shot

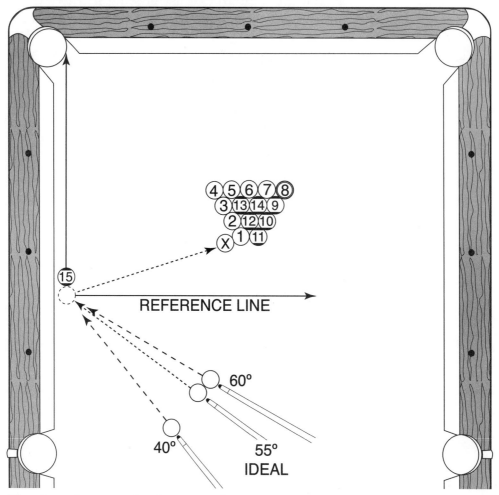

The first thing to check on a side-rail break shot is where the reference line is pointing. The reference line is a line that extends across the table at a 90-degree angle from the cue ball's point of contact with the break ball. In the diagram, the line points above the rack. With the break ball in this position, you would need some right english to pull the cue ball down into the rack.

The ideal angle for playing down-the-rail break shots is about 55 degrees. A cut angle greater than this adds speed to the cue ball, but at a loss of accuracy. With a cut angle of 40-degrees, you need to hit the cue ball with a hard stroke to break the rack, which also reduces the accuracy of the shot

There are exceptions to the rule regarding the ideal angle. If the balls are breaking open easily, or you have enough control to hit the top ball as shown, then you can get by with an easier stroke on a cut shot of less than 55 degrees.

Measuring the Cut Angle

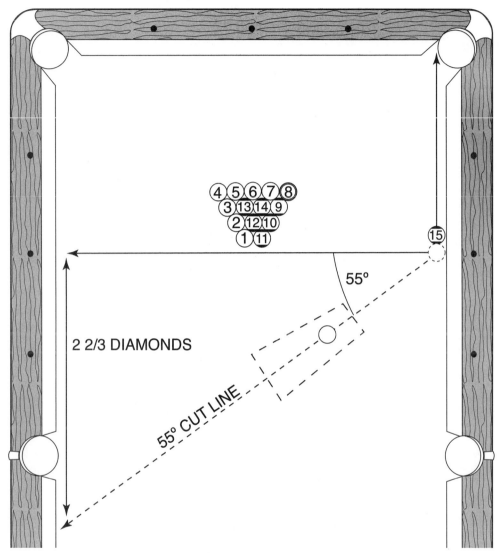

The illustration shows you an easy way to calculate the 55-degree angle. Extend the reference line to the opposite rail. Then find the spot 2 2/3 diamonds up the side-rail. The line formed by the point on the rail, and the cue ball's position at contact, is the 55-degree cut angle line. Any cue ball along that line, such as the one at Position A, is a 55 degree cut on the 15-ball. If the cue ball was located anywhere in the position zone, you would still have excellent shape on the break ball.

More Side-Rail Break Sots

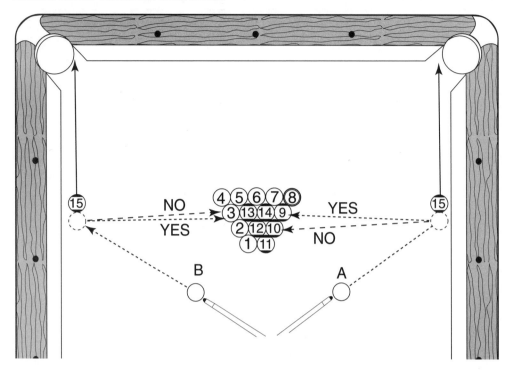

The position of the break ball in relation to the rack has a big bearing on how you play down-the-side-rail break shots. In this example, the break balls are further down the rail than in previous examples. In Position A the reference line for the break shot is pointing at the 10-ball. If you hit the 10-ball squarely, there is a good chance the cue ball will stick to the stack. A touch of left english will send the cue ball into the side of the 9-ball. The cue ball should then head towards the middle of the table. Although you now run the risk of traveling to the opposite end of the table, you should be ok as long as the cue ball stays within 4-5 diamonds of the foot rail.

The 15-ball in Position B is slightly further down the rail, but enough to make a difference in how the break shot is played. The reference line points at the middle of the 3-ball, which is in line with the 13, 14, and 9-balls. To avoid hitting this mass head on, you should use a touch of out-side (left) english so you can hit the edge of the 3-ball at an angle. This will help send the cue ball up-table. The harder you play this shot, the more you run the risk of going up-table. You will, however, open the balls better and reduce the risk of sticking to the rack.

Below-the-Rack Side Rail Break Shots

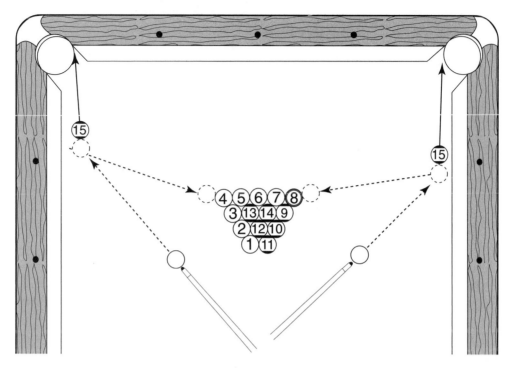

The break shots in this illustration are significantly more challenging than the other side-of-the-rail break shots we've just covered. The difficulty lies in making full contact with the corner ball. It is nearly impossible to hit and stick to the rack on these shots. What will happen, if you hit the upper side of the corner ball, is that the cue ball will roll uptable. And if you miss the corner ball and instead skim the side of the rack, the cue ball will most assuredly head to the far end of the table.

You could play these break shots perfectly. The majority of the time, however, you'll probably miss a full hit on the corner ball, and the cue ball will travel up-table. I'm not being pessimistic, just realistic. So you must be prepared to deal with the possibility of having a long shot, or of even scratching. It is really a shot you hate playing, but must play, so give it your best try and accept that the pool gods are largely in control of this one.

Down-the-Rail Break Shots With the Ball Off the Cushion

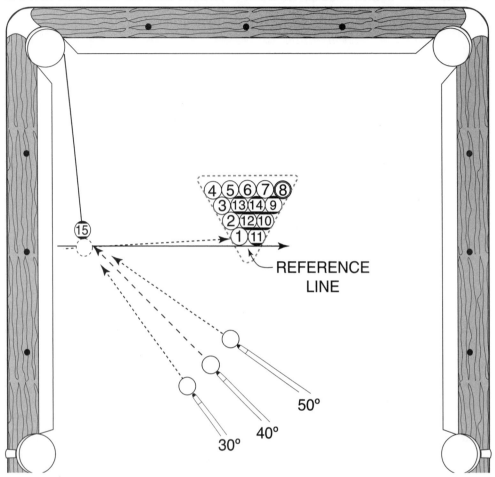

The dynamics of down-the-rail break shots change drastically when the break ball is even just a couple of inches off the rail. The cue ball's speed coming off the rail will be much less than when the break ball is adjacent to the rail, as in the break shots we've just covered. In addition, without using english the cue ball will rebound down a line well above the reference line.

The illustrations show three cut angles. At 50-degrees, you will need to apply at least half tip of english using a medium-hard follow stroke to send the cue ball down into the stack. The shallower cut angles of 30 and 40 degrees require even more english. You must carefully weigh the risk of sticking to the stack, with that of not hitting the rack, should you go for the head ball and miss on the high side.

Tip: I suggest you get familiar with this break shot by setting it up in the three positions shown. Use the donuts (hole reinforcements) so you can shoot the same shots over and over again. Next, set up the 1 to 4-balls in a row. Take note of where you are contacting the line of balls. The best place to contact the rack is slightly above the middle of the 1-ball, but this takes great cue ball control.

The Umbrella Break Shot

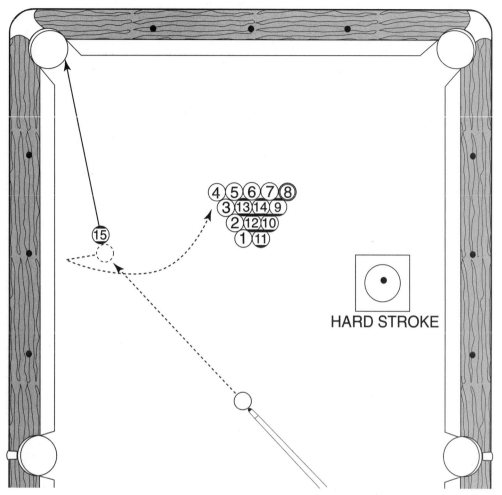

HARD STROKE

When the break ball is 3 fi" off the rail as in the position shown, you will be doing very well to knock out a few balls and have a shot. Your best bet is to play the shot with maximum follow and a very firm stroke. You want the cue ball to arc over and down into the stack at the angle shown. The cue ball's path will resemble the shape of an umbrella. The cue ball's angle of approach should work in your favor as it is will not be taking the mass of balls head on.

Behind-the-Rack Break Shots

• Inside Follow Three Rails

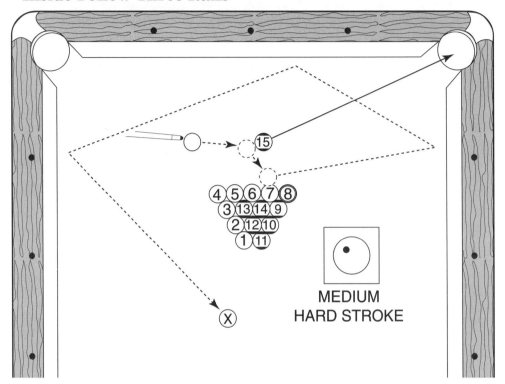

MEDIUM
HARD STROKE

The balls are going to head-up table on behind-the-rack break shots, so the cue ball must escape the end rail and travel to the middle of the table where shots will be located. When there is a straight-line relationship between the cue ball and the break ball, and the cue ball will be contacting any of the last four balls, play the shot with follow and inside english. The cue ball should travel three rails and out to the middle portion of the table. Don't make the mistake of slamming this break shot, as that greatly increases the chances of a miss. Use a medium firm stroke. The idea is to knock out 5 or 6 balls and go from there.

There are several advantages to behind-the-rack break shot even though they seem to be ignored by many players:
* They are easy to reach.
* You usually have a short, easy shot.
* Controlling the cue ball is not too difficult.
* There is little worry of scratching.
* There are many ways to easily get good position on these break shots.
* You won't stick to the stack because of the glancing blow.

• Behind-the-Rack Back-Cut Break Shots

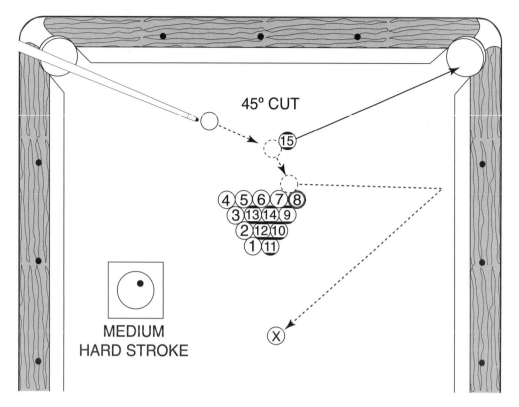

The advantages that we spoke of a moment ago on behind-the-rack break shots also apply to this break shot. Again, the goal is to knock out a few balls and leave the area of the end-rail. The 45 degree cut shot shown in the illustration is not too severe, and it will produce more damage to the rack than the shot in the previous section. Play this shot when you will be contacting either of the last two balls. Use top-right english. The cue ball will strike the rail where shown and the english will turn it towards the center of the table.

Behind-the-Rack Draw Break Shot

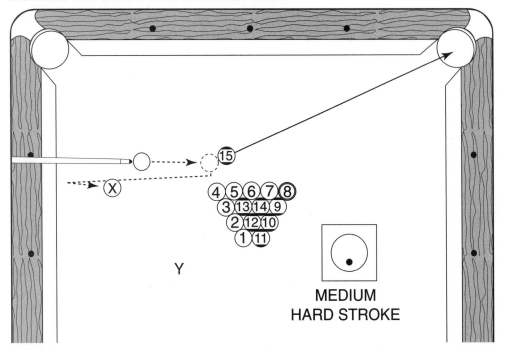

MEDIUM
HARD STROKE

When the break ball and cue ball are in the area of the positions shown, and you will be contacting the last ball, you can escape the back of the rack by using draw. The cue ball will come straight back to the rail. You should expect to have a shot in the opposite side pocket after this break shot with the cue ball at Position X. If you are confident using inside english, with draw, you could send the cue ball off the rail to position A.   This shot, like the previous two, is about controlling the cue ball and getting a few balls to work with.

Down-the-End-Rail Break Shots

The break shot in the illustration on the top of the next page scares many players for good reason. You can easily stick to the back of the rack if you take on the interior balls. You may also miss the shot if you try to take on the middle part of the rack with a hard stroke. The key to this shot is to hit the outer half of the second to last ball, or the end ball, at an angle as shown. The glancing blow will hit the rack in a weak spot, freeing enough balls for you to continue your run. Hitting the rack at an angle also insures that the cue ball will escape the back of the rack. Use a moderately sharp draw stroke. The emphasis should be on precision over power. Also remember that the cue ball will bounce off the rail at a wider angle when the break ball is an inch or more from the rail.

        This break shot makes a great secondary break shot. When insurance balls are available, you can take on the middle portion of the rack since the balls have already been loosened up.

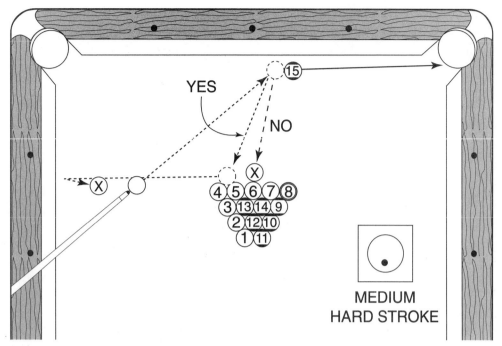

Down-the-Rail with Inside English

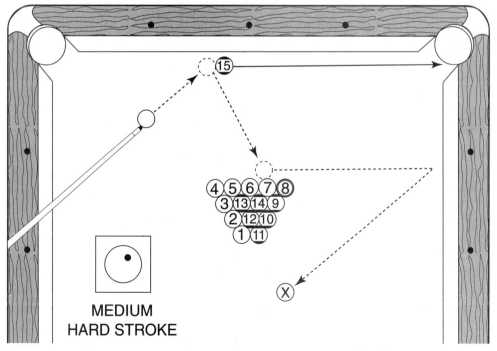

This break shot is really the opposite of the one in the previous section. The goal is to hit the last two balls at an angle and escape the back of the rack. Precision rules on this shot, especially because of the difficulty of playing a power shot with inside english. Use follow with inside english and a medium speed of stroke.

Down-the-Rail Cut Angles

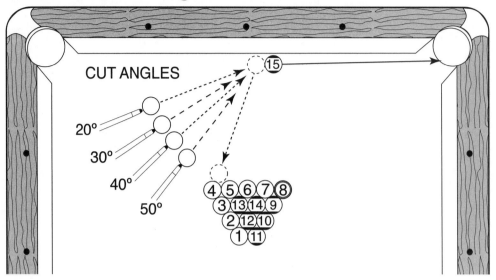

The cut angle can have a big effect on down-the-end-rail break shots. At 20 degrees, you need to provide most of the power because of the shallow cut angle. With such a small cut angle (for a break shot), you run the risk of either sticking to the rack, or, as is more often the case, applying too much draw and missing the rack altogether. This shot really calls for more of a stun/draw stroke. A cut angle of about 50 degrees is the best for playing this shot.

Tip: I recommend that you use the donuts to mark the four cue ball positions and the break ball. Place the 4-ball and 5-ball where shown and practice until you can consistently make contact with them. This practice will also help you to play secondary break shots with greater accuracy.

Straight Out to the Corner Ball

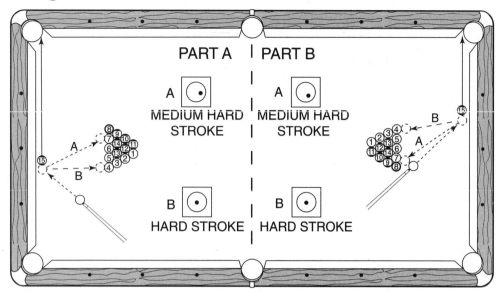

The cut angle is quite steep in Part A, which makes it difficult to pocket the ball, and hit the rack on the opposite end down Line A with inside english. This route might be preferable, however, if the balls are not breaking very easily, as it can help keep the cue ball from sticking to the back of the rack. You will have greater accuracy on the shot by using centerball to come straight out towards the corner ball. You will run the risk of sticking to the rack if you hit the 5-ball by mistake. This version of the break shot is the better choice when the balls are opening easily.

In Part B, a draw shot with outside english will send the cue ball into the last two balls down Line A. The key is to regulate the draw and english such that you avoid sticking to the back of the rack, or missing the rack altogether. This route should be chosen when the balls are not breaking very well. The break shot down Line B is nearly identical to the one in Part A, only the break ball is on the other side of the rack. Use centerball and a hard stroke. Again, this shot should be played when it doesn't take much to break open the balls.

Other Useful Break Shots

When the Break Shot is Very Close to the Rack

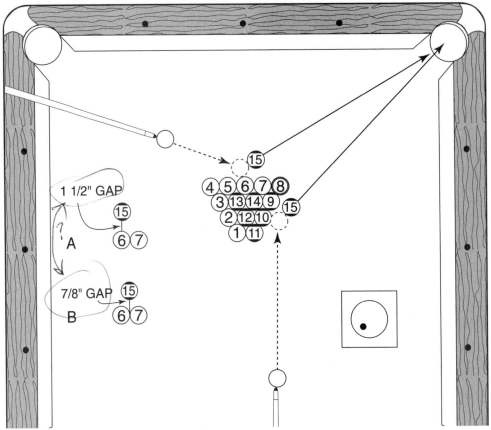

A break ball that's just outside of the rack can present you with it's own special set of difficulties. When the break ball is on the side of the rack and is just a hair outside the rack, there is very little room for the cue ball. You can choose to play the shot as a normal cut shot. The problem is the rack can be a visual distraction, making it difficult to see the shot. It might be easier instead to play ever so slightly into the ball opposite where the cue ball will be at contact. This would, of course, create too full a hit on the break ball. You can allow for the extra full hit by using some outside english to throw the ball into the pocket. You can guard against scratching by playing the shot with draw.

When the break ball is close to the back of the rack, there may not be enough room for the cue ball. You will need a larger gap between the break ball and the rack than with side-of-the-rack break shots because the back row of balls points farther up the rail from the pocket. When the break ball is directly opposite a ball in the row (Position A), then you need a gap of 1 1/2" between the balls to have enough room for the cue ball to fit. When the break ball is directly opposite the gap between two balls (Position B), you must have 7/8" clearance for the cue ball.

Pocket Hanger Break Shots

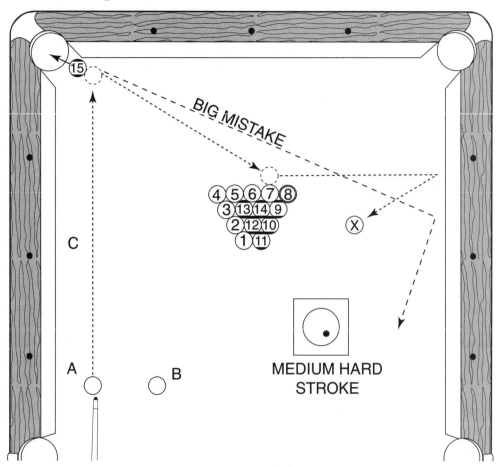

This break shot gets novices salivating at the prospect of a wide-open rack. They love to smash into a break shot that can't be missed. This shot, however, is loaded with danger. The big mistake comes from hitting the 15-ball too full and/or using too much outside english. The cue ball will then miss the rack on the opposite side and travel to the far end of the table, leaving you with no shot. Experienced players know that this shot must be played with great precision. The object is to hit the far side of the rack. Use low right english so the cue ball will go to the side rail and spin out to the lower center portion of the table after hitting the rack.

Play position for this break shot close to the rail, as shown by Cue Ball A. The shot is much more difficult to control from Cue Ball B. When playing position on this kind of break shot, you must consider which side of the table the break ball is on. You could play up-close to the 15-ball by leaving the cue ball at Position C if you were right-handed. In this position, a lefthander would have to stretch for the shot, use the bridge, or shoot opposite handed. Naturally the opposite is true on the other side of the table.

Head Spot Two-Rail Break Shot

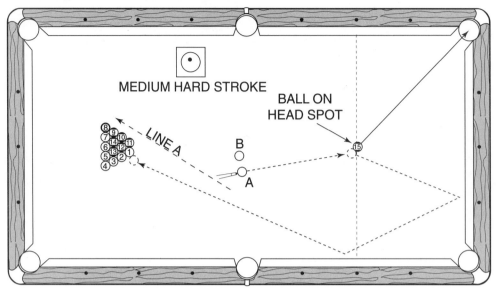

When the last ball is in the rack, it is placed on the head spot. You can occasionally keep a run going by remembering to play position for the break shot shown in the illustration when the last ball is going to remain in the rack. You want the cue ball just a little to the side of the break ball at Position A. Play the shot with a medium-hard follow stroke. If the cue ball was in Position B, which is a little close to the middle, use a / tip of inside (left in this position) english. With the cue ball in either position, the cue ball will swing wide of the rack down Line A if you hit the shot too firmly. Don't get greedy by trying to blast open the rack. What you are looking for are a couple of shots that you can work with to spread the rest of the balls.

A Tough Two-Railer

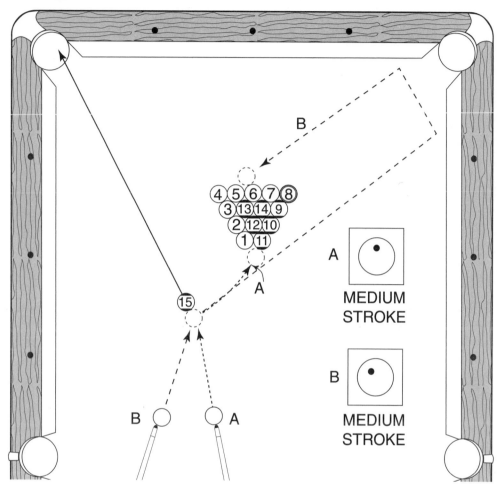

Break shots, like the ones in the illustration, are certainly not the kind that you would want to set up for if given a choice. They usually result from a tough rack where you must make the best of a less than ideal situation.

When the break ball is above the rack, you generally need less of a cut angle than if it was opposite the rack. If your cut angle is too great you may miss the top of the rack altogether. You can hit the rack from Cue Ball A providing you don't shoot excessively hard. Now move over to Cue Ball B and you have no chance of directly contacting the rack. You may still, however, be able to hit the back of the rack by going two-rails with top left english.

To Play or Not to Play

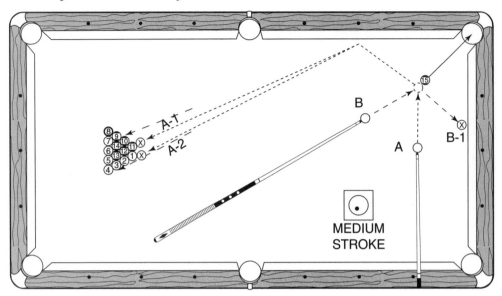

With the 15-ball in the position shown, you could choose to play shape at Position A for a long-distance break shot. When playing shape on long- distance break shots like this, your cut angle must be very precise so that you can play the optimal route down table to the rack. If you miss the ideal angle by just a few inches, it becomes much more difficult, if not impossible, to hit the rack.

In the example, you have a play off the side rail. You want the cue ball to hit the head of the rack on either the 1 or 11-ball. If you hit Side A-1 you might scratch. Should the cue ball skim Side A-2, it would do little damage to the rack. The best strategy may be to play safe when the object ball if at the far end of the table unless, of course, your record run is at stake. From Cue Ball B, it is easy enough to slide over to B-1 for a great safety.

Side Pocket Break Shots

• A Cut Shot From Center Table

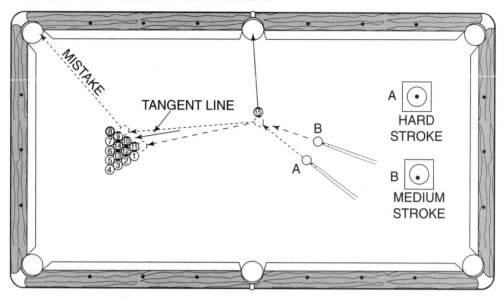

The break shot in the diagram can do some serious damage to the rack. In your excitement to blast open the stack, however, you must remember that contacting the head of the rack is no sure thing. You must cover those 2'+ from the break ball to the rack with great precision.

The key to playing this shot is deciding exactly where you need to strike the cue ball. The first step is to identify the direction of the tangent line. In this case, it is pointing slightly to the right of the head of the rack. With the cue ball at Position A, you should play a stun/draw shot using just a touch of draw. If you over-draw the shot, you'll miss the rack to the left. With the cue ball at Position B, it will hit the rack with plenty of speed using a medium stroke, so you should focus on precision. Resist the temptation to slug the shot.

A Cut Shot from off-Center

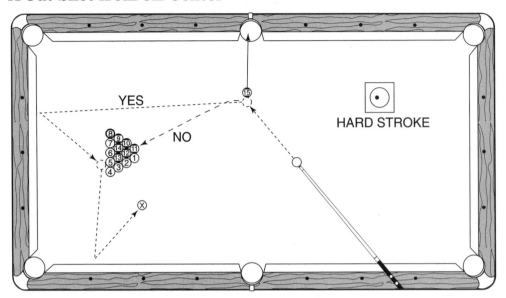

On this break shot it, is very difficult to control the curve of the cue ball. You could easily miss the rack if you tried to hit the head balls. Aiming for the head of the rack also increases the chances of scratching. The diagram shows a lower risk way to play this shot. Use just a1/2 tip of draw and some outside (left) English. The cue ball will spin off the end rail so that it contacts the back of the rack at an angle, then proceed to the side- rail and out as shown.

Side Pocket Hanger #1

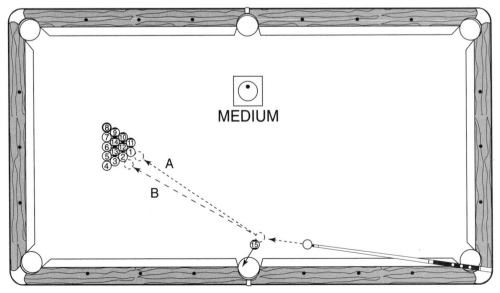

The temptation is to blast the rack apart because the break shot can't be missed. If your have excellent cue ball control, you could aim for the head of the rack down Line A. You could also use a firm follow stroke to send the cue ball down Line B into the side of the rack. The topspin should keep the cue ball from scratching in the lower left corner pocket.

Side Pocket Hanger #2

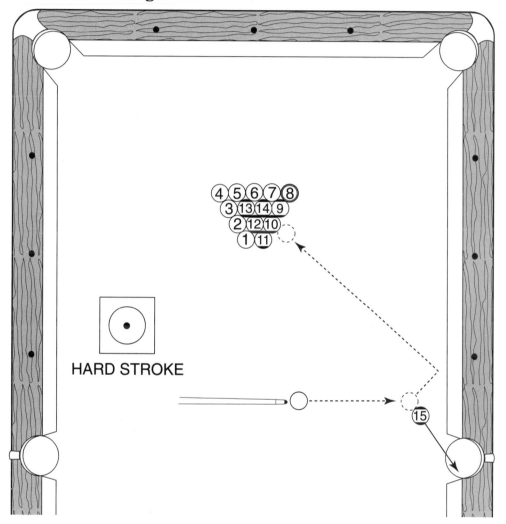

This can be a very effective break shot because the shot is easy and the cue ball will be approaching a big target at a high speed. There is some risk of sticking to the rack, but this can be reduced if you are able to hit the top part of the 11-ball. Naturally this controlled approach to playing the shot increases the chances of missing the top side of the rack. Play the shot with centerball, or slightly below, and a firm stroke.

Back Cut Near the Foot Spot

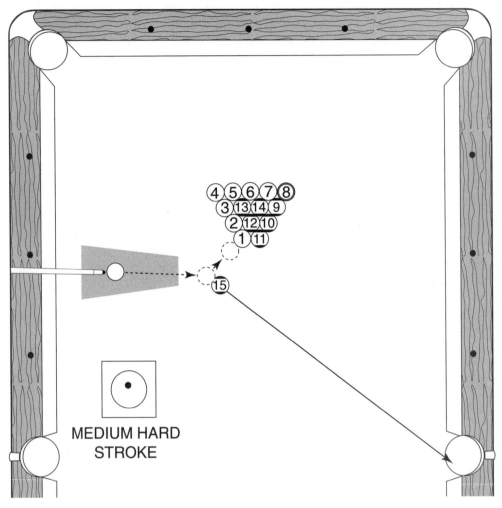

MEDIUM HARD
STROKE

When a ball is located above the rack in the position shown, it can serve as a highly effective side pocket break shot. The main challenge to this shot is getting position on it in the first place. Your ideal position zone is rather small and is not always easily accessible. The best way for getting on this break shot is a key ball that is located a little closer to the rail than the cue ball in the illustration.

The cut angle of the shot in the diagram is about 35 degrees, which is ideal for playing this break shot. If the cut angle is much greater, then you will be faced with a cut shot that does not appear very often, and which is quite difficult for most players. If the cut angle is less than 20 degrees, then it will be tough to control the cue ball and the balls won't open up nearly as well. Strange as it may seem, you must guard against scratching in the upper left corner pocket. It is best to contact the 1-ball slightly to the right of center. Use a medium-firm follow stroke.

Two Rails into the Back of the Rack

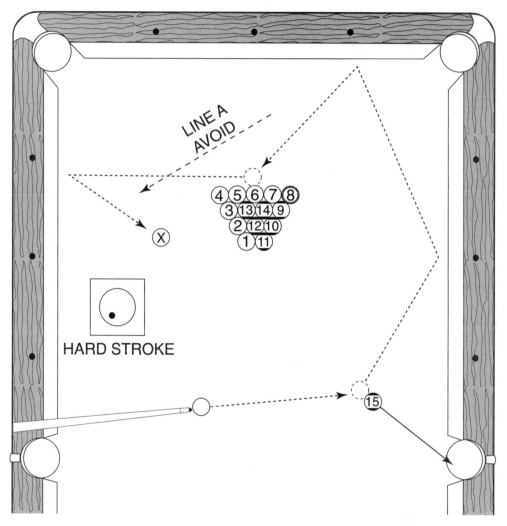

This break shot requires precise routing of the cue ball to hit any of the last three balls. The cue ball will be approaching the back of the rack at an angle, so there should be little chance of sticking to a ball. Use left english so the cue ball will spin towards the first diamond on the end-rail after bouncing off the side-rail. The biggest danger of this shot is swinging wide of the rack down Line A. This will happen if the cue ball hits too high up on the side-rail. You should experiment with this shot from a variety of locations to get a feel for the many routes that can take the cue ball into the back of the rack as shown.

Offbeat Break Shots

Two Rails With Inside Follow

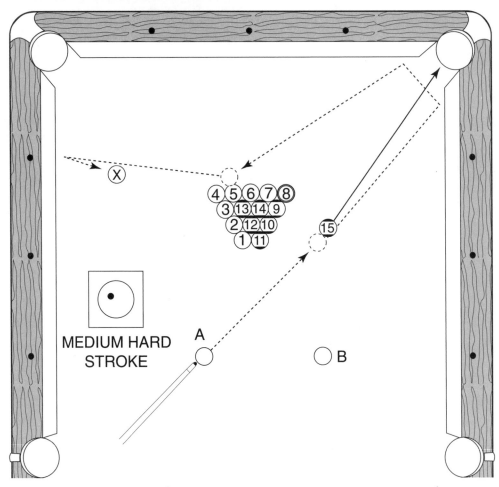

Throughout your Straight Pool career, you will rescue many runs with the surprisingly effective break shot at Position A. This break shot appears when you miss your position on the break shot at Cue Ball B. The two-rail follow shot from Cue Ball A won't exactly tear the rack apart, but it will give you an excellent opportunity to continue your run with another well played shot or two.

You have a very shallow cut angle on the opposite side of the break ball. Use follow with inside english (left in this position) and a medium firm stroke. The cue ball will follow the path shown and make contact with the corner ball.

The key to this shot is execution. Most players have a tendency to over-cut shots when using a firm stroke with inside english because they fail to allow for enough deflection. Remember that you must aim a little further to the left than if you were using follow with no english. Use your smoothest stroke. Also be sure not to twist or tighten your wrist as you go through the shot. Let your cue do the work.

Twice Across the Table

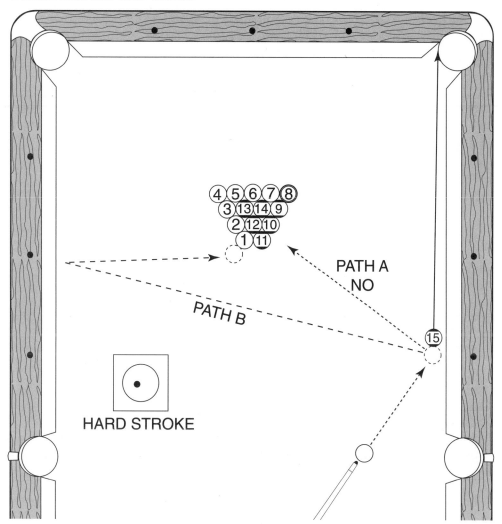

This break shot is a variation of the side-rail break shot I mentioned earlier. You could try sending the cue ball directly into the rack down Path A. However, pocketing the 15-ball on this shot would not be easy because of the amount of inside (left) english that would be required, and you would run the risk of missing the head ball or sticking to the rack. A creative solution is to use a half tip of inside english and a hard stroke. This should send the cue ball across the table down Path B and back into the rack. Hopefully it will hit the upper side of the 1-ball as shown.

Two Draw Shots Into the Rack

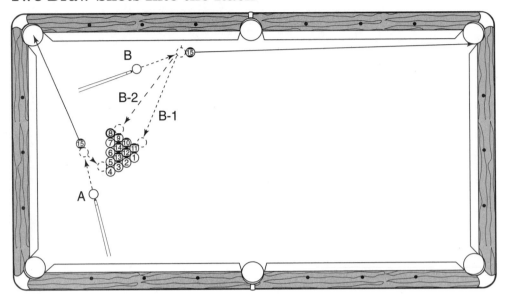

These two shots show that offbeat desperation break shots come in a wide variety of sizes and shapes. In Position A, you can still draw back into the outside edge of the corner ball despite the shallow cut angle. If you are successful, you could peel a few balls from the stack, enough to possibly continue your run

When playing the break shot in Position B the emphasis is on pocketing the ball. You will need to use a hard draw stroke to open the rack. If you have superb cue ball control, you can avoid the risk of sticking to the side of the rack by sending the cue ball into the rack at either Point B-1 or B-2.

Jump Into the Rack Break Shot

All is not necessarily lost when you're too straight on the break shot as shown in the illustration on the next page, providing the break ball is close to the rack. Just jack-up enough so that the cue ball will fly on top of the rack after contacting the 15-ball. The force of impact and the spin on the cue ball will enable the cue ball to burrow into the rack and spread the balls rather nicely.

The key to this break shot is to control the cue ball's flight pattern so that it pockets the 15-ball and has enough elevation to soar into the middle of the rack. You'll want to contact the 15-ball a little above its equator. There is definitely an element of luck to this shot. If the cue ball lands on the side of a ball, you should come away with a shot. However, if the cue ball skims off the top of a ball, it could bounce right off the table.

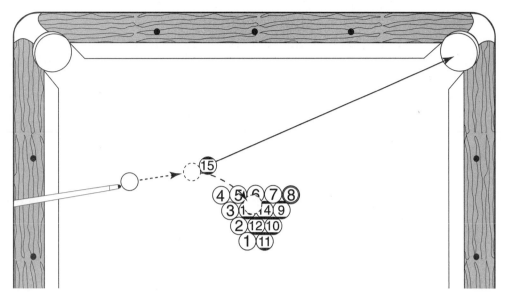

Jump Into the Lower Balls

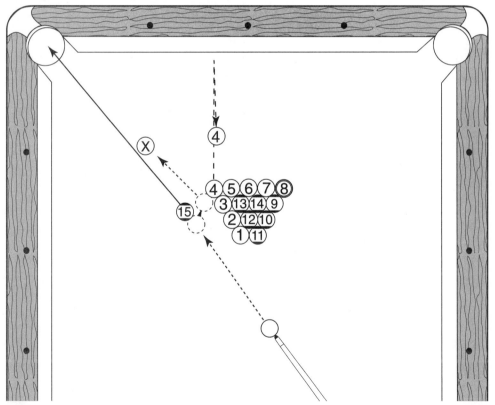

This break shot results from landing on the correct side of the break ball, but with an overly shallow cut angle. You can still knock a few balls out to the lower portion of the table, enough to continue your run. Use a powerful stroke with 1/2 tip of follow. Elevate your bridge so you are hitting slightly down on the cue ball. If all goes well, you could wind up with a secondary break shot like the one on the 4-ball.

Run Saving Odd-Ball Break Shots

The break shots in this section are a series of off-the-wall shots that will occasionally pocket the called ball, thus enabling you to continue your run. You should only consider playing these when your record run is at stake in practice, in a friendly game when you are not overly concerned about the outcome, or when your opponent is not likely to run more than a few balls should you miss the shot. Do not, I repeat, do not even think of playing these in serious competition. I will give you some advice on how to play these shots, but in all honesty the primary ingredient is luck. They do work sometimes (maybe 10% -20%) and they give you a better chance of making a ball than randomly picking a ball in the rack and blasting away.

Corner Ball Cross Side

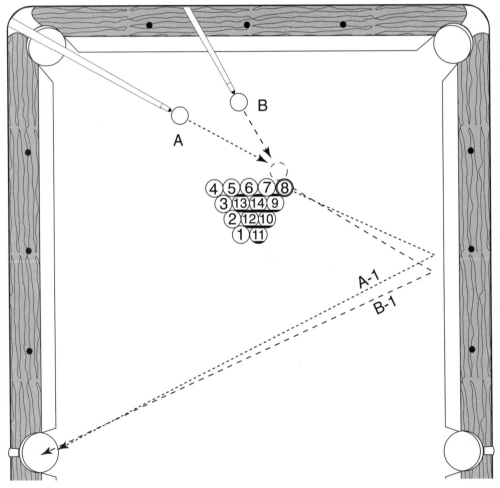

This rack shot goes a surprisingly high percentage of the time. From Position A, use left (outside) english and a medium hard stroke. With the cue ball in Position B you should now use right (inside) english and a medium hard stroke.

Top Ball Cross-Side

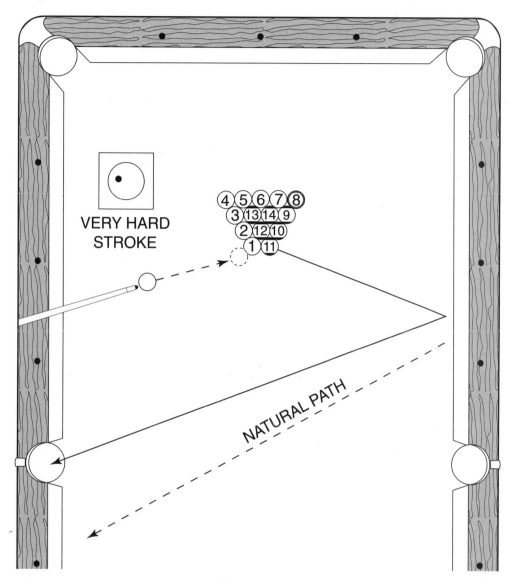

This is definitely a low percentage shot, but it does go occasionally. The problem lies in overcoming the natural path of the 11-ball when the rack is hit as shown. The 11-ball will usually head for a spot on the side-rail well past the side pocket. You must force the 11-ball to hit the rail farther down from the side pocket. Use a very hard stroke with left english and cut the 1-ball a little right of center. Good luck.

Long-Rail Corner Ball Bank Shot

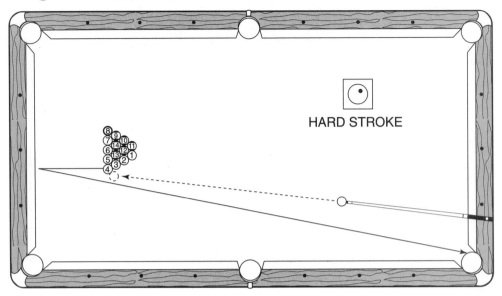

This shot is living proof that english on the cue ball is transferred to the object ball to a meaningful degree. Hit the cue ball with right (inside) english and the 4-ball will spin off the end-rail and travel towards the distant corner pocket. A top player told me that he expects to make this shot 30-40% of the time but would never, of course, shoot it in serious competition.

Carom off the Rack

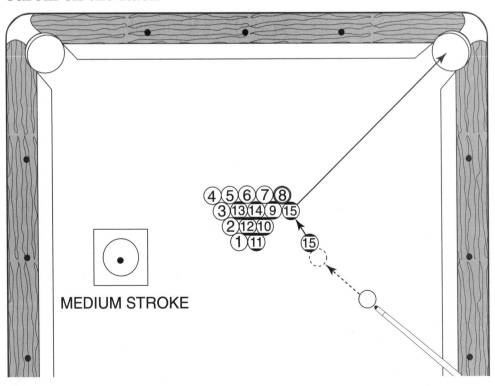

You have unfortunately missed position on the break shot in the illustration on the previous page. You do have a potentially run saving shot, which is bound to create some excitement because it almost always scares the pocket even when it doesn't go. Your target is the crack between the 8 and 9-balls. Use a medium speed of stroke with draw. You will open the rack on this shot, which is an added bonus assuming, of course, that you make the shot.

Two Rails After a Side Pocket Bank

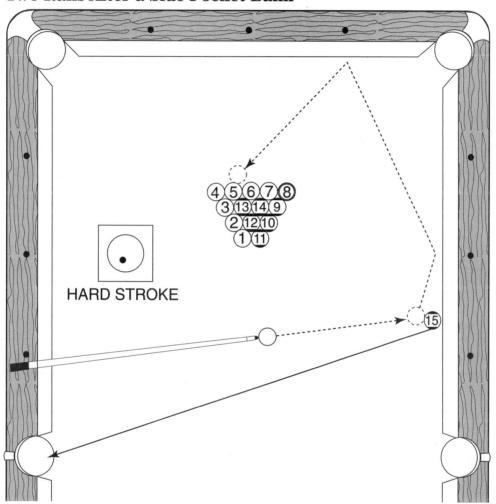

Nine-Ball players will love this shot. The bank shot is not too difficult on the 15-ball and you have a natural two-rail route into the back of the rack. The cue ball will be approaching the rack from an angle, so it there is little risk of sticking to the side of the stack. Use low left english and a hard stroke.

• The Opening Break Shot

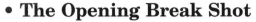

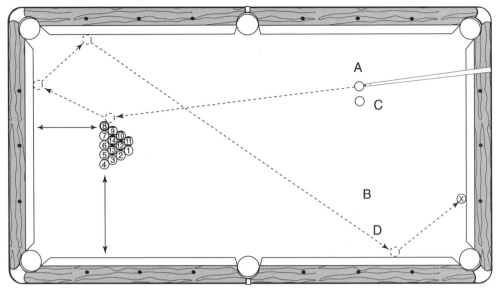

Since the odds of calling and pocketing a ball out of the rack are very slim, the opening shot of a game of Straight Pool is a defensive maneuver designed to give your opponent little, if anything, to shoot at. You don't want to offer your opponent a shot which could swing the early momentum in their favor. As a matter of record, in top-level competition, players have run 150 balls and out after the opening break while never giving their opponent a single offensive turn at the table!

You must play the opening break from behind the head string. You are required to drive at least two balls to the rail or else you lose two points (your score would be –2). If you fail to meet the requirements of the opening break, your opponent has the option of accepting the table or having you break again. You must continue in this fashion until you either make a legal break or your opponent accepts the table. If you drive two balls or more to the rail, but scratch, you lose one point and your opponent has cue-ball-in-hand behind the head string.

The diagram shows an opening break shot. The recommended position for the cue ball is one diamond in from the side rail. Some players favor Position A, while others prefer the other side of the table at Position B. There are also many players who feel they get better results by placing the cue ball a little further towards the middle, such as at Position C. Righthanders prefer Position A, while lefties like Position B.

The goal of the perfect break shot is to drive the two corner balls to the rail and back to their original positions. You should aim to hit about 1/3 of the corner ball. Use a medium speed stroke and cue slightly above center with a half tip of outside english. The cue ball will follow the path indicated on the diagram and ideally come to a stop at Position X.

One common mistake on the opening break is to hit the corner ball too thinly, which could fail to drive two balls to the rail. The opposite mistake is to hit the corner ball too full. You should balance the cost of making either error. Losing two points by failing to drive two balls to the rail is not that much of a penalty, especially if you are trying to keep a strong player from beginning a run on their opening inning. If you hit the corner ball too full, two bad things will happen: more balls will break loose, and the cue ball will not travel as far up the table. Position D shows a likely spot where the cue ball may come to rest if you hit too much of the corner ball. Because the opening break is such an important shot, you should devote at least a small part of your practice time to it.

• Determining Who Breaks

You can toss a coin to determine who breaks, but the method used in championship play is to lag for the break. The winner of the lag almost always elects to have their opponent shoot first, however, there can be exceptions depending on the conditions and the level of your opponent's game. For example, if the table is slow, the pockets are tight, and your opponent is weak at long shots, you may be wise to shoot the opening break. Because the lag shot plays such a critical role at the start of the game, you should practice lagging to develop a touch that can consistently leave the cue ball within a few inches or less of the head rail.

The lag is the only shot in pool where both you and your opponent are at the table shooting at the same time. There can be an element of gamesmanship during the lag. The rules state that you and your opponent are both supposed to lag at the same time. You could feel a little rushed if your opponent quickly plays their lag shot. On a delicate shot such as the lag, you don't want to feel rushed. I suggest you develop a routine for playing it quickly and efficiently. If you can be the one to pull the trigger first, you may gain an important edge in playing the lag. While on the subject of gamesmanship, it might not hurt to do an inspection of the rack before breaking the balls.

CHAPTER 6

How to Run a Rack

The 3 Phases of a Rack and Pattern Play in Action

I have covered the components of playing Straight Pool such as position play, pattern play and breaking clusters in previous chapters. This chapter shows you how to put those lessons to work. In the process, you will learn how to think your way through a rack. Before we begin, it is important for you to develop the proper mindset for playing Straight Pool. I recommend that you look at each rack as a puzzle that needs to be solved. Enjoy the challenge of creating a plan of attack for dealing with any and all problems, and relish the opportunity to put your plans into action.

The Three Phases of a Rack

You can simplify the process of shot selection in a rack of Straight Pool by recognizing the three segments of a typical rack: beginning, middle, and end. There are no hard and fast rules as to when one segment ends and another begins. For practical purposes, however, you can figure that each segment is about 4-5 balls.

There are certain objectives that should be met within each segment. In phase one, for example, you'll want to clear some balls and set up a secondary break shot. In phase two you might need to manufacture a break shot or break open a cluster on the rail. And in the final phase, you will likely be executing a precise pattern as you hone in on the key ball.

There will often be some overlap between the segments. It is important for you to note when you are in the transition from one phase to the next. We'll delve into the three phases in a moment, and analyze a couple of complete racks.

Phase 1   The Beginning - Balls 1-4

Before playing some break shots, you can actually begin thinking about position because of the their high degree of predictability. For practical purposes, however, we will begin the planning process by assuming the rack has already been opened.

Post Break Shot Analysis

After the balls have been broken, it is time to analyze what kind of rack you are dealing with and to develop a plan of attack. There are several main categories of layouts. They include:

Wide Open Racks

- The balls are wide open and there are no serious problems. This kind of layout is the closest thing to a breather in Straight Pool. Nevertheless, you still need to avoid knocking balls around and creating problems where none exist.
- The balls are mostly wide open, but there is a problem of two that needs to be solved when the timing is right.

Partially Open Racks

- The rack is partially open, but there are no major problems. The main concern is when and how you will break the rest of the rack apart.
- The rack is partially open and you have some problems outside of the triangle. Now you must plan how to open the rest of the rack while keeping in mind that there are some other problems that must be dealt with when the timing is right.

The Rack Has Been Barely Broken

- A few balls have broken loose, but you have a fairly clear-cut course to a secondary break shot. You will need to re-analyze the rack again once you've played the secondary break shot.
- A few balls have broken loose, but it's going to take a special effort to open the rest of the balls and keep your run alive. This is the kind of rack where survival is your first concern.

Planning Your Attack

After you have done a quick appraisal of the type of layout you have before you, it's time to devise a plan for the start of Phase 1.

   1] What shot(s) are available?

   2] What is the primary goal for the first shot? Answering this question will help you to select the best first shot.

   3] What's going to be your second shot? Some possibilities include:

- A secondary break shot.
- Another ball to be cleared prior to breaking a cluster.
- An insurance ball after breaking a cluster.
- A cluster break.

Possible Goals for the First Shot and for Phase 1
- Make a shot and get in play with the rack, especially if you are left with a tough first shot.
- Simplify the table by clearing a few balls prior to playing a secondary break shot.
- Clear one or more pockets.
- Choose and play a secondary break shot right away. Look for an insurance ball.
- Playing shape on a secondary break shot.
- Open a cluster.
- Take care of any other problems, such as a ball on the end rail.

Taking a few moments to consider the factors above is much more productive than just firing away at open shots. Thinking like a Straight Pool player will get you involved with the rack and its particular set of challenges right from the very start. Once you get past the first shot, or first few shots, you will need to re-assess the layout because a number of balls may now be in new positions.

Phase 2 - The Middle – Balls 5-9
During this stage you need to finish opening up any clusters and take care of most, if not all, of your problems. By the time Phase 2 is complete, all of the balls should be in the clear so you can focus on pattern play in Phase 3.

The Primary Activities in Phase 2
- Playing secondary break shots. Look for an insurance ball for the break shot.
- Continue to open pockets as needed.
- Planning for and clearing trouble spots.
- Choosing the break shot and key ball for the next rack.
- Selecting a key ball to the key ball.
- Manufacturing a break shot if needed. Also consider creating a second break shot.
- Manufacturing a key ball if needed.
- Eliminate balls at the far end of the table.
- Separate clusters.
- Setting up the rack for the last five balls.

While operating in the middle portion of the rack, you will often have several open shots. Nevertheless, you shouldn't get complacent. You'll always do better if you have a specific ball in mind for your next shot. I advise that you resist the temptation to play shape on several balls.

Mid-rack play features many changes in plans as the balls are moved around, or you miss position. So don't hesitate to adopt a Plan B if you're shape is a little off and another shot becomes the better choice. Even though you need to open the rack, that doesn't mean you should move balls unnecessarily. There's perhaps no bigger blunder than to create clusters once the balls are spread.

Phase 3 - The End - Balls 10-14

Your hard work will hopefully be over by the time you get down to the last 4 to 5 balls. When you enter Phase 3, the balls should all be separated. You should have a primary break shot, and perhaps a back-up break shot as well. In addition, there should be a key ball for getting on the break ball, and a ball that enables you to get on the key ball without too much trouble (a key ball to the key ball). When the balls are lying good, your primary tasks are to identify the best pattern or sequence of shots and then execute your position plays with precision. I recommend that you use the Process of Elimination method from Chapter 2 for planning your end-of-rack patterns. Decide what ball you're going to shoot first, which ones you're going to save for last, and then tie the two ends together with the shot(s) that link the beginning and end together.

As you proceed through an end-of-rack pattern, your position should be getting tighter with each shot. By minimizing or eliminating cue ball movement with stop shots or short-distance draw or follow shots, you can maximize you chances of getting perfect position on the break shot.

There will, of course, be many exceptions to the ideal scenario outlined above. When problems linger into Phase 3, your inning is in danger. You must be willing to slow down for a moment or two and come up with a creative solution. At times you will be required to raise your level of execution. You may, for example, need to play a long distance Nine-Ball type of position play to a Straight Pool sized position zone for shape on the break ball. The activities you will typically encounter in Phase 3 include:
- Basic pattern play leading up to the break ball.
- Breaking a troublesome cluster if needed.
- Cleaning up a ball or two from the far end of the table if necessary.
- Manufacturing a break shot if necessary.

A Blueprint for Running a Rack

The process for running a rack of Straight Pool is summarized below. You must make plans and execute them as well as possible. You must be able to constantly adapt to the many changes in the layout as balls are pocketed and moved about the table. In short, you've got to learn to think on your feet.

- Read the table after the balls have been broken.
- Devise a plan.
- Execute your plan.
- Be aware of the three phases so you can correctly plot your strategy. Shift gears from one segment to the next.
- Revise your plans as dictated by 1] the balls, 2] your execution. Develop a Plan B, or even Plan C, mentality. Always proceed based on what the table says now, not on what you planned to do before your execution changed things.
- Recognize problems (clusters, balls on the rail, etc.) and have a plan for solving them. Timing is key, but earlier is generally better.
- Take notice of the subtle challenges that can easily end a run if not dealt with correctly.
- Identify the common patterns which can help you choose the correct sequence for running the balls.
- Recognize when you can pick up the pace a little on easy layouts, as this develops rhythm, but don't get careless with either your planning or execution.
- There is no single right way to run a rack. Develop your own style. Your approach to running racks must meet one acid test: do you consistently get good shape on your break shots with a minimum of end-of-rack heroics?

• The Three Most Important Shots in Straight Pool

Every shot is important, but three particular shots stand out in most racks as being crucial to extending your run. Each therefore requires that little extra effort that ensures that you play them correctly. The three shots are:

- The key ball
- The break shot
- The shot after the break shot

- **The Stoplight Analogy**

As you proceed through a rack, you will develop a sense of the difficulty of the layout. If you have no problems, you can emphasize execution. But if you have problems that need to be solved, you will have to slow down a little and work out a solution for each one. The stoplight analogy may be useful in conceptualizing which kind of rack you are dealing with.

- **Green Light**. Everything is a go. Plan and execute several balls at a time. Concentrate on execution.
- **Yellow Light**. There is some work to be done, but the problems can be solved without too much trouble. This is typically the condition of most racks in Phases 1 and 2.
- **Red Light** Your run will most definitely end if certain problems are not solved which are far from routine. Creativity, planning and execution are all crucial to getting past a red light rack.

- **Problems that Appear Regularly**

While assessing the table, you will regularly encounter one or more of the problems from the list that follows. Learn to recognize each one as it appears, then develop a plan for systematically dealing with the problem.

- The tough shot that can't be avoided.
- Clusters.
- Unpredictable secondary break shots.
- No break ball.
- Stragglers at the far end of the table.
- Clusters at the end of the table can be especially troublesome.
- Balls on the rail.
- Ball frozen near the side pocket.
- No key ball, which means you'll have to play excellent shape to get on the break ball.

Run Out #1

Introduction

Now let's proceed together through a couple of racks of Straight Pool in which we'll discuss the three phases and point out the key concepts that apply to each shot. My goal is to have you thinking your way through a rack like a Straight Pool player. Before reading my explanation, try to analyze the layouts based on what you already know from reading the previous chapters, and/or your experience playing the game. You might try labeling the balls, such as the key ball, break ball, clusters and so forth. **Key concepts** from previous chapters are **in bold type**. The break shot has just been played and it's your shot.

Post Break Shot Analysis

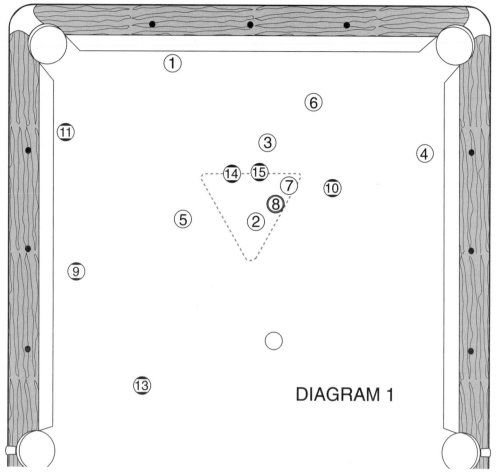

DIAGRAM 1

The balls are reasonably well spread, but the rack must still be handled with care. You have three potential shots, the 11, 4, or 13-ball. This rack demonstrates right away that there is more than one possible pattern, as is the case for most racks. Your need to sift through the options and pick the sequence you feel the most confidence in. Although the 11-ball goes, the 5-ball disrupts your vision slightly, just enough to possibly cause a miss. The 13-ball is a potential **key ball** for a break ball, or an **access ball** to the troublesome 9-ball. The 4-ball is a **useless ball on the rail**. The 4-ball is also an easy shot that enables you to play **two-way position** for either the 6-ball or 1-ball.

At this point, you have several **secondary break shots,** including the 3, 10, and 5-balls. The cluster in the area of the triangle is partially separated and can be broken with a controlled secondary break shot. Since there is no rush to re-break the remaining cluster, the wise thing to do is to **clear off some balls** and **eliminate some problems.** In actual practice, this post-break analysis of the rack takes but a few moments once you know what to look for, and have enough experience at evaluating racks. Now that our analysis is complete, it's time to start running balls.

Diagram #2   Phase #1

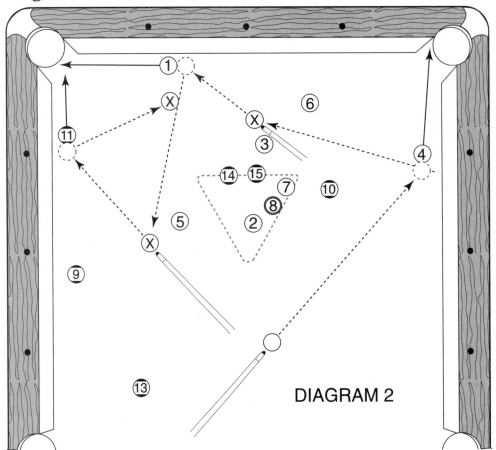

DIAGRAM 2

Ball 1: The first shot is the break shot, which has already been played.

Ball 2: Cut in the 4-ball and drift over for **two-way shape** on either the 1-ball or 6-ball.

Ball 3: You've got good position for both balls. The 1-ball is the better choice as it allows you to follow up the table for the 11-ball next. Play the 1-ball with a half tip of high left english. Shooting the 11-ball now **removes another ball from the rail** and **clears the pocket** for **long side shape** on the 9-ball.

Ball 4: You're now going to finish **clearing balls off the rail** and get ready for a **secondary break shot**. Play the 11-ball with a soft follow stroke with a quarter tip of right english. Use just enough spin to give you a shallow cut angle on the 6-ball. The 11-ball is a simple shot that can get you into trouble if you are not careful. Use too much english, and you will have a sharp cut angle on the 6-ball. Problems could also arise from getting too straight on the 6-ball as a result of not using english.

The Lesson: Never forget that Straight Pool is a game that's largely composed of simple looking little shots than can quickly destroy your pattern if misplayed.

Diagram #3   Entering Phase 2

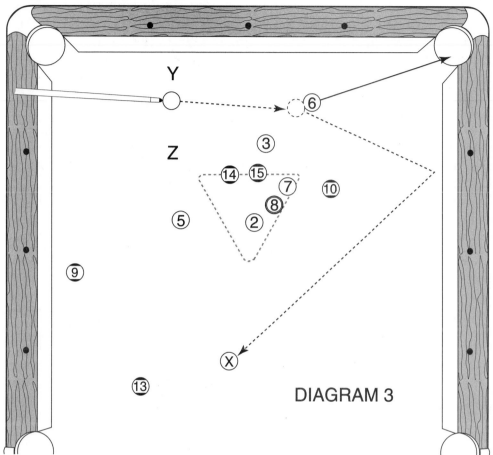

DIAGRAM 3

Analysis: Take a moment to compare the layouts in diagrams 1 and 3. Notice how the table is a lot less cluttered and how several useless or problem balls have been eliminated. By clearing out the 4, 1, and 11-balls and, in a moment, the 6-ball, you have made room for other balls from the cluster. In addition, you've also opened up traveling lanes for the cue ball.

The Lesson: It is often a good idea to simplify the layout as much as possible before playing a secondary break shot.

Ball 5: You've got perfect shape on the 6-ball. It's now time to **return to the center of the table** for the secondary break shot. (Note the troubles you would have encountered if you had missed shape on the 6-ball and wound up at either Position Y or Z.) The 6-ball was shot with follow and the cue ball landed at Position A. Your **speed was perfect** and you have great position for a **secondary break** shot on the 5-ball. Your position was **somewhat lucky** as the cue ball was **traveling across the position zone** for the 5-ball and it happened to stop just where you needed it. The 6-ball was a **three-way shot**. If you missed position on the 5-ball, you could have opted for **Plan B**, which was to use the 13-ball to get on the 5-ball. **Plan C** was to play the 10-ball and 13-ball to get a workable angle on the 5-ball.

Diagram #4 Phase 2 Continued

Analysis: The 5-ball could have been an excellent **break ball** for the next rack. The 13-ball was well positioned as a **key ball** to the 5-ball. But you're still early in this rack, so you have time to come up with another break shot. There is an urgent need to **separate the cluster,** and the 5-ball is best suited for the job. It might be tempting to first remove the ball on the rail (the 9-ball). Since you no longer need the 13-ball as a key ball, you could play the 13-ball now, follow over for the 9-ball, and come back out to Position A for the 5-ball. There is, however a major flaw with this pattern: it would be difficult to re-establish the perfect position you've got on the 5-ball now by shooting a ball as close to the rail as the 9-ball.

Lesson #1: Don't try to play position when you already have it.

Lesson #2: Solve problems when it's convenient <u>and</u> when the timing is right. (Note: the 13-ball is an excellent **access ball** to the 9-ball for later in the rack.)

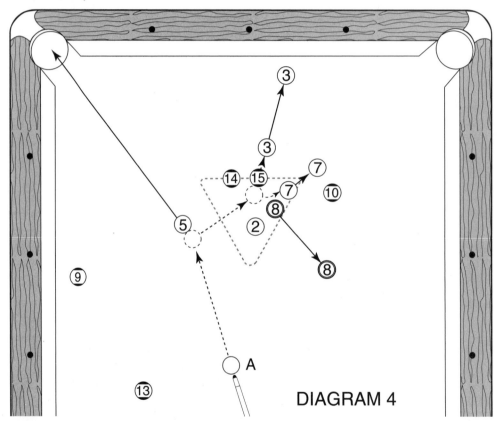

DIAGRAM 4

Ball 6: When the break ball is more than a few inches from the cluster and you have a relatively shallow cut angle, you can **adjust your path into the cluster** with great precision. Such is the case with the 5-ball. Take a moment to view the cue ball's path into the cluster down the tangent line, which is at position B, then make any adjustments in cueing that are necessary.

After inspecting the path of entry, you've decided to draw above the 14-ball and contact the 13, 8, and 7- balls. The 14-ball will serve as your **insurance ball**, even though it does not appear so obviously suited to the task at this moment.

Analysis: The rack has spread nicely and you are now in the later part of Phase 2. The 9-ball is still a minor problem. You have several possible **break balls**, including the 15, 10, and 8-ball.

Diagram 5   Ending Phase 2

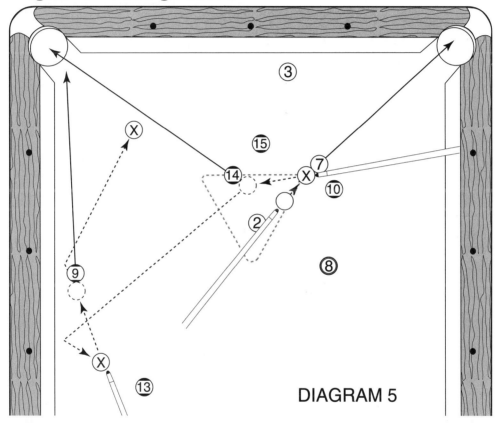

DIAGRAM 5

Ball 7: The 7-ball serves no purpose, so play it now with a **stop shot**.

Ball 8: The 14-ball was your **insurance ball** on the secondary break shot, but you chose to shoot it after playing the 7-ball first. You've got an ideal angle to float over for the 9-ball, which will **remove a ball from the rail**. Balls high up on the side-rail can be particularly troublesome late in a rack unless they serve some useful purpose, such as a key ball.

Ball 9: You could play the 13-ball now, but the cut angle is just a little steep. Besides, the 13-ball may come in handy later as a **Plan B** ball. Use follow with a quarter tip of right english to get position on the 3-ball on the bottom rail.

Diagram #6 Start of Phase 3

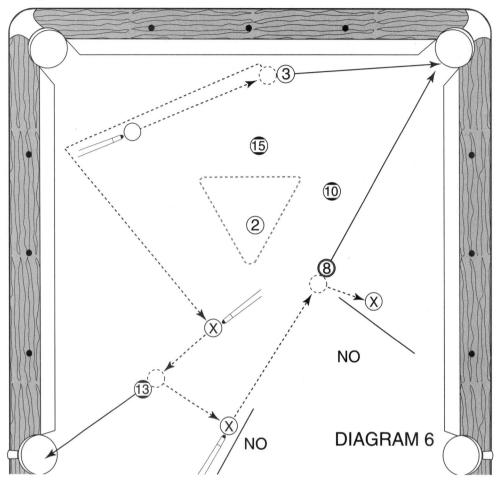

DIAGRAM 6

Analysis: The boundaries of **the three phases** can be a little arbitrary at times, especially when you are **in transition** from one phase to the next. With five balls left and all problems solved, you are now definitely in the early stages of Phase 3. From this point on it's all about **pattern recognition**, execution, and staying out of trouble. Here's the plan: play two-rail shape off the 3-ball for either the 2-ball or 13-ball. The 10-ball is your **key ball** for the 15-ball, which should be your **break shot**. Although the 8-ball is a potential **break ball**, it's a little above the rack and it doesn't have a key ball that is nearly in as good position as the 10-ball is for the 15-ball. (Take a moment to examine the position. Do you agree with this pattern, or do you have one you like better, and if so, why?)

Ball 10: The 3-ball is the last **multiple option ball** if all turns out as planned. If the cue ball had stopped short of Position A, you could still play the 13-ball in the far corner, or the 2-ball into the upper left corner pocket, but the cue ball came to rest at Position A. Now you're going to play the 13-ball into the side. At this point, the pattern for the final four balls is set: 13, 8, 2, 10, break with the 15-ball.

From here on you have short distance position plays. On each one, the goal is to have a small cut angle on **the right side of the object ball**. This concept is extremely important as it appears with great frequency at the end of Phase 3.

Ball 11: Play the 13-ball with draw. Make sure not to **cross over the line** as shown or you'll be on **the wrong side** of the 8-ball. Leave a little **margin for error** as shown in the illustration. Perfect.

Ball 12: The 8-ball is a longer version of the previous shot. Use draw with a medium soft stroke. Make sure not to draw back **above and across the line** (Note: if you had left a larger cut angle on the 8-ball, you would have had to send the cue ball to the side rail and back out.)

Diagram #7   Ending Phase 3

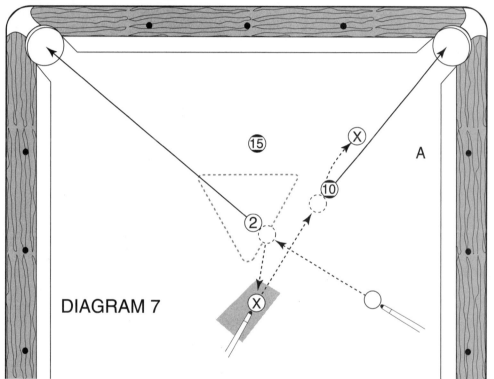

DIAGRAM 7

Now you're in the home stretch. Still, this is absolutely, positively no time to let up as it becomes increasingly difficult, if not impossible to cover your mistakes in the later stages of Phase 3. **Stay focused** 100% on perfectly executing these two simple, but extremely critical shots.

Ball 13: Before shooting the 2-ball, **survey the table** from Position A to determine where you want the cue ball for the 10-ball. Anywhere in the **position zone** would be ideal. There are a number of ways for getting on the 15-ball from outside of the position zone. At this stage of the rack, you want to **minimize cue ball movement** while at the same time maximizing your chances of getting ideal shape on the break shot.

Ball 14: You have excellent position on the 10-ball. Now all you have to do is use a **soft follow stroke** and ease the cue ball down for a **behind-the-rack break shot**.

Run Out #2
Diagram 1 Beginning of Phase 1

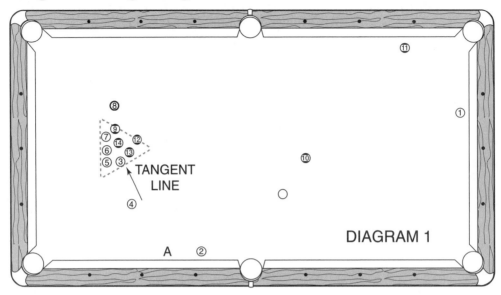

Analysis: This layout is completely different from the last rack due, in no small part, to the fact that you have played a behind-the-rack break shot. There are plenty of problems to be solved but, as the rolls would have it, some potential solutions.

The 11-ball is an **access ball** to the troublesome 1-ball at the far end of the table. You could play the 10-ball, then the 11-ball, which would enable you to get rid of the 1-ball on the far end rail. But these balls are minor concerns compared to the urgency to break open the cluster in the area of the triangle. Your decision to open the cluster this soon after a break shot is based on four factors: 1] you have perfect shape on the 4-ball to play a controlled break shot, 2] there are no other **secondary break balls** available, since the 8-ball is positioned too low to the cluster, 3] you have open spaces for the balls in the cluster at this end of the table, and 4] the distant 11-ball is close enough to the pocket to serve as an **insurance ball**, with the 10-ball as a secondary insurance ball.

The Lesson: Pool is full of exceptions to the rule. In our example you're going to rebreak the balls immediately after the break shot. Under "normal" circumstances a secondary break shot might not be played until several shots later. As you'll recall, the secondary break in the first rack did not occur until the sixth shot. You've got to play the hand you're dealt. Now get ready to bust the stack.

Diagram #1 (Continued) Phase 1

Ball 2: Before busting open the balls, you should take a moment to examine the **point of entry** into the rack. Altering the contact point on a break shot can significantly improve your results. From Position A you can see the cue ball will strike the 3-ball if it **travels down the tangent line**. Since the 4-ball is nearly 3 feet from the cue ball, it will be hard to hit this target exactly. Furthermore, you don't want to hit the lower half of the 3-ball since you could then easily **lose control of the cue ball**. The best course is to draw into the 13-ball. The 13-ball will proceed into the 6-7-9-14-ball part of the cluster while the cue ball will collide next with the 12-ball. Under a worst-case scenario, you should have a shot on the 11-ball.

The Lesson: Breaking clusters with a precise point of entry can greatly reduce risk.

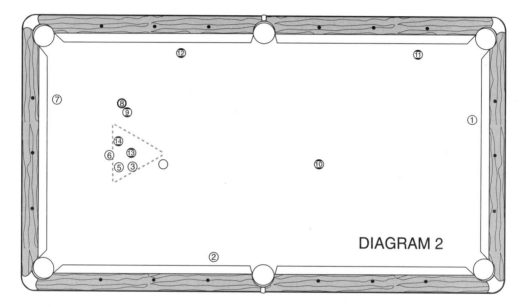

DIAGRAM 2

The balls loosened up somewhat but, as is often the case, you didn't get all you wanted from the break shot. But you can continue your run, which is the main thing. You can shoot the 11-ball, which was your **insurance ball**. Luckily enough, you've also got a **dead billiard** on the 3-ball off the 13-ball. The challenge is in hitting it precisely while using the **mechanical bridge**. Which shot to play next is somewhat of a **judgment call**. You could choose a long shot, or short shot with the bridge, which could be missed if you inadvertently put english on the "dead shot" (Note: the graveyards of pool are filled with players who managed to somehow miss "dead shots"). As part of your post break inspection, observe that the 13-5 combo and 14-6 combo are available. The 8-9 cluster which could also offer you an opportunity in the near future.

Diagram #3 Phase 1 Continued

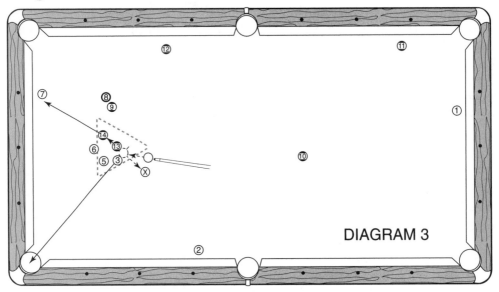

DIAGRAM 3

Ball 3: The shot is the 3-ball, which should be played with straight draw and no english. Use a **short stroke** for accuracy. Although the distant 11-ball once again is available as an **insurance ball**, you really shouldn't need it since you were expecting a shot from either the 13-ball or 5-ball.

The Lesson: As clusters get smaller and your contact points become highly predictable, you can often begin to play shape on balls you are about to break open.

Analysis: The complexion of the rack is changing rapidly (compare diagrams 1 and 2, and diagrams 2 and 3). While the balls have opened nicely, there are still several issues to be dealt with, most notably the 8-9 cluster and the balls at the far end of the table. But **first things first**, which is to play the 13-ball to its full advantage. As part of your inspection, perhaps you noticed that the 14-ball goes past the 7-ball.

Diagram #4 The Beginning of Phase 2

Ball 4: The 13-ball is one of those innocent looking shots that's full of danger if not played correctly. Your objective is to **bump** the 6-ball a few inches towards the rail and keep it out of the way of the 14-ball, which comes next. The shot calls for a follow stroke so soft that the object ball will reach the pocket with about 3" of rolling distance to spare. It would be a big mistake to draw the cue ball ever so slightly, so that it contacts the 5-ball and ends up behind the 6-ball.

The Lesson: Short shots in close quarters look easy, but are often filled with risk. Proceed with care.

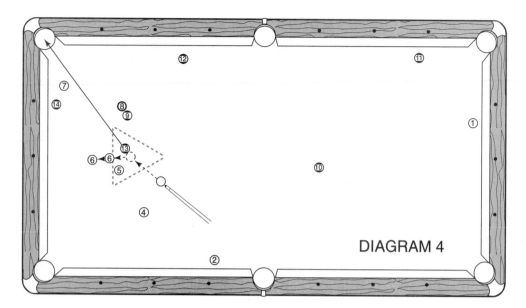

Diagram #5 Phase 2 Continued

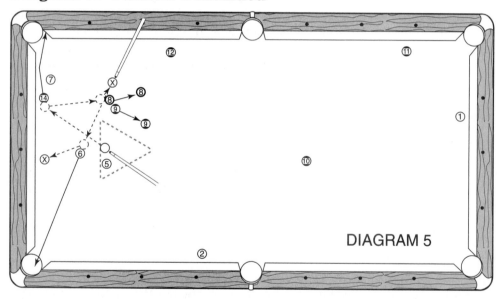

Ball 5: The play now is to **lag** the 14-ball gently into the corner. **Cheat the pocket** as a safeguard against running into the 7-ball. Your goal should be to separate the 8-9 **cluster**. In the process you can **manufacture two break balls** by hitting the 8-ball slightly left of center. The pattern suggests that you clear the area of the 6 and 7-balls next. The 7-ball is your **linking ball** to the **center of the table**.

Ball 6: It would be hard for you to go wrong on the 6-ball. A soft follow shot will give you an **ideal cut angle** for the 7-ball. The 6-ball is somewhat of a breather. Still, you wouldn't want to follow too far and leave yourself straight in on the 7-ball.

Diagram #6 Phase 2 Continued

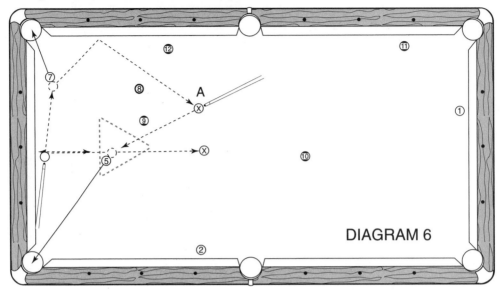

DIAGRAM 6

Analysis: You're at that critical juncture where there are several potential game plans for running the rest of the rack. A few things, though are certain at this point:

1] You need to still **chase down a few balls**, including the 10, 11, and 1-ball, as well as the 2-ball, resting in a troublesome position high up on the side rail.

2] Either the 8-ball or 9-ball is the **break ball**.

3] The 5-ball or 12-ball are potential **key balls**, as is the 8-ball for the 9-ball. The 9-ball could also act as a key ball for the 8-ball.

4] All plans at this point are subject to revision and entirely changeable. You have so many choices. Sometimes the best course of action is to play the shot you have and **let the result help determine your pattern**. In our example, after playing the 7-ball and **returning to the center** area of the table, you should have an even better handle on which way you want to go next.

Ball 7: You've played the 7-ball off the side-rail and out to Position A. If you had gone a little farther, you could have chosen the 10-11-1-2 for your next four shots. But in this position you are better off **letting the shot determine the pattern**.

Ball 8: You will need to use a quarter tip of left english when playing the 5-ball for position on the 9-ball.

Diagram #7 The End of Phase 2

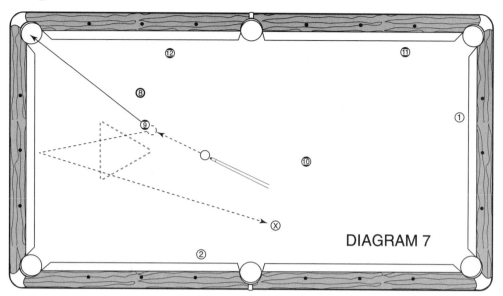

Ball 9: You've made a decision to remove the 9-ball now, which is one of your break balls. This decision is based on the fact that the 12-ball is a better **key ball** to the 8-ball. In addition you can now use a Nine-Ball type shot to get rid of the 2-ball next. The 9-ball is perhaps the most challenging shot of the entire rack as it must be played with a medium firm stroke to a distant position zone. You need to **keep the cue ball off the rail** and **avoid a scratch** in the side, which can be accomplished by **allowing for a margin for error** (away from the rail and the side pocket). This is the kind of shot where you could easily revert to a **Plan B** if you failed to get good shape on the 2-ball. Plan B could lead to either the 10-ball or 1-ball next.

Diagram #8   Phase 3

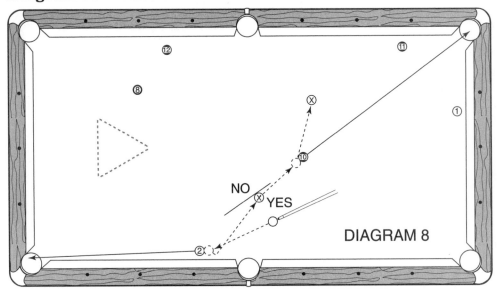

DIAGRAM 8

Analysis: You played a great shot on the 9-ball (with a little luck). As a result, you can now play the remainder of the rack with a specific pattern in mind. It's all about execution. The key is to get on the right side of the 10-ball. If that's done, the last four balls will fall perfectly in line.

Ball 10: A smooth draw stroke using a half tip of left english when playing the 2-ball will help keep the cue ball on the **right side** of the 10-ball.

Ball 11: You landed on the **right side** for the 10-ball. It should be all downhill from here. The pattern for the last four balls, barring any major mishaps, is etched in stone. When you have a pattern that allows for a fair amount of deviation from perfection, you can focus nearly 100% of your attention on execution. The thinking has been done, and there is little chance that you'll have to adjust your plans at this stage of a layout, such as the one we're facing. Now for the 10-ball. A medium soft follow shot will send the cue ball over for an **ideal angle** on the 11-ball.

Diagram #9   The End of Phase 3

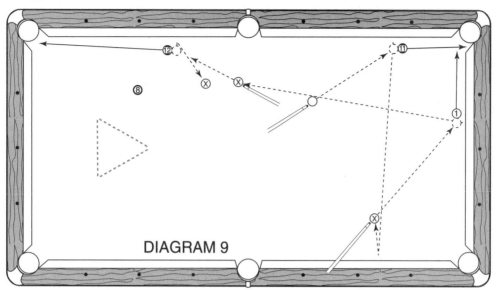

DIAGRAM 9

Ball 12: The 11-ball is the **access ball** to the **key ball to the key ball**. Use a centerball hit to send the cue ball across the table and back out for the 1-ball. It is easier to judge your speed on a shot like this by going to the rail and out.

Ball 13: The shot you're about to play will make you happy that you did-n't clear the 1-ball at the start of the rack when that was an option. You should take a moment to walk over and **survey the table** from Position A. From this location you can determine the path you want the cue ball to travel for shape on the **key ball**, which is the 12-ball. A follow stroke with a/ tip of left english will send the cue ball down the line for the 12-ball. As you'll recall, **down-the-line shape** enables you to play excellent position without the need for perfect **speed control**. Notice that you would have had good position on the 12-ball even if the cue ball had rolled a foot far-ther or stopped as much as 1fi" short of where it came to rest.

Ball 14: You're now about to play the all important **key ball**. At this dis-tance you should be thinking about where the "dime" is located that you want the cue ball to stop on, then go ahead and send the cue ball to that exact spot. A smooth draw stroke on the 12-ball has resulted in an excel-lent **break shot** for the third rack. Precision rules!

CHAPTER 7

SAFETY PLAY

How to Win the Battle for Control of the Table

Most players consider Straight Pool an offensive game. Indeed, the glamour is in high runs. But to get your chance to run balls, you've got to keep your opponent off the table. When you are up against a good player, you've got to play great defense to get your chance to turn your offense loose. Irving Crane, one of the finest Straight Pool players ever, was a great defensive player. He reportedly practiced defense 30 minutes a day. I suggest that you adopt a positive attitude towards safety play.

You should enjoy the opportunity to match your wits and skills with those of your opponent. Don't look at safety play as a necessary evil you must endure before starting your run, and don't view it as something you can't master that often costs you possession of the table. Don't just go through the motions and play halfhearted safeties. Instead, look for creative solutions that can possibly put your opponent in a bind.

Always be learning from safeties that are successful and from those aren't. That includes both yours and your opponents. Be sure to key in on your opponent's responses to your safeties. Did a particular move lead to an offensive opportunity? Was your opponent able to counter your tactics? If so, how did they manage to get the advantage?

Key Elements to a Safety

There are a wide variety of safeties you must master to achieve proficiency as a defensive player. Every safety in your defensive arsenal has one or more elements to it that are the key to it's success. When you are about to play a safety, it helps to know exactly what component(s) must receive special emphasis to make a successful safety.

The key elements of a successful safety include:

- **Strategy**. Knowing when to play the correct safety at the correct time.
- **Skill**. Some safeties rely mostly on skillful execution of the shot.
- **Combination safeties**. Some safeties require a combination of strategy and skill.
- **Cue ball control**. On many safeties your primary concern is where the cue ball ends up.
- **Object ball control**. The main ingredient for success may come from sending the object ball to a specific location on the table.
- **Controlling both balls**. Some safeties require that you exercise complete control over both the cue ball and object ball.

• Goals for a Safety

The layout, your opponent's abilities, and the game situation all can have a bearing on your goals for the safety you are about to play. Your objectives for a safety could be to:

- Lock up your opponent and get a makeable shot on your next turn.
- Begin to limit their responses, which can lead to a shot, possibly within the next two or three turns.
- Begin to chip away at their advantage if your opponent has the upper hand.
- Eliminate the areas on the table where they can leave the cue ball.
- Leave your opponent on the rail, which limits their responses.
- Leave your opponent with a tough shot.
- Leave a tough safety.
- Make your opponent take an intentional foul.
- Force your opponent to foul 3 times in succession.

Strategy

Smart safety play is really mostly about playing the percentages. That means playing both yours and those of your opponent. Before any game begins, you should be keenly aware of your capabilities. You should know what shots and which safeties are in your playbook, as well as those that are beyond your current level of skill. It also helps to know your opponents game. This knowledge can come from several sources including previous encounters and scouting reports.

The Chess Game

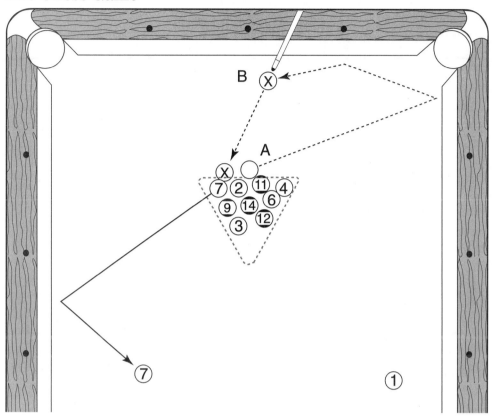

Safety play is a battle of wits with your opponent, much like a game of Chess. The big difference is that you are both playing with the same pieces. Nevertheless, you must be able to think ahead before playing a safety. Try to imagine the position of the balls after you played a safety. What would you do from the position your opponent will be in? It could pay to walk over to where they will be playing their next shot to determine exactly what you will be leaving them. Will they have an easy response, will they be in a jam, or will the difficulty of their reply be somewhere in between?

To carry this a step further, you may be able to play a sequence of two or three safeties with the idea of setting your opponent up for the crowning blow. Your first safety left the cue ball at Position A while knocking the 1-ball in front of the upper side pocket. Your opponent then sent the cue ball to Position B, which left it a couple of inches off the rail. If their execution had been a little more precise, they could have frozen the cue ball to the end rail. This would have prevented you from playing your second safety, which sent the 7-ball in front of the other side pocket while freezing the cue ball to the back of the stack. At this point, your opponent is in trouble, as there is nothing they can do to prevent you from having a shot, short of playing an intentional foul. In this position, an intentional foul would only stall your inevitable victory.

Skills Shots You Must Master

- **Skimming Balls**

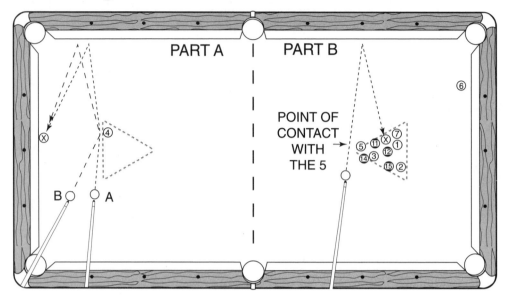

The master skill in playing Straight Pool safeties is skimming the cue ball off another ball with great precision. If you master skimming, your opponents will find themselves frozen to the rail much more often. In addition, you will tend to avoid the sellouts that occur when you hit the object ball too thickly, or not at all, when a thin hit is needed.

The majority of your skim shots will likely be played from behind the rack, but you must be prepared to play them from any position on the table at any time. Part A shows a typical skim shot (Note that other balls have been omitted). The shot here is to skim the 4-ball and send the cue ball to the end rail. From Position A, a very thin hit on the 4-ball with a half tip of left english will send the cue ball to Position X. You could achieve the same objective from Cue Ball A by hitting the 4-ball a shade fuller with no english and a little more speed. To reach Position X from Cue Ball B, you will need to hit the 4-ball about / full. A little left english will help spin the cue ball to X. You will need a little more speed to play this shot than with the cue ball at Position A.

Part B shows a game situation where your opponent has you in what appears to be a difficult position. The way out of this fix is to play a skim shot off the edge of the 5-ball. Use a quarter tip of right english and a very soft stroke. The cue ball will nestle into the stack, leaving your opponent in a much worse predicament than you were facing just a moment ago. The power to radically shift the odds to your favor at any time should be a prime motivator for you to master skim shots.

There are literally countless variations of the positions we've just covered and many more, making it impossible to cover all of them in this book. What is most important is for you to develop a complete understanding of how the cue ball behaves in a wide assortment of positions. These fine points will become a part of your game only by consciously looking for opportunities to play skillful and creative skim safeties.

Factors to Keep In Mind when Playing Skim Safeties

- **Your target.** Identify where you want the cue ball to go and how to get it there.
- **Possible changes in ball positions**. Analyze the layout and what impact your safety will have on it, if any. You want to guard against rearranging the balls in a manner that leaves your opponent a shot, or something he can work with.
- **Speed of stroke.** On the 1-10 scale (see Principle #1 in the chapter on Position Play), most skim safeties are played with a speed of stroke in the range of #1(extremely soft) to #3 (very soft). What often makes skim shots particularly challenging is the need to fill in the gaps for a safety to be successful. For example, a speed of 2.2 might be perfect, whereas a speed of 2.4 might leave your opponent with a shot. In short, you must acquire a fine touch for short-distance speed control.
- **Fullness of the hit**. You can change the cue ball's path and the speed of stroke by hitting various amounts of the object ball.
- **English.** English can greatly alter the cue ball's path as it comes off the rail, especially on slowly hit spin shots. Because of this, you must apply sidespin with great care. English can help you target the cue ball's final position with great precision. You can also change the hit on the object ball (fuller or thinner) by using english.
- **The conditions.** When the balls are separating easily, you must skim the rack with great care. When the balls are seemingly stuck together, you can skim the rack with less fear of leaving your opponent much to work with.

Masse Skim Safety

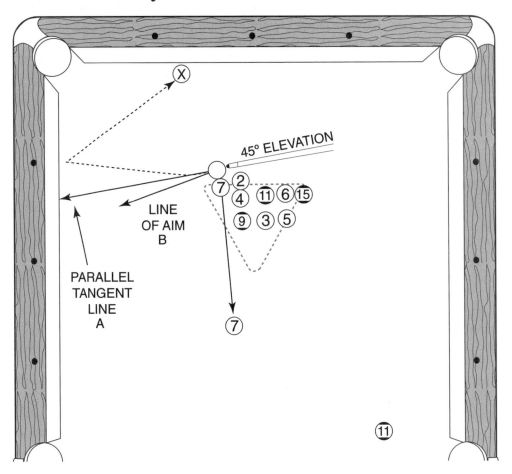

It looks as if your opponent has the upper hand. You can't play safe off the 2-ball because you would leave a shot on the 11-ball. The parallel tangent line (Line A) on the 7-ball is pointing up the rail, which also seems to rule out playing safe off the 7-ball. You could play an intentional foul and see what develops. A more creative solution, however, can quickly turn the tables in your favor. If you were to roll the cue ball away from the 7-ball while just barely brushing it, it would follow Line A. This, of course, would lead to a sellout. To change the direction of the cue ball, jack up to about a 45 degree angle and use right english. Aim a few inches above Line A along Line B. The cue ball will curve slightly as it approaches the rail. The english will take off the rail and propel the cue ball to Position X. In essence, you are using a half masse shot to send the cue ball along a path it could not follow by using of a conventional shot.

Skimming From Long-Range

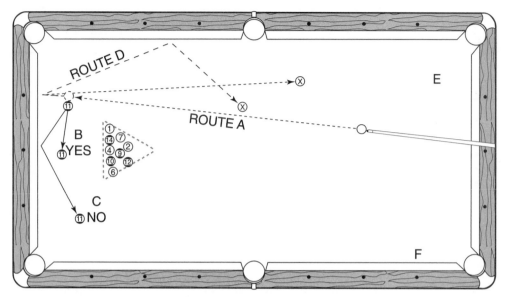

One of the most important and difficult safeties is the skim shot from long range. You have no choice except to skim off the 11-ball and send the cue ball down Route A. If you are successful, the 11-ball will be stationed behind the rack at Position B, leaving a long, tough safety for your opponent.

You must guard against two big dangers on this shot. Mistake #1 is to hit the 11-ball too full. This could knock it out in front of the pocket at Position C. The cue ball would follow Route D, which would leave your opponent with a relatively easy shot and a chance to open the rack.

Mistake #2 is to miss the 11-ball altogether. This often happens in your efforts to avoid Mistake #1. Should you miss the 11-ball the cue ball would return to the far end of the table to Position E. Your opponent could now roll the cue ball to Position F where you can't see the edge of the 11-ball. Since you would be on your first foul, you would have do something constructive, such as skimming off the side of the rack and sending the cue ball up-table. Be advised, however, that skimming the side of the rack at long-range in some positions is often one of the riskiest and most foolhardy "safeties" in Straight Pool.

Tip: You can develop the skill of long-range skimming by practicing hitting an object ball near one end-rail thinly with the cue ball a couple of feet away. Note how far the object ball moves. Gradually increase the distance until you can skim the object ball consistently from long-range.

• **End-Rail Safety Zones**

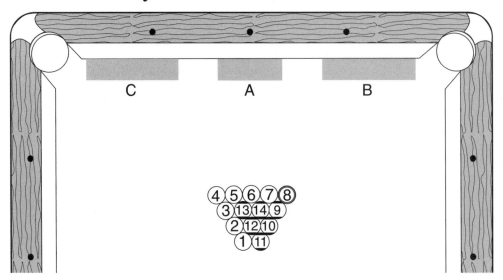

On behind-the-rack safeties the ideal position to leave your opponent is frozen to the end-rail. The best portion of the rail for the perfect safety zone really depends on the layout. If the rack is tight, your opponent could roll into a ball on the back row and drive a ball to the rail. In this case, you certainly don't want to leave them on the middle part of the rail, even if you can freeze the cue ball in Zone A.

The outer Zones (B and C) will force your opponent to skim the back of the rack at a big angle, which could turn into an advantage for you. If the balls were loosely scattered in the area of the triangle, then it would be very hard, if not impossible, for them to hit and stick on a ball while driving another to the rail. In this case, Zone A would be the best spot to leave the cue ball.

Hitting the Safety Zone

Knowing you want the cue ball on the end-rail is one thing, getting it to land there is quite another. We discussed earlier the importance of skimming balls with speed and directional control. What can also help you control the cue ball's final resting place is the angle of approach it takes to the safety zone. A shallow angle of approach gives you a better chance of leaving the cue ball very close to, if not on, the rail.

The diagram on the next page shows two identical positions on the 4-ball. In each one, the goal is to leave the cue ball as close to the end-rail as possible. You could follow Route A by barely skimming the 4-ball with right english. Notice the rather sharp angle of approach to the end-rail. The play in Route B is to hit the 4-ball 1/5 full with right (inside) english. The cue ball will hit lower on the side-rail and will approach the safety zone at a shallower angle. This shot allows you to hit the cue ball a bit harder than the shot in Route A, which could be an advantage to those who have trouble with soft-touch safeties.

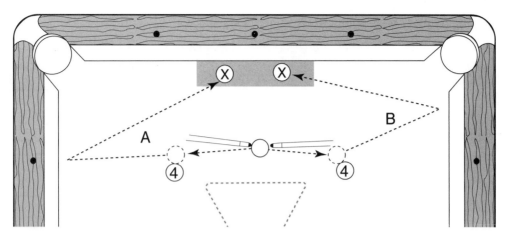

Snuggling Up Against a Ball in the Open

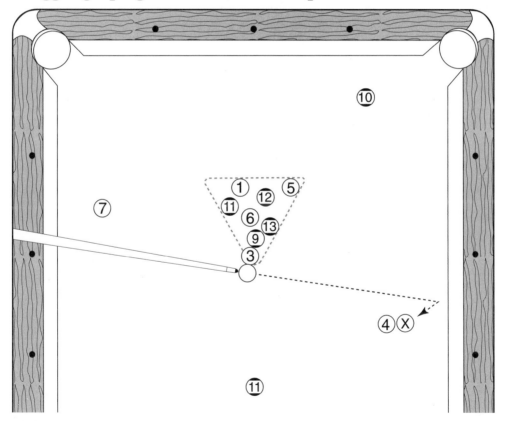

It looks for sure as if your opponent has you in Straight Pool checkmate. There are open shots on all sides of the rack. You certainly don't want to try the so-called shot on the 11-ball, which is next to impossible. Since you are now a creative skim safety master, you have a way out. You know that the 4-ball won't go past the 11-ball into the lower left side pocket. Furthermore, the cue ball, if skimmed off the 3-ball, would just miss the left side of the 4-ball. Perhaps the 4-ball could act as a hiding place for the cue ball, even though it is out in the open by itself. Voila, a creative winning safety! The big keys to this shot were creativity and a fine touch.

Controlling the Roll of the Object Ball

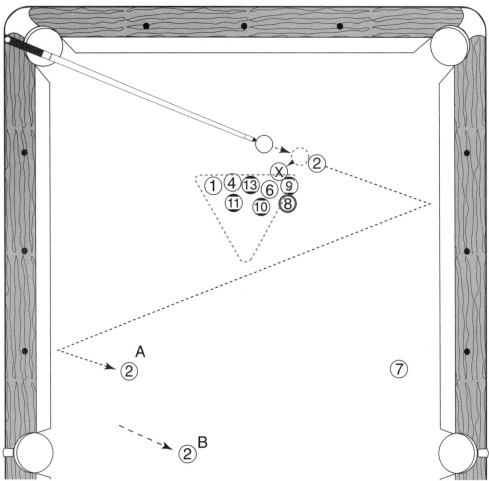

The 7-ball covers one side of the table. The 2-ball is in position for a devastating safety if you can control its direction and speed when traveling across the table. If you can bank the 2-ball short of the side pocket as shown with good speed, it will cover the other side of the table at Position A. The only place where your opponent can leave you without a shot is the zone behind the rack. With the cue ball at Position X, he will have a tough time sending the cue ball two cushions into the zone.

Controlling the direction and speed of the object ball is a valuable skill often ignored by many players. In our example, the tendency would be to aim straight at the 2-ball while being content to draw straight back behind the rack. The 2-ball might go in the side pocket (because you called safe, it would then be spotted), but it could also end up past the side pocket at Position B. In either case, the end result is an infinitely weaker defensive move.

Tip: you can strengthen your safety play by learning to spot opportunities to move the object ball to a more advantageous location, and then executing your plan with precision.

Choosing Directions on End Rail Safety Play

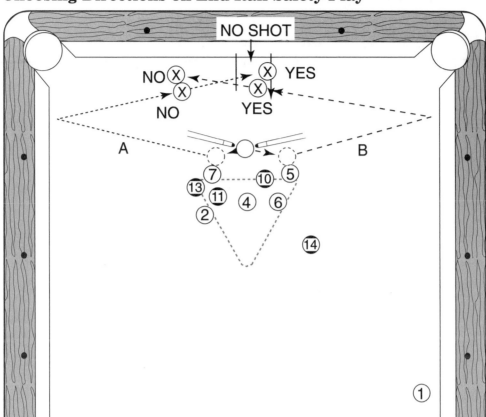

Your opponent has left you behind the rack with a ball on either side of the table. The first step is to find out if there is a no-shot zone on the end- rail. In the example there is a small area on the end-rail where your opponent won't have a shot at either the 15-ball or 1-ball.

You should try to leave the cue ball on the side of the zone on the same side of the table as the 1-ball. You could reach this position by following either Route A or Route B. Route A is probably easier for most players because the cue ball will be traveling away from trouble rather than towards it. The shot on the ball you will be skimming off should also be factored into your decision making. In this example, the skim shots are about equal in difficulty, making Route A preferable.

One big blunder in this position would be to leave the cue ball short of the zone on Route A. Another mistake would be to travel too far down Route B. In either case you would give your opponent an easy shot at the 15-ball. Even if you overrun the zone slightly while following Route A, your opponent still has to make a very tough shot on the 2-ball. This safety battle is particularly important because the winner will get a shot at opening the rack with the 14-ball.

Safety Maneuvers

Freezing To the Back of the Rack

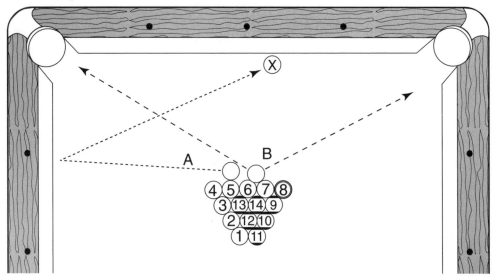

Cue Ball A is frozen to the bottom of the 5-ball. This is a weak leave as it makes it to easy for your opponent to send the cue ball to the middle of the end-rail, which severely limits your options. Freezing the cue ball in the gap between two balls at Cue Ball B is a much stronger move because it limits your opponent's responses.   In addition, they will be shooting jacked-up and may also have trouble avoiding a scratch.

It's Not Over Till It's Over

The illustration shows what should be an ideal ending to a safety battle. Your opponent is frozen on the end rail with a super difficult shot on the 11-ball.   Playing an intentional foul would probably only prolong the agony, but it also could enable a savvy player to wiggle out of a jam.   If your opponent rolled the cue ball into the 1-ball, you could turn around and send it right back to it's original location. You would need to return the cue ball to the rail or else you could make their shot on the 11-ball much easier. You might also open up the door for a stop shot on the 1-ball. Your opponent may then have a shot at sending a ball to the rail and freezing the cue ball up against the back of the 4-ball.

Your opponent might also "push out" to Position A in the hopes that you won't return the cue ball to its original location when you play your intentional foul. Their reasoning being if they must play the 11-ball, they might as well make it a little easier. Your reply, of course, would simply be to take a foul by nudging the cue ball back to its original location. The lesson is that you must press your advantage to the max, especially if your opponent is the cagey type who never gives up.

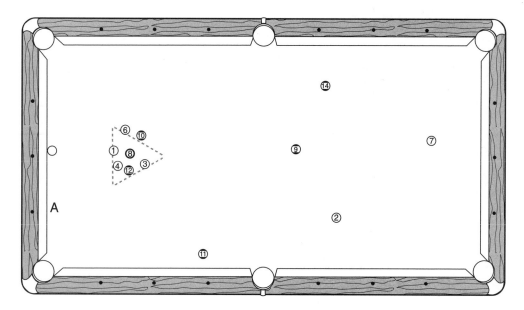

• Pocket the Ball and Call a Safety

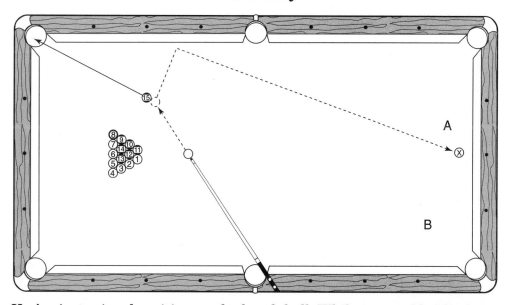

You've just missed position on the break ball. While you could still play a side-rail break shot, the odds are poor that you will come away with a shot. Another choice is to call safe. Let your opponent clearly understand your intentions. The 15-ball will be spotted at the top of the rack. With the cue ball at Position A, your opponent will probably play an intentional foul by sending the cue ball two-rails into the back of the rack.

Don't make the mistake of sending the cue ball to Position B. From Position B they could drive a ball out of the rack and to a rail. This would turn the tables and all of a sudden put you on the defensive.

Put Your Opponent in Jail

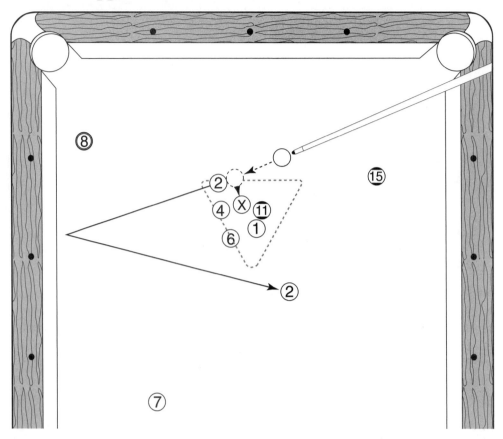

The play here is to slide the cue ball over a few inches into the middle of a group of partially broken balls. There is virtually no way that your opponent can escape from the "Pen". The key is to control the sideways movement of the cue ball so as to avoid disturbing any of the balls that make up the walls of the prison.

Creativity + Execution = A Winner

It looks as if you are stuck in the illustrated position on the next page. Your opponent has left you behind the rack with several open shots on the other end of the table. The 4-ball is well up the side-rail, but it's the kind of shot you would almost never attempt in Straight Pool. Controlling the path of the cue ball is often the key element in a safety. With this shot, execution is everything. A half-ball hit on the 4-ball using low left english will send the cue ball to Position X.

This rather unusual safety requires that you rely on your knowledge of how the balls react after contact. Often a moment of reflection will give you the time you need to see a shot you wouldn't ordinarily encounter. So when you are in jam, take a moment to allow your creative juices to flow and they will often provide you with the winning solution.

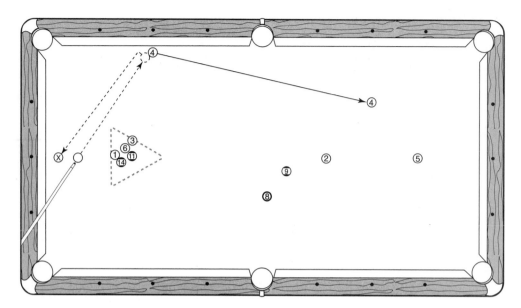

Off the Rail and Into the Stack

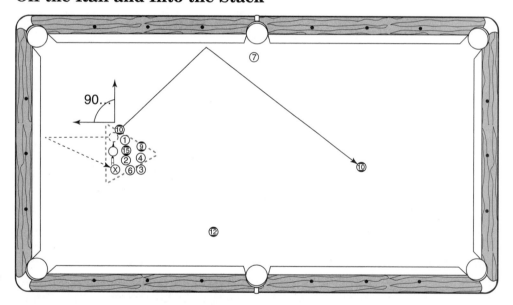

It looks as if you're in big trouble now. You've got no shot and there are balls in the clear on the other side of the table. You can get out of this jam and put your opponent in an even worse position. Use draw and a quarter tip of left english. Guard against using too much english as you could possibly miss the back of the rack on the opposite side.

The key to this shot is hitting just the right amount of the 10-ball. When the cue ball and object ball are in a direct line to the rail and you hit the object ball half full using draw, it will head toward the adjacent rail at about a 90-degree angle. In our example, the english then pulls the cue ball towards the back of the rack.

End-of-Rack Safety

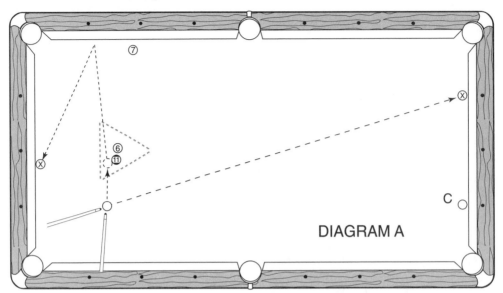

DIAGRAM A

Neither you nor your opponent is on a foul, and he's left you in the end-of- rack position shown in Diagram A. Since you have no shot, the obvious choice is to play a safety. You are blocked from direct contact with the 7-ball. You could try to skim off the 11-ball and try to leave your opponent with a difficult shot, perhaps at Position A. By separating the cluster you could, however, leave your opponent with a chance to run the last two balls and use the 7-ball as a break ball. In other words, a disaster could ensue from breaking the cluster apart. But what other choice is there?

It's time to "think outside the box" and devise a strategy that can keep you opponent from possibly launching a long run. In this position it pays to think like both a Nine-Ball player and a Straight Pool player. Your opponent does not get ball-in-hand anywhere on the table after a foul in Straight Pool. So now is the time to use the push-out strategy often employed after the break in Nine-Ball. You could roll the cue ball to Position B. If your opponent takes the bait, they could easily wind up missing this table-length shot. They could even leave you with a chance to run into the next rack should the 7-ball be banked two rails into the cluster. Should your opponent pocket the 7-ball, he could take an intentional foul by pushing the cue ball down to the far end of the table to Position C. Since you're on the first foul, you would probably be stuck with breaking the cluster. The good news is that both balls are in the rack. You could bank either the 6-ball or 11-ball to the other end of the table. If you do not disturb the other ball, your opponent would at best have a low percentage break ball from the head spot.

Now let's back up to Position B in Diagram B. You've just "pushed-out", taking an intentional foul. Your opponent could also take a foul. You would be left with a table length shot on the 7-ball with no chance of

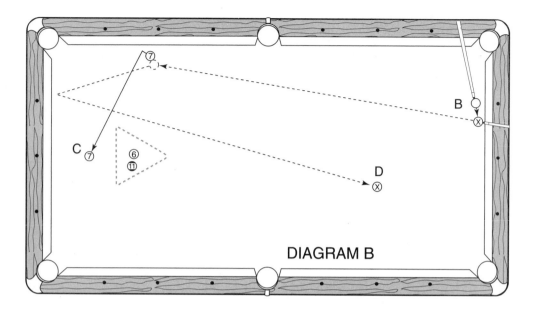

DIAGRAM B

breaking the cluster, unless, of course, you missed the shot. In this position, what would you do? One option is to cross-bank the 7-ball to Position C and leave the cue ball at Position D.

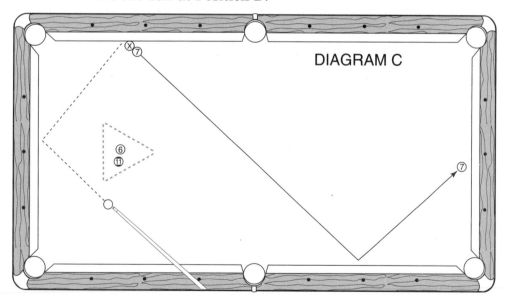

DIAGRAM C

Diagram C shows another creative solution to our original position. Now it's time to think for a moment like a Nine-Ball or One-Pocket player. The play is to kick two-rails for the 7-ball. This would remove the break ball. If executed perfectly your opponent would be left in the difficult position as shown.

These end-of-the-rack duels are really like a chess game in which you don't want to leave the "pieces" in a position where your opponent could start a long run. The least of your concerns should be losing a point or two to fouls, and/or the stray balls that your opponent picks off.

Go to the Far End-Rail and Back Out

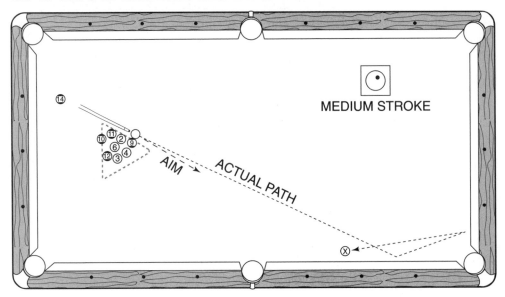

You are in danger of giving your opponent a long break shot on the 14-ball. If you play a conventional safety to the end-rail, the cue ball will end up at somewhere around Position A. While the break shot on the 14-ball is no easy proposition, it is still the kind of opportunity that could possibly get your opponent started on a run. You can eliminate his chances by playing to the end-rail and back out. Use the technique we covered in a recent section of aiming for a slightly fuller "hit" on the 9-ball. This will enable you to play the shot with a little more speed. Use follow and right english to send the cue ball to the end-rail and out to Position X. The distance principle says that you want to leave your opponent as long a shot as possible. In this example it is overridden by the principle that says you should leave your opponent with nothing to shoot at.

Tip: You can improve the accuracy of your safeties by using the diamonds as reference points. In the example, the shot was aimed 1fi diamonds up from the far corner pocket.

• Hitting Into the Side of the Rack and Stick

Whenever you play shape for a side-of-the-rack break shot and leave yourself with a straight-in shot, don't despair. What you have accidentally done is to play shape for one of the most devastating safeties in Straight Pool. From Position A in the diagram on the following page, roll the cue ball softly into the middle of the 3-ball. The 5-ball will pop-out to the end rail. A few more balls will come out on the other side of the rack. The end result is that you will almost always win this safety battle. Note that if the cue ball were in Position B, then you would roll into the 2-ball.

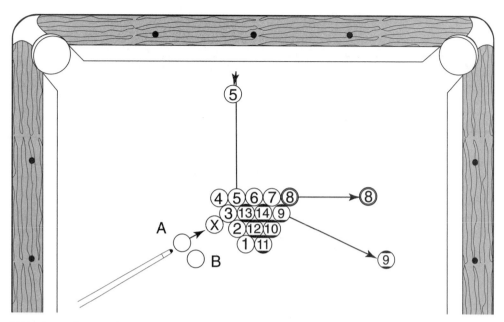

Hitting Into the Back of the Rack

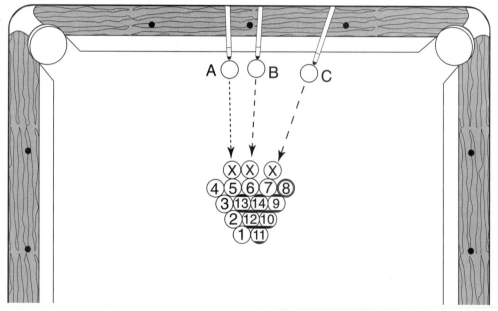

The illustration shows several ways for playing a safety into the back of a full rack. In Position A, roll the cue ball into the 5-ball just a little left of center. When the cue ball is directly opposite the middle ball as shown in Position B, roll into the middle of the 6-ball. With the cue ball in Position C, use a little right English and aim for a full hit on the 7-ball. In all three cases, the cue ball should stick to the back of the rack, and at least one ball should hit a side rail. This safety is reasonable effective, but not nearly as damaging to your opponent as the one in the previous section.

Cover Two Sides at Once

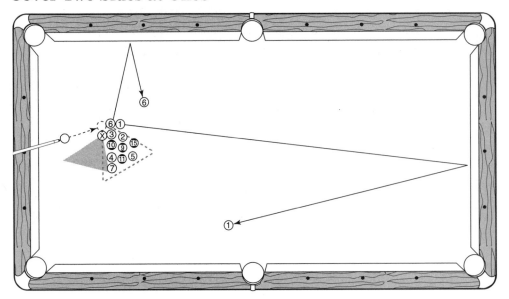

It is always a good idea to send a ball to the middle part of the table so that your opponent has fewer options when playing safe. This safety goes a step or two further by covering both sides of the table on one shot. Unless your opponent can send the cue ball off a cushion and back into the shaded area, they will give you a shot. One of the keys to this shot is hitting enough of the 6-ball to drive it to the rail and back out to Position A. The other key is to leave the 1-ball in front of the side pocket if possible.

Into the Top of a New Rack

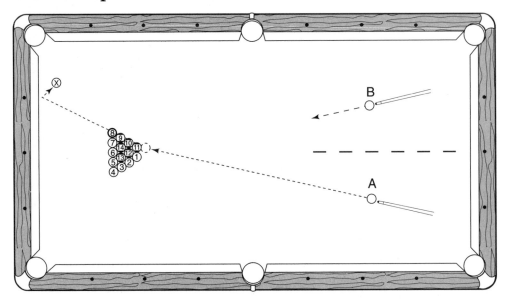

The opportunity to play the safety in the diagram on the preceding page can result from missing the rack on a break shot. With the cue ball in Position A, roll softly into a full hit with the 11-ball. Because of the distance of the shot there is the chance of missing the target from either a roll off or an aiming error. You may wish to use a drag draw shot so you can hit the cue ball more firmly and still have it hit the top ball at the required speed. The bigger mistake is to hit the 1-ball first as compared to hitting the 11-ball a little right of center. With the cue ball on the other half of the table at Position B, you would aim for the 1-ball.

- **Far End Rail Into the Back of the Rack**

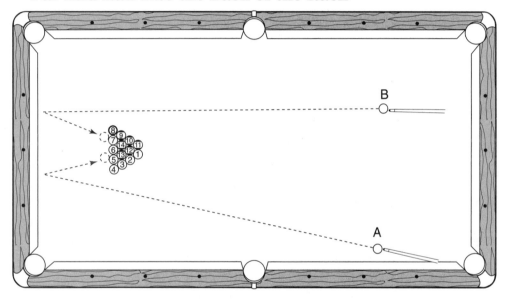

If your opponent pockets a ball and calls a safety on the first shot of a new rack, you may find yourself in one of the positions in the diagram. Unless you are on two fouls, don't make the mistake of trying to skim a corner ball and send the cue ball back to the far end rail. Ninety percent of the time this "safety" will leave your opponent with an open shot.

　　The play is to bank the cue ball off the foot rail and into the back of the rack. The idea is to knock a few balls out of the rack and to stick the cue ball to the back row. Occasionally you will drive a ball to the rail, which makes the shot a legal safety. Most of the time, however, this shot winds up being an intentional foul. That's ok. It is better to lose a point than to skim the rack and sellout.

　　With the cue ball in Position A, aim close to the corner ball and use a medium soft follow stroke. With the cue ball closer to the middle of the table in Position B, you will need to use a little softer stroke to avoid the risk of the cue ball slipping off the back row. Use a half tip of outside (left) english.

Two Rails Into the Back of the Rack

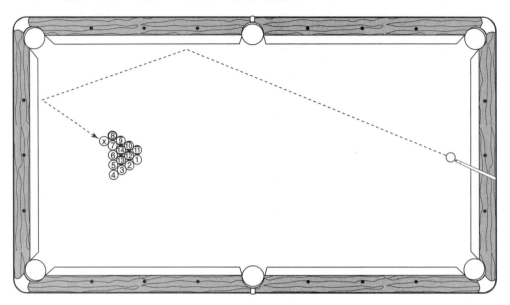

If your opponent calls a safety on the first ball of a new rack and is able to leave the cue ball close to the middle diamond on the head rail, that's a good indication you are up against a savvy competitor. When the cue ball is in this position on a full rack, the play is to go two rails into the back of the rack.

This shot is always played as an intentional foul because of the angle that the cue ball will be approaching the back row. If you used enough speed so a ball from the rack could reach a rail, chances are the cue ball would slip off the back row and possibly leave your opponent a shot. Use a half tip or more of outside english and aim well up the side rail as shown. Notice the angle that the cue ball approaches the back of the rack. The english will help keep the cue ball from slipping too far down the back row.

Freeze the Cue Ball at a Pocket

You can really gain the upper hand by freezing the cue ball against a ball so that it is pointed directly at the pocket. Notice that the cue ball in Position A in the diagram on the next page is frozen against the 6-ball and is pointing at the corner pocket. If you find yourself in this situation, you could take a foul and nudge the cue ball over a bit to Position B so that it is no longer pointing at the pocket. It would be quite difficult for your opponent to push it back to its original location. On your next turn, you might have the option of playing off the 6-ball and sending the cue ball towards the end rail. This safety is most potent when there are open shots on the other sides of the rack and your opponent is on two fouls.

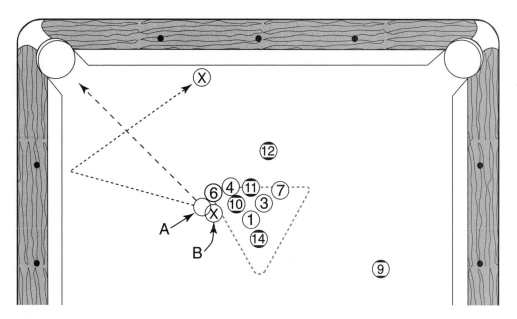

Pass on a Long Shot that Leads Nowhere

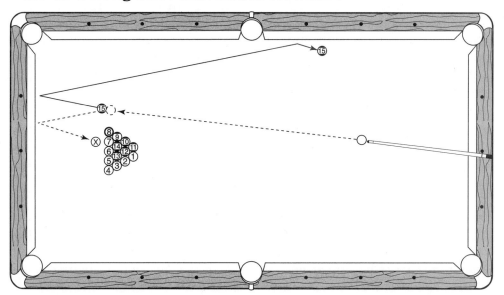

You could try to pocket the 15-ball but there is no chance of hitting the rack unless you use tons of right english and overcut the 15-ball. You could also attempt to pocket the 15-ball and call a safe. If successful, your opponent will be facing a long safety from the far end of the table. If you miss the shot, there is always the possibility you could leave your opponent something to work with. The best bet is to bank the 15-ball up table and send the cue ball into the back of the rack as shown. This safety is an easy shot. It is a somewhat neutral play in that it may not gain much in terms of a strategic advantage, but loses nothing either.

Frozen to the Rack

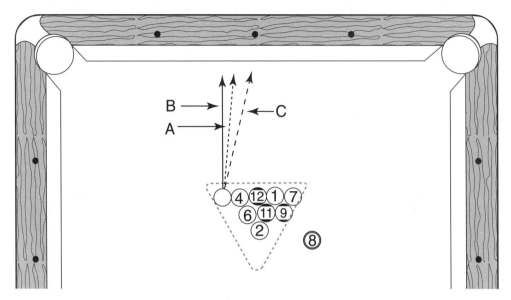

On many occasions you will find yourself frozen against the rack. Strangely enough, you must guard against making a bad hit. This is easy to do if you aim slightly outside of the parallel tangent line (Line A), as shown by Line B in the diagram. On shots like this where the object ball is not going to budge, you better have an iron clad case that you did, indeed, hit the 4-ball. This is especially true if your opponent is the kind of player who likes to call everything, including imaginary fouls.

You should make a show of lining up the shot. Your theatrics can be part of your case should a dispute arise. Demonstrate that you are going to be aiming along Line C, which is slightly inside the tangent line. By aiming down this line, you guarantee a good hit.

Tip: If you want to shoot to the rail with a little more force and kill the cue ball's speed ever so slightly, try aiming just a little further inside the tangent line. The fuller "hit" will slow the cue ball down slightly. Remember, when you are operating on the spectrum of speed where a very fine touch is required, tricks like this could make the difference between success and failure. Using our 1-10 scale, a 2.5 stroke speed may be what's needed while a 2.6 could result in a sell out. I mention this as a way of stressing to you the importance of having at your disposal the powerful weapon of a "safecrackers" touch.

CHAPTER 8

STRATEGY

How to Play Smart and Outthink Your Opponent

In many situations there is one strategy that should be used by virtually all players. On other occasions, however, your choice of strategy is dictated by several factors including the score, your ability, your opponents ability, the layout, the playing conditions, what's at stake, etc. There is no one correct strategy for all skill levels or game situations. Many of your strategic decisions occur during the battle for control of the table. Others center on how you should play certain shots while you are on the offensive. Part of your skill as a player is the ability to weigh all relevant factors so you can make the best decisions no matter what the situation.

Early Game Strategies

Your want to make your opponent earn everything in the early part of the game. The opening break can often set the tone for the contest. If you can leave your opponent a long tough shot, you could quickly seize the table after a miss. And if they break the opening rack, your ability to make a long shot can enable you to grab the early momentum, and possibly even launch a long run.

In the early going you may be wise to emphasize pocketing balls. The idea is to get your stroke in gear while you get familiar with the speed of the table. You may also be wise to play farther away from the balls to get the correct angle. As the game progresses, your position should get tighter and tighter. On your first couple of break shots, you should consider sacrificing power for accuracy by playing for a little less angle.

Straight Pool is largely a game of momentum. The opportunity to control the table via defense or for long periods of time with a long run can turn your opponents game to stone. Of course, the same thing might happen to you. Therefore, it is crucial that you make every effort to establish momentum at the start, and maintain it for as long as possible. A strong start does not guarantee victory. Your opponent's job will be much tougher, however, if they have to rise from their chair after cooling off from their pre-game warm-ups for any length of time.

In the early stages of a match, you want to get loose and get rolling. At the same time, you also want to send a message to your opponent that you are ready to play. A strong start may be just enough to cause them to blow their first couple of scoring opportunities, which can build on your early game momentum.

Middle of the Game

Once you reach the middle stages of a game, you should be familiar with the playing conditions. In addition, your stroke should be good and loose. Now is the time to take a little more risk on offense. If you are leading, it is time to really push your advantage. You might just put the game out of reach. You should not, however, take foolish chances that could let your opponent back into the game.

If you are trailing, the middle stages of the game are the time to launch a comeback before the game gets completely out of reach. Let's assume you are trailing 65-38 in a game to 100. Even though you are down, you are certainly not out. A deficit of 27 points may seem like a lot, but it's amazing how quickly it can disappear once you start pocketing balls. In no time you could find yourself in the lead. You could also initiate a comeback with tight defense that cuts off your opponent's offense. So by all means don't panic when you are behind in the middle part of the game. Realize that you still have enough time to overtake your opponent and win the game.

End of the Game

As a game nears completion, there are certain mental aspects that must be dealt with successfully. If you are leading by a sizeable margin and you only need 10-15 points, there could be a tendency to let up. There is perhaps no worse feeling than to see a game start to slip away that you knew you had won. Even though you may feel the game if yours, it is not really yours until you've scored the game ball. You must not panic when you see your opponent slicing away at your lead. Stay positive and keep making the best decisions on both offense and defense. The idea is to protect your lead without losing the confidence that put you ahead in the first place. You don't want to get so overly cautious that you wind up employing a Straight Pool version of Football's much maligned prevent defense.

When you are trailing at the end of a game by a large margin, you should adopt the attitude that you have nothing to lose. You might as well relax and let your game out. Play one ball at a time, one rack at a time, and before you know it, you could find yourself right back in the game.

When you are locked in a close battle, you must weigh your decisions carefully on both offense and defense. As an example, let's figure that both you and your opponent need about 10 points, and you have a tough break shot that you expect to make 70% of the time. You might shoot this shot every time in the middle stages of the game, but with the game now on the line, you might want to consider playing safe. If your opponent is weak on defense, and you feel you can win the safety battle 80% of the time, then the odds say play it safe. If they play defense like Irving Crane in his prime, then you've got no real choice but to shoot the break shot.

It helps build your confidence when you enter the later stages of a game if you know the range at which you feel you can get out with a decent run. Let's assume you at least occasionally run 20-30 balls. If your opponent leaves you a shot with the score 75-90 their favor in a game to 100, you should take the table with the feeling that you can run out the game. The 100th point is well within your range. Tell yourself that you are a closer and can smell the finish line.

The score can definitely have an impact on your decision making as the game draws to a close. It is important to know the key numbers for both you and your opponent. For example, if you have 85 points with a full rack in a game to 100, you know that you don't need to save for a break shot for the next rack. This could dramatically change how you play the rack. Instead of saving break shots for yourself, you would now want to clear them from the table so they won't be left for your opponent should you miss.

Your confidence can also get a boost if you know you only need to play one more break shot. If you take the table needing 15 points and there are 6 balls on the table, it is comforting to know that you only need to pocket 5 more balls in this rack, and 10 (including the break shot) in the next rack.

It is also important to know your opponents score as well as their ability to set up break shots and run balls. Let's say you are in a battle for the table and your opponent only needs the 8 balls that are left on the table. If you can force them to take a foul or two, they will have to run into the next rack even if they win the safety battle.

Tip: Remember to always make your opponent do the most difficult thing you can to make them beat you, especially at the end of the game.

Establishing Your Game Plan

• Never Let Up

Momentum is such a valuable and hard won commodity in Straight Pool so you must do everything to preserve it. This can be difficult for some players who have a natural tendency to let up, especially after a long run, or after they have jumped to a big lead. The "nice guy" impulse may tell them that they should give their opponent a chance. After all, their opponent came to play, and they've been patiently waiting their turn. If this describes your attitude at times, then you need to get a little more selfish, because Straight Pool is a selfish game. At the highest levels of play, players relish the thought of a perfect game in which their opponent never gets back to the table after the opening break.

Shot Selection

When Straight Pool is played correctly, it is largely a game of relatively easy shots, but that doesn't mean your shotmaking abilities won't be severely tested several times during a game. When you are faced with a particularly tough shot that is far less than a sure thing, you must carefully consider the situation before pulling the trigger. The valid reasons for shooting a tough shot include:

- You are playing great and feel in your heart that it's a go.
- There is a reward for shooting the shot at least equal to the risk. You want to avoid high risk, low reward shots.
- It is early in the game and you want to grab the momentum.
- You want to avoid a safety battle with a tough defensive player.
- You have no choice. Your opponent has put you in a spot, or you perhaps got a bad roll.
- Your only other alternative is to take 3 fouls and lose 18 points.
- Your all time record run is at stake and it means more to you than the game.

• Playing Your Game

You no doubt have a particular style of play with which you are very familiar. Your style dictates your shot selection and how you play position. For the most part, you will get your best results if you play your game. When you try to go against the grain by playing risky shots or position plays that are out of character, it can lead to disaster. Strangely enough, the more you know about the game, the more often you will pass on shots you played at an earlier stage in your career when you weren't aware of the risks involved with a particular shot.

Never Leave the Table on a Miss

One of the goals of many top players is to never leave the table via a missed shot. When a top player misses position or gets a bad roll, they will play safe rather than take a very tough shot that could open the door for their opponent. Even though the average player must expect to miss some shots during the course of the game, they can still establish strategic goals for limiting their opponents offensive opportunities. One strategic goal could be to never leave a wide open table by, for example, playing a foolish high-risk break shot. Another strategy could be to never shoot a ball out of the rack that's almost dead.

Your Opponent

Straight Pool may seem like a solitary game when you are in the midst of a long run. During a typical game, however, you must deal successfully with your opponent in order to gain possession of the table in the first place, and to minimize their offensive opportunities. It is therefore wise to evaluate your opponent's game and style of play so you can fine-tune your strategy to minimize their strengths and take advantage of their weaknesses.

Some of your opponent's characteristics, and the appropriate strategies for dealing with them are:

High Run Artist:

- If they consistently run a lot of balls, you've got to play tight defense and minimize their opportunities.
- If they run a lot of balls, but are inconsistent, it could be a sign that they take lots of chances, or they just run hot and cold. Be prepared to weather the storm of a high run, knowing that you'll get your opportunities for scoring.

Defensive Specialist:

- If your opponent is highly skilled at defense, you need to recognize those situations where they are likely to prevail. You must then decide if it's better to play a somewhat risky shot or trade safeties with them.
- If your opponent is weak on defense, then you should pass on even moderately difficult shots in favor of defensive maneuvers.

A Risk Taker:

- If your opponent likes playing aggressively, you can take advantage of that by leaving him shots that are slightly out of his comfort zone. You should also take comfort knowing that he'll likely leave you with many scoring opportunities. This relieves some of the pressure when they are running balls.
- If you play a tight game against a risk taker, they may get impatient and go for low percentage shots that can give you excellent opportunities to run some balls.

A Conservative Player:
- You don't have to worry as much about your opponent embarking on a long run if they are likely to duck at every opportunity. You do have to guard against getting impatient because of the constant need to play safety after safety. You've got to enjoy matching wits with a conservative player.
- You can break the spirit of some defensive players by excelling at offense. If you run enough balls so it will take them several innings to catch up, they could become discouraged. They might even abandon their style of play and start taking risky shots.

A Consistent Player who Knows the Game:
- These are the players who are toughest to beat, as they make few mistakes on both offense and defense. Be prepared to play your best game by making sound decisions on both offense and defense.
- Understand that you will have to earn most of what you get. Be patient and enjoy the opportunity to match skills with a worthy opponent.

A Fast Player
- Fast players can be very dangerous if they get their rhythm going. They are prone to making errors. If your opponent plays fast, you may expect to get more turns than usual because of their errors.
- You should not have to wait as long between turns, which should help keep your game from cooling off.
- You should resist the temptation to copy their pace of play.

A Slow Player
- Slow players can drive you nuts, especially if they are the kind that seldom make mistakes. Recognize, however, that their pace of play usually works against them running lots of balls, for it is hard to develop rhythm when you are moving at a snails pace.
- Once again, don't let another player's pace affect the way you play.
- Try to remain patient while sitting in the chair.

A Straight Shooter
- You must reconsider what you feel is a tough shot when playing safe. What may be difficult for you, or your typical opponent, may be a routine shot for someone who is a very straight shooter.
- Some straight shooters tend to over-rely on their skill at pocketing balls, which takes away from their position play, so don't be intimidated by their shotmaking. Tell yourself that it's skill at the overall game that counts.

A Poor Shotmaker
- You can tease poor shotmakers with shots that are somewhat out of their comfort zone, but that they feel they should be making and must shoot.
- Skimming the stack and sending the cue ball to the far end rail is a winning strategy against players who dislike the long green.

You're Opponents Play

How you look at your opponent's game can go a long ways towards improving your level of play. There are four possibilities listed below, two of which can improve your game, and two that can prove harmful. It's all really a matter of which perspective you wish to adopt while awaiting your turn.

- Your opponent's poor play gives you the confidence to excel.
- Your opponent's poor play causes you to let up and play below your best.
- Your opponent's good play motivates you to play your best pool.
- Your opponent's good play intimidates you and causes you to play poorly.

Interestingly enough, no matter whether your opponent play well or poorly, you can gain strength or suffer as a result of how you respond to their game. Naturally it pays to always adopt the perspective that helps your game no matter what is the current state of your opponent's game.

While in Your Chair

I find that one of the most amazing accomplishments in pool is when a top player gets out of their chair after watching their opponent run 50 or 100 balls and embarks on a run of a similar nature from a standstill. Obviously they were not spending too much time in their chair feeling sorry for themselves or engaging in any other form of destructive self-talk. But what do they do, and what can you do to maximize your chances of a successful inning after your opponent's kept you seated for any length of time? Below are some ideas that can help you prepare for your next turn.

- You can gain valuable information about how the table is plating by watching how the balls separate on break shots, how the cue ball reacts to English coming off the rails, and the speed of the table
- Observe the layout. Get actively involved in the planning process so you can keep your mind engage in the thinking side of the game. This could prepare you to finish a rack should they miss on an open table.
- If your opponent is a fine player, you have the opportunity to learn something about the game.
- Appreciate your opponent's fine play rather than stressing out while secretly praying that they miss any time soon.
- Pump yourself up for your next turn with some positive self-talk.
- Drink some water, take a few deep breaths and relax.
- Find some reason to believe that you can beat the person you're playing.

Preparing for Competition

You will be much more confident going into any serious competitive event if you take the necessary steps to bring your game to a peak levels. Top players know that a layoff or a decline in hours at the table has a definite impact on their game. So to get razor sharp, you should practice two or more hours a day for at least two weeks just prior to the competition. Much of your practice time should be by yourself, because this allows you twice as much time at the table, and it enables you to work on your weak spots. Part of your practice time should also include visualizing yourself playing you best game in as complete detail as possible while in the comfort of your easy chair.

If possible, you should plan on arriving at the tournament site early enough so you can get used to the playing conditions. Part of your preparation should include plenty of rest and a healthy diet that gives you the stamina to play game after game with no loss of effectiveness.

How to Maximizing Your performance During Competition

- The first match of a tournament is always the toughest because you need to get used to the equipment and because of first match jitters. Don't get down on yourself, because your opponent is likely to experience the same difficulties.
- There is a carry over effect from match to match. If you played well in a previous match, let your confidence rise with your accomplishment. If you played poorly, try to regain your confidence at the practice table pior to the next match.
- Winning is one thing, performing is another. Concentrate on the performance and the winning will take care of itself.
- Try to let your stroke out as soon as possible to combat the natural tendency to shorten your stroke under pressure.
- When you're on offense, don't play the opponent, play the table. When you are in a battle for the table, play to your strengths and your opponent's weaknesses.
- Momentum is nearly everything in Straight Pool. When you have it, work to retain it. And when you don't, try to turn it around as soon as possible.
- When you are facing a large deficit, remember that comebacks happen one ball at a time. Tell yourself you have everything to gain and nothing to lose.
- Recognize the need to elevate your game when you are facing a critical shot that could largely determine the outcome of the match.
- Realize that different events carry with them different levels and types of pressure.
- Remember that the more you compete, the less that pressure will effect you.
- Follow you routine and natural tempo to alleviate pressure.
- Enjoy playing in the competition and believe in yourself.
- Attack the ball. Be aggressive.
- You can help your concentration by always keeping your eyeds on the table.

• Your Pace of Play

Learn to recognize when you can pick up the pace. Sometimes easier conditions and/or the current level of your game may lend themselves to a faster pace of play. When the conditions are tough and/or you are in a defensive battle, it pays to slow down a bit and think each shot through very carefully.

Running Balls and Playing Safe

One of the toughest decisions to make is to play safe while on a long run. There is a tendency to go for even low-percentage shots, rather than end your run with a safety. It's all right to gamble if you are in a friendly game where winning or losing is no big deal, but if you are in a serious competition, you should always play the smartest shot, even if that means playing a safe after running 20, 30, 50 or more balls.

Strategic Maneuvers

Leaving a Shot that Leads Nowhere

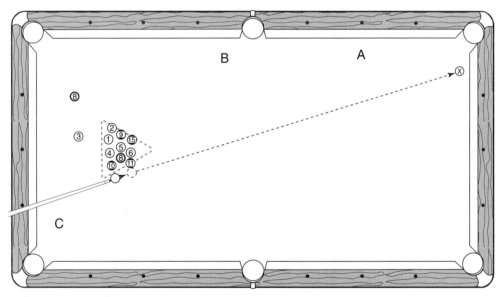

The shot in this diagram is another form of bait for your opponent. If they shoot the 8-ball and make it, the cue ball will return back up-table. The net result is that they have played a safe on themselves. And if your opponent misses, chances are you'll have a shot. If you get put in this position, you could skim the 8-ball on the right side, which would put it behind the rack while sending the cue ball to Position A. You could also try a more aggressive tactic of hitting the 8-ball slightly full. The idea is to leave the cue ball at Position B while the 8-ball relocates at Position C. If you can pull this one off, you will have two sides of the rack exposed to open shots.

Baiting Your Opponent with Table-Length Break Shots

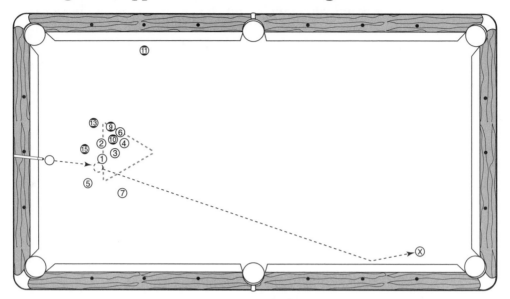

Your strategy should take into account the conditions, the score, and your opponent's game. Let's assume you need only 8 points, which means that you can get out without going into another rack. Your opponent needs 40 points. They are not known for making long, tough, pressure shots, but they see themselves as the hero-type who likes to shoot risky shots when they should play safe.

In this position you could choose to draw back to Position A off the 13-ball. This would force your opponent to play safe, which would not be all that easy. After considering all relevant factors including their game, the best strategy is to skim the 1-ball and send the cue ball to Position X. The reason for leaving the cue ball short of the end-rail is that even a complete fool might not go for a break shot from the end cushion. You've baited the hook with a shot that your opponent will go for, but that the odds say they will miss more often than not. And even if they make the shot, they still have 39 more to go. In short, your opponent could make winning easy for you while your chances of losing are very slim. Note: If you were playing a world-class player, you would most likely choose to play the safety on the 13-ball.

When the Game Is On the Line

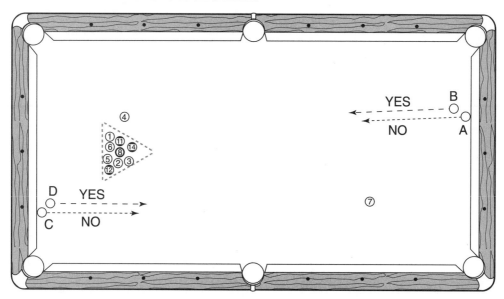

There are occasionally those defining moments in a game of Straight Pool when the outcome may hinge on a long and difficult shot. Your decision of whether or not to risk the outcome of the game on a single shot could rest on a 2" difference in the position of the cue ball, or possibly even less.

In the diagram, you have a possible break shot on the 4-ball from the end-rail. With the cue ball frozen to the rail at Position A, the shot is a no go. Move it out a couple of inches to Position B and the little bell could go off in your mind that says "I can make this shot, I'm going for it". You, and only you, are best qualified to make the decision to play the shot at this moment in time. If you do go for it, give it your best shot with no regrets. Don't look back and say, "I coulda this and I coulda that". The fact is you played that shot, so accept the results and move on.

The cue balls in Positions C and D are two more examples of game-winning and losing shots. From Position C, the shot is a gamble for even the very best players in the world. From Position D, I would guess that a top player would probably expect to make this shot 60-70% of the time. Even though it is no sure thing, this shot could give you better odds than waging a safety battle, especially if defense is a strength of your opponent's game.

• Remember Your Opponent's Fouls

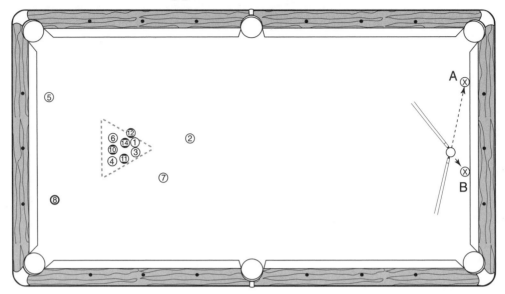

You are on a run of 35 balls, which means you've been shooting for a while. You've just broken the rack and committed the cardinal sin of drawing all of the way back to the end-rail. It looks as if you're going to be forced into playing a very difficult shot that has sellout written all over it. Since you've been in a totally offensive mode, this could make it easy to make mistake #2, which is to forget you're opponent left the table on a foul. Now imagine for a moment how the outcome of the game could be altered by taking and missing the 7-ball, especially when you don't even have to shoot the shot.

Of course you remember details like your opponents fouls. The prudent move is to take an intentional foul. If you bump the cue ball to Position A, you're opponent will have a tough shot with little or no reward. If you nudge the cue ball to Position B, your opponent has an even tougher shot. This shot, however, gives them a better chance of continuing their turn at the table if they are able to make the ball. Once again, when you are in a tough spot, check to see if your opponent is on a foul. Remembering their fouls could only mean the difference between winning and losing, that's all

The Last Rack

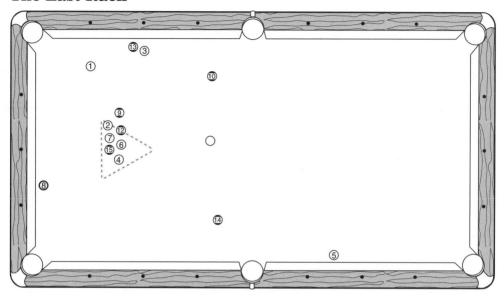

There is a definite strategy for playing the last rack that differs significantly from your pattern play throughout the rest of the game. When you are in the last rack, you need to be primarily concerned with ball count. In the example, there are 6 open shots. If you need 6 points or less, you should pick off the open balls while leaving the clusters alone. This tactic will lower your risk while making it tougher for your opponent should you fail to get out. One possible pattern for playing this layout is 1, 8, 10, 14, 5, and the 9-ball for last. How would you play for 5 or 6 points in this situation?

Now let's assume you need 8 points. You might start with the 9-ball break shot because you have the 10-ball as an insurance ball. You would be wise to use it for insurance when you need only 8 points. If you needed the entire rack, you might want to use the 10-ball to break the 3-13 cluster.

Tips for Playing the Final Rack

- Know how many points you need.
- Count the number of open shots.
- Leave problems for your opponent should you miss.
- Don't worry about setting up a break ball for the next rack.
- Shoot break shots if they are not needed to break clusters.
- Keep your patterns as simple as possible.
- Work around the edges of the rack.

Now for the exception to the above strategy: you are on a high run and you want to continue it after the game has been decided. You must weigh the situation as to whether your opponent might consider this a breach of etiquette. I remember trying to continue a game ending run of about 50 balls. My opponent would have none of it as he scattered the balls about the table after handing me the green.

To Shoot or to Try to Outmove?

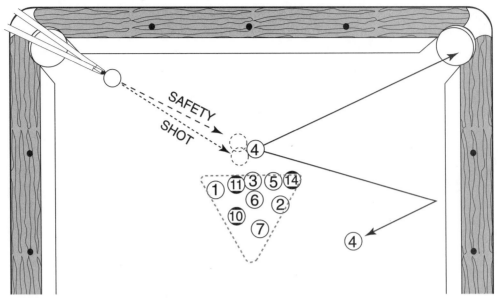

The behind-the-rack break shot on the 4-ball is certainly no cinch. But if you can make it, you should be well rewarded. You could also play safe by rolling the cue ball into the 4-ball and leaving the cue ball behind the rack. So which is the better choice? It really depends on your skills and those of your opponent. If you are a strong shotmaker and your opponent is likely to outmove you in a safety battle, then you might as well go for it. If you can outmove your opponent, then you should probably roll the 4-ball to Position A and play safe. Thin-cut break shots like the one in the example are one of the most vivid examples of the calculated gambles you will encounter in Straight Pool.

• Intentional Fouls

The intentional foul is one of the knowledgeable Straight Pool player's most powerful strategic weapons. The value gained from purposefully losing one point is probably recouped by a factor of 10 in the long run. Properly deployed, an intentional foul can help you press your advantage if your opponent is on the first foul. And when you must take the first intentional foul, it can often turn the tables in your favor, especially if your opponent doesn't know the correct response to a particular situation.

Some Common Scenarios for Intentional Fouls

There are numerous scenarios that encompass the use of intentional fouls. In some cases you will have the upper hand, while in others your opponent will initially have the advantage. Below are just a few of the examples that will serve to give you an idea of the type of thinking that goes into using fouls as a defensive measure.

You Have the Advantage
- You have no fouls, your opponent is on a foul, and it's your shot. You should probably force their hand by taking a foul.
- You're have no fouls, or are on 1 foul, your opponent is on 2 fouls and it's your shot. Make them take a third foul or leave you a makeable shot.

Your Opponent Has the Advantage
- You have no fouls, your opponent has no fouls, and it's your shot. They have left you tough. Is there a safety or should you take a foul? How can you reposition the balls to wiggle out of trouble on the next shot? Will your opponent fall for a bluff?
- You're on one foul, your opponent has none, and it's your shot. Should you take another foul or do you have a safety? Is there a spot they can put you where it will be difficult to avoid a third foul? If so, what can you do to prevent that from happening with your second intentional foul?
- You're on one foul, your opponent is on one foul, and it's your shot. Play a foul with the idea of setting up the balls so you can avoid giving up a shot or committing a third foul on your next turn.
- You're on two fouls, your opponent is on two fouls or less, it's your shot, and you are left tough. Now is the moment of truth. Should you take a third foul and go back another 16 points or not? The answer is not always so obvious. For example, if you only need 3 points and your opponent is out of their normal range for running out, you may be wise to leave them as tough a shot as possible. They will be under extra pressure knowing you need only 3 points and not 19. Should they miss at some point, the game should be yours.

When Your Opponent is on the First Foul

There is no reason to gamble when your opponent is on the first foul and it's your shot. And, of course, the same is true when they are on two fouls and you have no fouls or are on one foul. Now is the time to press your advantage to the limit. In most case that means you should take an intentional foul by tapping or rolling the cue ball to the worst spot you can think of from your opponent's perspective. Rolling the cue ball gives you maximum control in placing it exactly where you want it, especially when compared to sending the cue ball off another ball and to the rail.

Give Your Opponent the Chance to Do Something Dumb

There is an element of bluffing when using intentional fouls. Often you may move the cue ball slightly just to see what your opponent will do. They may pleasantly surprise you by playing a "legal" safety when they would be much better off taking a foul. You might disturb the pack slightly, which will give your opponent something to think about. In doing so they may reposition the cue ball to where you have a better angle for playing a legal safe following their foul. They could even graze the stack and wind up leaving you a dead ball in the rack.

Put Them Back Where They Were

When your opponent is behind on fouls and they take an intentional foul, quite often your best move is to send the cue ball right back where it was, if possible. There could be a very good reason why they didn't like the spot the cue ball was at, so that would be a good place to return it to.

When To Take Three Fouls In a Row

The idea of taking three fouls in a row, which costs 18 points (3 points for the 3 fouls + the 15-point penalty) is not a pleasant thought, especially when you know how hard it can be to grind your way through a rack. Still, you need to keep in mind the strategic value of this potentially game- saving tactic. Whenever you are in doubt about taking three fouls, just ask yourself what is worse: going back 18 points or losing the game.

Your opponent is an excellent player who needs only 9 more points while you need over 38. You're stuck in the middle of the rack (see diagram on the next page) and there are open shots seemingly everywhere. You'll almost certainly lose if you give them a shot at this layout. In this position, your only chance is to accept your 18 points of medicine. Here is the rationale for taking 3 fouls in this position:

- You can't give them a shot at the table when it is this inviting.
- If you play a strong opening break (after the third foul) you could recapture the table.
- It doesn't matter if you lose by 38 or 56 points – a loss is a loss.
- Your comeback run will be that much more spectacular because you've got 18 more balls to run.

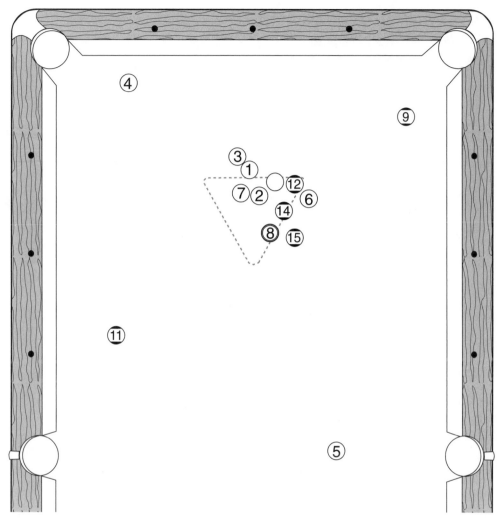

There will be times when you will be in a less drastic position than our example where taking three fouls still makes sense. For instance, let's assume that the tables are playing very easy and you and your opponent are both capable of running lots of balls under these conditions. You might consider taking 3 fouls early in the game because you don't want your opponent to blast off to a big lead. You also know that under the conditions, it will be easier for you to recoup the 18 points with a long run of your own.

The real secret to using the 3-foul rule is to be able to weigh all the appropriate variables so you can make the best strategic decision. You are more likely to use 3 fouls when:

- Your opponent is near victory, or possibly within their runout range.
- The conditions are easy.
- You are playing well and are confident in your ability to run balls.
- Your opponent is an excellent player.

• **Use a Foul to Set Up a Safety**

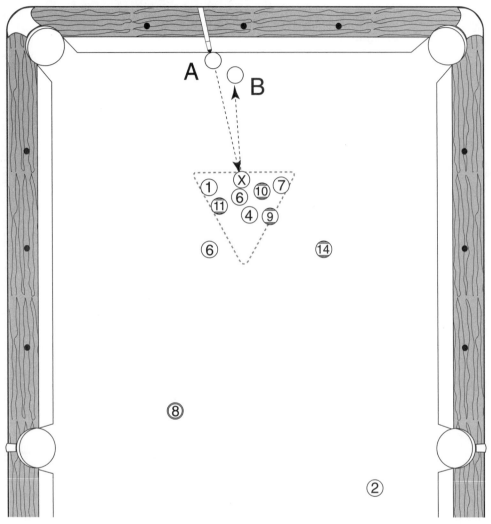

Your opponent has got you in a tough situation with the cue ball at Position A. The cue ball is frozen to the end-rail and there are open shots in the middle of the table. Your options are very limited with the cue ball in this position. In fact, there is no way to play safe without leaving a shot. When in a predicament such as this, you can often set up a safety by first taking an intentional foul.

Let's assume you roll the cue ball gently into the 6-ball. Your opponent counters by trying to push the cue ball back to where it now rests. It will be difficult for him to freeze the ball on the rail while shooting jacked-up over the rack. If he pushes back to Position B, you now have 2" of daylight from the rail to work with. Now you could knock the 7-ball and 14-ball up-table while drawing the cue ball behind the 10-ball. Let's back up to the beginning. Again, the play is to roll the cue ball into the back of the cluster. Your opponent may then counter with an intentional foul. If they are not particularly careful with their push-shot, they could leave you with a chance to play off either the 10-ball or 1-ball and send the cue ball back to the end rail.

When you are in a situation like the one we've just covered, you can often turn the tables in surprisingly quick order. In the first part of the example, your opponent was unable to send the cue ball back to it's original location. In the second part, you took advantage of his failure to play an intentional foul with the utmost of care. Maneuvers such as these can turn a whole game around. I suggest that you learn to enjoy these "little shots" and the battle to outwit your opponents.

End Game Score Reduction

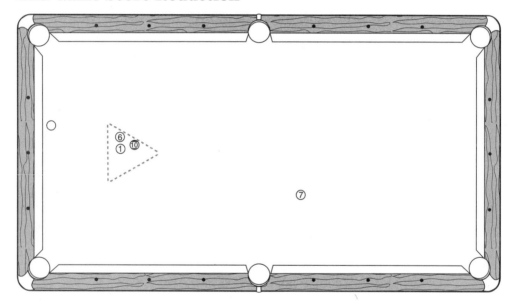

Here's the situation: you need 15 points, you're opponent only needs 4 points and it is your shot. Neither you nor your opponent is on a foul. It would be a mistake to play a safe off the cluster as this could give him the chance to end the game without having to run into the next rack. An intentional foul does you little harm anyway, as you must still score over 10 points out of the next rack. The move is to nudge the cue ball an inch or so. Be sure to keep the cluster between the cue ball and the 7-ball so your opponent can't play safe off the 7-ball. His only choice now is to play an intentional foul. Now he needs 5 points, which means that he will have to get into another rack to beat you. That's a big plus, especially when there is no high-percentage break ball currently available.

From this point forward there are several possible moves and counter moves, too many to mention. The important point is that you're opponent is going to have to do considerably more to win the game now because of that not-so- inconsequential 1-point reduction in their score.

Playing an Intentional Foul After a Scratch

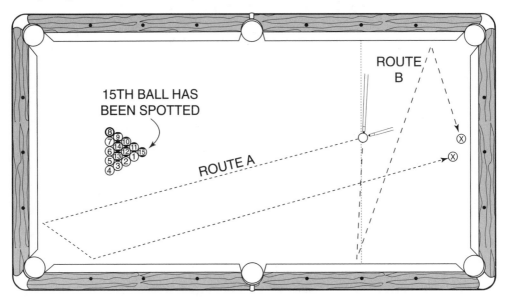

After a scratch in Straight Pool, you get ball-in-hand behind the head-string. This limits the attractiveness of ball-in-hand compared to other games such as Nine-Ball. Nevertheless, you still can maintain the advantage, even if no shots are open down-table, providing you didn't leave the table on a foul on your previous turn. In the diagrammed position, your opponent made the "break shot", missed the rack, and scratched. The 15-ball was spotted at the top of the triangle. (Note: some players will re-rack the balls when this happens if the 15-ball does not freeze against the top two balls.)

The best strategy here is to take a foul and leave the rack undisturbed. The rules state you must send the cue ball over the headstring even when playing an intentional foul after a scratch. The goal is to send the cue ball to the middle diamond on the far end-rail. The two most common routes are shown in the diagram. Use top left english on Route A. Route B also requires top left english. My suggestion is to give each shot a couple of tries in practice. Then use the route you like best when it comes up in a game.

The example shows how to play an intentional foul after a scratch with a full rack. Keep in mind this is a useful strategy even with clusters as small as two balls when there are no open shots down table. The only difference is that you may wish to send the cue ball to another part of the table.

• Adapting to the Playing Conditions

Many great players have commented that Straight Pool is a different game when played under widely varying conditions. Your ability to adapt to the conditions and plot your strategy accordingly can make the difference between winning and losing. Understanding the conditions can also help you to manage your expectations for running balls. If you are playing on unfamiliar equipment, you can learn the conditions in pregame practice, by watching other games, and in the early stages of your matches. Do the conditions match your style? How will you adjust to the conditions if they aren't perfectly suited to your game? Do the conditions help or hurt your opponent? Correctly answering these questions and adopting a game plan suited to the conditions can, everything else being equal, give you the winning edge.

Matching Your Stroke to the Table Speed

Speed control is the critical component of position play in Straight Pool. You can gain an important edge by learning to adapt to the speed of any table as quickly as possible. You should take a few moments to learn how far the cue ball travels up and down the table when you strike it with your favorite speed of stroke on the tables in your homeroom. When you travel to compete, test the tables using this speed of stroke. This will tell you if the tables are playing fast, average, or slow. When you are warming up, play a few of the most basic position routes and assess the results. If you are coming up short, for example, that's an indication that the table is playing slowly. Once you know the speed of a table there are numerous strategies you can use to fine-tune your game.

Table Speed is Fast
- Shoot easier.
- Go an extra rail occasionally.
- Play break shots with less speed and emphasize control.
- Go to the rail more often because it slows down the cue ball.
- Play further away from the object ball until you've adjusted to the table.
- Play for smaller cut angles.

Table Speed is Slow
- Shoot with a firmer stroke.
- Make sure to avoid coming up short of your position zones.
- Limit your cue ball movement.
- Play away from the rails more often.
- Use a firmer stroke on break shots.
- Set up break shots so you will hit the end balls.
- Look for dead balls in the rack more often.
- Play more kill shots.
- Play for larger cut angles.

The Pockets

Straight Pool is largely about pocketing balls consistently and confidently. The size and cut of the pockets therefore plays a big part in formulating your strategy. If you are comfortable with the pockets, you can go about playing an offensive game without worrying about jawing shot after shot. When the pockets are tight, however, pocketing balls can become a major concern. Let's assume that you play regularly on tables with average pockets. When you encounter tables with either tight or easy pockets, you should consider making the following adjustments:

Tight Pockets
- They can effect your shot selection, especially on break shots and long shots
- Shoot extra softly down the rail to avoid jawing the shot.
- Never take even the easiest shot for granted, not that you should under any conditions.
- Play a more defensive game.
- Realize that you're opponent's game may also be affected by the conditions.
- Try to avoid down the rail break shots if possible.
- Play your best position to minimize shot difficulty. Play up closer to the object ball.
- Give each shot you're best stroke. Don't dog stroke it.

Easy Pockets
- Shoot with complete confidence, but don't get careless.
- Realize that it's going to be an offensive game, especially if the balls are breaking reasonably well.
- Fine-tune your position by cheating the pocket when it's called for.
- You can be aggressive playing down-the-rail break shots.
- Be extra careful which shots you leave when you play safe.

How the Balls are Breaking Apart

One of the biggest factors in determining your chances for running lots of balls is how the tables are breaking. The easier a rack comes apart on a break shot, the better your chances of running balls. When it's humid or the balls are unclean or unpolished, they won't come apart nearly as well. When you are playing under these conditions, make an effort to enjoy the chalenge. Tough conditions can offer you a chance to learn something new about the game. For example, you may learn how to pick a rack apart in sections. When the balls aren't breaking well, it is much easier to play safeties, especially off the stack, without selling out. Play a defensive game, and let your opponent get flustered, not you. The tips bellow should help you to adapt quickly to how the balls are breaking open.

The Balls Are Breaking Open Easily

- Play break shots with less speed since you don't need to clobber them to get the balls apart.
- Set up break shots with less of a cut angle so you can control the cue ball better.
- Don't fire away with reckless abandon after a break shot just because the balls are scattered widely.
- Study the layout after the break shot. Be on the lookout for clusters on the side-rails and end-rails, as well as for balls at the far-end of the table.

The Balls Are Tough to Break Open

- Play for a little more cut angle on the break shots.
- Emphasize hitting the end balls, especially on end-rail break shots.
- Avoid shooting too hard on break shots. Don't miss just for the sake of getting the balls open.
- Play a defensive game.
- Be patient.
- Pick the rack apart in sections.

Cleaning the Cloth

Keeping the cloth free of little pieces of debris keeps the cue ball from "turning over" on a piece of chalk as it slows down. Fastidious players should also make a point of removing lint, as it can be very distracting when you are down over a shot. If the palm of your hand starts turning the color of chalk after playing for a little while, it's a sign the table's not very clean. A damp cloth can effectively remove excess chalk and brighten the color of the cloth, but it can take awhile for the moisture to completely dry. When the cloth is filled with chalk, the balls might be especially dirty, which increases the chances of shots skidding and of the rack not breaking very well. These conditions are particularly acute when the humidity is high.

The Balls

Clean and brightly polished balls are a Straight Pool players dream because they spread more easily and are far less prone to skidding. Before playing, take notice of the balls. If they shine and look like new, then they should break open easily. If they are they dull, have pits marks, or the numbers stick out, then your game may suffer as a consequence.

Tip: I suggest you take a few moments to wipe chalk and smudge marks off the balls before starting play.
Tip: If you play in a poolroom, you may wish to consider buying your own set of balls. Then you can clean and polish your set on a regular basis so they play great every time.
Tip: If you don't want to buy a complete set of balls, then I recommend you at least purchase a blue circle cue ball.

Lighting

The heat and quality of the lighting can have an impact on how the table plays, and on your shot selection. For example, contestants at the 2000 BCA U.S. Open were able to run more balls on the table where matches were being filmed because the heat from the lights dried out the table. When checking the lighting, be apprised that florescent lights are not nearly as hot as bulbs. The amount of light cast upon the table could affect your shot selection. If you see shadows next to the balls and the table looks particularly dull, it may make it tough to play thin cut shots, for example.

The Not So Little things

The mechanical bridge is an important tool in Straight Pool. Unfortunately, many places use inexpensive ones that offer insufficient support for your cue. You may be wise to carry with you a quality bridge head that can be placed on the end of a house cue.

Many players prefer to carry their own chalk, rather than leave it to chance. There is nothing more annoying than playing in a room where every piece of chalk seems to have a crater in it. When in a game, you should also beware of the little games your opponent may play with the chalk. For example, when leaving the table, many players will place the chalk on the rail in line with your next shot in an attempt to create a visual distraction.

• Handicapping Straight Pool

Straight pool is one of this easiest game to handicap because of the scoring system. You and your opponent simply need to agree on a specific number of points that the better player is going to be giving. If you play in a league or tournament that uses a handicapping system, then the work of determining the spot has already been taken care of. How much you give or receive in a "friendly" game is a matter of your negotiating skills and the results of previous encounters. Bear in mind that Straight Pool lends itself to lopsided scores, especially when better players are involved. As an example, at the 2000 U.S Open, the average score was 150-82.

The table below should give you some rough guidelines as to what is a fair spot between players of varying levels of skill. Note that the percentage changes in a longer game because in Straight Pool, the longer the game, the better the chances are of the superior player.

Players	Game to 100	Game to 150
A gives a B	40	65
A gives a C	50	85
B gives a C	35	60

CHAPTER 9

SHOTMAKING

How to Adapt Your Shotmaking to Straight Pool

Your success at any pool game rests largely on your ability to pocket a wide variety of shots and to judiciously select shots that are within your unique capabilities. When playing Straight Pool, you must be especially careful about which shots you select because of the often high penalty for missing. It follows that you need to be completely confident and capable of pocketing the vast majority of shots you do choose to play. Like any pool game, however, there will be times when you will have no choice but to go for a difficult shot. In this chapter I'll discuss how you can specifically adapt your shotmaking to Straight Pool.

• Fundamentals

Those of you who mostly play Straight Pool will naturally develop your fundamentals in such a way as to maximize your chances for playing the game as well as possible. This probably means using a shorter bridge for most shots than those who specialize in Nine-Ball. Back in the days when Straight Pool was the main game, champion players used a bridge about 8" long.

If Straight Pool is just one of many games that you play, then you must consider the pros and cons of adapting your shooting style for each game. Can you easily adapt to a shorter bridge for Straight Pool when you mostly play Nine-Ball? Are you comfortable shooting with less english when playing Straight Pool than you normally use in One-Pocket? These are just a couple of questions to ask yourself if you are the type of player who plays several games. Your goal should be to maximize your results in each game without unduly burdening yourself with excessive changes in technique.

Some Thoughts on Technique for Playing Straight Pool
- Consider using an 8-10" bridge for most shots.
- Use a shorter stroke on most shots.
- Learn to use a short pop-stroke for forcing the cue ball short distances.
- If you are primarily a Nine-Ball player, use your long bridge power stroke on selected shots.
- Most shots are generally shorter and easier in Straight Pool than in other pool games. It may be a good idea, therefore, to stand a little taller when playing Straight Pool. You can afford to give up a little in aiming (which you can gain back with a shorter bridge) to get better peripheral vision of the table.
- Learn to recognize when to cinch shots. Put 100% of your attention into making the ball (and, of course, not scratching).
- Beware of developing a Straight Pool poke stroke that causes you to fear long shots. No matter how well you play, you'll still have to occasionally pocket a long shot to keep a run going.
- Shots that are routine in Nine-ball are not so in Straight Pool because of the penalty for missing.

• Developing a Straight Pool Rhythm

As your game develops and your runs become longer and longer, you will come to experience a true Straight Pool player's shooting rhythm. In conversations with several players who have high runs of over 200-300 balls, they singled out shooting rhythm as one of the key ingredients to playing the game at the highest level. These masters excel at entering a zone where they shoot with a pace that is perfectly in sync with their personality. These players all feel that the first 2-3 racks of a long run are really just a warm-up for establishing their rhythm, flow, confidence and feel for the table. Experiencing this kind of rhythm requires that you learn the game inside and out, and that you develop a stroke in which you feel very confident. With extensive knowledge and a dependable stroke in place, you can optimize the process of thinking and shooting, thinking and shooting, over and over again. It also helps if you develop a consistent shooting routine.

Once you find yourself effortlessly shifting gears as you play your runs will grow longer and longer. Think, shoot. Plan, execute. Over and over again with your mind and body in perfect balance. You'll always be required to think, but this part won't take away from your ability to execute. When you are confident about your shooting, you won't feel pressured to play 100% perfect position. Playing Straight Pool on automatic pilot doesn't just happen, at least not until your game is ready, but it is definitely something to look forward to.

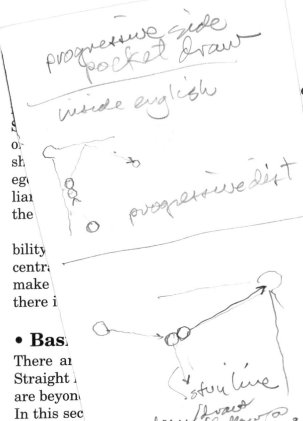

e table (versus the chair) will
s based on the requirements of
shots which have little chance
m to those who feel they can
r example. You must put your
still make combinations, bil-
u shoot in Straight Pool are
ling shots.
ame of 95%-99.8%+ proba-
sy ones that you fail to con-
to rise to the occasion and
of going, especially when

• Bas

There ar
Straight
are beyon
In this sec
that are co
long shots,
binations.

t master to bring your
he details of these shots
in *Play Your Best Pool*.
most important shots
ould include cut shots,
roms, banks and com-

• Shooting Softly

A fine touch will enable you to achieve many positional objectives. It can
also allow you to slide balls into the pocket when an obstruction blocks
part of the entrance to the pocket. A super-fine touch that sends the object
ball into the pocket with only 1-3" to spare requires that you become familiar with the object balls rolling distance after contact. This is a concept
that may be somewhat foreign to Nine-Ball players who are used to using
a full stroke on most shots.

I suggest you practice shooting some straight in shots with the object
ball 2' from the pocket and the cue ball 1' from the object ball. Try having
the object ball barely topple into the pocket without stopping short. This
will refine your touch for playing shots with a very soft stroke.

• Shooting Over a Ball

You simply must get comfortable shooting over balls because the congestion factor in Straight Pool guarantees that you will shoot jacked up on
many occasions. A firm bridge is a must. It is much tougher to get your
bridge just right when you are shooting jacked up, so you need to patient
as you set up for these shots. It also takes a little more time to get properly aligned for the shot. So don't make the mistake of shooting until

you are quite comfortable with your stance and alignment. I suggest that you use as short of a stroke as possible. If you need some power, try to generate it mostly with your wrist.

On nearly every shot, you should be looking at the object ball as you let the shot go. Some players, however, are successful shooting jacked up shots by looking at the cue ball last. If you have trouble shooting over balls, perhaps this method will work for you.

There are certain occasions when there are several balls lined up in front of the object ball which prevent you from placing your bridge hand on the table, or even from using the mechanical bridge. In this circumstance, you would normally chose another shot or play safe. If your hands are rock steady, you could use an air bridge to play the shot. Hold your bridge hand within a few inches of the cue ball and use the lowest degree of elevation possible that still enables you to make solid contact with the cue ball. It can help add stability to the shot if you cock your wrist backwards. In case there are any doubters, I saw the great Johnny Archer make a shot using this technique in a major Straight Pool championship.

Shooting Opposite Handed

If you are ambidextrous or have a penchant for hard work and practice, then you can develop the ability to play shots with your opposite hand. This skill really comes in handy in Straight Pool as it allows you to use a fuller stroke than you may be able to generate with a mechanical bridge. You can also play position on shots that you might otherwise avoid. You will also have a higher degree of effectiveness on those shots where you wind up with an opposite handed shot because you failed to consider the stretch factor when playing position.

You should develop a keen awareness of your ability to play shots with your opposite hand. Some players will only play the easiest shots opposite handed, or even avoid them altogether. Other players, on the other hand, may feel comfortable shooting a break shot opposite handed. If you have any doubts about playing a shot opposite handed, I suggest you reach for the bridge. A so-so stroke with a bridge is almost always better than a poor stroke with your opposite hand.

• The Mechanical Bridge

You should make an effort to become very effective using the mechanical bridge. The keys to the bridge are a short stroke with a little more wrist action than on a normal shot. I also advise that you use somewhat of a sidearm stroke as this helps keep the cue as level as possible. Try to make your stroke as smooth and relaxed as the stroke you use for shots without the bridge. Unless you are shooting over a ball, you should use the lowest rung on the bridge, as this will help keep you from shooting excessively down on the cue ball.

When you must shoot over balls using a mechanical bridge, take extra care in setting up for the shot. Get the bridge exactly where you want it. Use a couple of practice strokes to make sure the position feel right. Then pause for a moment to regroup before going into your shooting routine.

Tip: When you must use a mechanical bridge to shoot over several balls, and the highest rung is still not high enough, you can place a second bridge on top of the first. Play this shot with extreme care.

Behind the Back

There seems to be two groups of players who play shots behind their back: novices who think they look cool and who think shooting this way will impress onlookers, and very fine players who have mastered the technique and who can use it very effectively. The main difficulty with shooting behind your back is getting lined up properly using what is inherently such an awkward position. I don't recommend shooting behind your back, but if it works, and I mean really works for you, then by all means use this technique when it's appropriate.

• Long Shots

There will be many occasions when you will play long shots into the far corner pockets with the cue ball and object ball close to each other, and with little or no cut angle. These long shots are not very difficult, they just require that you concentrate on the shot.

The long green shots that terrify some Straight Pool players are the kind where there are several feet of distance between the cue ball and object ball. The main ingredients for success on long green shots are proper technique, confidence and concentration. On long shots, it's all about balancing your priorities. Use little, if any, english and play for adequate shape on the next ball. When you are facing a long shot, you should concentrate primarily on pocketing the ball. Stay down on the shot and give it your best stroke.

Use a Short Stroke for Accuracy

Many excellent players have long favored the short stroke because of it's high degree of accuracy. When your backstroke is only 2-4" long, there is not much room for anything to go wrong with your stroke. With a short stroke, the main factor in pocketing the shot is aiming properly. When using a short stroke, you must guard against poking at the cue ball. You may also have some difficulty with speed control. The short stroke is highly effective on longer stop shots and shots where you need accuracy, not power. A short stroke can also be effective on softer shots as it can help keep you from decelerating into the cue ball, which can rob a shot of accuracy.

The Wrist Stroke

When the cue ball is close to the object ball and you use a full follow through, there is a danger of double hitting the shot. This can pose a problem if you need at least a moderately powerful stroke. The solution is to use a short stroke with a pronounced snap of the wrist. Be sure to limit your follow through so you don't foul. You will be pleasantly surprised at how much power can be generated with this kind of stroke.

The Dreaded Skid Shot

Every so often the cue ball will stick to the object for just a fraction of a second longer than normal before the object ball continues on its way. Chalk on the cue ball and/or object ball is the primary reason why a ball skids. The faster cloth now being used also contributes to skidding. It is easy enough to spot a skid: you will undercut the shot by a wide margin even though you know you hit it right, and the balls will make a sickening sound (at least to a pool players ears) at contact. Skids happen mostly on softly hit cut shots, especially those hit with inside english.

Many excellent players avoid skids by using outside on softly hit cut shots. Before adopting this preventive measure, you should carefully consider whether the cure is worse than the problem. You may eliminate skids by using english, but you may also wind up missing even more shots by using english than you missed due to skidding while hitting the cue ball on the center axis.

Tip: Since the cue ball is hit 15 times more than each ball, and because chalk is applied directly to the cue ball from contact, I suggest you wipe off the cue ball after every scratch shot.

Tip: The majority of skids occur because of chalk on the cue ball. If you and your opponent agree, you could accurately mark the position of the cue ball at the end of each rack and wipe the cue ball. This is really no different than a golfer marking and cleaning their ball before putting.

Viewing Obstructions Accurately

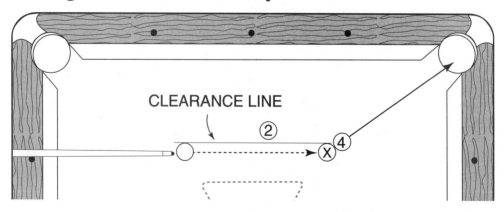

The 4-ball can be made, but it may not appear that way because of the presence of the 2-ball, which obscures the left edge of the 4-ball. In this situation, many players will overcut the 4-ball just to make sure they don't run into the 2-ball You can avoid this mistake by visualizing the cue ball's position at contact. Remember that you must allow for contact-induced throw, which means that you can hit the 4-ball slightly more to the right than you may think.

Once you've determined the cue ball's position at contact, line up the left edge of the cue ball with the left edge of the imaginary cue ball at contact. Does the line pass by the 2-ball with at least a 1/8" or 1/4" to spare? If so, you should now be able to play the shot as you normally would with no concern for hitting the 2-ball.

• Cut Shots

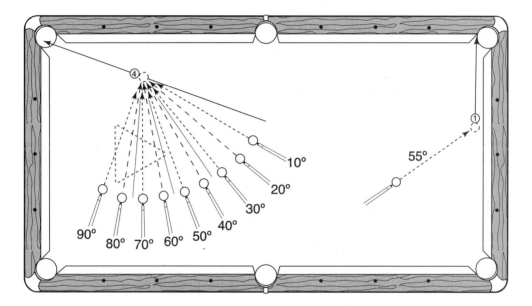

When playing Straight Pool, you don't want to be playing position for thin cut shots on a regular basis. But what cut angle is the kind that puts you at risk of missing? That largely depends on your game. The diagram shows a series of cut shots from 10 degrees to the theoretical limit of 90 degrees. In Straight Pool, most shots are played with a cut angle of less than 35 degrees. These fairly shallow cut shots are not a problem for average players. Cut shots in the 35-55 degree zone are not difficult for experienced players.

At some point, however, every player reaches an angle where a cut shot begins to really test their capabilities. For most players that range falls between 55-75 degrees. Even world-class players seldom, if ever, play cut shots above 75 degrees. I suggest you study the various cut angles on the diagram to determine you own comfort range. You may even wish to set up the shots on a table.

The 55-degree cut shot on the other side of the diagram shows what this angle looks like. Higher cut angles like this are used in Straight Pool mostly for breaking balls apart, not for playing shape.

• **Frozen Cue Ball Table Length**

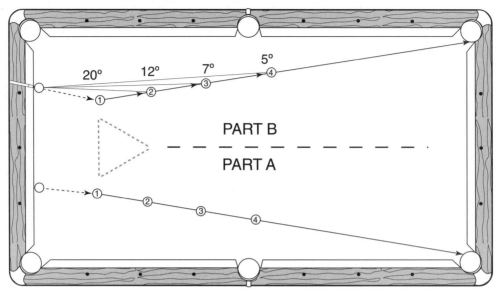

When you are engaged in a safety battle on the end-rail, you will quite often find yourself facing a table-length shot off the rail. In some instances you may have the option of playing safe, but in others you will have little choice except to go for the shot. Since ownership of the table is at stake, skill at frozen-to-the-rail shots like the ones on the diagram will give you a big offensive weapon. Skill at frozen shots will also reduce your opponent's options for playing safe.

The degree of difficulty factor rises dramatically the farther the object ball is stationed from the rail. A frozen-to-the-rail shot reaches it's maximum degree of difficulty when the ball is opposite the side pocket. In Part A, the 2-ball is more difficult than the 1-ball, while the 4-ball is much tougher than the 2-ball. Part B shows a series of cut shots that you might typically encounter from the end rail. The secret to playing this shot is to use a short stroke of no longer than 4", a short bridge, and a level cue. Many players feel that an open bridge gives them a better look at the shot.

Your main concern is to pocket the ball, so use the speed that maximizes your accuracy. Normally you need not be concerned too much with position on this shot because there will usually be at least a couple of shots available in the middle part of the table. This shot is worth spending some time on in practice. I suggest you start with the 1-ball and work your way up to the 4-ball.

• Combinations (P)

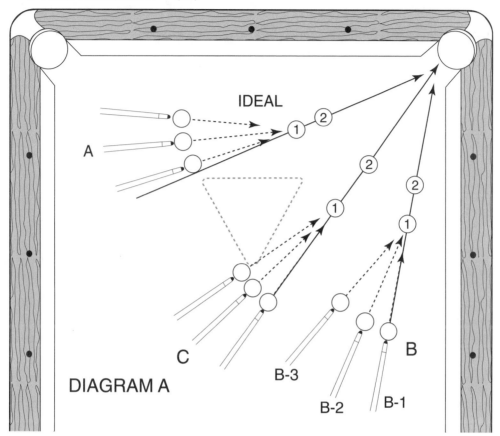

DIAGRAM A

You will be playing combination shots ("combos") quite often in Straight Pool. You must therefore become skilled at playing the easier versions of these shots. At the same time, the accuracy requirements of the game severely limit which combos you should be shooting. In other words, you must master the easy combos, and pass on shooting the tough ones. Naturally your definition of which combos are easy and which are not is a highly individualistic matter. Don't hesitate to shoot what you know you can make. But don't balk at passing on a combo if a higher percentage shot or a safety is available.

Part A of Diagram A shows a series of the most basic Straight Pool combinations. The balls are about 1" apart, and there is very little cut angle. These are the type of combos you should always play and almost never miss. In Part B, the balls are now 2" apart. The shot is not hard with the cue ball in Position B-1. The difficulty factor rises significantly though with the cue ball at Position B-2. When the cue ball is over a few inches at B-3, this shot can be easily missed by even the best of players. The chances of missing are greater still with the two balls about 5" apart in the three position in Part C. The object balls in our examples were all lined-up at the pocket. The combos would have naturally been that much more difficult if you had to cut the first ball into the second ball.

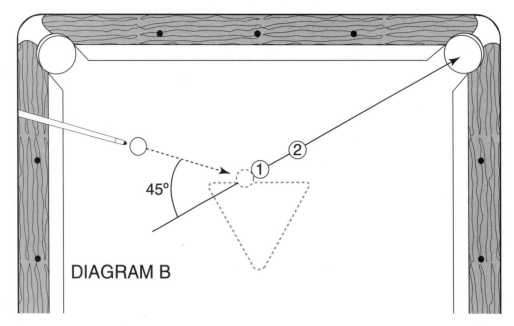

DIAGRAM B

Diagram B shows a combo that's missed often, even when the player is certain they have hit the first ball at their chosen contact point. The problem is they mistakenly believe that the contact point is in a direct line through the back of the second ball. The cue ball, however, will be approaching the first ball at a 45-degree angle, which is going to throw the 1-ball slightly to the right. By the time the 1-ball contacts the second ball, it will be far enough to the right of the contact point to cause the 2-ball to be missed to the left of the pocket. The solution is to hit the first ball a little fuller to compensate for the contact induced throw.

• Frozen Combos

Part A of Diagram A illustrates a frozen combination that is lined up directly with the pocket. To pocket the shot, just shoot at the 4-ball as if you were playing it. The beauty of this shot is that you can be slightly off with your aim and still make the shot. You can also play this shot with a hard stroke without worrying about missing. This can be helpful if you are using the shot as a secondary break shot into a thick cluster.

In Part B, the object balls are lined up to the right of the pocket. You can still make this frozen combo by contacting the 1-ball to the right of center as shown. The 8-ball will be thrown to the left into the pocket. If the combo was lined up to the left of the pocket, you would aim at the left side of the second ball. A soft stroke enables the second ball to be thrown farther. When the combo a couple of feet or more from the pocket, the second ball can be thrown a few inches into the pocket. Pocketing long distance frozen combos using a soft stroke requires experience and good judgment.

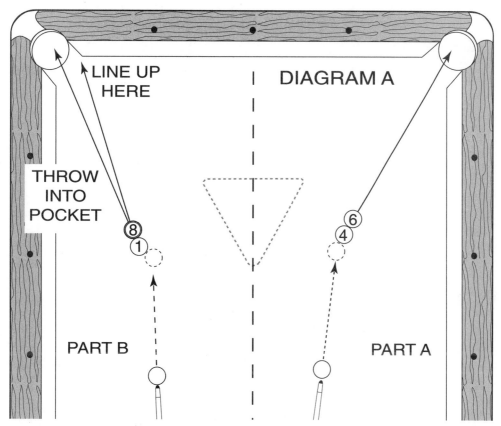

Diagram B below shows a steeper cut angle on a frozen combo than the shots in Diagram A. You could aim as usual down Line A. The cue ball would continue to the rail and out to the center of the table after contacting the 5-ball. If you needed the cue ball to remain near the point of contact with the combo, you could aim straight at the 5-ball down Line B. You can keep the 11-ball from being thrown to the left by using a hard stroke, which severely reduces the throw.

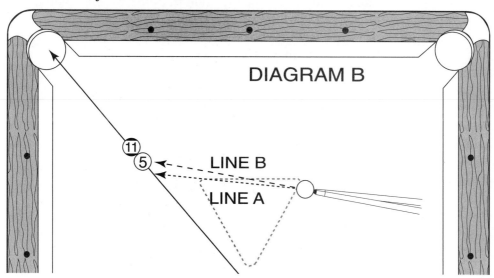

• The Critical 1/8th Inch

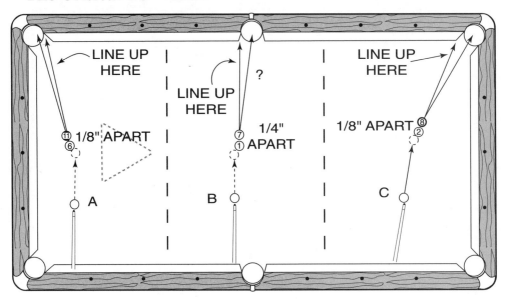

Frozen combos are a snap once you understand how they can be thrown into the pocket. When the balls in a combo are within about 1/8 of an inch of each other, you can still apply throw to the second ball. In Part A of the illustration, the 6-ball and 11-ball are 1/8" apart, and are lined up at the right edge of the pocket. You can make the shot by cutting the 6-ball as shown. Hitting the 6-ball to the right of center applies right english to it, which throws the 11-ball to the left and into the pocket.

In Part B, the 1-ball and 7-ball are⁄" apart. Hitting the 1-ball to the left of center will put left english on it, which will help throw the 7-ball to the right. This action, however, will largely be canceled by the fact that the 1-ball is cutting the 7-ball to the left. When two balls are over 1/8" apart, it becomes very difficult, if not impossible to throw the shot into the pocket. At the same time, the balls are not far enough apart to allow you to hit the opposite side of the first ball to cut the second ball into the pocket.

The combo in Part C is very similar to the shot in Part A except that it is lined up a little further above the pocket. In this case, you can augment the throw that comes by cutting the 2-ball on the left side. Use right english, which will turn into left english on the 2-ball. The left english will, in turn, help throw the 8-ball to the right and into the pocket.

• Bank Shots

Bank shots are a mainstay of many pool games, including Nine-Ball and One-Pocket. Even if you miss a bank in either game, you may still end up with a safety, or you might even gain some other strategic advantage. In One-Pocket, banks are missed routinely while the cue ball is stationed on the

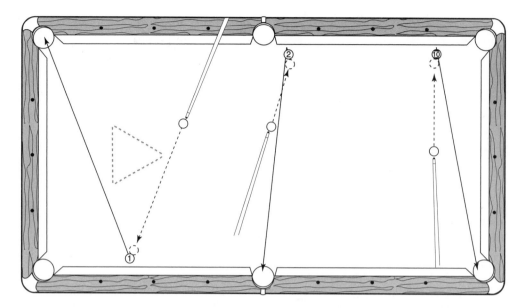

other side of the pack. In Nine-Ball, a bank may be combined with a hook (a two way shot) to create an offensive/defensive maneuver. In Eight-Ball a missed bank could block an opponent's pocket.

In Straight Pool, however, a bank shot is an altogether different animal. A bank is looked upon as a high-risk shot, even if the odds of making it are 80% or even 90%. In Straight Pool you want an unending series of 95%+ shots. That's how you run balls and keep your opponent off the table. However, it is a game loaded with exceptions to the rule. I remember watching Lou Butera make 4 bank shots in one rack of Straight Pool during the 1974 U.S. Open in Chicago.

When playing Straight Pool, even the easier bank shots seem tough to most players. Perhaps that's because the penalty for missing (the chair) can be so great. Banks shots are also tougher because you are not used to playing them in Straight Pool. In championship play, the crowd will cheer wildly for a bank shot that would go almost unnoticed in a game of Nine-Ball.

Still, there are times when you should play a bank shot. The diagram shows a couple of typical short-rail banks that you should be able to pocket a very high percentage of the time. The cross side bank on the 2-ball is particularly inviting because the pocket is so big when approached from this direction. The cross-corner bank is a little tougher as the 10-ball is nearly a diamond up the rail. You will raise your accuracy by shooting this bank softly, which reduces the chances of the ball rattling in the jaws of the pocket.

The bank shot on the 1-ball is played all of the time in Nine-Ball and One-Pocket, but is rarely played in Straight Pool. As a rule of thumb, you should avoid most bank shots when the ball is more than a diamond up the rail from the pocket, opposite the one you would be playing the ball into.

• Carom Shots

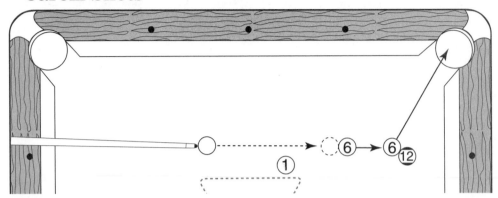

When you don't have a ball that can go directly into a pocket, a carom shot may be the answer. The 1-ball prevents you from cutting the 6-ball into the corner pocket. The 12-ball is in a good position for a carom shot. You want the 6-ball to hit the spot on the 12-ball that is at a 90-degree angle to the pocket. When the ball you are caroming off of is any farther from the pocket than the 12-ball, the object ball will tend to drift forward after contact. You can avoid this problem by playing the shot with a firm stroke. After the 6-ball contacts the 12-ball, it will behave like the cue ball does after it contacts an object ball when hit with a stun stroke.

• Dead Carom Shots

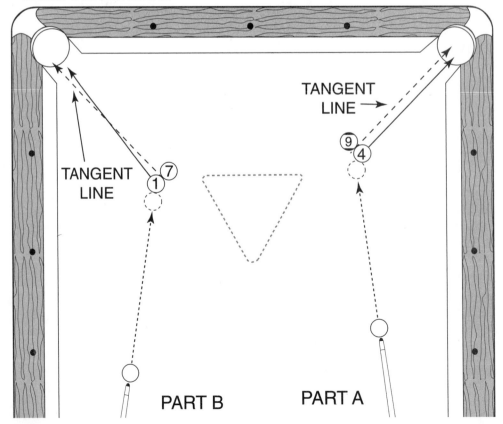

The 4-ball is dead in Part A of the diagram on the previous page. All you have to do is contact the 4-ball anywhere near the position shown with a follow stroke. When two balls are frozen such as in the diagram, extend the tangent line between the balls to the pocket. If it lines up about an inch towards the far edge of the pocket, then the shot should split the pocket. Notice that the center of the 4-ball points almost directly at the center of the pocket. In Part B, the tangent line is pointing at the left edge of the pocket. You can still make the shot by hitting the 1-ball full with draw. The 1 and 7-balls will be pushed slightly forward before the 1-ball squirts off towards the pocket.

• Billiards

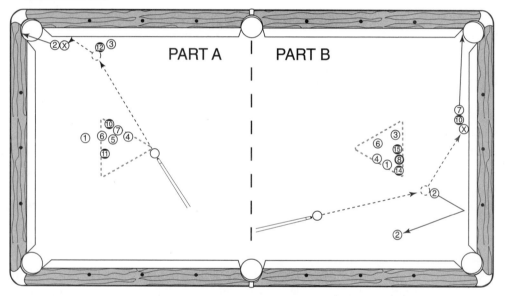

The cluster blocks a direct shot on the 2-ball in Part A of the diagram. In addition, the 3-ball prevents you from using the 12-ball to play a combination. You can still pocket the 2-ball by sending the cue ball off the side of the 12-ball and into the 2-ball as shown. The often congested quarters of a rack of Straight Pool will give you plenty of opportunities to play billiards like this throughout your career.

When playing billiards, you can predict the cue ball's path with great accuracy when it is within about 2' or less of the first ball. The key here is to use centerball and a firm stroke. In essence, you are playing a billiard with a stun stroke. The cue ball in Part B will travel precisely down the tangent line as shown after contacting the 2-ball. Shots like this billiard/combo are a means of combining concepts to create a solution to a potentially troublesome situation (see the previous section).

Near Dead Billiards

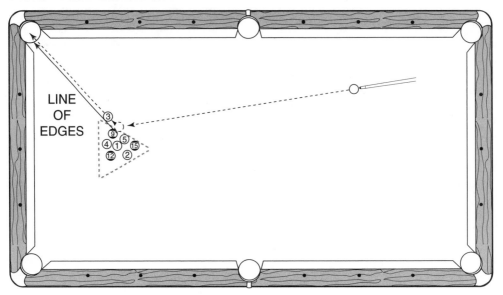

When a ball sticks out slightly from a partially broken rack, you may have a dead billiard that can also serve as a break shot. In the diagram, you have what appears to be a long tough break shot on the 3-ball. The 9-ball up next to the 3-ball may give you a shot at a dead billiard. Line up the outside edge of the 9-ball with the inside edge of the 3-ball. If they line up at the left center of the pocket, you have a dead billiard. (Note: you must allow for the width of the 3-ball in lining up the shot).

If the edges of the two balls lined up further to the left of center than is shown, you could throw the shot in with outside (left) english. And if the edges were pointing a little to the right, you could throw the shot in with inside (right) english. Use a firm stroke with draw so the cue ball doesn't follow the object ball into the pocket.

Miscellaneous Shotmaking

Rail-First

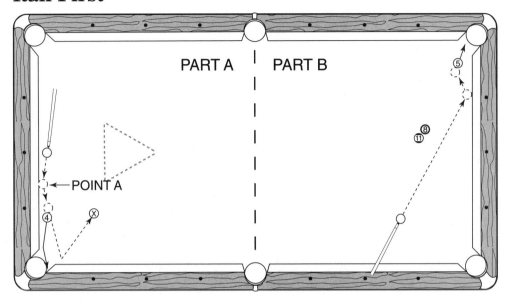

Rail-first shots are often used to escape the cushion when you've left your-self a straight-in shot, as shown in Part A. When both the cue ball and object ball are about the same distance from the rail, the target on the rail is a spot slightly ahead of the midway point between where the cue ball is now and it's position at contact. You can increase the cut angle coming off the rail on the 4-ball by aiming a little ahead of Point A and cheating the pocket. The 4-ball will brush the lower rail before continuing into the pock-et. Cheating the pocket will help send the cue ball a little farther up the table.

Another technique many players favor is to aim at about the mid-point between the two balls and use running (left) english. This helps the cue ball turn up table after it hits the side-rail. The shot we've just cov-ered can also be very useful in helping you to escape the side rail. You might use it, for example, if you're straight-in on a key ball shot and you need to come off the rail for shape on the break ball. Also keep in mind that you can play rail-first shots with centerball or draw if that's what's need-ed to get the position you're after.

In Part B, the 11-8 cluster blocks the 5-ball. You can still pocket the shot by aiming at the rail ahead of the 5-ball. Again, many players seem to feel that running english (left) helps to make this shot a bit easier. You really don't need to adjust your aim when using english because the throw on the object ball is canceled out by the shallower angle of approach the cue ball will have into the 5-ball (thanks to the english flattening out the rebound angle).

Combining Shots

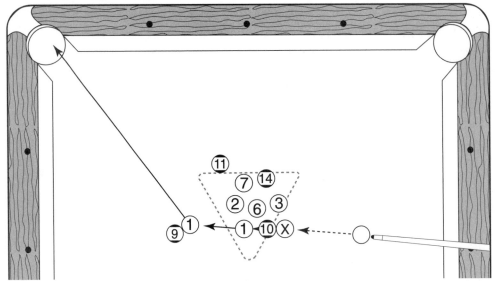

You can combine different shots to form a hybrid, such as the one in the diagram. The 10-ball and 1-ball are lined up at the right half of the 7-ball. Furthermore, it looks as if the 1-ball can be played as a combination into a carom off the 7-ball into the upper left corner pocket. At this distance you would need to aim the 1-ball to hit slightly to the right of the pocket because it will drift forward of the tangent line. If you are quite confident in the shot in the illustration, you might also consider using a hard follow stroke so you can scatter the pack. We have just created a combo/carom/break shot! A shot like this is admittedly a bit of a gamble, but even in Straight Pool sometimes you've got to take a risk.

The list below gives you a few more hybrid shots that appear with some regularity in Straight Pool. Note that the elements of the shots are in the order in which they occur. The illustration was of a combo into a carom, so the shot is a combo/carom. All of the combos in the list below are either dead or can be easily thrown into the pocket.

- Combo/ carom
- Billiard/combo
- Kick/combo
- Rail first/combo
- Bank/pocket hanger

Curve Shots

The 6-ball is blocking just enough of the 1-ball in Part A on the diagram on the next page such that you can't make the shot by conventional methods. You can, however, still pocket the 1-ball by curving the cue ball around the 6-ball. Aim away from the 6-ball to allow for the curve to the right. Jack-up slightly and use right english. You don't need a big swing in the cue ball or anything resembling a masse shot. A nice gentle curve will work fine. The right english will throw the 1-ball to the left, so you really don't have to curve the cue ball quite as much as you might have

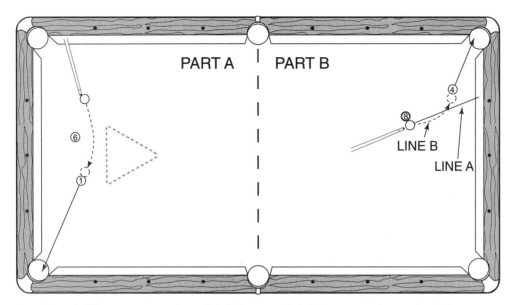

imagined. You can create a highly predictable curve by using the same speed and technique for almost all of your curve shots. One method is to lightly drop the cue into the shot at consistently the same angle.

In Part B the cue ball is frozen up against the 8-ball. The cue ball is pointing down Line A if you played it off the edge of the 8-ball. In doing so, you would miss the 4-ball. You could aim away from the 8-ball and curve the cue ball back towards the 4-ball down Line B. An easier way to play the shot is to send the cue ball down Line A off the edge of the 8-ball. Jack-up slightly and use left english. This method enables you to better control the path of the cue ball. In addition, you don't need to curve the cue ball nearly as much.

Curve the Object Ball Shot

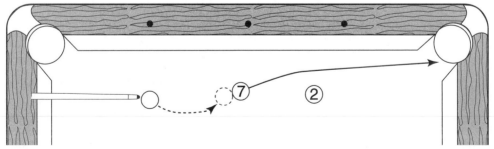

The 2-ball is blocking just enough of the pocket so that the 7-ball can't be made, at least by means of a conventional shot. You can pocket the 2-ball by jacking up slightly and using left English with a sharp stroke. You can aim almost directly at the 7-ball. The cue ball will deflect to the right and then curve back to the left. The spinning cue ball will throw the 7-ball to the right. It will also put enough right spin on the 7-ball to enable it to curve around the 2-ball on its way to the pocket. Note: don't play this shot without first mastering it in practice.

Rack Shots

I love to watch players study the rack for a dead ball. There is a certain intrigue and intensity as they peer at the balls from one angle, then another. What are they looking for? What do they see? What do they know or not know? And then comes the big decision: to shoot or not to shoot what may or may not be a dead ball in the stack. This all leads up to the grand finale when they give it their best shot. Will they be starting or continuing a run, or will they blast open the balls for their opponent? Yes, there is perhaps no more dramatic moment in Straight Pool than when a player exposes their knowledge for the world to see and puts the game on the line by playing a "can't miss" dead ball in the rack.

Finding dead balls in the rack, and then having the conviction to shoot them, is a must to reach your full potential as a player. But that does not mean that you should test your knowledge by playing everything that you hope will go, think will go, or has some remote chance of going. No, you must learn to study the rack for dead balls with the cold calculation of an Investment Banker. Is this shot a good deal, or not? You must carefully study all of the relevant factors before risking a shot that could largely determine the outcome of the game. Your decision to play a rack shot may be influenced by several of the following criteria:

- Does the object ball line up directly at the pocket, or at the edge of the pocket?
- Can the shot be thrown into the pocket if it is a little off?
- Can the shot be thrown out of the pocket?
- Is the shot frozen?
- What english should I use, if any?
- What speed should be used?
- Am I going to blast the rack or play a more controlled break shot?
- Is there a risk of scratching? If so, how can it be eliminated?
- Could the cue ball get stuck in the stack?
- Can the cue ball be controlled, or am I going to have to turn it loose?
- Is there possible interference from other balls in the rack?
- What kind of shot is it? Is it a combo, billiard or carom, or even a hybrid, such as billiard/combo?

Let's examine the shot in the diagram using items from the checklist presented above. For starters, it looks as if the 4-ball and 12- ball are lined up at the left side of the pocket. There is about a 1/8" gap between them. You can't aim directly at the combo, but you could play a billiard off the 8-ball into the 12-4 (Shot A). Because the 12-4 are so close together, you could throw the shot towards the center of the pocket by using some right english (which will turn into left english on the 12-ball).

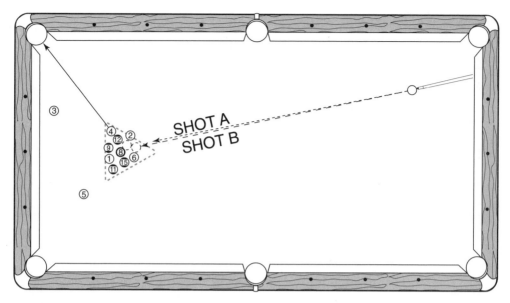

There is no risk of scratching, but you might get stuck in between the balls if you shoot too softly. Shot A will open 6 of the balls, but will leave the 6, 11, and 15-balls untouched. You could open these balls at the same time by playing Shot B, which is a billiard off the 6-ball and 8-ball into the 12-4 combo. This shot is riskier, but it offers a bigger reward. A percentage player would choose Shot A, figuring they can open the other 3 balls later in the frame. This player might also realize that the 6, 11 and 15-balls can all go into the same pocket once the other balls have been removed.

Irving Crane played a backward combo out of the rack to start a run of 150 and out versus Joe Balsis at the 1966 U.S. Open. I was also fortunate enough to have a dead ball in the rack that got me started on a decent run when playing Mr. Balsis in an exhibition match in the early 70's. He, of course, went on to win the game, but the shot still makes me smile twenty-something years later. Perhaps one day you will start a long run in an important match with a similarly crowd pleasing shot out of the rack.

Finding Dead Rack Shots

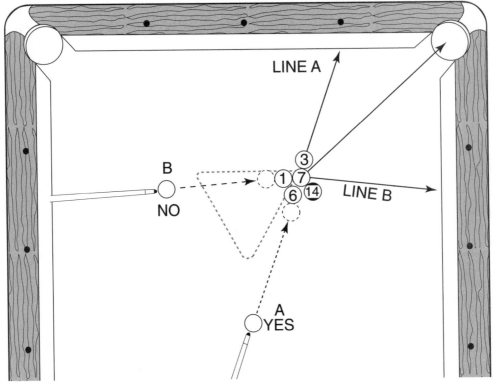

Your ability to pick out dead shots from unlikely positions could help you start or preserve a run. In the diagrammed position, it looks like nothing will go in the five ball cluster. With the cue ball at Position A, however, the 7-ball is dead! The cue ball's force at contact with the 6-ball will drive the 2-ball towards the end-rail down Line A. The 7-ball will be squeezed at the left edge of the 14-ball. The 7-ball has now been turned in to a dead carom off the 14-ball. The 7-ball will not go with the cue ball in Position B because the initial force of contact with the 1-ball would drive the 14-ball away, destroying the dead carom. The 7-ball would travel down Line B.

Jump Shots

Jump shots are a favorite of Nine-Ball players, but are seldom used in Straight Pool because of their inherently risky nature. Still, there is a time and a place for everything. The diagram on the next page illustrates the ideal conditions for playing a jump shot in Straight Pool:

- You must only clear the outer edge of the blocker.
- You have a long landing strip.
- The ball you are playing is near the pocket.
- There is a ball on which you can easily get position.

In the example, a jump shot is easier than a long distance curve shot since the cue ball will be traveling directly at the object ball. This eliminates the need to calculate the amount the cue ball will be curving over a span of about 5'.

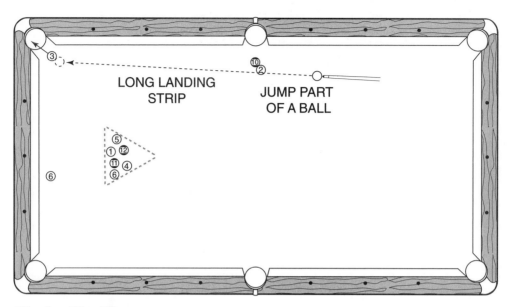

Choke Up Shot

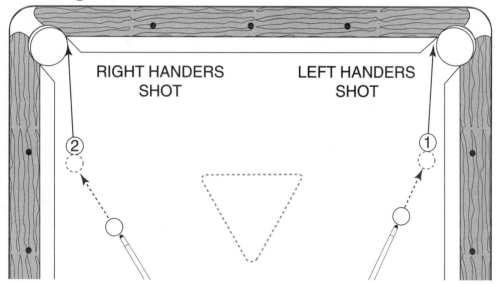

You can avoid using the mechanical bridge and gain additional power if needed when the object ball is located near the side rail and the cue ball is a little further from the rail. The diagram shows typical positions for the choke up shot for both righthanders and lefties. Lean over the table and use a closed bridge for stability. Place your bridge hand about 5" from the cue ball. Choke up with your grip hand to a position near or at the joint. The goal is to be able to lean over the table and shoot with your head directly over the cue so you don't lose any accuracy. In this position, you can shoot with surprising power and accuracy.

• Stretch Zones

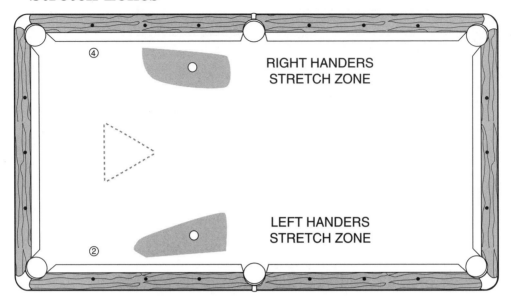

In Straight Pool, the balls are primarily located at one end of the table so you will be shooting them mostly towards the corner pockets on the foot rail from either the side of the table, or while leaning over the head rail. Because of this, if you are not careful when playing position, you may find yourself unable to reach a particular shot. Even though you can still use a mechanical bridge if you are unable to reach a shot, you may often find you need the power and accuracy of your normal stroke to play the shot the way you really need to.

For this reason and others, it is important for you to discover those areas on the table where you can't reach a shot without stretching excessively or using a mechanical bridge. Part A of the diagram gives you my stretch zone on the 2-ball (Note: I'm 6' tall). If the cue ball is anywhere within the zone, I have a long stretch or a shot with a mechanical bridge. The zone in Part B shows where I would encounter a stretch shot on the 4-ball if I were right-handed. I suggest you place the cue ball and an object ball in various locations to determine your individual stretch zones, which will be based on your unique physical characteristics.

Tip: When you are in a game, wondering if the position play you are considering could lead to a stretch shot, take a moment to make a stance where the next shot will be played. If you find you are playing position for a stretch shot, you may want to choose a new position zone.

Tip: If you find yourself with a long stretch shot, set up just to the left or right of the shot and take a couple of practice strokes to get a better feel for the action required. This approach is much like a golfer's practice swings. Remember, the more you need to stretch for a shot, the less power you should use in order to maintain your accuracy.

Leaning Out Over the Table

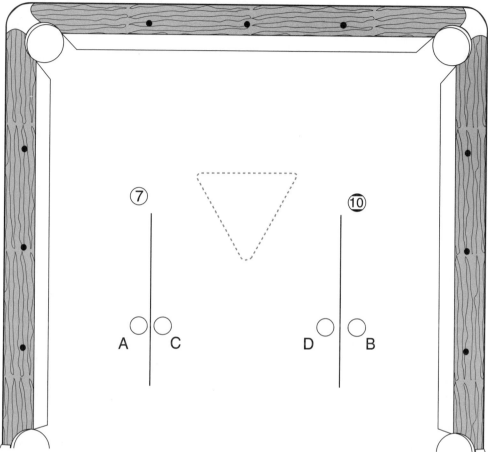

There are two nearly identical cue ball positions for the 7-ball break shot for righthanders. The same is true for the 10-ball, which is a lefthanders break shot. In fact, the 3" difference in the location of the cue ball in each position completely changes the shot. With the cue ball at Position A, a righthander can easily lean over the side of the table without compromising their aim. The same is true for a lefthander with the cue ball at Position B.

With the cue ball at Position C, a righthanded player will have to lean over the head rail and stretch for the shot. The same goes for a left-handed player with the cue ball in Position D. You cannot use nearly as much power with the cue ball in Positions C or D. When playing position, you must factor into your planning those critical few inches where a lean-over-the-table shot turns into a stretch shot down the length of the table.

Kick Shots

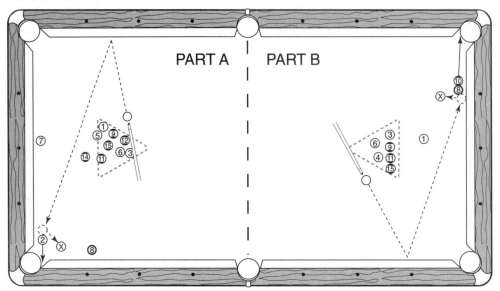

Kicks shots are normally considered to be a defensive maneuver in One-Pocket, or a means of avoiding a foul in Nine-Ball. Kick shots are seldom played in Straight Pool because the chances of pocketing the ball are usually very slim. The diagram shows two instances where a kick shot is probably your best choice.

In Part A, you are stuck behind the rack. The 2-ball is near the lower left corner pocket, which makes it a reasonably large enough target to consider playing a kick shot. If you feel the odds of making the 2-ball are better than winning a safety battle from this position, then it is your best shot. Should you pocket the 2-ball, you will be rewarded with a secondary break shot on the 14-ball. If the 2-ball were a little closer to the rail, you should aim for the gap between the 2-ball and the rail, which gives you a big margin for error.

The kick shot in Part B is very similar to that in Part A, except that now you are kicking into a frozen combo. Aim to hit the rail and the 8-ball at the about the same time as this will throw the 10-ball to the left into the pocket. The only kick shots you should ever consider playing in Straight Pool should be the absolute simplest versions of this high-risk shot.

When a Frozen Cluster Can Be Made

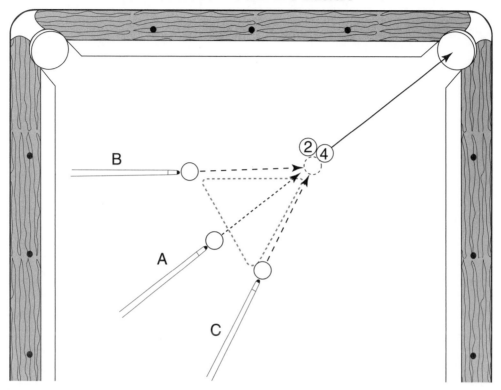

The 2-ball and 4-ball are frozen together, which may cause you to pass on shooting the 4-ball. It will still go, however, as long as the 2-ball only blocks 1/8 or less of the 4-ball from full view. Position A shows what the shot looks like with the cue ball directly in line with the pocket. Notice how the cue ball fits with the 2 and 4-balls.

The 4-ball can also be made up to a cut angle of a little over 30-degrees on the side shown by the cue ball in Position B. When the cue ball is on the other side of the 4-ball as in Position C, you must apply some outside (left) english to offset the contact induced throw. The 4-ball can be made from a much greater cut angle on Side C than on Side B.

• A Shot to Avoid

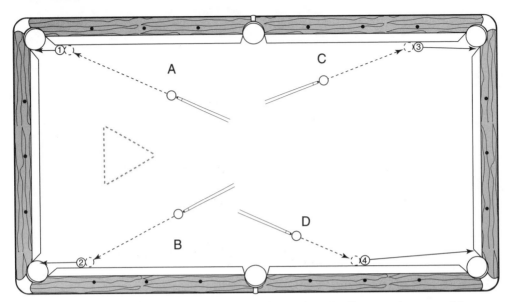

There are a great many players who like to spin balls in using outside english, especially when cutting balls down a rail. This may be doubly so in Straight Pool, since one of the main objectives of using english is to exert maximum control over the cue ball. But when the object ball is frozen to a rail, outside english virtually guarantees that you'll miss the shot if the ball is much more than a diamond away from the pocket.

The illustration shows 4 different locations for shots that are frozen to the rail. When the ball is close to the pocket, as in Position A, you can use outside engligh because the margin for error is so great. You are also reasonably safe using outside english in Position B. With the object ball a little past the first diamond, as in Position C, your risk of missing is now great. And with the object ball in Position, the shot has little chance of going with outside (right) english.

CHAPTER 10

LEARNING TO PLAY STRAIGHT POOL

How to Make Your Practice as Productive as Possible

• There is a tendency to over simplify the process of leaning most pool games. Some "instructors" contend that all you need is a solid stroke, a few key principles and away you go. Top players know better. They know that mastering Straight Pool, or any other pool game for that matter, takes years and years of play and study with a dedication towards always improving their game. There is a seemingly endless body of knowledge to be learned, all of which can improve your game.

The way to raise your game to it's highest level is to enjoy the learning process. Understand that with every day you play there is an opportunity to learn something new about the game which can make you an even better player than the day before. If you adopt this attitude with Straight Pool, as well as an other games you play, pool will fascinate you and never bore you for as long as you play. Straight Pool is a game for a lifetime, so you needn't be in a big hurry to learn it all at once. There are no short cuts. Never forget that winners are willing to do what others won't.

• Practicing Straight Pool

If you are serious about improving, and you enjoy practicing, then you are in luck, because Straight Pool is the ideal pool game for solitary practice. You can easily simulate actual game conditions without the need for an opponent. There is no need to distinguish between solids and stripes as in Eight-Ball, or between pockets as in One-Pocket. You and your "opponent" both shoot any ball in any pocket. Because of the offensive nature of the game, once you gain control of the table, your turns often last much longer in Straight Pool than in other pool games. When you are in the middle of a run during practice, you are really playing the table and not an opponent, which is exactly what you would be doing in competition.

A number of the very best players contend that Straight Pool is the best game for learning the all-around skills that can be applied to other games. These would include speed control, pattern play, defense and shot-making. One other big plus in practicing Straight Pool is that it helps you to develop the ability to concentrate on pocketing balls. Once you get a run going, the last thing you want to do is end it by missing a relatively easy shot due to a lack of concentration. You also don't want to hand the table over to your opponent because you let up on an easy shot for whatever the reason.

• Running Balls by Yourself

There are several approaches you can take to practicing the game by yourself. The most common is to set up your favorite break shot, open the rack and start running balls. When your "turn" ends, just start another. Using this approach gives you practice in all three phases of a rack. You may wish to note how many balls are on the table when you start a new run so you can keep track of them. Just don't let counting interfere with your play.

After each turn ends, you may wish to set up a break shot and start over. You can set up the same break shot until you have it mastered. Another approach is to set up a variety of break shots. For those who like to keep track of their runs, setting up a new break shot makes this an easier process.

I recommend that you get into the habit of playing the game as well as possible. Spend some time just playing. Don't bother to keep track of your runs. Realize that by playing the game you'll get the high runs you're after. You may even discover on many occasions that you have no clue as to how many balls you've run because you were so wrapped up in the game that you failed to keep count.

I have a friend who has run in the 100's many times, including a neat little 126 against me. I recently asked him what his high run was, and he wasn't sure. He said he was so lost in the game when it happened that he could only guesstimate it at 175-200. If you adhere strictly to never counting balls, there should come a time when an onlooker or an opponent will keep track and be able to tell you how many balls you've run after your run has ended. You could be surprised and very pleased with the number.

While you are running balls by yourself, be sure to take breaks periodically, especially if you are in the midst of a long session. A few minutes away from the table can refresh your game and your spirits. Breaks also help simulate the time you will spend in the chair when playing in competition. And most important, when you feel you've had enough, quit practicing. Bad practice is worse than no practice.

• Dissect Your Game

The time to dissect your game is while you are practicing. Take notice of why each runs ends. Did you miss an easy shot? Why? Did you miss position? Does this particular position play give you trouble? What could you do differently next time to make the shot a success? The idea is to learn where things go wrong so you can play a similar shot successfully when it comes up again. You may even wish to set up the errant shot again and try it until you get it right.

• Let Go

While practicing, devote some of your time to completely letting go and running balls at a pace that seems most natural to you. Your goal is to establish your ideal rhythm. This kind of practice helps you build trust in your game and your stroke. It is designed to resemble the way you would be playing if you were in dead stroke and in the midst of your record high run. Some players do best with a consistent and measured pace of play, while others prefer to pick up the speed when they "get hot". If you like playing fast, just be sure not to play so quickly that you make the kind of silly little mistakes that seem to plague many players who prefer this style of play.

• Emphasize a Skill

You must combine many skills and trains of thought into one big bundle to play Straight Pool really well. You need to play position, read the table, pocket balls, and so much more, all at the same time. This becomes more and more of an automatic process as your knowledge and skill at the game grows. In the process of learning the game, it can help to focus on one particular skill while you are practicing running balls. For example, at the start of practice you could tell yourself that today you're going to emphasize speed control and that you are going to excel at this phase of the game. Speed control would then become the focal point of your practice session. Below are some additional trains of thought that can build your skills in various aspects of the game.

Today I'm going to:
- Plan my patterns to perfection.
- Play precision position.
- Shoot every ball with my very best and smoothest stroke.
- Exert control over the table.
- Read the table and label every ball correctly.

You will discover that your skills in each of the areas above will exceed the norm on the days that you emphasize it. Ideally that higher level of expertise will stay with you as you go on to work on other facets of your game. Imagine what it will be like when all of the skill sets listed above work together without you having to consciously think about them one at a time.

• Practicing with a Friend

There are a number of techniques you can use while practicing with a friend to improve your game. These include:

- Play a friendly game for the competition, or nominal stakes.
- Ask each other for suggestions on how to play certain shots or patterns.
- Suggest an alternative to the shot your friend is about to play if it looks like the wrong shot.
- Analyze certain shots after they've been played. Go over both the successes and failures.
- Practice break shots. Rack for each other. Have the observer watch for how the balls move.
- Set up safety battles. When one person wins by pocketing a ball, re-rack the balls and start over.
- Help each other with your fundamentals.
- Set up position play contests.

• Keep a Journal

Straight Pool is by far the best and easiest pool game for quantifying your results. Your daily high run(s) are a fairly accurate barometer of your game. I suggest you keep a journal of your results. Set goals for yourself in your sessions. You might want to run a minimum of 20, 30 or more balls before ending practice. Choose a number that is in line with your level of play. Write down your best runs in each practice session. Was there anything that you learned during the run? How did it end and why? You can compute an average for your sessions and chart your progress. It is quite satisfying to see your average increase over time. You should also record anything you learned about the game that was particularly memorable. This could include information on fundamentals, how to play a break shot, or a particular safety, for example.

• Making Your Own Diagrams

I suggest you make copies of the blank pool table diagram on the opposite page. I use a circle template from Staedtler (about $3) to draw balls on my rough diagrams. Your can ensure that your diagrams are perfectly to scale by drawing circles whose diameter (width) is 2.25% of the length of the pool table. When choosing the circle, you must allow for the thickness of the pen or pencil. I use a pen with a medium point. If you use a 5/32" circle with a medium pen with the diagram on the following page, they will be perfectly proportioned. The edge of the template is prefect for drawing directional lines. The lines beneath the diagram are for writing notes.

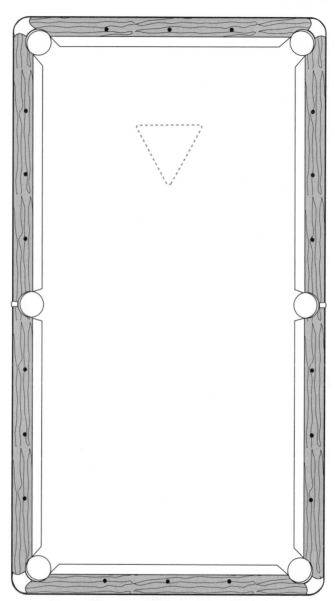

PHIL CAPELLE'S *PLAY YOUR BEST STRAIGHT POOL*

Notes_____

_____

_____

_____

_____

_____

• Learning the Game

Pool players have never had it so good when it comes to learning the game, what with the abundance of books and tapes now on the market. The cost of an education is minimal, especially when you consider the decades of enjoyment you will get from playing pool at higher and higher levels. In addition, there are opportunities to learn from qualified teachers, competition and watching top players that can all serve to enhance the learning process.

Some students say they learn best from playing, some from watching, while others learn best from books or videos. I suggest you remove any barriers or preconceived notions you have about learning and instead make use of any and all means at your disposal. If you feel you learn best from books, you should still watch videos, even if they aren't the mainstay of your approach. And of course, the opposite is true if you prefer videos. A well-rounded approach to learning would include the following:

- Read books, including, of course, *Play Your Best Straight Pool*.
- Watch good players. You may have to make some calls and visit your local rooms to find where the better Straight Pool players play in your town.
- Take lessons from acknowledged masters of the game. Call some of the local pool rooms and start asking around. You may have to be prepared to travel out of town to find an instructor who is especially competent in Straight Pool.
- Play good players for nominal stakes. Excellent Straight Pool players will often play for far less than Nine-Ball players because for them the game is the thing.
- Watch videos. Accu-Stats (800-828-0397) has a library of over 50 tournament matches featuring the best Straight Pool players in the world. (See the Appendix for more information.)
- Practice regularly.

• Developing Your Skills

We've already talked about developing your game by practicing running balls. In the following sections are some drills and routines for learning specific skills. These are all vital components of your game, such as position play or safeties. In addition, throughout the book there are shots and skills that could be improved from practice. A list of them appears at the end of each section along with the page on which they are located.

• The Donuts – a Reminder

Throughout this chapter I will be referring to donuts that you can place on the table for marking the position of the balls. They are sticky backed circles that are reinforcements for three-hole binder paper.

Position Play

• Speed Control (1)

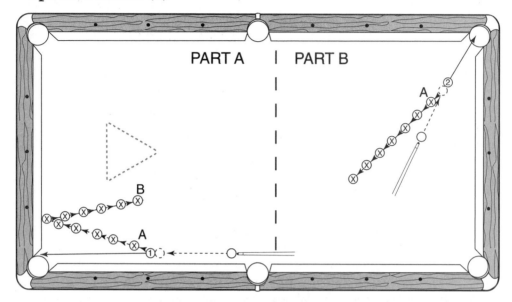

In the chapter on position play I presented the spectrum of speed. The scale is a handy means of visualizing the wide variety of speeds required in Straight Pool. A soft stroke is a #3 while a medium soft stroke is a #4. In between these ranges are several additional grades of speed. You should not be thinking about the scale when playing. Your sense of speed is something you feel based on your experience playing thousands of similar shots. Speed control can be developed by using progressive drills. In the next few diagrams, I'll cover 6 of the most common position routes in Straight Pool. When practicing progressive drills, try to increase or decrease your speed of stroke in small increments.

Part A is a drill for developing your touch on follow shots. A very soft follow stroke (a #2) will send the cue ball to Position A. A medium speed stroke (a #5) will send the cue ball to Position B. In between are 9 additional positions that lie between #2 and #5 on the scale. Try practicing the drill in both directions. Work your way from A to B with a progressively firmer stroke, then reduce the power as your go from B back to A. If you are able to land within a couple of inches of each X, you have an excellent feel for distance. Imagine what that can do for your game.

Part B shows a progressive drill for developing a fine touch on draw shots. If you can send the cue ball to within a few inches of each position as you work your way back from A to B and beyond, you have the feel for draw of a world class player. Drawing the cue ball precise distances is perhaps the most challenging position play in pool, so don't become too discouraged if it takes hours of practice (not all at once, of course) to master this drill.

• Speed Control (2)

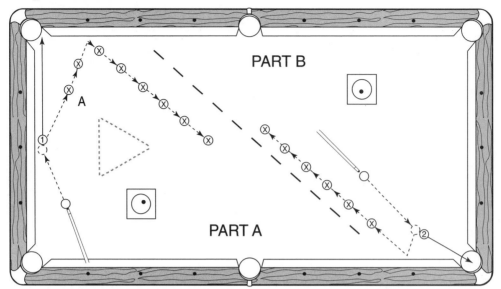

Part A is shows a position route that comes up over and over again. It requires follow with inside english. This series of shots promotes a smooth stroke and a sense of touch. When using inside english, you simply must avoid poking at the ball. The progressive drill in Part B is a draw shot off the side rail. This position play is also used regularly in Straight Pool.

• Speed Control (3)

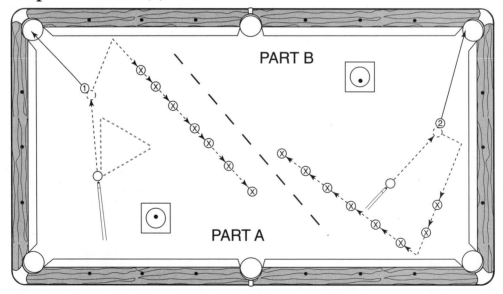

Part A is a cut shot of about 40-degrees that's played with follow. This valuable shot requires a relatively easy follow stroke. The position play in Part B shows a commonly played shot that requires a fairly powerful stroke, which makes precision speed control quite challenging.

• Hitting the Big X

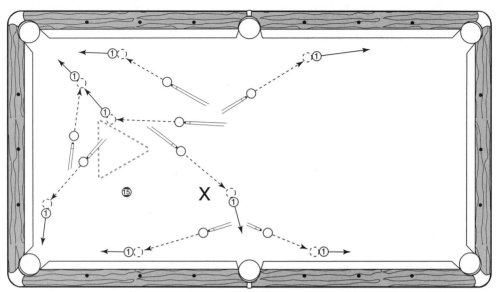

In a perfect world, you would always have a stop shot into the side pocket for position on a side-of-the rack break shot. In the real world, however, you will often find yourself playing the most important position shot in pool from a distance. It is imperative, therefore, that you master some of the most common position routes to a side-of-the-rack break shot, such as the ones shown in the diagram. Set up the break ball as shown. Also place donuts for the cue ball, 1-ball and the spot on which you want the cue ball to stop, as shown by the Big X. Try shooting these shots and any others with which you have trouble. This drill is a great reality check. Can you get shape or can't you? Play each shot until you can get within a few inches of the Big X. Your ability to hit the Big X when needed will extend countless runs during your Straight Pool career.

Diagrammed Position Plays to Practice from Chapter 1

Cueing
- Stop shots, and Adjusting Them
- Soft Outside Draw
- Inside English
- Draw Speed Control
- Stun Shots
- Draw-Stun shot
- Follow-Stun Shot
- Pounding balls with Speed and Accuracy
- Holding Up the Cue Ball
- Drawing Across the Table and Out
- Floating Follow at Higher Speeds of Stroke
- Pounding with Follow
- Floating the Cue Ball for Precise Shape

Position Concepts
- Using the Rail Increases Your Options
- How Pocketing Affects Position
- Using the Cue Ball as a Target

Hitting Other Balls
- Bumping Balls – Basics
- Playing Position on the Bumped Ball
- Bumping Balls with Spin

• One-Rail Directional Control

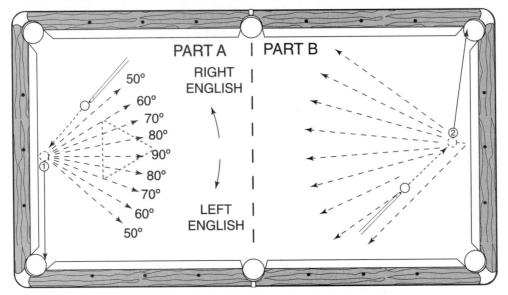

The drills in this diagram can teach you to control the cue ball's path off the cushion with a high degree of accuracy. In Part A, the 1-ball is very close to the rail. It is not too difficult to control it's path off the rail when you have a reasonably sharp cut angle and want to come straight back off the rail. The real test of your cue ball control is in applying the correct amount of english to send the cue ball down the various routes shown. Inside (left) english will send the cue ball to the bottom part of the table while outside (right) english will guide it towards the top half. Mastering one-rail directional control is vital for playing position and especially for playing secondary break shots.

The position in Part B is somewhat similar, only the 2-ball is about 3" off the rail. This slight difference in position from Part A makes directional control significantly more difficult, but this is a shot worth mastering.

• Side Pocket Circle Drill

This drill can help hone your short-range draw speed and directional control. Place the balls in a semi circle. Start at one end of the circle and proceed the other, shooting the balls in order. Your cut angle will naturally vary slightly from shot to shot. This means that you will have to change your approach slightly for each shot so that you can get as close as possible to the ideal angle for the next shot. In the process, you will need to employ such techniques as changing speeds of stroke, holding the cue ball, using inside or outside english, and cheating the pocket.

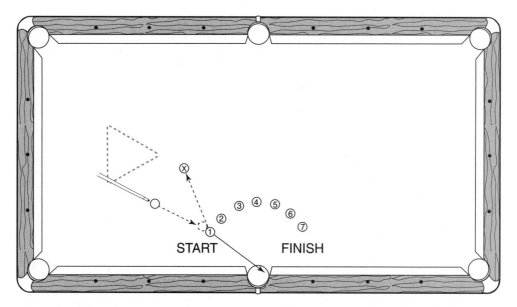

One Corner Pocket Drill

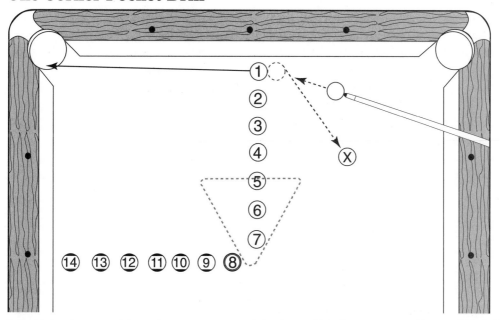

Place 14 balls in the positions shown in the diagram. To complete this drill, you must pocket all 14 balls in succession into the same pocket. You will need to use a wide variety of positional skills to complete this drill. Some techniques include draw, follow, english and one or two rail position. In the process you will hone your skill at maneuvering the cue ball at close range.

• Practicing Pattern Play

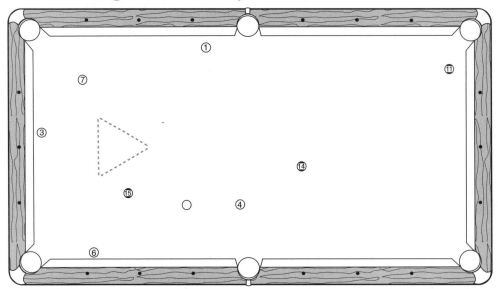

Most of your end-of-rack pattern play practice will come from running racks in practice. If you feel this part of your game needs extra work, use this routine. Place balls in ideal positions for a break ball and key ball, then spread another 5-6 more balls randomly about the table. Place a ball or two on the rail, and perhaps one or two in the area of the triangle.

Study the layout carefully and devise a plan for running out the rack. Remember to use the process of elimination method to planning your run. Pick out your opening shot or two as well as your last couple of shots, then tie the two ends together. The next step is to put your plan into action. Observe both your successes and failures. If your plan fails, was it because of poor execution, or did you choose the wrong pattern? And if you run out, internalize what worked so you can use what you know when a similar pattern shows up in competition.

The diagram shows the kind of layout you will encounter when doing this drill. The 15-ball is the break ball. Take a moment to devise a solution before reading the answer. Got it? Ok, here's how I would play this rack: 6, 3, 7, 14, 11, 1, 4, and the15-ball for the break shot.

Things to Practice from Chapter 2

Planning
- Process of Elimination Planning
- Labeling the Balls Correctly
- **Manufacturing Break Shots**
- Manufacturing a Break Shot
- Skillful Ball Bumping to Create a Break Shot
- Manufacturing Break Balls From All Angles

Position on the Break Ball
- An Excellent Second Choice Key Ball
- The "Can't Go Wrong" Key Ball
- Side Pocket Key Balls
- The Magic 20-Degree Cut Shot
- Which Way Is Better?

• Breaking Clusters

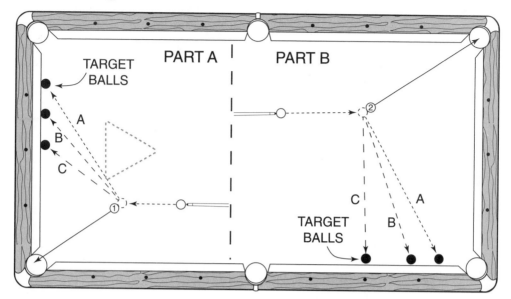

After the initial break shot of every rack, you will almost always have balls that are still clustered together. Breaking clusters while maintaining control of the cue ball is an art in and of itself. You can increase your skill at breaking clusters by learning the cue ball's precise route after it contacts the object ball.

In Part A, your goal is to break a cluster on the end-rail. A stun shot would send the cue ball down Path A. A medium speed follow shot would propel the cue ball along Path B. A soft follow shot would cause the cue ball to roll down Path C. I suggest you set up the cue ball and break ball in different locations. Play each shot using soft follow, follow and stun strokes. This will quickly teach you the path of the cue ball. Also place target balls to simulate the clusters you are trying to break.

In Part B, the objective is to hit the target balls on the side-rail, which simulate clusters. Use a stun shot to send the cue ball down Path A. A draw/stun shot will result in Path B. Use a full tip of draw to send the cue ball down Path C. You can fill in the gaps between the target balls by refining your ability to control the cue ball's direction after contact.

Shots to Practice from Chapter 3
•Secondary Break Shots
•Cueing Adds to Your Precision
•Off the Rail Secondary Break Shots
•The Overdrive Follow Break Shot

A Shot to Practice from Chapter 4
How the Cut Angle Determines the Path Into a Cluster

Break Shots

The rack opening break shot is the most important shot in Straight Pool. Most players, however, never shoot break shots except in a game. This makes it difficult to learn how to play them correctly. To fully understand break shots you should spend some time practicing the various break shots until you have at least mastered the most common break shots.

The 9/16" Solution

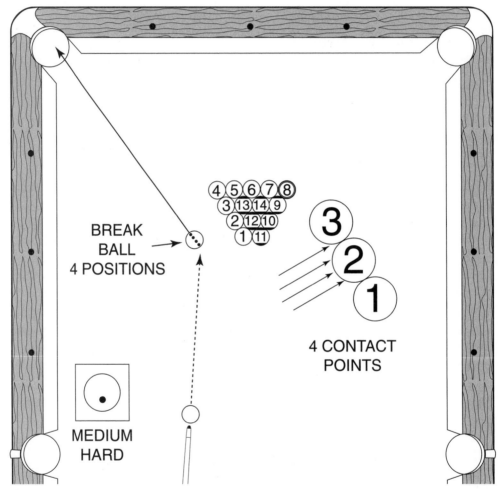

The donuts, which I've recommended several times throughout the book, are 9/16" in diameter, which is 1/4 of the diameter of the balls. The donuts can be used to show you how the cue ball reacts when it strikes each of the four basic contact points on a specific ball in a new rack. The four basic points of contact are:

- The upper part of the ball
- The middle of the ball
- The lower part of the ball
- Simultaneous contact with an adjacent ball

The inset shows the four basic contact points. Place the four donuts in a line facing towards the pocket and within 3" or so of the rack. Use another donut to mark the position of the cue ball.

Place the break ball on the first donut and shoot the break shot with a medium hard stroke with 1/2 tip of draw. Repeat the procedure, but each time move the break ball to another donuts. Note the action of the cue ball on each shot. After you complete this drill, you will know why the cue ball goes in different directions on break shots that appear to be exactly the same.

Break Shots Part Two

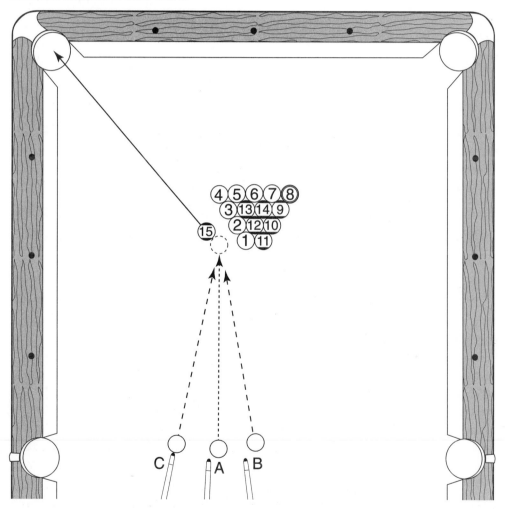

Set up a break ball in a position where the cue ball will be contacting the outside edge of a ball in the side of the rack. Use the donuts to mark the position of the balls. Shoot the break shot from Position A first. Then move the cue ball over about 4" to Position B. Finally, move the cue ball 4" to the left of Position A and play the shot from Position C. Try using half a tip of draw and a medium firm stroke on each shot. Notice how the cue ball reacts in each instance.

Practicing Long Distance Break Shots

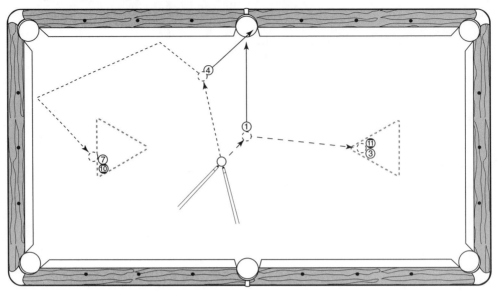

The diagram shows two of the most common long-distance side pocket break shots. On break shots when the cue ball must travel some distance to the rack, the main ingredient to success is in controlling the path of the cue ball. On most long-distance break shots, the objective is not just to hit the rack, but also to make contact with a specific ball or part of the rack.

You can practice these shots without going through the trouble of racking the balls after every shot. Set up a break shot and place two or three balls in the area of the triangle where you would want to be contacting the rack. Set up the exact same shot and try it several times. Make any necessary adjustments in cueing and speed until you can consistently hit the contact point where intended.

How a Rack Breaks Apart

The best players play position for certain balls on a break shot when they are not just obliterating the rack. There is an easy way get an accurate read on how a rack breaks apart without having to shoot numerous break shots. Aim the cue ball at a specific ball in the rack, and then choose the angle of approach that would approximate that of an actual break shot.

In most cases you will want to use a soft to medium soft stroke. This will compensate for the fact that a good deal of the cue ball's energy is spent on the object ball when you play a break shot. Play the "break shot" and observe which balls leave the stack and where they go. After shooting a few of these "break shots", you will gain some valuable knowledge of which balls break loose and where they wind up.

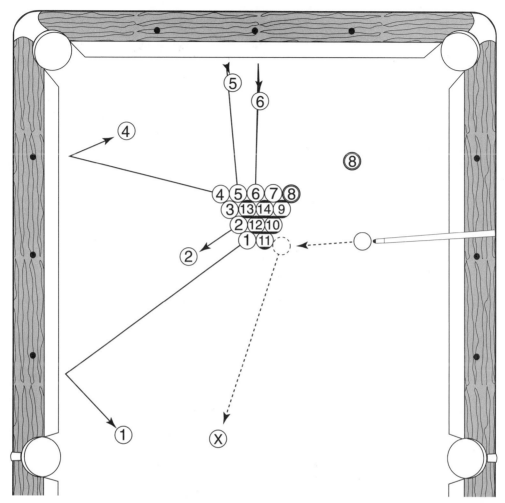

The diagram shows how the balls would break on a side-rail break shot. The cue ball hit the 11-ball slightly on the left side, which is why the cue ball traveled to Position X.

Break Shot Practice Tips

Certain break shots appear very often. You can try to learn them as you play. Another approach, however, is to systematically practice each shot. Take 3 or 4 each practice sessions and run through the 25 or so most common break shots (see Chapter 5). Use the donuts to mark the positions of the cue ball and break ball. Shoot each shot 2-3 times. Then move the balls to new locations so you can get a little different look at the shot. While you practice, pay special attention to these items:

- Your cueing and speed of stroke.
- The cue ball's route and where it comes to a stop.
- Which balls leave the stack and what shots do you have.
- Any mistakes that you make such as scratching or not having a clear shot.

Break Shots to Practice from Chapter 5

Side of the Rack Break Shots
The Classic Break Shot
•A Control Break Shot
•Back Cut Rack Blaster
•Close To the Rail Break Shots
•Shallow Cut Angles
•Above the Rack
•Follow Back Out Off the Low Balls
•Shallow Angle Follow Shot
•Ball in Hand Break Shots
Side Rail Break Shots
•Side Rail Break Shots
•More Side Rail Break Sots
•Below the Rack Rail Break Shots
•Down the Rail Break Shots
•With the Ball Off the Cushion

Behind the Rack Break Shots
•Inside Follow Three Rails
•Behind the Rack Back Cut Break Shots
•Down the End Rail Break Shots
•Straight Out to the Corner Ball
Other Useful Break Shots
•Pocket Hanger Break Shots
Side Pocket Break Shots
•A Cut Shot From Center Table
•A Cut Shot from off Center
•Back Cut Near the Foot Spot
•Two Rails to the Back of the Rack
Offbeat Break Shots
•Jump Into the Rack Break Shot
•Two Rails Using Follow With Inside English
•Jump Into the Lower Balls

The Opening Break Shot

The opening break shot (page 246) is one of the most important shots of the game. Play it well and your opponent is immediately in trouble. Misplay the shot, and your opponent may launch a momentum-building run right out of the starting gate. I suggest you occasionally spend a few minutes shooting a couple of opening break shots in practice. This will reinforce how this important shot is played, since you will only get to shoot it in competition about once every other game. You might also practice lagging. If your lag shots consistently end up near the rail, your opponent will be the one breaking the balls most of the time.

Shotmaking Practice

Straight Pool requires that you consistently make a wide variety of shots, due largely to the congestion factor at the foot-end of the table. Most of the specialty shots, such as combinations and caroms are the easier version of these shots, but that does not make them a cinch. Each of the shots below must be mastered. The explanations for each appear in Chapter 9.

•Frozen Cue Ball Table Length Viewing •Obstructions
Accurately
•**Cut Shots**
•**Combinations**
•Frozen Combos
•Taking the Throw Out of Three Ball Combos
•The Critical 1/8th Inch
•**Bank Shots**
•**Carom Shots**

•Dead Carom Shots
•Combining Shots
•**Billiards**
•Dead Billiards
•Curve Shots
•Rail First
•Rack Shots
•Finding Dead Balls
•A Dead Rack Shot

Safety Play

You skill at defense is largely what gives you the opportunity to launch your offense and start a run. The better your opponent's game, the more important this facet of the game becomes. Most players "practice" defense only when they are playing. If you want to win more safety battles and separate yourself from the competition, then I suggest you devote at least 10-15 minutes of your practice sessions to working on defense.

Skimming Drills

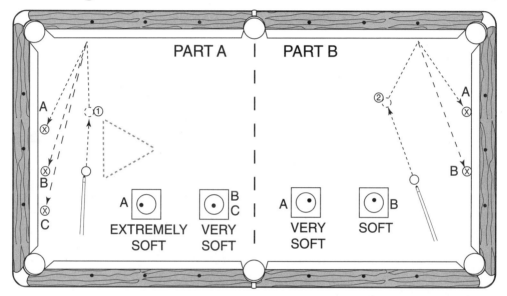

Skimming balls with precision is a most valuable skill in playing defense. The diagram shows just a couple of the wide variety of possible drills that can sharpen your ability to hit the object ball thinly and control the cue ball. In Part A, a thin hit on the 1-ball with a full tip of left english will send the cue ball to Position A on the end-rail, providing your speed is perfect. Also try landing the cue ball at Positions B and C, which require less english and a bit more speed.

In Part B, you are hitting nearly half of the 2-ball. This will slow the cue ball down and alter it's path to the end-rail compared to the shots in Part A. Once again, try to hit two or more locations on the end-rail. On these and other skim shots, you must control both the speed and direction of the cue ball. This is accomplished with your speed of stroke, english and the amount of the object ball you hit.

Ball Control Drills

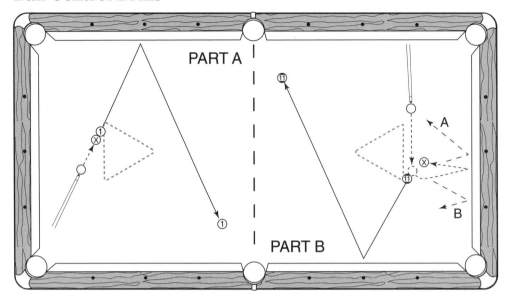

The ability to control the direction and rolling distance of the object ball off of which you are playing safe can enable you to considerably strengthen your safeties. Part A shows a common safe in which your goal is to send the object ball close to the side pocket on the foot side of the table. Use a full tip of draw and a very soft stroke. The cue ball should stop dead or draw back slightly. The low hit on the cue ball enables you to hit this shot with a little more speed, which makes it easier to control the rolling distance of the 1-ball.

You want to send the object ball to the same place in Part B, only this time you have a 30-degree cut shot on the 11-ball. Play this shot with a half tip of draw. You will need a little firmer stroke than in Part A because you are hitting only about half of the object ball. On this shot you must also control the route of the cue ball. If you send the cue ball down either Path A or B, you might leave your opponent with a shot.

Safeties to Practice from Chapter 7
•Skimming Balls Must Be Mastered
•A Masse Skim Safety
•Skimming From Long Range
•Hitting the Safety Zone
•Hitting Into the Side of the Rack and Sticking
•Into the Top of a New Rack
•Far End Rail Into the Back of the Rack

Strategy
•The strategic foul below appears on page 312 of Chapter 8
•Playing an Intentional Foul After a Scratch

CHAPTER 11

ALL ABOUT HIGH RUNS

How to Go About Setting Your Personal New Record

When playing Straight Pool, the object of the game is obviously to win, even if that means clawing you way to victory with a series of short runs and tight safety play. Still, there is a certain mystique about high runs. Spectators at tournaments all want to see runs in excess of 100 balls. Great players are all justifiably proud of their record runs of several hundred balls even though they have almost always occurred in practice or in an exhibition. Likewise, you should also feel proud of your record run no matter what the figure, for it is the product of many hours of work and devotion to the game. And make no mistake about it, every serious Straight Pool player wants to break their personal record or has a goal of how many balls they would like to run at some point in their career.

There will be times when the stars align properly, the table will be breaking perfectly and you'll be in dead stroke. Under these conditions you may well run many more balls than is typical of your game. While it's great to run lots of balls no matter what the reason, to consistently produce high runs, you've got to really know what you're doing. You've got to study the game and all of the fine points and then you've got to execute what you know with the ultimate of consistency and precision.

The good news is that once your game reaches a certain point, further improvement has a geometric effect on your ability to run balls. As an extreme example, an excellent pro player may probably have a high run of around 200 balls. If they could improve just 2% to close to world champion status, their record run could soar to above 300-400 balls, for an increase of over 50%. A player with a high run of, let's say, 20 balls, could some day up that to 30 or more with a modest improvement in their game.

The real secret to running lots of balls, perhaps many more than you ever imagined possible, is to become the best Straight Pool player that your time, talent and desire can produce. That means learning all you can about the game. It also means developing both your physical game and your mental game as well.

In the beginning, your physical game receives the major emphasis. When you have developed a stroke with which you are confident, then the emphasis switches to learning about how the game is played. This includes position play, patterns, and break shots. Finally, once you reach a certain level, then continued improvement comes largely from improvements in your mental game. To runs lots of balls, you've got to have the four C's working together: capability, consistency, confidence, and concentration.

• How to Prepare for High Runs

There are many diverse factors that can all contribute to you achieving a new record run. To set the stage for it to happen in the first place, you've got to be playing some of your best pool. It also helps to have favorable conditions, and you've to be at least just a little bit lucky. Below is a complete game plan for achieving your new record run.

Your Attitude

How you truly feel about the game goes a long ways towards determining how well you play and how many balls you can run. If you play Straight Pool because you love the game, then you will always be seeking ways to improve your game which could, of course, contribute to a new high run. You must also enjoy working at your game. It will take many hours of practice to develop the skills that can enable you to reach higher levels of play.

Desire

Your new record run is a significant achievement, no matter what the total. Like anything you accomplish in life that has meaning, it only comes after much hard work. So if you truly want to improve your game and set a new record run, you've got to have the desire to make it happen. You've got to practice and work on those areas of your game that can contribute most to your success. You can add fuel to your desire by setting a goal for how many balls you want to run within a certain time frame.

Get in Stroke

High runs will almost always come only when your physical game is at peak levels. To get in stroke, you've simply got to play and practice on a regular basis.

Increase Your Skills

One of the most fascinating aspects of Straight Pool is how both position play and shotmaking complement each other. When you play excellent position, you take the pressure off your shotmaking. And when you are a great shotmaker, you don't stress out every time you miss shape by a few inches or more.

You can really only run a limited number of balls if you are very deficient with either your position play or your shotmaking. Great position play keeps you from shooting shots that could easily be missed. Nevertheless, great shotmaking is a must for achieving long runs as it will bail you out when you get a bad roll or miss shape. While you are building your game, be sure to give both of these critical areas of skill the proper attention.

Pattern Recognition

Our brains process the information on the table to determine the best sequence of shots. This is commonly referred to as pattern recognition. Like any other skill, it can get better with practice. Planning and executing you patterns with great precision, particularly in the later stages of a rack, is one of the most important components of achieving high runs. Even though pattern play is a mental skill, your ability to plan your patterns may fluctuate from day to day, just as your physical game does. Don't let this upset you, as it also happens to even the very best players.

Learn the Game

When you know the game and know what you are doing, then your mind looks at the layout in a completely different way. It can make sense of the endless variety of positions and come up with a solution to the Straight Pool puzzle on the table. In short, knowledge gives your mind many things to think about, all of which help keep you focused on the task at hand.

Visualization

Top athletes almost all use visualization to improve their performance. Before playing, spend some time relaxing while you see yourself playing Straight Pool at your very finest. Try to make the experience as real as possible. Imagine yourself moving about the table analyzing the layout and choosing a pattern. Then experience each shot and each stroke in as much detail as possible. This mental exercise could help get you primed for peak performance.

When You Are Playing

The Conditions
The ultimate conditions for achieving a record run are: a fairly fast and level table with generous pockets; very low humidity; a set of polished Centennial Balls; excellent lighting; and sufficient room between the tables. The degree to which running balls becomes more difficult depends on how much the conditions deviate from those listed above. You can increase your chances of setting your personal record by playing under the most favorable conditions you can find within your area. When the playing conditions are particularly poor, you might as well accept the fact that you're high run is not in jeopardy.

Play High Percentage Shots
You can't run very many balls by playing too many low percentage shots. The law of averages will catch-up with you very soon if the pressure of having to make many difficult shots doesn't. The only way to achieve your record run is to control the cue ball well enough that you are shooting mostly easy shots. Even though the very best players, who are also great shotmakers, could not run close to a 100 balls on a regular basis by leaving themselves several tough shots during their runs.

Playing in Competition
Most truly fine players find that competition heightens their level of concentration. If you are playing in formal competition, you may have an excellent opportunity to slip into the zone where you are running balls without a clue as to the total. Under these conditions, you may continue well past your previous record while you remain in a Straight Pool player's fog. When playing in competition, if you must relinquish the table when the game is over, the point at which you begin a run can determine whether or not you will have a chance for setting a new personal record.

Good Rolls
No matter how well you play, there is always an element of luck to any pool game. During a long run, you will probably get at least a few good rolls. And even if you don't get any good rolls, not getting any bad rolls also requires an element of luck. The rolls, as you well know, are not evenly distributed throughout a pool game or , for that matter, a long run. You should count this as a blessing, because it means that good fortune will often come to you aid in your quest for a record run.

One of the best examplea I can recall of how a good roll can extend a run took place at the 1974 U.S. Open in Chicago. Richie Florence, a fine player from California, took his seat with a slight smirk on his face after running 105 balls to take a 105-12 lead over Hall of Famer Joe Balsis. Balsis replied with a long run of his own that had exceeded 100 balls when he set to play a side-of-the-rack break shot. Balsis was known for clobbering his break shots, and this one was no exception. He pounded the buster, missed, and watched in astonishment as the ball banked 4-rails around the table and into the called pocket. He proceeded to run 138 and out.

Play Each Ball One at a Time

One of my favorite quotes is from the Chinese Philosopher Lao-tzu. It is:

A journey of a thousand miles must begin with a single step.

Lao-tzu

Since we're talking Straight Pool, here is my adaptation of the quote as it applies to your game:

A run of a 100 balls must be played one ball at a time.

Phil Capelle

When great athletes are asked about their game plan, either before or after competition, you will hear a consistent message no matter what the sport. And in most cases, it has to do with staying focused on the task at hand. Typical comments include:
- I'm going to play one shot at a time.
- I want to stay in the present moment.
- I 'm going to concentrate on playing my game.
- I've got a job to do.
- I don't want to get ahead of myself.

How Runs Get Started

In practice, you will certainly have many chances to run balls. When playing in competition, certain situations are conducive to launching a run. If your opponent misses a break shot, that usually gives you a great opportunity to get a run going. Your opponent could also leave you with a dead ball in the rack or a few balls that lead up to a break ball. You could also grind your way through a tough opening rack to a break ball and then explode from there. In short, a long run can start at any time. You never really know when the pieces will all come together, but before you know it, you may be well on your way to a new record.

Rhythm

Top players all seem to agree on one point: long runs come when you are playing at your optimal pace of play. For most players, this is usually a little faster than your normal pace. When you are playing a notch or two below your best, there is a tendency to grind a little. You have to work at running balls. When your game is totally in sync, it takes far less effort.

As a result, your pace will quicken somewhat. You will get a rhythm going. When you are in gear and are playing at a faster tempo you should still remain within a range of what "normal" for you. If your typical pace is 6 on the 1-10 scale, you might speed up to a 7 if things are really going your way.

Someone's Racking for You

One of the benefits of competition is that you don't have to rack the balls. This short break between racks can give you just enough of a breather to recharge your batteries. If you are practicing and embark on a long run, it may be helpful to have a friend come over and rack the balls for you. I've seen this courtesy extended among friends on many occasions.

Don't Count the Balls

Counting the number of balls during a long run is really is at odds with playing the game. It's results oriented, not process oriented. You want to get lost in the game. When you are in competition, this should not be a problem, especially if no one is reminding you of the current total. If you embark on a long run in practice, it may be helpful to have a friend keep track of the run for you so you can concentrate fully on running balls without visions of your personal record dancing in your head.

In big time competition, interestingly enough, the referee calls out the length of the run after every shot. This seems to have little or no negative impact on players of this caliber. In fact, the referees voice calling out their run could become a part of their routine and it might even help keep them retain their focus on the game.

The Formula for High Runs

Knowledge + Dead stroke + Concentration + Rolls + Favorable conditions = High runs

Analyzing Your High Runs

After you have set a new record run, you should bask in the glory of your achievement. There is nothing like relaxing in your easy chair and visualizing some of your best moments in living color. Soak it all in. After all, it's not every day that you set a personal record. In addition to enjoying your accomplishment, you would be wise to take a few moments to analyze your run. This can help you confirm what you did right so you can repeat the experience. This exercise also can build your confidence.Your post game analysis should also reveal those areas of your game where you still have room for improvement.

How to Your High Runs

- What were the key shots that sustained the run?
- How was your position play?
- Were you playing your patterns particularly well?
- How did your stroke feel?
- What break shots did you play? How did they work out?
- Did you get some key rolls?
- What were the conditions like?
- Were you in the zone?
- Did the game seem easy? Why?

Why Runs Usually End

Some runs end because of plain old fashion bad luck. The great majority, however, end because of a mistake in planning or execution. You can discover flaws in your game by carefully analyzing how and why your runs come to an end. It also can be instructive to see what stops the runs of others as well because this can show you what mistakes to avoid. When you watch tapes of the matches of top players, you may also wish to pay close attention to how their runs came to an end.

The list below includes some of the most common reasons why a run ends. See if you can find a commonly recurring problem or two that may be harming your game.

Your skills are not fully developed. Your runs may be ending because you are still early in the learning process. Be patient and keep working on your game.

Bad rolls. Some of your runs will end due to bad rolls. But there will be times when you may have, upon further analysis, discover that you created your own bad luck.

Lapses in concentration. Develop a precise shooting routine and use it consistently.

Carelessness. This can cause you to miss easy shots. This usually happens when you are playing faster than your ideal pace of play. Slow down and maintain your ideal rhythm.

Poor planning. Work on your pattern recognition, especially in practice. (See Chapter 2).

Poor position. Missing shape comes from poor directional control and/or speed control. It may also result from choosing the wrong route. Failure to take care of trouble soon enough. You need to carefully assess where problems lie and develop a sensible plan for dealing with them. Remember, when dealing with trouble, timing is crucial.

Lack of shotmaking skills. If you are missing too many shots you feel you should be making, perhaps you need to reevaluate your fundamentals.

Fear of success. Perhaps you have a mental barrier once you reach a certain number of balls or come within range of your current record. You need to focus on playing one ball at a time and learn to enjoy playing the game.

Tough conditions. There is not much you can do when the conditions are difficult. Play your game and accept that your new high run may have to wait.

A ball skids. Some players advocate using outside english on cut shots hit with a soft stroke.

• Significant Milestones

Athletes in all sports gauge their progress by reaching certain milestones. Golfers first want to break 100, then 90 and so forth. Bowlers may shoot for their first 200 game or 600 series. Straight Pool, unlike most other pool games, allows you measure your progress with a high degree of accuracy.

Your high run is like a golfers low round. There are a number of significant milestones that mark a players progress. Each of these gives you a meaningful and measurable goal. When playing Straight Pool, you don't have to resort to saying you are playing some of your best pool. Instead, the game gives you an objective measurement of your progress. The table below lists some of the most significant milestones in a player's career, from beginner to world champion and all points in between. What's your high run? What are your plans for breaking it?

- 14 balls   Your first complete rack.
- 20 balls   A rack plus several from another rack (could have 2 break shots).
- 30 balls   Over 2 racks. Means you set up 2 break shots (possibly 3) and ran over 2 complete racks.
- 40 balls   Means you set up 2-3 break shots and ran almost 3 racks.
- 50 balls   You ran over 3fi racks and reached half of a hundred. This is a big goal for many amateur players.
- 75 balls   Over 5 complete racks. Shows potential for 100.
- 100 balls   The first big hurdle of all great players. A verysignificant achievement.
- 150 balls   The equivalent of a complete championship game.
- 200 balls   A level reached by skilled professional players.
- 300 balls   Puts you in the class of a world beater

Runs by the Numbers

The table shows how many racks go into runs of various lengths.

- 1 rack = 14 balls   6 racks = 84 balls   11 racks = 154
- 2 racks = 28 balls   7 racks = 98 balls   15 racks = 210
- 3 racks = 42 balls   8 racks = 112 balls   22 racks = 308
- 4 racks = 56 balls   9 racks = 126 balls   29 racks = 406
- 5 racks = 70 balls   10 racks = 140 balls   36 racks = 504

Appendix A

The Rules of Straight Pool

Straight Pool is more fun once you have a reasonably thorough understanding of the rules. Knowing the rules helps avoid unpleasant disputes or can prevent your opponent from pulling any questionable moves against you. An in depth understanding of the rules may also give you a competitive advantage. You will also have the confidence to step forward and make the tough calls during a game that can make the difference between winning and losing.

The discussion below is an overview of some of the most important rules of play. Where appropriate, there are also references to local rules or amendments to the rules that you and your opponent must agree upon prior to beginning play. For a thorough discussion of the rules, I highly recommend that you obtain a copy of *Billiards, The Official Rules and Records Book* that is published by the Billiard Congress of America. (Note: Straight Pool is also called 14.1 Continuous, which is what it is called in the rulebook.)

Length of the Game

In formal competition, the length of a game is already predetermined. In professional tournaments, games are usually played to 150 points. When you are playing for fun or for a few dollars, you and your opponent are free to set the number of points to which you will be playing. Generally speaking, the better you and your opponent play, the longer the game. A longer game enables both players to have a number of scoring opportunities, and it allows a player a chance to come back after his opponent has run a lot of balls. The most popular length of game for average players seems to be 100 points. Your available time may also be a factor in setting the length of the game.

Determining Who Breaks

The opening break is decided by by lagging for the break. Each player stands side by side at the head rail and simultaneously banks a ball from behind the head string to the foot rail and back. The player whose ball stops closest to the head rail wins the lag. You and your opponent may also chose to flip a coin to determine who breaks. In either case, the winner has the choice of breaking or of having their opponent break.

Racking the Balls for the Opening Rack

The 1-ball goes on the right corner closest to the person racking the balls. The 5-ball goes on the left corner closest to the racker. The other 13 balls are placed at random.

Scoring

You score one point for each ball you pocket. You must designate the pocket in which you are playing a shot. As a practical matter, most players only require you to call shots that are not completely obvious. These include shots out of the rack, banks shots, billiards, caroms, and combinations. Any shot counts providing it goes in the designated pocket.

At times a ball can be made by a variety of methods other than being shot directly into the pocket. Even so called slop shots still count, as long as they go in the in the designated pocket. Any other balls that you pocket in addition to ball you called also count towards your score.

Requirements for the Opening Break

The breaker must drive at least two balls from the rack to the rail. In addition, the cue ball must strike a rail. If these requirements are met, it is a legal break even if they scratch. The breaker loses a point on a scratch, and would now have a score of -1. If the breaker fails to drive at least two balls to the rail, their opponent can accept the table as is, or rerack all 15 balls and have the breaker break the balls again.

Whenever the breaker fails to drive two balls to a rail, they lose two points. The breaker who fails to meet the requirements for a legal opening break would have a score of -2. Should they fail once again to meet the requirements on their second attempt, they would now have a score of -4, etc. A foul committed on the opening break does not count towards the three fouls in a row rule.

The person playing the opening break may also elect to attempt to call a shot out of the rack, but this is almost never done because of the risk involved.

Starting a New Rack

A rack of Straight Pool is complete when the 14th ball has been pocketed. The 15th ball remains on the table along with the cue ball. The other 14 balls are reracked. The apex of the triangle is the spot left vacant.

Legal Shot

You have met the requirements for a legal shot when you pocket a ball, providing you don't scratch. You also meet the requirement for a legal shot when you miss a shot providing either the cue ball or object ball hits a rail after contact, providing you don't scratch.

Legal Safety

A player must declare their intention to play safe before executing a safety. To play a legal safe, either the cue ball or any object ball must strike a rail after the cue ball has made contact with any object ball. A player can also meet the requirements by calling a safety and then pocketing any object ball. The ball is then respotted.

Scratches and Other Fouls

You lose one point when you scratch. If you made a shot and scratched, you lose one point and you do not receive credit for the ball you pocketed. The ball you pocketed would be respotted. After a scratch, your opponent has cue ball in hand behind the head string. Many players refer to that part of the table as the kitchen. **The base of the cue ball must be placed behind the head string.**

You commit a foul and lose a point if you fail to drive an object ball to the rail or if the cue ball fails to hit a rail after the it makes contact with an object ball.

If an object ball is within a ball's width of a rail, you can only play a safety off that ball two times in succession while using the nearest rail. On the third safety, the rules for a frozen ball apply (see below).

Intentional fouls are used regularly as a defensive measure. When playing an intentional foul, the shooter must contact the cue ball with the tip of their cue. Failure to do so in championship results in a 15-point penalty. The player who committed the violation must now meet the requirement of the opening break.

When the Object Ball is Frozen to the Rail

When you are playing a safety and the object ball is frozen to the rail, the cue ball must hit a rail after contacting the object ball. The cue ball can hit the same rail that the object ball was on. You can also meet the requirements for a legal safety by driving the ball that's frozen to the rail into another rail, even if the cue ball fails to hit a rail. The ball that was frozen can also knock another ball to a rail to meet the requirements of a legal safety.

Cue Ball Fouls and Object Ball Fouls

In championship play, any contact with the cue ball or an object ball while setting up for a shot or in playing a shot is considered a foul. This results in a one point penalty and loss of turn. Otherwise, you and your opponent are free to determine whether or not you will call fouls for incidental contact.

You could play cue ball fouls only, for example. In this case, should you accidentally make contact with an object ball, your opponent would have the option of leaving the ball in its new position, or they could replace it as close to the original spot as possible. If you accidentally touched the cue ball, it would result in a one point penalty and loss of turn. In very friendly competition, sometimes the players will even waive the penalty for this infraction.

Balls in the Triangle at the End of a Rack

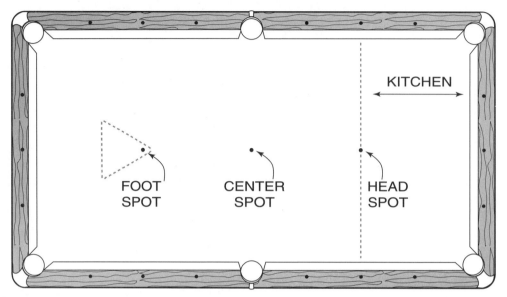

When a rack is complete, quite often either the cue ball or the last object ball will be in the triangle. A ball is in the triangle when any part of the ball interferes with the racking of the balls. Understand, however, that you can slide the rack in very carefully from the opposite side of the triangle to avoid touching the last ball, unless, of course, it is in the rack. A ball is in the rack even if only the edge of the ball is overlapping the triangle.

This is one area of the game that is really open to dispute, especially if there are no pencil lines to determine the exact location of the rack. I advise that you proceed with great care when you are checking the position of a ball that is close to the triangle when you are getting ready to rack the balls. During the course of a play, you and your opponent may check to see if a ball is in or out of the rack when pencil lines have not been drawn. This is done by placing the triangle as close as possible to where it will be when the balls are actually racked without disturbing any balls on the table.

There are a number of potential scenarios involving balls in the triangle at the end of the rack. Rack ending positions Number 2 and Number 8 in the table below probably occur 95%+ of the time among the nine possibilities. The table lists the position of the 15th ball and the cue ball. It then tells you where to move either or both balls. The diagram should help you to visualize the many different possible positions for both balls.

Position of the Balls		Action	
15th Ball	Cue Ball	15th Ball	Cue Ball
1 In rack	In rack	Foot spot	In kitchen
2 In rack	Not in rack, Not on head spot	Head spot	Leave alone
3 In rack	On head spot	Center spot	Leave alone
4 Pocketed	In the rack	Foot spot	Kitchen
5 Pocketed	Not in rack, not on head spot	Foot spot	Leave alone
6 Pocketed	On head spot	Foot spot	Leave alone
7 In kitchen, Not on head spot	In the rack	Leave alone	Head spot
8 Not in kitchen, Not in rack	In the rack	Leave alone	In kitchen
9 On head spot	In the rack	Leave alone	Center spot

On a Foul

When your last turn ended with a foul (see above), you are said to be on a foul. You will be off of a foul on your next turn if you play a legal shot or safety at the very start your next turn. You could go right back on a foul if, after pocketing one or more balls, you committed another foul. You would then be on one foul.If you are on a foul and you commit another foul at the very start your next turn, you are now on two fouls. If on your next turn, you play a legal shot or safety at the very start of your turn, both fouls are removed at once. If you are on two fouls and you commit another foul at the very start of your next turn you have committed three fouls in a row. Now the rule for three fouls in a row takes effect (see below). Once you have committed a third consecutive foul, you are no longer on a foul.

Three Fouls in a Row

Each foul (either scratching or failing to hit a rail) results in the loss of a point. If you are on two fouls (see above) and commit a third foul, you also lose an additional 15 points. After you commit a third foul, your opponent can accept the table as is. Your opponent also has the choice of reracking all 15 balls and making you play a break shot. You must then meet the requirements of the opening break by driving at least 2 balls to the rail, as well as the cue ball. If you fail to drive two balls to the rail, then the rules for the opening break continue to apply. 36

Double Hits

This continues to be an area of debate, despite what the rulebook says about double hits. According to the BCA Rule Book:

> When the distance between the cue ball and object ball is less than the width of a chalk cube, special attention from the referee is required. In such a situation, unless the referee can positively determine a legal shot has been performed, the following guidance may apply: if the cue ball follows through the object ball more than fi ball, it is a foul.

Spotting Balls

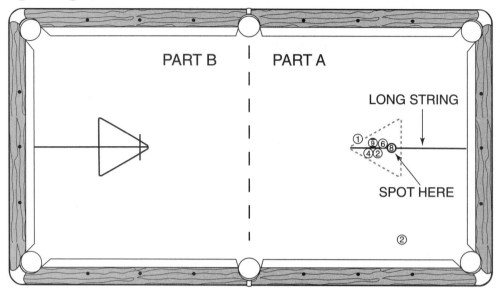

Balls are respottted on the foot spot. If the foot spot is fully or partially obscured by another ball, the ball would be spotted as close to the foot spot as possible on a line (the long string) that extends down the middle of the table. Part A of the diagram shows the 11-ball being spotted on the first available spot on the long string.

Pencil Lines

In championship play and in locations where Straight Pool is played regularly, pencil lines are drawn on the table that mark the position of the rack. These lines, which are shown in Part B of the diagram above, are useful in determining if a potential break ball is in or out of the rack. They also help insure that the balls are racked in the correct position. A pencil line also extends from the foot spot to the foot rail at a point opposite the middle diamond. This line is very use for spotting balls accurately (see above).

Referees

Whenever you are in an event that is being referred, chances are the person watching over your match is someone who is getting paid little or anything to do their job. They have likely volunteered for the job because they love pool and want to help out. This attitude could help you keep your cool if and when they make an incorrect call, which happens occasionally.

The decisions in Straight Pool are a little more clear cut than in other pool games, thanks to the fact that there are no disputes over which ball was hit first. Nevertheless, referees are prone to error. I saw a referee on tape at a major tournament fail to call an obvious double hit, perhaps because they were intimidated by the shooter's reputation. Referees are human, which means they'll at some point make a mistake that hurts your chances of winning. That's life. You've got to shake it off and continue playing as well as possible. The pool gods owe you one, and perhaps you'll be the beneficiary of a referees error in judgment at some point in the future.

The Most Common Areas Where Disputes Arise

The majority of the time you will probably be playing without a referee present. Under these conditions, disputes can arise as each player has their own perspective of what has taken place, and both may feel that their opinion is 100% correct. It can help your chances of winning if you are familiar with the most common areas where disputes arise.

You can solve some disputes by having a rulebook handy. If you feel there a shot you are about to play could be questioned by your opponent, it can some times help to explain what you are about to do before the shot rather than after. You may also ask a neutral party to call the shot. Naturally, your opponent must agree to your selection.

- Double hits.
- Spotting balls.
- Pocketing a rack shot without clearly stating your intentions.
- Racking the ball properly.
- Forgetting the number of fouls either player is on.
- Replacing balls that have been accidentally moved
- Balls in or out of the rack.
- Lack of knowledge on some obscure rule that one player claims to know, but that you can't resolve because neither has a rulebook handy.
- Unsportsmanlike conduct, otherwise known as sharking.

Etiquette

The rulebook states during championship play, players must remain seated while their opponent is at the table. Furthermore, if a player leaves the area of the table when it is not their turn without permission from the referee, 15 points will be deducted from their score. I bring these points up only to underscore the seriousness with which the rule makers consider the proper etiquette of the game. If you are serious about your game, as I certainly hope you are, then you should insist on proper etiquette from your opponent.

Appendix B

Keeping Score

The first step is to keep track of each player's score during a particular rack. This number will always add up to 14 at the end of the rack. (Note: I don't think I've ever seen someone make both balls on the last shot of a rack, although it could happen, in which case the total would be 15 balls). At the end of each rack, each player's total is then added to a second score (the game score), which is a running total for the entire game. Any loss of points resulting from fouls is subtracted from the game score.

On some tables devices have been installed for keeping score. You can also purchase freestanding devices that keep score in the exact same manner. If neither of these devices is available, you may want to use the scorecard on the following page. I suggest that you blow it up to 133% of the size in the book to give you more room to write your information.

The example shows how the scorecard works. Each time there is a change in a rack score, write it in the appropriate space. In the first rack, Joe ran 4, then 4 more, for a total of 8. His game score is also 8. Fred ended the rack with a 6 ball run for a game score of 6. In the second rack, Fred broke and ran all 14 balls and now has a game score of 20. Joe remains at 8. In the third rack, Fred ran 4 and missed. Joe scored 10 balls in the third rack and now has a game score of 18. Fred scratched during the rack, and a point was deducted from his game score on the previous line. He ended the rack with 4 points, which when added to his game score of 19, gives him a game score after three racks of 23.

If you and/or your opponent like to keep track of your runs, it is easy to do with this system. In our example, Fred ended rack #1 on a run of 6 balls, which is marked with a R6 in the third column. He ran the entire next rack, and is on a run of 20 balls. His run ended 3 balls into the next rack, which is shown by E23. Joe ended rack #3 on a run of 4 balls.

When the game is over, it is interesting to see how it progressed. You can spot where runs occurred, and where leads were overcome or lost. If you are getting or receiving a spot, just write the amount of the spot on the first line of the game score and place a 0 in the column of the player giving a spot.

Phil Capelle's Straight Pool Scorecard   (Sample)

Player #1 __Joe Player__   Player #2 __Fred Opponent__

Rack #	Rack	Game	Run	Rack	Game	Run
1	4-8	8		6	6	R6
2	0	8		14	20-19	R20
3	6-10	18	R4	4	23	R24

Phil Capelle's Straight Pool Scorecard

Player #1 _____   Player #2 _____

Rack #	Rack	Game	Run	Rack	Game	Run
1						
2						
3						
4						
5						
6						
7						
8						
9						
10						
11						
12						
13						
14						
15						
16						
17						
18						
19						
20						

Comments _____

_____

_____

Appendix C　　Glossary for Straight Pool

The majority of terms in this glossary are related to pool in general. In many cases, however, the definition for the term is as it relates to Straight Pool. Since this is a book on Straight Pool, many of the terms only apply to that game.

A

Access Ball　A ball that enables you to easily get position on another ball that would otherwise be in a troublesome location.

Across the Line　A position play in which the cue ball is traveling across the position zone. It is very difficult to accomplish.

Area Shape　An extra large position zone that is used to keep the cue ball out of trouble.

B

Back Cut　When the cue ball is closer to the rail adjacent to the pocket than the object ball.

Ball in Hand　A rule that allows a player to place the cue ball anywhere behind the head string (in Straight Pool) after his opponent has scratched or committed three fouls in a row.

Bank Shot　A shot in which the object ball contacts one or more cushions before going into a pocket.

Behind the Line　Any ball that's between the head string and the head rail.

Billiard　A shot in which the cue ball glances off one ball before driving another ball into the pocket.

Body English　Twisting and turning the arms and/or body in an attempt to influence the shot.

Break (The)　The first shot of the game. In Straight Pool it is also the first shot of a new rack.

Break Out　A shot that removes a ball(s) from a cluster.

Bridge　Using the front hand to support the shaft of the cue.

Bridge Hand　For a righthanded player it's their left hand. Vive versa for lefties.

Bumping　A shot that sends a ball a short distance to a more advantageous location.

Bye　In a tournament a player without an opponent advances to the next round.

C

Call　The act of designating a specific pocket for a shot.

Called Ball　The designated shot.

Called Pocket　The designated pocket for a shot.

Carom　A shot in which the object ball glances off another ball on its way to the pocket.

Chalk　A small cube with a tacky substance that is applied regularly to the cue tip to help prevent miscues.

Cheating the Pocket.　Shooting the object ball into either side of the pocket.

Choke Up Shot　A shooting technique for playing hard to reach shots.

Closed Bridge　A bridge with a loop for the cue, formed by connecting the tips of the thumb and index finger on the middle finger.

Cluster　A group of object balls that are touching or are very close together.

Combination　A shot that involves two or more object balls. Two ball combinations are the most common.

Combo　(See combination).

Complementary Angles　A cut shot with an angle that makes it ideal for playing position on the next shot.

Connecting Ball　A straight-in shot which, when played with a stop shot, leaves you with a straight-in shot on the next ball.

Contact Induced Throw　Friction between the cue ball and object ball on cut shots that alters the path of the object ball.

Contact Point　The spot on the object ball that the cue ball must hot to make the shot.

Corner Hooked　A cue ball that's deep in the jaws of the pocket. When the edge of the pocket blocks the cue ball's path to the object ball.

Cross-side　A bank shot into the side pocket.

Crutch　(See mechanical bridge).

Cue　The stick with which you shoot.

Cue Ball　The all white ball which you shoot with the cue.

Curve　What happens when you hit down on the cue ball with english.

Cushion　The raised surface that surrounds the playing surface.

Cut Shot　Any shot that has an angle to it.

D

Dead Combination　A combination shot that's lined up to the pocket which virtually can't be missed.

Dead Shot　A shot that's lined up to the

Dead Stroke When a pool player is playing at peal levels and his stroke is on automatic pilot.

Deflection Hitting the cue ball with english that causes it to take off to the opposite side of the English.

Diamonds Markings along the top of the rails.

Domino Effect (The) When one little mistake at the wrong time can cause your whole pattern to begin to unravel.

Double Elimination A tournament in which a player must lose twice to be eliminated.

Double Hit Hitting the cue ball two or more times in succession. It's a foul.

Down the Line Shape A technique for playing position that minimizes the chances of not getting ideal shape.

Draw(the) Used to determine the pairings at a tournament.

Draw Shot Hitting the cue ball below center and applying backspin. On a straight-in shot the cue ball will come directly back at you.

Draw/Stun Shot A shot that is part draw and part stun.

E

Elevated Bridge Raising the palm of the bridge hand off the table so you can shoot over an obstructing ball.

End Rail Either the head rail or the foot rail.

English Side spin that results from stroking the cue ball on either side of its vertical axis.

Explosion Ball A ball in a cluster that, when struck, sets off a chain reaction within the rest of the rack.

F

Fan It In To make a very thin cut.

Feather Shot A very thin cut shot.

Ferrule The hard white piece of plastic or ivory at the end of the shaft to which the tip is attached.

Float the Cue Ball A shot that sends the cue ball in a sideways direction with a soft stroke.

Floating Follow A shot in which the cue ball rolls slowly forward after being hit with a firm stroke.

Flow Chart It is used to keep track of the progress of a tournament.

Follow Top spin that causes the cue ball to roll forward after contacting the object ball. It's applied by striking the cue ball above the horizontal axis (above center).

Follow/Stun Shot A shot that is part follow and part stun.

Follow Through The final phase of the stroke. Extending the cue tip past the cue ball's original location.

Foot of the Table The end of the table on which the balls are racked.

Foot Rail The rail at the end of the table where the balls are racked.

Foot Spot The spot on the table that's on the middle of the foot string. It's where the head ball of a rack is located and where balls are spotted.

Foot String An imaginary line that cross4es the table two diamonds up from the foot rail. It goes directly over the foot spot.

Force Follow Hitting the cue ball extra hard above center creating lots of top spin.

Force Shot Making the cue ball travel a good distance sideways with only a small cut angle with which to work.

Foul Scratching or not meeting the legal requirements of a legal shot or legal safety.

Frame A player's turn at the table.

Free Wheeling Very close to dead stroke. When a player is loose and confident, partly due to their opponent's poor play.

Frozen Ball A ball that is in contact with another ball or a cushion.

Full Ball Sending the cue ball into 100% contact with the object ball.

G-H

Getting In Line A demanding shot that puts the cue ball into good position for the next shot.

Hanger A ball that's sitting in the lip of the pocket.

Head of the Table The end of the table from which you play the opening break shot.

Head Rail The rail between the two corner pockets on the end of the table from which you break.

Head String An imaginary line that runs across the table two diamonds up from the head rail. You must place the ball behind on scratches.

High Run The most consecutive balls made by a player in a game of Straight Pool. It can also be a person's career best run.

Hold-up English Spin that sharpens the cue ball's rebound off the cushion. It slows the cue ball down.

Hold-up A technique that retards the roll of the cue ball.

Hooked When another object ball is blocking the cue ball's direct access to the designated object ball.

Hot Seat The winner of the winner's bracket in a double elimination tournament. They are guaranteed no worse than second place.

House Rules   A set of local rules by which you are expected to abide.

Hug the Rail   When a ball frozen to the cushion remains frozen as it rolls towards the pocket.

I

In Jail   When the cue ball is in a position where your opponent has neither a shot nor a safety. Pool's equivalent of checkmate.

Inning   A player's turn at the table.

Inside English   Applying sidespin on the same side of the cue ball as the direction of the cut shot.

Insurance Ball   A ball that's in a position that virtually guarantees you'll have a shot after breaking a cluster.

Intentional Foul   A strategic maneuver in which you deliberately lose a point.

J

Jacked Up   When you must raise your bridge to shoot over an obstructing ball. Raising the backhand and shooting a draw shot when the cue ball is near a rail.

Jagged Edge   A large cluster which has a ball sticking out from the rest of the pack.

Jaws   The area of the playing surface that is inside the edges of the pocket.

Jump Shot   A downward stroke that causes the cue ball to leave the bed of the table and sail over obstructing balls.

Jumped Ball   An obstructing ball that's been cleared.

K

Key Ball   A ball that's used to get position on the break ball for the next rack.

Key Ball to the Key Ball   A ball that makes is relatively easy to play position on the key ball.

Kick Shot   Shooting the cue ball into one or more cushions before contacting the object ball.

Kill Shot   A type of draw shot that checks the cue ball's roll after it rebounds off the cushion. Sometimes English is also used with the draw.

Kiss   When the object ball glances off another ball.

Kitchen   The area of the playing surface between the head string and the head rail. It's the area from which you break.

L

Lady's Aide   (See mechanical bridge).

Lag   A very soft stroke. Easing the ball into the pocket.

Lag for the Break   Each player simultaneously rolls the cue ball down the table and back. The player whose ball stops closest to the head rail wins. Used at the start of the game.

Leave   The position of the balls that one player receives as a result of another's shot.

Linking Balls   A linking ball makes it much easier to move from an area of the table where your work is complete to another area.

Long   When a bank shot misses to the far side of the pocket. Also when a player runs the cue ball past the ideal position zone.

Long Rail Bank   A table length bank shot.

Long Side Shape   When the cue ball is positioned so you can shoot to the closer pocket.

Long String   An imaginary line that runs down the middle of the table. Balls are spotted along the long string, starting at the foot spot.

M

Manufacturing a Break Shot   A shot that sends a ball into position for a break shot for the next rack.

Masse   A shot in which the cue ball curves radically as a result of a nearly vertical stoke.

Mechanical Bridge   A long handled implement with an attachment that has several ridges in which the cue is placed. It is used for shot that can't otherwise be reached.

Miscue   What occurs when the tip fails to stick properly on the cue ball at impact.

Miss   A shot that fail to go into the pocket.

N

Nap   The degree to which parts of the cloth rise above the rst of the playing surface.

Natural Position   Shape that results from allowing the cue ball to roll without using English.

Neutral Ball   A ball that is easy to get shape on from a variety of positions and it is doing no harm in its present location.

Nip Draw   A special draw stroke in which you use a short punch-like stroke.

O

Object Ball   The ball at which you are shooting.

On a Run   The number of ball made in your current turn.

Open Bridge   A bridge formed by laying the hand flat on the table and placing the cue in a vee formed by the thumb and index finger.

Open the Angle   English that causes the cue ball to rebound at less on an angle than the angle of approach.

Opening Break (The) The very first shot of the game.

Out of Stroke When a player is off their game and their stroke does not fell right.

Outside English Applying side spin on the opposite side of the cue ball than the object ball is traveling.

Overdrive Follow A technique for applying extra follow to the cue ball. It is used for breaking clusters.

Over Cut Missing a shot because the object ball was hit too thinly.

P

Pattern Play Playing the balls in a specific order and/or a certain style of playing position.

Pinball Effect (The) The churning like action of the cue ball as it bounces off several balls when breaking a cluster.

Plan B Resorting to a different shot or pattern as a result of a shot not being executed exactly as intended.

Player A person who plays very well, especially under competitive conditions.

Pocket Billiards The formal name for pool.

Pocket Speed Hitting a shot with just enough force so that the object ball drops with a few inches to spare.

Pool Games that are played on a rectangular table with six pockets, a cue ball and several colored ball.

Pool Gods Mythical characters who control the rolls and the luck factor in each contest. It is not wise to upset them.

Position Where the cue ball is located in relation to the next shot.

Position Zone An area of the table in which the cue ball is well placed for the next shot.

Pound Shot A shot that uses a very hard stroke to send the cue ball off a cushion when the cut angle is very shallow.

Pounding the Ball The act of using a pound shot.

Process of Elimination Planning A technique for planning patterns.

Pyramid A full rack of balls at the start of a game. The front ball is located on the foot spot.

R

Rack A triangular shaped object that is used to put the balls in place at the start of a the game and for each new rack. Also refers to the position of the balls once they've been placed in position and the rack had been removed.

Rack Shot Playing a shot out of the rack. It.

Rake (See mechanical bridge).

Rail The raised surface that surrounds the playing surface. It includes the cushions.

Rail Bridge A bridge that's formed by placing the bridge hand on the rail.

Rail Shot When the cue ball is frozen to the cushion or is very close to it.

Rail Target A spot on the rail that is chosen as a place where you want the cue ball to hit.

Regulation Sized Table A 4fi' x9' sized table.

Reverse English Side spin that causes the cue ball to rebound off the cushion at a sharper angle that the approach angle.

Rock The cue ball.

Roll Off When an irregularity in the table or a not perfectly level playing surface causes a slow moving object ball to roll off line.

Row Blocker A ball that prevents several other balls from being played into the pocket that is blocked.

Run The number of balls made on any particular turn.

S

Safety A defensive maneuver that's designed to leave your opponent with a tough shot or safety, or perhaps no shot at all.

Safety Zones A place on the table where your opponent cannot pocket a ball.

Score How a match stands at any time.

Scratch When the cue ball disappears into any of the six pockets.

Scratch Shot A shot in which a scratch is very likely or is unavoidable.

Secondary Break Shot A shot that's used to separate a cluster after the initial break shot of a new rack in Straight Pool.

Shape (See position).

Shark A tactic that's designed to distract or throw an opponent off their game. A player who hustles pool.

Sharking The act of using shark tactics.

Shooting the Lights Out When you are shooting very straight and playing perfect pool.

Short A bank shot that misses on the near side of the pocket. When the cue ball fails to reach the intended location for good position.

Short Side Shape Position for the more distant pocket.

Shotmaker A very straight shooter who emphasizes making balls over playing position.

Short Rail Bank A bank across the width of the table.

Side Rail The rails that run along the length of the table.

Side Rail Break Shot A break shot where the object ball is close to or on the ra

Skid When the cue ball and object ball maintain contact for a fraction of a second longer than normal. This almost always results in the shot being under cut.

Skimming Balls Rolling the cue ball very softly off the edge of an object ball. It is a defensive measure.

Slate The hard playing surface that rests under the cloth.

Slug A loose rack.

Snookered When the cue ball rests behind a ball which blocks a direct hit on the designated ball.

Spectrum of Speed A 1-10 scale used for measuring the various speeds of stroke.

Speed Control The ability to control the cue ball's rolling distance. Good speed control is essential for playing good position.

Speed of Stroke The force that you apply to the cue ball.

Spin Your Rock Applying English to the cue ball.

Spot A location on the table. The foot spot and the head spot.

Spot Up Placing a ball on the foot spot. Usually occurs after a ball has been pocketed and a foul has been committed.

Stack Same as the rack. The group of balls prior to the opening break.

Stance The position that you take for a shot.

Stick It Stopping the cue ball dead in its racks upon contact with the object ball.

Sticking to the Rack When the cue ball sticks to the side of the rack on a break shot, leaving the shooter without a shot.

Stone Slang for the cue ball.

Stop Shot (See stick it)

Straight In Refers to a shot where the cue ball and object ball are lined up directly at the pocket.

Straight Pool Also known as 14.1. A game played to a specific number of points. One point is scored for each ball pocketed.

Stroke The swing of the arm, wrist and hand that propels the cue through the cue ball.

Stun Shot A firmly hit shot in which the cue ball slides across the cloth.

Sweat Watching a pool game. For example, sweating the action.

T

Table Roll (See roll off).

Thin Cut A shot that requires very little of the cue ball contacts the object ball.

Throw Friction between the object ball and cue ball that changes the path of the object ball. english can cause throw, as can contact.

Tip The small round leather item that is attached to the ferrule. Also refers to how much English is used on a particular shot.

Triangle Another term for the device used to rack the ball. The area in which the balls are racked.

Through Traffic Skillfully maneuvering the cue ball past a number of potentially obstructing balls.

Two Way Shots A position play that gives you the luxury of playing position on either of two possible targets.

2 1/4" Rule (The) It states that everything about a shot can and very often does change within the space of 2 1/4".

U

Umbrella Break Shot A break shot using s hard stroke with follow. The cue ball arcs into the rack after striking the side rail.

Under Cut Missing a shot because the object ball was hit too fully.

Useless Balls Balls that serve no purpose and that are not a problem.

W

Warm Up Strokes A series of movements of the arm, hand and wrist that prepares the shooter for the actual stroke.

Weight A handicap that one player gives another in a money game.

Whitey Slang for the cue ball.

Appendix D   Great Straight Pool Players

The champions listed below are players who excelled at Straight Pool, many of which also played other cue games at a similar level. There accomplishments provide the sport with a long and rich history. In the modern area, there are a number of great players who are not listed below only because they tend to excel at games other than Straight Pool, mostly I would suppose as a matter of personal preference. The players are listed alphabetically.

BCA's Hall of Fame Members who Excelled at Straight Pool

Joe Balsis was a consistent contender at the U.S. Open, winning the title in 1968 and 1974. He also captured a World title in 1965.

Lou Butera won the World Championships in 1973. In one game, Butera, nicknamed "Machine Gun Lou", ran 150 balls and out in 21 minutes.

Jimmy Caras was five times a World Champion from 1935 to 1949. In 1967 he captured The U.S. Open.

Irving Crane was a master of position play and defense. In 1966, in a match captured on film, he ran 150 and out against Joe Balsis to win the U.S. Open. He won six Worlds titles from 1946 until 1972. In 1939 he established a then record high run of 309.

Arthur Cranfield won the world title in 1965. He is the only person to win a world title, the National Junior, and the National Amateur.

Alfred De Oro won World Championships at both Straight Pool and Billiards in the late 1800's and early 1900's.

Ralph Greenleaf was a perennial World Champion from 1919 until 1937. He ran what was then a record 272 balls in 1935.

Luther Lassiter excelled at both Nine-Ball and Straight Pool. He won the Straight Pool title five times and the Nine-Ball title four times at Johnston City between 1962 and 1972. Lassiter also won numerous World Championships and the U.S. Open in 1969.

Ray Martin, a master of position play, won three World Ttitles between 1971 and 1978. He is the co-author the *99 Critical Shots*.

Steve Mizerak won four consecutive U.S. Opens in the early 1970's and two World Titles in the 1980's.

Jimmy Moore was a runner-up five times in world championship events. He won a national title in 1965.

Willie Mosconi set what the record book says is the record high run of 526 balls in 1954. From 1940 to 1957 he won fifteen World's Titles at Straight Pool. Considered by many to be the best pool player ever.

Cisero Murphy won a World Title in 1965 and was a runner-up on several occasions. He won numerous prestigious titles in the 1950's and 1960's.

Andrew Ponzi won three World Titles from 1934 to 1943

Erwin Randolph beat kingpin Ralph Greenleaf to win the first of his four World Titles in 1926. The last came in 1933.

Frank Taberski won the World's Title on numerous occasions from 1916 until 1928. In 1921 he was the first to run 200 balls, at the time a record.

Mike Sigel won three World titles in Straight Pool from 1979 until 1885. He has two perfect games in competition. Sigel won the 1992 U.S. Open. He has won numerous major titles in Nine-Ball and other games as well, and has claimed over 100 professional titles.

Nick Varner won World Titles at Straight Pool in 1980 and 1986. Varner is a strong all-around player, having won numerous titles in Nine-Ball and other games as well.

Dallas West was twice a winner of the U.S. Open in 1975 and 1983. He has been active as instructor for many years.

Harold Worst was a great all-around player who won major titles in Johnston City and Las Vegas

Top Straight Pool Players of Today
Any or all of the players listed are all viable candidates for the Hall of Fame base on their accomplishments in Straight Pool and other pool games.

Allen Hopkins, a strong all-around player, won a World Title at Straight Pool in 1977 to go with his many titles in Nine-Ball and One-Pocket.

Oliver Ortmann from Germany won the U.S. Open in 1989 and 1993.

Jim Rempe, one of the most consistent all-around players, has won several major titles in Straight Pool and Nine-ball.

Efren Reyes from the Philippines, who excels at all games, won The Maine Event 14.1 Championships against a stellar field in 1995 to go with his numeous titles at Nine-Ball and On-Pocket.

Ralf Souquet from Germany captured the 2000 U.S. Open to go with his World Title at Nine-Ball in 1995.

Women Members of the Hall of Fame
Jean Balakus dominated women's pool until her retirement, winning six World Championships and seven U.S. Opens in the 1970's and 1980's.

Ruth McGinnis was a perennial World Champion in the 1930's who posted a high run of 128 balls.

Dorothy Wise won the U.S. Open five straight times in the late 1960's and early 1970's.

Top Women Straight Pool Players of Today
Allison Fisher, the dominant player in women's pool, won the 2000 U.S. Open. In the process, she recorded the tournaments high run of 60 balls.

Loree Jon Jones is a former Women's World Champion at Straight Pool who, like Jeanette, has run over 100 balls. She has won the U.S. Opens in 1989 and 1992 and was a runner-up at the U.S Open in 2000.

Ewa Mataya Laurence holds the women's record at the U.S Open with a high run of 68 at the U.S. Open in 1992.

Jeanette Lee has fared well against top men players in Straight Pool tournaments, and has run in excess of 100 balls.

Appendix E
Learning by Watching Videos

There are many sources for learning pool in addition to books like the one you are reading. One of the best ways is to watch videotapes of top professionals playing in serious competition. Pat Fleming and his team at **Accu-Stats** (800-828-0397) have toured the country filming the professional tournaments. As this book is being written, they have a compiled a library of over 50 Straight Pool matches that include over a half dozen members of the BCA's Hall of Fame as well as many other domestic and international superstars.

If you like watching long runs (and what true fan of Straight Pool doesn't), then you will find plenty for your viewing pleasure. There are 14 100+ runs in the Accu-Stats library, including two runs of 150 and out by Mike Sigel and another by Johnny Archer. In addition there are another 17 runs in excess of 80 balls. Accu-Stats filmed the 2000 BCA U.S Open, which produced an excellent 13 tape series of matches.

100 Ball Runs on Tape

2000 U.S. Open
141 Efren Reyes
120 Ralf Souquet (unfinished)
129 Oliver Ortmann

1995 The Maine Event
102 Grady Matthews (unfinished)
123 Efren Reyes

1993 Cleveland 14.1 Invitational
101 Pat Fleming
115 Mike Zuglan

1992 U.S. Open
150 Mike Sigel (unfinished) (H)
111 Mike Sigel (H)
109 Mike Zuglan
150 Johnny Archer (unfinished)
148 Mike Zuglan

1989 U.S. Open
150 Mike Sigel (unfinished) (H)
104 Steve Mizerak (H)

- The letter (H) signifies that this player is a member of the B.C.A.'s Hall of Fame
- An unfinished run (as noted) means the player ran out the game. In most cases, these runs could have been significantly higher were the player to continue shooting.
- All games played by the men in the Accu-Stats matches filmed by Accu-Stats were to 150 points except for the finals of the 1989 U.S. Open, which was played to 200 points. Two games were taped in the 1992 U.S. Open in the women's division. In one game, Ewa Lawrence set a U.S. Open record 68. In the other match, Loree Jon Jones ran 49 in winning the finals.
- To run a 100 in tournament competition, you have to start your run by the 51st ball. This, of course, limits your opportunities.

Player Review Matches

This series of matches features commentary by players who participated in the match. Their comments can be very helpful to your game. I particularly enjoyed the commentary of Dick Lane and Jim Rempe.

1992 U.S. Open
Mike Zuglan defeats Cicero Murphy (H), 150-26
Dick Lane defeats Johnny Archer, 150-121

1993 Cleveland 14.1 Invitational
Grady Matthews defeats Pat Fleming 150-118

2000 U.S. Open
Jim Rempe defeats George SanSouci, 150-(-12)

Photo Finishes

When top players compete at Straight Pool, the winning margin is typically quite large. One player will usually gain the momentum at some point in the match and carry their advantage to the games conclusion. This can and does happen despite some fine play by their opponent. Occasionally, however, a game will go down to the wire. The matches listed below from Accu-Stats were all decided by less than 20 balls. These are the Straight Pool equivalent of a golfer winning a tournament by one stroke or a football game being decided by a field goal.

1989 U.S. Open
Oliver defeats Nick Varner (H), 150-135
Oliver Ortmann defeats Steve Mizerak (H), 200-186 (finals)

1992 U.S. Open
Dallas West (H) defeats Nick Varner (H), 150-146
Jim Rempe defeats Allen Hopkins, 150-143

2000 U.S. Open
John Schmidt defeats Mike Sigel (H), 150-131
Oliver Ortmann defeats Jim Rempe, 150-144

Tips for Learning by Watching Videos

- Use slow motion for observing the path of the cue ball and for observing how the balls break apart.
- Notice the patterns and how the player gets position on the break ball.
- Observe how each player conducts themselves at the table.
- Carefully observe the fundamentals of those players whose styles you like.
- Rewind and play over any parts that you didn't fully understand on the first viewing.
- Take notes and make diagrams of things tou want to work on.
- Keep a timed contents so you can easily return to certain parts of the tape that have key shots.
- Install a tape player in your home pool room.

Appendix F

Your Straight Pool Game Plan

PositionPlay
- Emphasize speed control
- Get the correct angle on the right side
- Plan several balls ahead
- Enter the wide part of a position zone
- Playing down the line shape
- Survey the table
- Plan your position route
- Allow for a margin for error
- Use the rail to increase your options
- Remember the 2/inch rule
- Minimize cue ball movement
- Bump balls into position

Pattern Play
- Play the table
- Labeling the balls correctly
- Take care of first things first
- Simplify the table
- Manage risk
- Be sure you use the side pockets to full advantage
- Think diagonally when playing patterns in the area of the triangle
- Have a Plan B ready
- Play two-way shots
- Clear pockets
- Work one area at a time
- Take care of multiple objectives in congestion
- Shoot easy combos to preserve your pattern
- Grind it out on tough racks
- Take balls off the rails
- Clear balls off the end rail
- Use access balls to get to trouble balls
- Manufacture break shots
- Look for key balls with the ideal characteristics
- Manufacture key balls

End of rack Pattern Play
- Use process of elimination planning on the last 4-7 balls
- Use key balls to the key ball
- Emphasize the three-ball end of the rack pattern
- Leave balls in the area of the rack

Secondary Break Shots
- Know when to stop breaking the balls
- Use three ball patterns to get on secondary break shots
- Play secondary break shots with precision
- Have an insurance ball available
- Partially break clusters
- Break clusters on the good side
- Look for explosion balls

Cluster Management
- Using the tangent line
- Determine the path into a Cluster
- Bust clusters when the timing is right
- Precision rules over power

Break Shots
- The contact point on the ball in the rack affects the path of the cue ball
- Use the correct speed of stroke for each kind of break shot
- Cueing affects the cue balls path after contact
- Use the distance principle on break shots
- Break shot stretch distances
- Ball in hand break shots

At the Start
- Be prepared to lag
- It is better to lose two points than to hit the corner ball too fully
- Get psyched for the first long shot after the break

How to Run a Rack
- Be aware of the three phases when working the table
- Emphasize execution on the key ball, break ball and the first shot after the break
- The stoplight analogy can help you size up a rack
- Be aware of problems that appear regularly and know how to deal with them successfully

Safety Play
- Have a goal for each safety
- Skim balls precisely
- Hit the end rail safety zones
- Control the roll of the object ball
- Creativity and execution = winner

- Hit into the side of the rack and stick
- Cover two sides at once

Strategy
- Never let up
- Choose your shots wisely
- Play your game
- Put your opponent in the proper perspective
- Use your time wisely while in the chair
- Prepare for competition
- Know when to pick up the pace
- Get psyched for gamewinning shots
- Always remember your opponent's fouls
- Use last rack runout strategy
- Use intentional fouls
- Adapting to the playing conditions

Shotmaking
- Fundamentals for 14.1
- Establish your ideal rhythm
- Shot selection for 14.1
- Emphasize making the ball on long shots
- Use a short stroke for accuracy
- Beware the dreaded skid shot
- Know your limits on cut shots
- Use a short stroke on frozen table length shots
- Play only easier combos
- Look for frozen combos
- Remember the critical $1/8^{th}$ inch on combos
- Play only easy bank shots
- Look for carom shots
- Look for billiards
- Look for rack shots

Practicing Straight Pool
- Practicing Straight Pool by running balls
- Dissect your game
- Let go
- Emphasize a skill
- Practice with a friend
- Keep a journal
- Make your own diagrams
- Use he donuts

High Runs
- Play one ball at a time
- Don't count the balls
- Play under ideal conditions
- Get in top form